SAVING FOR DEVELOPMENT

How Latin America and the Caribbean Can Save More and Better

Edited by

Eduardo Cavallo and Tomás Serebrisky

Inter-American Development Bank

Inter-American Development Bank
Washington, DC, USA

ISBN 978-1-349-94928-1 ISBN 978-1-349-94929-8 (eBook)
DOI 10.1057/978-1-349-94929-8
Library of Congress Control Number: 2016942088

Cover image © Dave Cutler / Illustration Source
Cover design by Dolores Subiza

Printed on acid-free paper

This Palgrave Macmillan imprint is published by Springer Nature
The registered company is Nature America Inc. New York

Contents

List of Tables

List of Figures

List of Boxes

Preface

In discussions about saving in Latin America and the Caribbean, a common critique is that the region saves little. Indeed, the data support this statement: the region saves from 10 to 15 percentage points of GDP less than the most dynamic countries of Emerging Asia. At the Inter-American Development Bank (IDB), we know that understanding why this occurs and, above all, how and in what way Latin America saves is crucial for the region's economic growth and the well-being of its people. That is why we have decided to devote the 2016 edition of our institutional publication *Development in the Americas* (DIA) to studying this topic and to proposing solutions to address this critical problem.

We believe this publication comes at an opportune moment. The engines of economic growth in Latin America and the Caribbean following the most recent financial crisis have been gradually weakening. The region can no longer count on a favorable external environment, and so it is time to look for new domestic sources that can drive our economies forward.

The standard response to the relative lack of saving in the region is that its impact on growth is low since countries ultimately can turn to external saving to finance the region's investment needs. We believe that this view ignores a crucial consideration: it is very difficult to attract external capital on favorable conditions if Latin Americans themselves do not save or invest in their countries. Besides, in the current environment, when interest rates in developed nations are rising and capital is no longer abundant, the prescription to turn to external financing as a palliative for our low saving is probably more uncertain and risky than in the immediate past.

Saving in Latin America and the Caribbean is low not only in comparison with other regions; it is also fundamentally low in relation to the region's need for development and its need to improve equity. The low level of saving also reinforces the very low level of productivity growth, since whatever scarce resources are generated from saving are for the most part not invested in projects that would increase levels of long-term growth. Consequently, this nonproductive allocation of saving keeps the region from reaching the levels of income and well-being of more prosperous countries.

For all of these reasons, one of the greatest challenges for Latin America and the Caribbean is to increase saving levels in a way that is sustainable and improve the allocation of that saving to more productive activities so as to boost overall productivity. All of these challenges are closely linked. It will not be possible to invest more if we do not generate the resources to finance that investment; but neither will it be possible to sustain higher levels of saving if we do not generate productive opportunities for investment.

One of the main contributions of this publication is to focus the discussion within a framework that identifies the source of the problems affecting different agents—households, businesses, and governments—and proposing concrete solutions for each one of them.

Saving more and saving better are not necessarily associated either with the traditional recommendation to undertake a fiscal adjustment or with the traditional recourse of providing tax incentives to promote certain types of saving. Nor is such saving associated with paternalistic public policies. What "saving more and better" really means is rethinking public policies, especially in the area of social security; increasing the efficiency of public expenditures and giving investment more weight over current spending within the structure of public expenditure. It also means eliminating distortions that impact the effective functioning of the financial system, the labor market, and fiscal and regulatory systems.

One cannot talk about saving in Latin America and the Caribbean without making reference to pensions. Contributions to pensions are the main mechanism by which people save for retirement. The region has long debated whether pension systems should be pay-as-you-go (PAYG) or fully-funded, defined-contribution schemes. However, this is not necessarily the most relevant debate. Many contribution systems in the region, whether based on PAYG or funded contribution schemes, have structural problems that require immediate correction. It is an illusion to believe that saving can only be generated through funded contribution systems. Transitions to such systems can also generate large fiscal costs that reduce national saving, so these systems need to be carefully designed. At the other extreme, PAYG systems can and should increase savings while they have surplus contributions to ensure long-term sustainability and guarantee that they generate adequate returns. This, in turn, requires that the management of these systems be strictly professional and without political interference.

At present, the debate needs to revolve not around whether pension systems should be PAYG or funded contribution schemes, but around the fact that less than half of the Latin American population contributes to any type of pension system. This reflects serious problems in the functioning of the region's labor markets, beginning with high levels of informality. It is urgent to refocus the debate on reforms that can help all pension systems improve coverage, as well as increase saving. The population is aging rapidly, and if action is not taken now, resources will not be available to address the growing needs of this population segment.

Another major topic addressed in this publication is that in Latin America and the Caribbean there is not only little saving, but that this low amount of saving is not effectively channeled toward the economy. This stems in part from a lack of instruments that are adequate for long-term saving, given the underdevelopment of our financial markets. An example of this problem is the lack of investment instruments to channel public and private saving to infrastructure. In Latin America and the Caribbean, there is a significant investment gap in infrastructure: transport, telephone networks, energy generation and distribution, and potable water, among other sectors. This gap constrains long-term growth because if the investment is well planned and executed, the returns to investment in infrastructure are very high and encourage private investment in the economy. However, it is difficult today to channel national saving toward infrastructure because there are no instruments with which to do so. To foster this process, it is necessary to adapt the regulatory framework for infrastructure investment so as to generate the mechanisms and vehicles to remove the bottlenecks that currently exist in the region.

Despite advances in recent decades, financial systems in Latin America and the Caribbean are still small, expensive, and inefficient. Not surprisingly, many families do not use those financial systems as a preferred vehicle for saving, and businesses face significant problems obtaining financing at reasonable rates and terms. Low saving is the flip side of scarce credit, and the poor allocation of that credit is, for its part, a product of inefficiencies in the operation of financial systems. In order to expand the use of financial systems, and above all to promote saving through formal financial systems, a culture of saving must be developed. This effort should be supported by interventions that, on the one hand, help reduce the costs of operating with the financial system and increase returns for savers, and on the other hand, mitigate the problems that drive families and businesses away from banks. One of these problems is the lack of trust. No one can blame those who have been harmed in the past by recurring financial crises that have wiped out their savings. However, financial systems in general today are much more solid, in part because they have learned the lessons from past crises. The lack of trust today is more related to the lack of understanding about how banks operate and about the advantages and opportunities, as well as the risks, of using formal financial systems. Financial education, particularly at an early age when cognitive capacity is still being developed, represents a good opportunity to foster a culture of saving.

On the fiscal front, the good news is that the region has enormous opportunities to improve the delivery of public services with fewer resources. This could generate significant savings without the need to turn to traditional fiscal adjustment recipes that translate into higher taxes and reduced expenditures. What is needed now is to redirect public expenditure, placing more emphasis on investment than in the past. In turn, there is a margin to increase public saving by eliminating waste in expenditures related to subsidies, tax expenditures, and social assistance programs. Those efforts can complement one another, increasing the efficiency of expenditure in such sectors as health and education. This publication presents new data that allow policymakers to identify sources of waste and opportunities to increase the efficiency of expenditures.

This publication does not aim to be a recipe of good practices or to indicate a single path that all countries should follow. Every country is different, and in each case the emphasis should be placed on those aspects that are most relevant. The objective of this publication is to generate awareness among public officials, business persons, and workers that promoting saving—and particularly the efficient use of resources that are generated through saving—is an essential part of the solution to the problems of low growth, little investment, and the growing needs of a rapidly aging population. More and better saving is the path that leads toward a region with greater stability and confidence, and where lack of capital is no longer a constraint for economic and social development.

Luis Alberto Moreno
President
Inter-American Development Bank

Acknowledgments

Development in the Americas (DIA) is the flagship publication of the Inter-American Development Bank (IDB). This issue was produced under the direction of Eduardo Cavallo, lead research economist of the Research Department, and Tomás Serebrisky, sector economic advisor for the Infrastructure and Environment Sector.

This book would not have been possible without the exceptional editorial work of Rita Funaro, the publications coordinator of the Research Department. Rita worked tirelessly and patiently to translate complicated technical concepts into a language accessible to a broader audience. She made this book possible, and much, much better. Rita was assisted by Cathleen Conkling-Shaker, Nancy Morrison, Matías Marzani, and Jaime Ramírez Cuellar. John Dunn Smith edited many background papers and technical notes associated with this book.

Orazio Attanasio, Peter Montiel, and Klaus Schmidt-Hebbel were external advisors. Their advice throughout all the phases of this book has been invaluable.

Santiago Levy, vice president for Sectors and Knowledge, José Juan Ruiz, the chief economist and general manager of the Research Department, and Andrew Powell, principal advisor of the Research Department, provided constant guidance and technical advice throughout the life of this project. Valuable comments and suggestions were also provided by the IDB's Programming Committee of Management.

The principal authors of each individual chapter are as follows:

Chapter 1   Eduardo Cavallo and Tomás Serebrisky
Chapter 2   Eduardo Cavallo, Verónica Frisancho, and Jonathan Karver
Chapter 3   Andrew Powell and Eduardo Cavallo
Chapter 4   Tomás Serebrisky, Diego Margot, and Ancor Suárez-Alemán

Chapter 5 Eduardo Fernández-Arias, Eduardo Cavallo, and Matías Marzani
Chapter 6 Solange Berstein, Mariano Bosch, and María Laura Oliveri
Chapter 7 Solange Berstein and Mariano Bosch
Chapter 8 Alejandro Izquierdo
Chapter 9 Verónica Frisancho
Chapter 10 Matías Busso, Andrés Fernández, and César Tamayo
Chapter 11 César Tamayo and Eduardo Cavallo

Carola Pessino was the author of the box on taxation and saving (Box 8.1). A special word of gratitude goes to her for stepping in to provide her expertise and knowledge on this difficult and important topic.

Special thanks go to Aglae Parra, the administrative coordinator of this project. She devoted immense effort and provided efficient administrative support. Other members of the administrative team provided invaluable support throughout the life of this project, in particular, Mónica Bazán, Beatriz Contreras, Myriam Escobar-Genes, David Gómez, Elton Mancilla, Sofía Meléndez, Mariela Semidey, and Federico Volpino.

Javier Caicedo, Camila Fonseca Sarmiento, Melany Gualavisi, Jonathan Karver, Pamela Mendoza, Liu Mendoza Pérez, Mathieu Pedemonte, Dario Romero Fonseca, Mariano Sosa, Maria Laura Oliveri and Juan Miguel Villa all provided excellent research assistance. Matías Marzani and Jaime Ramirez Cuellar deserve special recognition for their dedication to this project.

Pablo Bachelet, Carlos Gerardo Molina and Kyle Strand helped immensely with the communication and dissemination strategy.

Many other people contributed their technical input to this report, including Joshua Aizenman, Jorge Alonso, S. Gabriela Andrade, Raúl Andrade, Gabriela Aparicio, Martín Ardánaz, Edna Armendáriz, Daniel Artana, Viviane Azevedo, Nick Barr, Alberto Barreix, Ricardo Bebczuk, Óscar Becerra, Juan Luis Bour, Rodrigo Cerda, Juan José Cruces, Fernando de Olloqui, Edgardo Demaestri, Víctor Dumas, Barry Eichengreen, Emilio Espino, Antonio Estache, Vicente Fretes, Rodrigo Fuentes, Lourdes Gallardo, Néstor Gandelman, Gustavo García, Martín González-Rozada, Catalina Granda Carvajal, Werner Hernani, Diego Herrera Falla, Ayse İmrohoroğlu, Luis Carlos Jemio, Enrique Kawamura, Juan Ketterer, Mariano Lafuente, Carlos Madeira, Ángel Melguizo, Alejandro Micco, Alejandro Morduchovicz, Oscar Natale, Fernando Navajas, Sergio Navajas,

Andrés Neumeyer, Ilan Noy, Carmen Pagés, Mónica Panadeiros, Ugo Panizza, Diana Pinto, Lucas Ronconi, Gabriel Sánchez, Alfredo Schclarek Curuchet, Miguel Socías, Marco Stampini, Nuria Susmel, Miguel Székely, José Tessada, Jorge Tovar, Verónica Trujillo, Patricio Valenzuela, Fermín Vivanco, and Rodrigo Wagner.

The opinions expressed in this publication are those of the authors and do not necessarily reflect the views of the Inter-American Development Bank, its board of directors, or the technical advisors.

Contributors

Solange Berstein, a citizen of Chile, holds a PhD in Economics from Boston University. She is a principal specialist in the Labor Markets and Social Security Unit of the Inter-American Development Bank.

Mariano Bosch, a citizen of Spain, holds a PhD in Economics from the London School of Economics. He is a lead economist in the Labor Markets and Social Security Unit of the Inter-American Development Bank.

Matías Busso, a citizen of Argentina, holds a PhD in Economics from the University of Michigan. He is a lead research economist in the Research Department of the Inter-American Development Bank.

Eduardo Cavallo, a citizen of Argentina and the United States, holds a PhD in Public Policy from Harvard University. He is a lead research economist in the Research Department of the Inter-American Development Bank

Eduardo Fernández-Arias, a citizen of Uruguay, holds a PhD in Economics from the University of California at Berkeley. He is a principal economist in the Research Department of the Inter-American Development Bank.

Andrés Fernández, a citizen of Colombia, holds a PhD in Economics from Rutgers University. He is a research economist in the Research Department of the Inter-American Development Bank.

Verónica Frisancho, a citizen of Peru, holds a PhD in Economics from the Pennsylvania State University. She is a senior research economist in the Research Department of the Inter-American Development Bank.

Alejandro Izquierdo, a citizen of Argentina, holds a PhD in Economics from the University of Maryland. He is a senior advisor at the Research Department of the Inter-American Development Bank.

Jonathan Karver, a citizen of the United States and Mexico, holds a MA in Economics from the Instituto Tecnológico Autónomo de México (ITAM). He is a research fellow in the Research Department of the Inter-American Development Bank.

Diego Margot, a citizen of Argentina, holds a PhD in Economics from the University of Illinois at Urbana-Champaign. He is an economist in the Infrastructure and Environment Sector of the Inter-American Development Bank.

Matías Marzani, a citizen of Argentina, holds a postgraduate degree in Economics from Universidad Torcuato di Tella (UTDT). He is a research fellow in the Research Department of the Inter-American Development Bank.

María Laura Oliveri, a citizen of Argentina, holds a MS in Economics from Universidad Nacional de la Plata, Argentina. She is a consultant in the Labor Markets and Social Security Unit of the Inter-American Development Bank.

Carola Pessino, a citizen of Argentina, holds a PhD in Economics from the University of Chicago. She is principal specialist in the Fiscal and Municipal Management Division of the Inter-American Development Bank.

Andrew Powell, a citizen of the United Kingdom, holds a DPhil. (PhD) from the University of Oxford. He is the principal advisor in the Research Department of the Inter-American Development Bank.

Tomás Serebrisky, a citizen of Argentina, holds a PhD in Economics from the University of Chicago. He is the sector economic adviser for the Infrastructure and Environment Sector of the Inter-American Development Bank.

Ancor Suárez Alemán, a citizen of Spain, holds a PhD in Economics from the University of Las Palmas de Gran Canaria. He is an economist in the Infrastructure and Environment Sector of the Inter-American Development Bank.

César Tamayo, a citizen of Colombia, holds a PhD in Economics from Rutgers University. He is a research economist in the Capital Markets and Financial Institutions Division of the Institutions for Development Sector at the Inter-American Development Bank.

1 Saving for a Sunny Day

Why should people—and economies—save? The typical answer usually focuses on the need to protect against future shocks, to smooth consumption during hard times, in short, to save for the proverbial rainy day. This book approaches the question from a slightly different angle. While saving to survive the bad times is important, saving to thrive in the good times is what really counts. People must save so they can invest in their own and their children's health and education, live productive fulfilling lives, and end their days in comfort and peace. Firms must save so they can grow productive enterprises that employ more workers in better jobs to produce quality goods for domestic and international markets. Governments must save to build bridges, highways, and airports that support a productive economy, to provide quality services such as education, health, water, and sanitation to their citizens, and to assure their senior citizens a dignified, worry-free retirement. In short, countries must save for a sunny day—a time when everyone can bask in the benefits of growth, prosperity, and well-being.

To have even a chance of reaching that sunny day, this book argues that Latin America and the Caribbean must save more and save better. It contends that saving in the region is too low and that the savings that do exist can be used more efficiently to enhance growth and development. The purpose of this book is to raise awareness about the urgent need to promote more and better saving to address several of the region's most pressing issues including lackluster growth, low investment rates, and the growing need to care for an aging population.

Why should economies care about how much they save? After all, if economies can always borrow from abroad, then national saving rates should not matter. However, borrowing from abroad may be more costly and may raise the risk of crises. Foreign financial flows are fickle, and history shows that they dry up just when they are needed most. Latin

America and the Caribbean is no stranger to the currency and financial turmoil generated by external debt. Importing saving from abroad is far from a perfect substitute to boosting saving at home.

Given the limits to external borrowing, countries that save more also invest more. In other words, there is a positive association between national saving and domestic investment (investment in the real economy, not purely financial investment). From a policy perspective, it is useful to understand which drives which: whether higher saving leads to more real investment or whether better investment opportunities lead to increases in saving. This book argues that causality runs in both directions. Or more precisely, that Latin America and the Caribbean suffers from two reinforcing problems: low saving supply and weak investment demand. Solving these problems and breaking the vicious cycle between them demands concerted and swift policy action to increase saving and investment.

Savings: The Sum of its Parts

National saving is the sum of all the individual saving decisions of the agents in the economy: households, firms, and government agencies. While a macroeconomic analysis is instructive, in the end saving decisions are made by individuals and reflect the information they have and the many real-life considerations that may influence their behavior. To fully understand the problem of saving, it is imperative to break down and analyze how the savings generated by households, firms, and government agencies is aggregated and channeled to the economy.

The financial system is the middle man: it moves the resources from people who save to those who need the resources to invest. Small and inefficient financial systems, like those in Latin America and the Caribbean, jack up the costs for financial services, which in turn depress both saving (by reducing effective returns to savers) and investment (by increasing the cost of credit to borrowers). In such contexts, households that lack access to good financial savings instruments may opt to save in other ways—by accumulating cash or jewelry, by buying durable goods, or by investing in the family firm— which may not be the most productive. These mechanisms reduce the collective efficiency with which the existing savings are used. A good financial system not only mobilizes savings but also pools them and allocates them efficiently to finance the projects with the highest returns. If savings are not pooled within a well-functioning financial system, then the overall economy suffers a loss, as do the individuals and firms in that economy. Efficient financial intermediation encourages more saving and ensures that savings are used in the most productive fashion, supporting growth and development.

Despite the financial deregulation and reforms of recent decades, financial systems in Latin America and the Caribbean remain very shallow by international standards. While the median banking system in the region has grown to provide approximately 30 percent of GDP in loans to the private sector, this level remains much lower than the banking systems of the median OECD or Emerging Asia economy, which provide approximately 80 and 100 percent of GDP in loans to the private sector, respectively.

Households in the region, especially lower-income households, have limited access to adequate financial instruments to save. They face relatively high costs to access and use the available instruments and often do not trust formal banks. As a result, households save less than they otherwise would; or when they save, they do so using nonfinancial vehicles.

The lack of development and coverage of pension systems in the region is another severe constraint for saving. Less than half the population in Latin America and the Caribbean saves for retirement through a contributory pension system. Households simply do not save enough for retirement, and do not make up for the lack of pension saving through nonpension saving instruments. This situation is a crisis in the making that will worsen as the region inevitably ages. Pension regimes by and large have failed to prepare countries for the demographic transition underway in their societies. In addition to low pension coverage, extensive labor informality, widespread financial illiteracy, and lack of trust in financial systems seriously hamper household saving.

In the case of firms, saving decisions are intimately connected to their investment needs. Firms save (that is, retain earnings) because internal funds are cheaper: they are free from the intermediation costs of bank credit. When the cost of external credit is too high, self-financing may become the only feasible way for firms to finance investments. But when firms lack sufficient retained earnings or external credit in the form and amount they need, they forego productive opportunities. Removing distortions in financial markets that prevent firms from accessing the funding they need at a reasonable cost would enable firms to take on productive investment projects with high returns. This, in turn, would encourage more saving, as both households and firms would want to save more to benefit from the higher returns to investment.

Distortions in labor and product markets also set the stage for misallocating economic resources and, therefore, limiting productivity growth. Scores of small, informal, and unproductive firms in Latin America and the Caribbean limp along on the crutches of lower input costs or higher product prices thanks to taxes and poorly enforced regulations. Removing these preexisting distortions would put everyone on an even footing, improve the business environment, boost investment and, eventually, saving.

Government agencies also save. The political economy literature abounds with theories as to why governments consume too much and save and invest too little. Governments with short time horizons may shy away from long-term investments. Governments with windfall revenues (say, from commodity price booms) may be tempted to dole out the proceeds to their constituencies today, rather than risk others spending in a different fashion tomorrow. Adding to the problem, governments tend to spend inefficiently. Subsidies and/or social transfer programs may be poorly targeted, or the quality of spending is low. These inefficiencies lead to government overspending. Reducing spending inefficiencies would amount to increasing public saving: more money would be freed up for higher quality and more productive public outlays.

Impediments and distortions to saving by households, firms, and government agencies take a toll on the efficiency with which available savings are used. The absence of long-term saving instruments can steer investments away from projects with long horizons that are necessary to raise economic productivity and growth.

A case in point is infrastructure investment such as ports, roads, railways, energy, communication networks, and water and sanitation. Latin America and the Caribbean suffers from the dual problems of low-quality physical infrastructure and insufficient annual investment to close the infrastructure gap. The region must increase investment by between 2 and 4 percentage points of GDP per year for decades to loosen this binding constraint on growth. Low national saving limits the financing available for building and maintaining productive infrastructure. Poor infrastructure, in turn, results in the inadequate provision of services such as potable water, sanitation, health, communications, transportation, and even public safety. These deficiencies prevent households from living the productive, healthy lives that they aspire to. It also slows entrepreneurs with good ideas from expanding their businesses and adding capital and high productivity jobs to the economy.

Saving also matters to the day-to-day life of individuals. Households that either do not save, or save primarily through informal mechanisms, usually have more difficulty dealing with shocks such as losing a job or illness; it is harder for them to invest in education or other forms of human capital; and they do not have the reserves to ride out hard times (smooth consumption). For many individuals, it is too difficult to save when they struggle to make ends meet. However, low-income households do need adequate saving instruments; the problem is that they are not available.

On top of all these pressing needs, the population of Latin America and the Caribbean is aging fast. For the past four decades, most countries in the region have benefited from a bonus in the form of an increase in the working-age population. More workers made it easier to take care of a relatively smaller pool of elderly people through intergenerational transfers (either arrangements within the family, or to a lesser extent, through pensions). This bonus has now ended in many countries, or will end very soon for the rest. Population graying will fuel the demand for resources to meet the greater needs of an expanding group of elderly people. The policy challenge is to ensure that the necessary savings are mobilized now. The alternatives are sad indeed: siphon off more resources from a shrinking working-age population through significantly higher taxes, or face the moral challenge of relegating a large share of the elderly population to live in poverty. The region's aging is inevitable. Saving now is an antidote for the looming aging crisis.

Why Care about National Saving?

National saving is the vehicle through which the region can become stable and confident in its own future. Yet countries in Latin America and the Caribbean are falling short of this goal. They save less than 20 percent of their national income. By contrast, the high-growth countries in East Asia save about 35 percent of national income. Latin America and the Caribbean saves less than every other region in the world, except Sub-Saharan Africa. At the same time, investment rates are lower than what would be needed to sustain high rates of economic growth.[1] The region is not putting aside enough resources today to build a better, brighter future.

Can countries substitute low national saving rates by importing savings from abroad? Not perfectly. Few countries have been able to import savings for prolonged periods of time without abrupt reversals or without incurring severe external indebtedness problems that lead to recurrent financial crises. Crisis-related volatility generates disincentives to save locally because the real value of savings usually falls after crises. People naturally want to protect the real value of their hard-earned savings; thus, they often channel savings abroad, purchase durable goods, or step up consumption rather than invest locally when there is too much volatility. High volatility may also discourage foreigners from lending at longer terms and lower cost. A negative cycle sets in whereby low national saving fuels the need for more foreign savings, which becomes ever more difficult to attract, increases external borrowing costs, induces financial fragility and crises—and feeds back into another shaky cycle. Mobilizing national saving would help break the cycle and set into motion the opposite dynamic. Foreign saving can be a necessary and useful complement to national saving, but it is far from a perfect substitute.

Sharing the Blame for Low Saving

Demographic factors—such as the number of working to non-working age people in a country at a given point in time—matter for saving. Are demographic factors to blame for the region's low saving rates? The answer is no. Beginning in the 1960s, the region embarked on a "saving-friendly" demographic transition (with decreasing age dependency ratios), very much like high-saving countries in Asia. In 1965, for each 100 individuals of working age, there were 90 dependents, either young or old; today there are fewer than 50.Yet, unlike Asia, national saving rates in Latin America have not increased much. If favorable demographic factors had been fully exploited, the average saving rate in Latin America and the Caribbean should be about 8 percentage points of GDP higher. [2]

Various nondemographic factors have kept the saving rates in the region from rising, despite the demographic bonus. One is the lack of adequate saving instruments. The perennial problems of lack of trust in financial institutions and high costs of doing business with banks discourage households from placing their savings in formal financial institutions. Only about 16 percent of the adult population in Latin America and the Caribbean report saving through a bank, compared to 40 percent in Emerging Asia, and 50 percent in advanced economies.[3] Instead, households in the region—especially relatively poorer households— save more through informal mechanisms, or just give up on saving altogether.

Another factor that has depressed saving is the state of the region's pension systems. They cover less than half the population, and many of them face long-term sustainability challenges. Most people in Latin America and the Caribbean do not save through pension systems, or they do not save for enough years to qualify for a contributory pension at the end of their working lives. Importantly, they do not make up for the lack of pension contributions with higher voluntary saving. The pension crisis in Latin America and the Caribbean is effectively a saving problem, with serious social implications.

Fiscal policy has also been a drag on saving in the region. Two long-standing problems of public finance remain largely unaddressed and have a direct bearing on public saving. First, the composition of public expenditures is more oriented toward current expenditure (consumption) than to public investment (saving). Distorted incentives bias public expenditures toward current spending and away from capital investment over the economic cycle. In good times, political economy incentives encourage governments to increase spending across the board. In bad times, it is usually politically more expedient for governments to cut (or postpone) capital expenditure projects than to reduce other expenditures. For example, total expenditure in Latin America and the Caribbean from 2007 to 2014 increased by a very significant 3.7 percent of GDP, but more than 90 percent went into current expenditure, and only 8 percent was devoted to longer-term public investment.

Second, there is considerable leakage in spending areas such as social assistance, tax expenditures and subsidies to energy that average about 2 percent of GDP in the region. In addition, inefficiencies in health and education expenditures average approximately 1 percent of GDP. These leakages and inefficiencies are in essence public saving that is forgone. In good times, nobody pays much attention to these inefficiencies because they are hidden behind positive headline fiscal numbers. But when tax revenues fall, these inefficiencies loom large.

Taxation also directly impacts saving because tax revenue is one of the components of public saving (see Box 1.1). And it indirectly impacts saving through the incentives it provides to individuals and firms to save. Widespread tax evasion in the region is a problem on both fronts: it reduces tax revenues, and it distorts the incentives of compliers versus noncompliers. Tax evasion is, on average, about 52 percent of potential tax collection in Latin America: that is, about half of potential revenues are lost through tax evasion.[4]

BOX 1.1. DEFINING SAVINGS AND ITS COMPONENTS

Total saving in an economy is the current national income that is not consumed. Therefore, it is equal to domestic (real) investment. In turn, total saving can be broken down into national and foreign saving. National saving is the sum of the saving of households and firms plus the saving of public sector agencies. Foreign saving is the net capital that inflows to the economy (that is, net external borrowing). Figure B1.1 illustrates these fundamental accounting relationships.

Total saving has two main components: gross national saving (GNS) and foreign saving (FS).

Gross national saving is the national income (gross national income, GNI) minus private and public consumption (C and G, respectively). Private saving is GNI minus taxes (T) minus private consumption (C). Public saving is taxes (T) minus public consumption (G).

Foreign saving is equal to the current account deficit (CAD) in the balance of payments. This is the net of gross capital inflows to the economy (defined as the changes in the stock of international liabilities) and gross capital outflows from the economy (defined as changes in the stock of foreign asset holdings by residents).

Figure B1.1 Fundamental Accounting Relationships of Savings

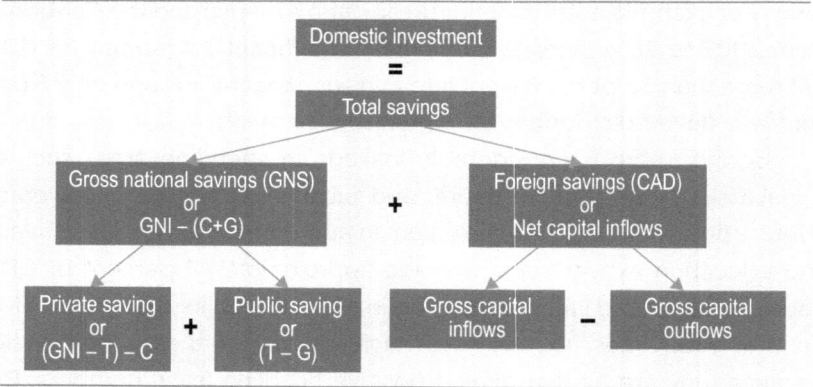

Note: C = private consumption; CAD = current account deficit; G = public consumption; GNI = gross national income; T= taxes.

The result is a misallocation of economic resources and lower aggregate productivity. This, in turn, generates disincentives to save because an economy with low productivity growth is essentially an economy in which returns to saving and investment are also low. Distortions beyond financial markets also matter for productivity growth and saving. Labor markets distorted by high levels of informality, inefficient or inequitable social policy regulations, special tax regimes, or a combination of these factors, change the private profitability of investment projects and lead to socially inefficient investments. Removing these distortions would increase productivity, investment, and savings.

How to Promote Saving for Development

This book outlines how to increase saving for the future in sustainable ways. A comprehensive agenda to mobilize saving combines public policies to stimulate saving directly, such as measures related to fiscal policy and pensions, with policies that operate indirectly by removing constraints that impede agents from saving—and particularly from saving efficiently, in ways that support economic growth and welfare. Improving the efficiency with which savings are used also requires eliminating the distortions that waste economic resources and restrain productivity growth—and thus reduce investment demand.

Tackle the pension problem. A solution to Latin America's saving problem requires fixing broken pension systems. Countries in the region have promised to pay very generous pensions to their retirees, but they have not saved enough to fulfill those promises for everyone. Most pension systems in the region face structural challenges associated with informality and low contribution rates. The public debate in the region largely revolves around whether pension systems should be based on individual accounts (fully funded) or pay-as-you-go (PAYG) approaches. However, that is not necessarily the most relevant debate.

Countries with pension systems based on individual saving accounts—or that want to move in that direction—must realize that these systems per se cannot resolve their saving woes. First, if too few people are covered or contribute to the system, and/or contributions throughout the working life of an individual fall short of providing adequate pension benefits at retirement (either because contributions are low or because the returns to those contributions during the investment period are low), then the government will have to shell out resources to make up the deficit. This will continue to be a drag on national saving. Moreover, transition costs have piled up from shifting pension systems from pay-as-you-go structures (which is how all pension systems in the region began) to systems based on individual accounts because the commitments made to contributors under the pay-as-you-go systems must be fulfilled. This can be a substantial drain on public resources.

Countries with pay-as-you-go systems must adjust the systems' parameters (such as the retirement age, level of benefits, and required years of contributions) to avoid unfunded and/or unsustainable systems down the road. So far, the problem has been hidden behind favorable demographic trends (with relatively more contributors to the pool than retirees receiving benefits). Yet despite the favorable demographics, pay-as-you-go systems have not built adequate reserves by saving (and investing) the excess contributions. Pay-as-you-go pension systems should and must save, creating adequate reserve funds to ensure their long-run sustainability. Importantly, the inevitable fixes to the systems' parameters should come before expanding benefits to more people; otherwise, adding beneficiaries, without addressing the underlying problems of the system, increases the demands on a shrinking pool of resources.

Because pension coverage is inadequate in the two types of contributory pension systems that coexist in Latin America and the Caribbean, noncontributory pension programs are proliferating. Noncontributory pensions provide payments to people who have either not contributed, or do not qualify for a contributory pension. Today, noncontributory pensions account for one-third of pension coverage in the region. In several countries, more people receive noncontributory pensions than contributory pensions. The noncontributory pensions with the highest coverage cost between 0.7 percent and 1 percent of GDP. This cost will more than double by 2050 if generosity and coverage remain constant, just to account for changes in demographics.

The possible effects that noncontributory pensions may have on incentives to save are also important. The emergence of these pensions has yielded some very relevant insights into how individuals and households react to changes in benefits. Noncontributory pensions steal beneficiaries away from contributory systems, and in some cases decrease their savings. They also reduce the transfers that beneficiary households receive from other households.[6] To minimize unintended negative consequences on saving either through excessive fiscal costs, or indirectly by crowding out saving, these programs must be carefully designed and funded, and targeted only to the population at risk of old-age poverty.

Increasing pension saving can also help solve another perennial problem of the region: the lack of long-term funding in local currencies available to finance investment. Infrastructure investment is a highly productive form of investment in short supply in Latin America and the Caribbean. To be viable and sustainable over time, infrastructure investment requires long-term financing—precisely the type of financing that comes with national saving. As countries raise pension saving, the accumulated resources—which by definition are locked up for some time—can be increasingly channeled to finance infrastructure investments.

To do so, policymakers in the region must set up the rules of the game. The first step is to promote the development of an "investible asset class" that permits accumulated savings to be channeled into investment in infrastructure. Since well-planned and executed infrastructure investment is highly productive, the returns on saving generated by these investments can potentially be very large and support the long-term sustainability of pension systems.

However, the region is starting from a very low point, as many countries still have amassed few resources in pension funds, particularly in countries with pay-as-you-go systems. Therefore, the expectation that higher pension saving by itself will solve the region's infrastructure gap is unrealistic.

Focus on infrastructure and capital spending. To increase investment to close the infrastructure gap, the region needs to boost public saving and investment. The public sector is the main source of financing for infrastructure investment in the region and in the world. Increasing public investment requires designing fiscal rules and targets that direct a higher share of total expenditures to public investment and counter the political economy forces that bias expenditures toward current expenditures in both good and bad times.

Over the last two decades, improved fiscal frameworks have delivered higher public saving in many countries. Yet more effort is needed just when a challenging economic environment has made doing so more difficult. The good news is that substantial public saving can still be generated without having to rely on the traditional tools of raising taxes or reducing expenditures across the board.

First, governments must realize that the composition of public expenditures is a direct determinant of the level of public saving. Governments have room to boost public saving by increasing the share of capital expenditures, which is low in the region, with respect to current spending, which is high. This requires a more prudent approach to fiscal policy. As a general rule, only a small fraction of any change in commodity prices or other external factors should be considered permanent. Then, current expenditures will be expanded relatively less in good times (the upside of the typical business cycle) and reduced more in the downturns.

Second, savings of approximately 2 percent of GDP on average could be generated by reducing leakage in current expenditures in areas such as social assistance, tax expenditures, and subsidies to the energy sector. That means making sure that spending reaches its intended beneficiaries only. Designing and implementing reforms to make public expenditures more efficient should rank high on the policy agendas of governments throughout the region.

Target tax policy better. Governments can also encourage saving through tax policy. Income taxes are levied on both individuals (personal income tax) and firms (corporate income tax). But households collectively own firms; therefore tax policy should consider integrating personal and corporate income taxes, and avoiding double taxation of savings: first, when it is generated by the firm, and then when it is distributed to households as dividends.[7] Personal income taxes across the region should continue evolving into a dual system,[8] with a lower flat tax on capital, in which all forms of capital income (interest payments, dividends, and capital gains) receive equal tax treatment. Corporate income tax rates should fall in line with international trends to facilitate the formalization of informal firms.[9] This would help expand the tax base, which is currently low.[10]

Countries in the region must also reconsider tax preferences that favor investing in housing rather than financial instruments such as stocks, bonds, and term deposits in banks. Loopholes in the tax codes in many countries discriminate against nonhousing saving vehicles while mostly benefiting high-income households. Leveling off tax incentives for housing with other forms of financial saving is generally a better option than introducing new tax incentives for certain types of financial saving. In the past, many advanced countries introduced tax-preferred savings accounts, sometimes designed to encourage saving for education, life insurance contracts, and other purposes. The evidence shows that these tax preferences did not increase saving. By and large, only the relatively rich used these vehicles, primarily to reduce their tax payments, with limited to no impact on total saving.[11]

Promote household saving and create a savings culture. At the household level, saving rates in the region are distorted by a number of factors: high costs of accessing and using the financial system; lack of confidence in the financial system; poor financial regulation; little understanding about banks and how they work; and social pressures and behavioral biases. Successful financial inclusion requires more than just opening new bank accounts. It means tailoring saving products to the demands of potential clients, taking into account the various real-life constraints they face to save, and creating incentives to channel more savings through the formal financial system. Preliminary but encouraging evidence of public policy interventions and financial product innovations shows an increase in household saving, as well as promising initiatives to encourage more financial saving in particular. Making more and faster progress in these areas requires more dynamic regulation and supervision of the financial system and the collaborative efforts of financial regulators and bankers to implement reforms and promote even more innovation.

Government initiatives to pay social transfers through bank accounts and to channel remittances through domestic financial systems are useful first steps. Additional progress in encouraging more financial saving demands improvements in the design of the programs: for example, by pairing payments with programs that provide financial education, and/or with instruments to help users overcome the behavioral and social biases that constrain saving. Innovation and technology provide another opportunity to encourage more saving through the formal financial system. While the penetration of mobile telephones is high in Latin America and the Caribbean, the region still lags behind in using mobile technology for financial services and as a tool for financial inclusion because policy and regulations have not kept pace with the mobile telephone revolution.

A promising avenue for creating a saving culture in Latin America and the Caribbean is financial education, with a focus on children and youth. Positive saving habits are easier to instill during the early years, when the brain is still developing and learning is easier.

Improve productivity growth. Increasing national saving is necessary to achieve the region's aspirations, but it is not enough. Evidence from around the world shows that historically, an increase in national saving rates coincided with higher economic growth only when the saving surges were accompanied by higher aggregate productivity growth.

This relationship underscores two points. First, a surge in saving rates can be sustained for long periods of time when it is associated with permanent incentives for individuals to save. And the incentives to save are higher when productivity grows faster. Second, in order for more saving to impact growth and development, the savings must be put to good use. That is, savings must be channeled to productive investment opportunities.

Total factor productivity (TFP) is ultimately the weighted sum of the productivity of the existing population of firms in the economy. TFP can grow because either firms in the economy become more productive, more resources are channeled to productive firms, or the market allows more productive firms to survive and less productive firms to exit. Latin America and the Caribbean is cluttered by a large number of small, informal, and unproductive firms that survive because they enjoy cheaper inputs and/or higher product prices. These factors, in turn, arise from distortionary taxes and regulations that are not properly enforced. Increasing aggregate productivity requires reducing those distortions. Doing so would improve the allocation of resources in the economy and increase aggregate saving and investment.

Fix the financial system. Efforts to create and sustain a culture of saving in the region must be complemented by efforts to help the financial system pool and allocate savings efficiently. Only by fixing the problems that discourage the use of financial systems for saving and limit the availability of financing for productive firms, can more saving turn into better saving for development.

Financial frictions are like sand in the wheels of the economy; they slow down economic progress. Two types of financial distortions are particularly acute in Latin America and the Caribbean and are amenable to policy action. First, banks do not have access to quality information about potential borrowers. While the region has made progress in extending the coverage of credit bureaus that provide this information, the quality and timeliness of the information available through such bureaus is still poor in many countries. On average, the regulatory framework in Latin America is less conducive to information sharing than in other regions of the world.

A second problem is the high cost of enforcing financial contracts in the region. The effective protection of property rights is particularly weak in Latin America. The good news is that examples of successful reforms in the region have helped alleviate this constraint. Bankruptcy reforms in Brazil (2004–05), Colombia (2012), and more recently Chile (2014) appear to be lowering the costs of enforcing financial contracts.

The Many Faces of Saving

This book considers how changes in the different components of saving (see Box 1.1) contribute to total saving and investment in the overall economy. This approach allows a more comprehensive understanding of how public policies can affect saving by households, firms, and government agencies, while recognizing the important interrelationships between the different components. There are four possible interrelationships to consider:

- **Between private and public saving.** While government thrift would increase public saving, this usually leads to an offset in private saving because households and firms anticipate that with higher government saving today, lower taxes will be required in the future, and therefore they increase consumption today.
- **Between household and firm saving.** Households, which own firms, may factor firms' saving decisions into their own consumption decisions. Thus, higher saving by firms may be offset by lower saving by households.
- **Between mandatory and voluntary household saving.** Households may choose how much to save for retirement, using both pension and nonpension saving instruments interchangeably. Therefore, any saving done through pension instruments may just be forgone saving through other instruments.
- **Between national and foreign saving.** If national and foreign saving were perfect substitutes, a shortage of national saving would simply be made up by higher imports of foreign saving.

Box 1.2 discusses the theoretical and empirical evidence for each of these interrelationships. Here, suffice it to say that the collective evidence indicates that multiple possible offsets are only partial. Thus, increases in either public or private saving will increase national saving, but not on a one-to-one basis. And an increase in national saving will support higher domestic investment.

A Policy Agenda for the Future

The book identifies six strategic goals for households, firms, and governments in the region.

First, governments must create an enabling environment for saving. This should become a high priority in the region's policy agendas. The "saving glut" in other parts of the world will not make up for the saving deficit in the region because foreigners cannot be expected to invest for the long term in countries where their own citizens are not confident enough to save.

Second, governments across the region can generate more saving by spending more efficiently. In fact, during difficult economic times, targeting public expenditures may be the only politically viable way to increase public saving in many countries because it avoids the unpleasantries of traditional fiscal tightening such as raising taxes or cutting expenditures.

Third, governments should promote and facilitate the development of financial systems that offer a full range of saving and investment instruments for households and firms. Banks can support these efforts by reaching out to more people with better financial instruments.

Fourth, governments, pension regulators, supervisors, and public and private sector managers must collaborate to fix broken pension systems. Population aging poses a great threat to economic stability and prosperity. Pension systems across the region must become sustainable, equitable, and more inclusive.

Fifth, people in Latin America and the Caribbean must develop a saving culture. Saving is difficult because it involves sacrificing current consumption. If people do not internalize the benefits of saving more, it will be hard, or impossible, to overcome inertia. Right now, too many people across the region fail to see the benefits of saving. A culture is built from the bottom up. Starting early in life with financial education on the role of saving is a critical element for success.

Sixth, saving more will not be enough to support development. The additional saving must be put to good use. The investment distortions that plague the region and that weaken investment demand must be eliminated. These distortions include inefficiencies in financial markets, high informality in labor markets, lack of adequate and predictable regulations, and special tax regimes. These distortions squander economic resources and impede productivity growth, which in turn feeds low investment demand and reduces saving.

BOX 1.2. THE INTERRELATIONSHIPS BETWEEN THE COMPONENTS OF SAVING

Public versus Private Saving: Ricardian Equivalence

Do increases in public saving increase national saving? Governments' actions on fiscal policy are usually offset by private saving. In fact, the offset could be one to one, under the conditions specified by Barro (1974) on "Ricardian Equivalence," such as complete capital markets and perfect foresight. For example, any increase in the fiscal deficit financed either by lower taxes or higher debt—both of which would leave permanent income of households unchanged— would result in an equivalent increase in household saving, such that the net impact on national saving would be null.

However, the conditions that would enable a perfect offset are too stringent. Since Barro's paper, the literature has focused on assessing the degree of offset.[a] Estimates vary across studies, but they tend to cluster in the range of 0.4 to 0.6, suggesting that for every dollar by which public saving is reduced, private saving tends to increase by 40 to 60 cents.[b] While the offset is significantly less than one to one, the fact that there is a partial offset suggests that putting the burden of rising national saving on fiscal policy alone is wrong. Governments should not overlook policies to mobilize private savings as well.

Firm versus Household Saving: Piercing the Corporate Veil

Within the private sector, part of the saving is generated by households and another portion by firms through retained earnings. Poterba (1987) noted that firms contributed a high share of private saving in the United States and went on to posit the "corporate veil hypothesis," according to which households take full account of the saving made by businesses: that is, households "pierce" the corporate veil.

The argument rests on the fact that households are the ultimate owners of firms, and thus they adjust their saving plans in accordance with changes in firms' saving decisions. However, various problems can invalidate the full piercing of the corporate veil in practice, such as asymmetric information and bounded rationality (Poterba, 1987). The resulting empirical prediction was that an increase (reduction) in firm saving will give rise to an increase (reduction) in private saving, albeit not one to one.

A handful of papers have researched the empirical nexus between household and firm saving, concluding that the offset is only partial. Grigoli, Herman, and Schmidt-Hebbel (2014) find that an additional dollar of firm saving translates into an increase of 42 cents in private saving. Using a different sample, Bebczuk and Cavallo (2016) find that a $1 increase in firm saving reduces household saving by 40 cents—thereby increasing private saving by as much as 60 cents.

(continued on next page)

BOX 1.2. *(continued)*

The bottom line is that the saving decisions of households and firms are intertwined. An association between the two sectors should be taken into account, but the two forms of saving are not perfect substitutes.

Mandatory versus Voluntary Household Saving: The Pension Offset

Household saving includes a mandatory component in the form of pension contributions. The potential substitutability between mandatory and voluntary saving matters for policy. If they were perfect substitutes, then retirement policies would have no incidence on the level of saving: that is, every dollar saved through a pension instrument would be offset by an equal amount of forgone saving in nonpension instruments. What is the extent of the offset in practice? In this area as well, the evidence points to only partial substitution, although the magnitude remains contested.[c]

This is a relevant and contentious policy issue in Latin America and the Caribbean. Beginning in the 1980s, the region was a pioneer in reforming pension systems from unfunded pay-as-you-go to fully funded regimes based on individual accounts. The objectives of the reforms were to increase pension coverage and reduce long-term fiscal vulnerabilities associated with the old systems. The reforms were also expected to increase private and national saving.

With the benefit of hindsight, researchers can evaluate the extent to which saving increased in the aftermath of the reforms. The evidence shows that private saving rose only moderately.[d] The increase in private saving was weak because the number of contributors to the reformed systems remained low, as, in turn, informality in labor markets remained high. In addition, the reforms created a deficit during the transition period (to fulfill the promises made to people who had contributed to the old systems) that persists in several countries, and that lessened the positive impact of the reforms on national saving.

Foreign versus National Saving: Imperfect Substitutes

There is a high positive correlation between national saving and domestic investment across countries (Feldstein and Horioka, 1980). Numerous studies have found— with very few exceptions—that the correlation is systematically greater than zero across countries and over time. The positive correlation reveals imperfect financial integration across countries: changes in national saving are not completely offset by changes in foreign saving. Therefore, while the correlation does not prove if higher national saving leads to investment or vice versa, it does underscore that an increase in national saving can be expected to be at least partially retained domestically, thereby ending up as additional investment, rather than completely exported abroad through capital flight.

(continued on next page)

BOX 1.2. *(continued)*

For countries that need to raise domestic investment, the robust positive correlation between national saving and domestic investment shows that recourse to importing foreign saving can be a helpful remedy, but is not a cure to low national saving. This conclusion is reinforced by two additional pieces of evidence presented in this book. First, for most countries, the net absorption of foreign saving is small relative to the volume of domestic investment (see chapter 2). Second, the financing of the domestic capital stock in each country has been predominantly national.[e]

---

[a] For a recent survey of the literature, see Röhn (2010).

[b] Background research conducted in the context of this project confirms this range. Becerra, Cavallo and Noy (2015) conduct reduced form regressions of the determinants of private saving rates using panel regressions. One of the determinants of private saving is the public saving rate. Their coefficient estimate on public saving is approximately –0.60, in line with previous estimates in the literature.

[c] Two strands of the literature have tested this hypothesis. The first strand analyzes the relationship between pension wealth and private savings using country case studies. Attanasio and Rohwedder (2003) and Attanasio and Brugiavini (2003) find evidence for Italy and the United Kingdom of a high degree of substitution between pensions and voluntary saving. For some groups of workers, the elasticity of substitution is close to 0.9. Using similar methods, Coronado (1998), Aguila (2011), and Sandoval-Hernández (2012) find high offset coefficients for workers in Chile and Mexico. The second strand exploits cross-country evidence of variation of pension arrangements (and saving) and aggregate saving. Examples include Bailliu and Reisen (1998); López-Murphy and Musalem (2004); Bebczuk and Musalem (2006); Clements et al. (2011); and Bebczuk (2015a). A common thread across these studies is that they uncover a positive but very small impact of funded pension regimes on nonpension saving.

[d] See Bebczuk (2015a).

[e] Aizenman, Pinto, and Radziwill (2007) show that on average 90 percent of the stock of physical capital in developing countries has been self-financed through the accumulation of national savings. Background research conducted for this book confirms this result for Latin America and the Caribbean.

In the end, measuring success in achieving these goals boils down to creating an environment where everybody shares the vision that more saving, and a better use of existing savings, is the solution to the region's economic woes—and the path to a stable and confident region in which any aspiration is possible.

Notes

[1] See Commission on Growth and Development (2008).

[2] See Cavallo, Sánchez, and Valenzuela (2016).

[3] See World Bank (2014b).

[4] Corbacho, Fretes Cibils, and Lora (2013).

[5] See World Bank and PwC (2015).

[6] See Juárez (2009).

[7] Integrating corporate and personal income taxes proved to be very successful in encouraging saving in Chile. See Cerda et al. (2015).

[8] For example, the dual income tax in Nordic countries combines a flat tax on capital income with a progressive labor income tax schedule. Several countries in Latin America and the Caribbean have a dual or semi-dual system, but most are not integrated (Corbacho, Fretes Cibils, and Lora, 2013).

[9] Corporate income tax rates have declined over the last 40 years from an average of 40 percent in 1980 to about 30 percent in the 2000s, and to 24 percent in 2014. Among the reasons for the decline, ongoing research points to profit-shifting concerns and the attraction of investment and tax competition.

[10] High taxation of formal firms can lead to both less saving and lower formal employment. In Colombia, Granda and Hamann (2015) show that lower taxes on profits increase firm saving in the formal sector, and increase labor formalization and entrepreneurship. Reducing payroll taxes achieves similar qualitative results.

[11] See OECD (2007); McDonald et al. (2011); Boadway (2015).

2 The State of Saving in Latin America and the Caribbean

Savings in an economy matter for development. At the macro level, savings determine how much a country can invest, and they have implications for growth and economic stability. At the individual level, savings give people a cushion to withstand unexpected income shocks, smooth consumption, and plan for the future.

Despite their significance, determining how much a country should save is not an easy task. Just like the "right" flying altitude of an airplane depends on factors such as wind speed, distance to destination, and weather conditions, aggregate saving rates in an economy depend on several factors that vary across countries and over time. In particular, saving rates are driven by: (a) demographic trends; (b) income growth and how that growth is distributed across generations; (c) people's income at different ages and stages of life; (d) pension and old-age living arrangements; (e) asset markets that permit households and firms to shift consumption from the present to the future; (f) individual preferences and varying levels of tolerance for uncertainty; (g) growth expectations; and (h) the institutional framework, among other factors.[1] The interaction of all these factors determines the differential saving patterns across economies and over time.[2]

This book tells a story of unrealized potential and the role savings has played in the region's search for elusive growth. This chapter sets the stage for this story by describing household and aggregate saving patterns in the region and by defining the main terms and concepts that will be used throughout the book (see Box 2.1). It is the starting point for the discussion, the base on which policy must build.

BOX 2.1. WHAT IS SAVING?

At the aggregate level, national saving (Sn) is defined as gross national disposable income (NDI) minus total consumption, based on national accounts data. This is the flow of saving generated within a period of time, usually a year. The saving rate is generally defined as the ratio of national saving to gross domestic product (GDP).

Aggregate national saving may be further decomposed into its private and public components, depending on who generates it:

$$S_n = S_{pri} + S_{pub}$$

Private saving (S_{pri}) is defined as the sum of household (Hh) and firm saving (Bs).

$$S_{pri} = Hh + Bs$$

Household saving is the portion of the disposable income of families that is not devoted to current consumption; it comprises voluntary household saving and pension contributions. Firm saving is defined as cash flows—net revenues plus depreciation—minus dividends or firms' retained earnings. In practice, national accounts data in many countries do not permit the sub-components of private saving to be identified separately. This reflects, among other factors, the prevalence of large informal sectors in developing countries that blur the boundaries between households and firms. When disaggregation can be done, the saving generated by firms that operate in the informal economy, such as family firms and self-employed workers—to the extent that it is measured—is bundled together with household saving.

Public saving (Spub) is defined as total public sector income minus current government expenditures. National accountants typically approximate this by adding up the overall fiscal balance of the public sector (OB)—including interest payments on debt—and public sector investment (PI).

$$S_{pub} = OB + PI$$

By definition, aggregate saving equals domestic investment ("real investment," which is the so-called "gross fixed capital formation") in closed economies because both concepts refer to national income that is not consumed when it is generated. Instead, open economies can rely on foreign saving as a complementary source of investment financing. Therefore, in open economies:

Domestic Investment = Total Saving (TS) = National Saving (Sn) + Foreign Saving (FS)

where FS is the counterpart of the current account deficit in the balance of payments: that is, when a country runs a current account deficit, it imports

(continued on next page)

BOX 2.1. *(continued)*

savings, (FS > 0); when it runs a current account surplus, it exports savings, (FS < 0).

Some components of savings, such as pension contributions, are directly measured, but in most cases, savings are not directly observed. Thus they are usually approximated as the residual between measured income and consumption, which implies a double measurement error in the computation of saving flows. Notwithstanding, the international harmonization of national accounts records across countries allows for meaningful cross-country comparisons of saving rates.

---

[a] Gross National Disposable Income is equal to the Gross National Product (GNP) plus all net payments from abroad (i.e. net factor payments and net current transfers).

[b] Business saving is also referred to as corporate saving, retained earnings, undistributed cash flows, and the accumulated stock of saving as internal funds (or own funds).

[c] A country's GDP (Y) is divided into four components of expenditure: consumption (C), Investment (I), government purchases (G) and net exports (X – M). In closed economies, X – M = 0, and therefore (Y-C-G) = I, where the left-hand side of this equation is national saving.

[d] In open economies, the wedge between Saving (S) and Investment (I) is the current account balance (CAB). CAB = (X –M) plus net total payments from abroad. Therefore, saving equals investment plus the current account balance.

National Saving Rates: Comparatively Low

Over the last 30 years, national saving rates in Latin America and the Caribbean have hovered below 20 percent of GDP, well below Advanced Economies and fast growing Asian countries (Figure 2.1).[3] Even after controlling for factors such as demographics, income per capita, and growth performance, Advanced Economies and countries in Emerging Asia save, on average, 3 and 9 percentage points of GDP more, respectively, than countries in Latin America and the Caribbean.[4]

National saving rates in Latin America have varied significantly in recent decades. During the debt crises of the early 1980s, they fell to their historical minimum (11.5 percent of GDP in 1983), and during the 2003–06 commodity price boom, they temporarily surged above 20 percent of GDP. Although average saving rates in Emerging Asia have also fluctuated throughout this period, they have been consistently higher than in Latin America and the Caribbean by between 10 and 20 percentage points of GDP. In Advanced Economies, average saving rates have been relatively stable at slightly over 20 percent of GDP.

Figure 2.2 shows the distribution of average national saving rates from 1980 to 2014 in select regions. The line at the center of each box

Figure 2.1 Gross National Saving Rates (percent of GDP), Simple Averages by Region

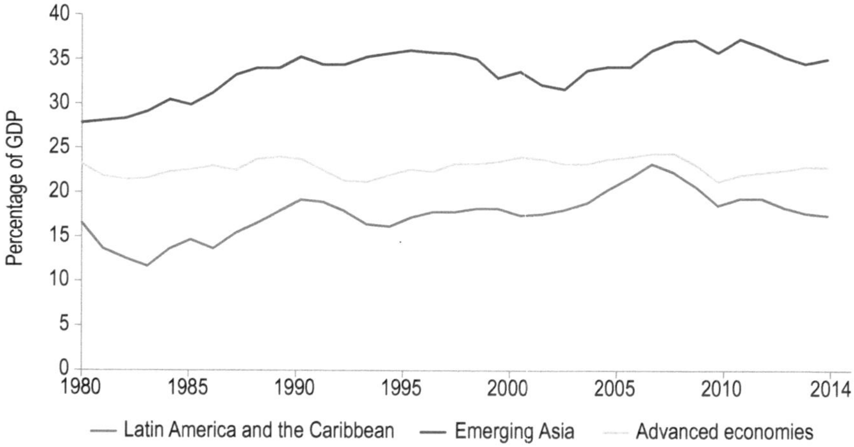

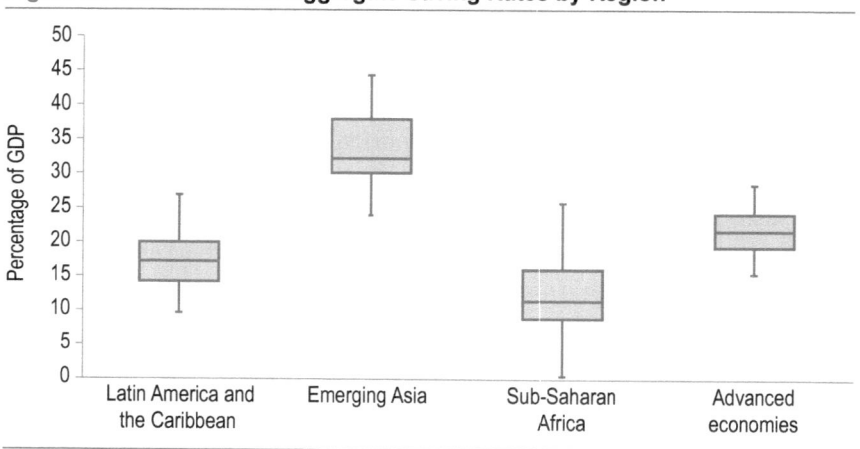

Source: Authors' calculations, based on data from World Economic Outlook database (IMF, 2015).

is the median of the regional distribution. The top and bottom edges of each box are the 75th and 25th percentile of the regional distribution respectively, and the line-ends plot the minimum and maximum.[5] Tellingly, the median saving rate in Latin America and the Caribbean is closer to that of Sub-Saharan Africa and Advanced Economies—two

Figure 2.2 Distribution of Aggregate Saving Rates by Region

Source: Authors' calculations based on data from World Economic Outlook database (IMF, 2015).
Note: Aggregate saving rates (percent of GDP) are computed as country averages of annual saving rates over the period 1980–2014. Each country's average is then grouped by region.

Figure 2.3 Gross National Saving Rates in Latin America and the Caribbean

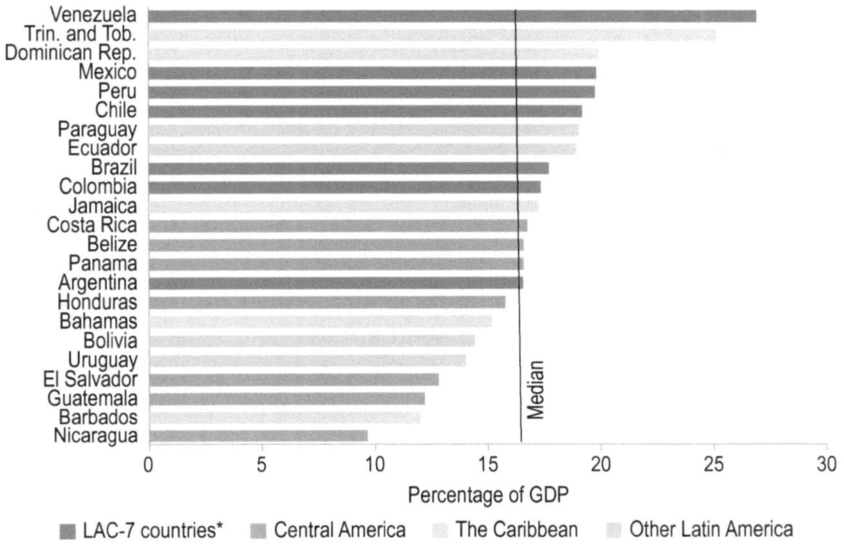

Source: Authors' calculations based on data from World Economic Outlook database (IMF, 2015).
Notes: Aggregate saving rates (percent of GDP) are computed as country averages of annual saving rates over the period 1980–2014. The horizontal line is the sample median.
LAC-7 includes Argentina, Brazil, Chile, Colombia, Mexico, Peru, and Venezuela.

regions at opposite extremes of the world distribution of income per capita—than to Emerging Asia, a more comparable region in terms of income level. All told, national saving rates in Latin America and the Caribbean pale compared to almost every other world region, except Sub-Saharan Africa.[6]

Across subgroups of countries in Latin America and the Caribbean, median saving rates range between 14.7 percent of GDP in Central America (excluding Mexico) and 20 percent in the Caribbean region. Among the seven largest countries by income (LAC-7),[7] median saving rates lie between these two extremes at 18.2 percent of GDP (Figure 2.3).

The Private Sector: Taking the Lead

The private sector does most of the heavy lifting when it comes to savings in Latin America—and throughout the world for that matter. Table 2.1 presents the shares of each subcomponent of total saving—public, private, and foreign—averaged over the period 1980-2014 for Latin America and the Caribbean, Emerging Asia, and Advanced Economies. Across these three regions, private saving leads the way, representing between 70 and 90 percent of total saving. Clearly, private saving plays a pivotal role in determining the level of total saving rates in all regions.

Although private saving rates represent the largest component of total saving in Latin America and the Caribbean, they are lower there than in both Emerging Asia and Advanced Economies. On the other hand, average public saving rates in the region are higher than in Advanced Economies and lower than in Emerging Asia. Compared to the other regions, foreign saving in Latin America and the Caribbean represents a relatively large share of total saving (3.5 percentage points out of 21 percentage points of GDP of total saving) and contributes a positive amount to total savings—meaning that, on average, the region has been a net importer of foreign saving for the past three decades (in sharp contrast to Emerging Asia).

While public and foreign components of saving contribute quantitatively less to total saving in Latin America, they nonetheless influence the variation of saving rates over time. Figure 2.4 shows that the importance of foreign saving in the region has been declining since the 1980s. It also shows that a temporary surge in saving rates, fueled by the 2005-09 commodity price boom, was driven largely by the expansion of public saving.

Figure 2.4 Composition of Total Saving in the Region, 1980–2014

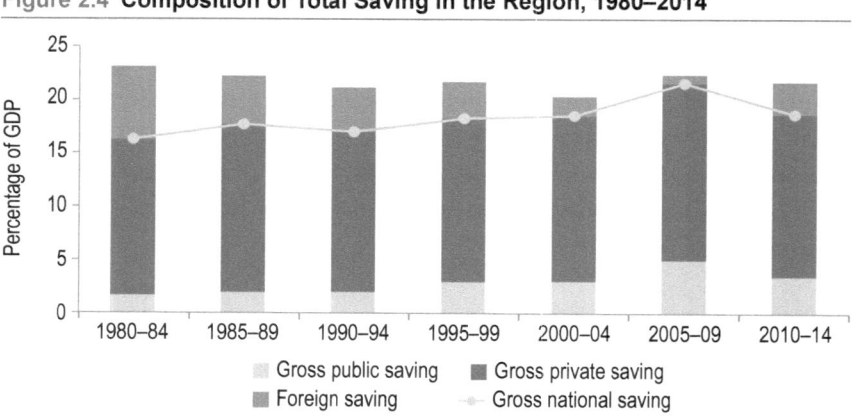

Source: Authors' calculations based on data from World Economic Outlook database (IMF, 2015).
Note: Quinquennial averages computed over regional yearly averages.

Foreign Savings: A Secondary Actor

Foreign savings can complement or decrease national savings, depending on whether a country is a net importer or exporter of foreign savings. Between 1980 and 2014, the median country in Latin America and the Caribbean was a net importer of savings (as in Sub-Saharan Africa and Advanced Economies), while the median country in Emerging Asia was a net exporter of savings (see Figure 2.5).

However, foreign savings are not high enough to pick up the slack for comparatively lower national saving rates in Latin America and the Caribbean (see Table 2.1). In fact, foreign saving rates (in absolute terms) are significantly lower than national saving rates in all regions.

Figure 2.5 Distribution of Foreign Saving Rates by Region

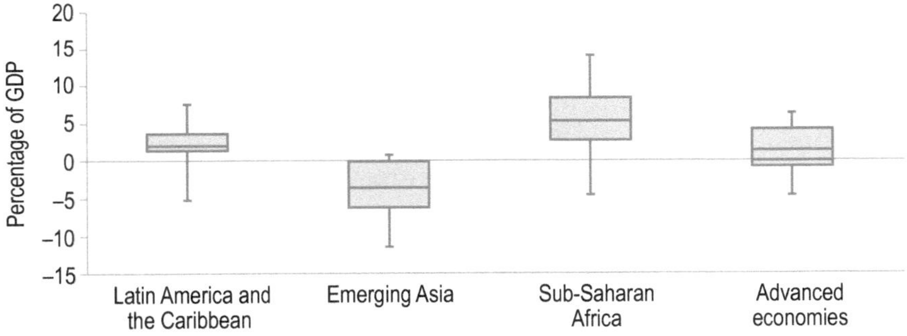

Source: Authors' calculations based on data from World Economic Outlook database (IMF, 2015).
Note: Aggregate saving rates (percent of GDP) are computed as country averages of annual saving rates over the period 1980–2014. Each country's average is then grouped by region.

Table 2.1. Saving Rates by Sector, 1980–2014 (percentage of GDP)

Saving rates by region	Latin America and the Caribbean	Emerging Asia	Sub-Saharan Africa	Advanced economies
1. Gross national saving	17.5	33.7	13.8	22.8
1.1 Gross public saving	2.8	7.9	2.8	1.5
1.2 Gross private saving	14.7	25.8	10.9	21.2
2. Foreign saving	3.5	-3.8	5.4	0.8
3. Total saving	21.0	29.9	19.2	23.6

Source: Authors' calculations based on data from World Economic Outlook database (IMF, 2015). Gross national saving (1) is equal to gross public saving (1.1) plus gross private saving (1.2). Total saving (3) is equal to foreign saving (2) plus gross national saving (1).
Note: Statistics computed over country averages.

Businesses: The Biggest Savers—Worldwide

The prevalence of large informal sectors in developing countries blurs the boundaries between households and firms. Many households are supported by self-employed workers who run their own businesses, usually in the informal economy. This limits the availability of cross-country data on private saving for clearly distinguishing between households and businesses. Despite the difficulties, two recent papers (Bebczuk and Cavallo, 2016; Grigoli, Herman, and Schmidt-Hebbel, 2015) compile the available data from international and national sources.[8] While the studies have different samples and assumptions, both reveal that, on average, business saving is the largest contributor to aggregate private saving in most countries, including Latin America and the Caribbean (see Figure 2.6).[9]

Firms save because internal funds are a cheaper source of investment financing than external credit, which includes the costs of financial intermediation (see Myers and Majluf [1984] on the pecking order theory of finance). Households, in turn, are the owners of the firms, which means that, in principle, the distribution of savings within the private component should not be particularly relevant.

However, as discussed in detail in Chapter 1 (Box 1.1), business saving and household saving are not perfect substitutes. There are many

Figure 2.6 Composition of Private Saving, World and Latin America and the Caribbean

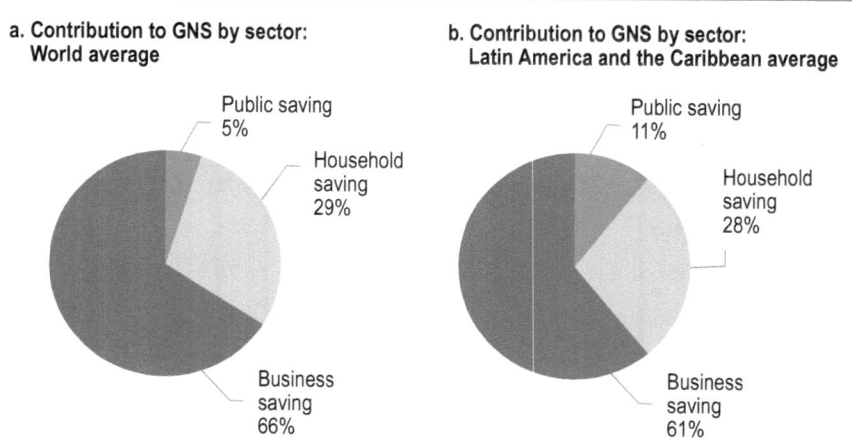

a. Contribution to GNS by sector: World average

Public saving 5%
Household saving 29%
Business saving 66%

b. Contribution to GNS by sector: Latin America and the Caribbean average

Public saving 11%
Household saving 28%
Business saving 61%

Source: Authors' calculations based on data from Bebczuk and Cavallo (2016).
Note: The figure shows the contributions to Gross National Saving (GNS).

reasons why households do not perceive the saving done by firms as their own. For instance, the majority of households are not direct owners of firm shares; there is asymmetric information between firm owners and managers; and, in many countries, there is differential taxation of corporate profits and capital owner income.[10]

Importantly, household savings per se have important welfare implications. Households use savings to smooth consumption and to cope with unexpected income shocks. Savings help households manage risks better, especially when they face liquidity and/or credit constraints. Therefore, although their relative contribution to aggregate saving is smaller than the saving generated by businesses, fostering the accumulation of household savings is important to sustain an equitable development path. With this in mind, the rest of the chapter is devoted to the analysis of household savings (see Box 2.2 on measurement issues related to household savings).

Farewell to the Demographic Dividend

According to the most well-known theory of consumption and saving behavior, Modigliani's Life-Cycle Hypothesis (LCH), individuals borrow when they are young, save during their working years, and then deplete their savings once they reach retirement. When economies are growing, younger generations tend to be wealthier and save more, leading to a positive relationship between growth and aggregate saving.

During a demographic transition, a country moves through three broad phases (see Bloom, Canning, and Sevilla, 2001) that vary in their impact on the dependency ratio (the ratio of the young and old-age populations to the working-age population). In the first phase, advances in healthcare reduce mortality rates, particularly infant mortality, thereby increasing the ratio of dependents (in this case, children) to the working age population. In the second phase, lower fertility leads to a decrease in dependency rates, as the number of incoming (young) cohorts declines while the number of adults entering the labor force rises. In the last phase, longer average life expectancy leads to an aging population and a corresponding increase in old age dependency rates and, therefore, overall dependency rates. This cycle lasts several decades, but the duration of each stage varies across countries.

During the second phase (also known as the "demographic dividend"), age dependency rates decline. This, in turn, implies that the

BOX 2.2. HOUSEHOLD SAVING RATES: MEASUREMENT ISSUES

National accountants rely on indirect data sources and make simplifying assumptions to construct disposable income and consumption statistics from which they can derive saving as a residual between the two. Consequently, there is considerable measurement error in the resulting estimates of saving rates.[a]

Alternatively, household saving rates can be computed using micro-level data from household surveys. Since these surveys focus on measuring living conditions, they typically collect detailed income and expenditure modules that in turn can be used to compute saving rates. These surveys are generally representative of the country as a whole and, as such, the estimates they provide are comparable to those coming from national accounts.

However, several studies show that there are significant discrepancies between household saving rates computed from national accounts and those computed from household surveys.[b] On the one hand, household surveys have the potential to provide more accurate measures of both disposable income and consumption at the household level because they can capture transactions in informal sector transactions. On the other hand, there are misreporting biases in income or consumption that may be more salient among specific income or occupational groups.[c] For example, higher-income households may have a more varied consumption basket; consequently, they could have a higher likelihood of forgetting or misreporting these expenditures than poorer households. In addition, estimated saving can be negative for households that can finance expenditures using credit or accumulated savings over a given time frame, or among those that tend to underreport household income. This is sometimes reflected in negative national average saving rates, particularly when wealthier segments of the population are underrepresented in the sample.

What then is the informational value of household saving rates computed from household surveys? The advantage of these data sources is that they allow the definition of household consumption to be fine-tuned by taking into account the heterogeneity in saving vehicles used in different contexts. For example, in countries with limited access to diversified saving instruments, some households may choose to save by purchasing durable goods. Similarly, in countries with deficient public education and health services, households may choose to invest in these services to accumulate human capital. Although not all expenditures in durables or health and education are undertaken as a form of saving, the alternative saving rates (computed by excluding certain types of expenditures) can be informative, especially in settings where non-traditional forms of saving are expected to be important, as is the case in Latin America and the Caribbean.

Figure B2.1 reports the ratio of alternative definitions of household saving rates to standard definitions (i.e., saving rates using all categories of consumption without discriminating) for select Latin American and Caribbean

(continued on next page)

BOX 2.2. *(continued)*

countries, and for a smaller set of Asian countries and Advanced Economies used as comparators.[d] Excluding the consumption of durable goods from expenditures generates a substantial increase in saving rates in all regions. On average, saving rates computed assuming that durables are an alternative form of saving, increase by 50 percent, relative to the traditional definition in Latin America and the Caribbean. This increase is even larger amongst the comparator countries: the ratio of the alternative definitions to the traditional definition of saving rates is approximately 2.0 and 2.4 amongst the control groups in Asia and Advanced Economies, respectively. The regional differences reflect the fact that households in countries of the comparator groups spend a higher fraction of their incomes on durable goods.

Excluding education and health spending from total consumption has a comparatively larger effect on the resulting saving rates proxy in Latin America and the Caribbean than in the control groups. On average, saving rates in the region are 1.6 times higher after removing education and health expenditures from consumption, while they are 1.3 and 1.4 times higher in Asian and Advanced Economies in the comparator samples, respectively.

In summary, household saving rates are estimated to be higher when computed using a different definition of saving that considers expenditures in durables or in health and education as alternative forms of saving rather than

Figure B2.1 **Alternative Definitions of Saving Rates vs Traditional Definition**

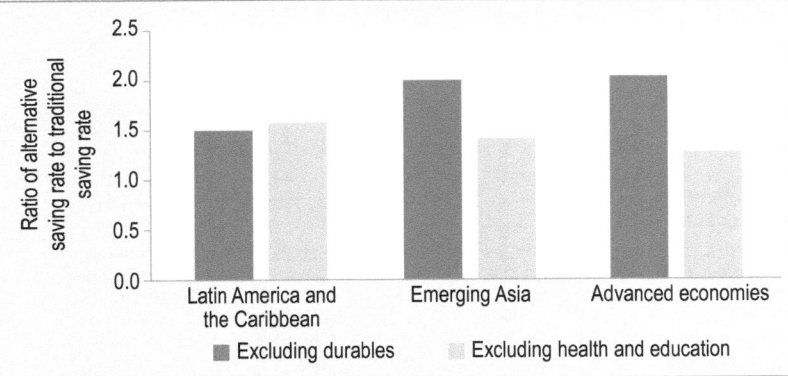

Source: Authors' calculation based on data from Bebczuk et al. (2015); Székely, Mendoza, and Karver (2015); Hernani-Limarino, Jiménez, and Mena (2015); and Centro de Estudios Educativos y Sociales (CEES). Estimates for Mexico come from Székely, Mendoza, and Karver (2015) and for Bolivia come from Hernani-Limarino, Jiménez, and Mena (2015). Estimates for all other Latin American and Caribbean countries (Argentina, Brazil, Colombia, Ecuador, El Salvador, Guatemala, Nicaragua, Panama, Peru) come from Bebczuk et al. (2015). Estimates for Emerging Asia (Sri Lanka, Taiwan, Thailand) and advanced economies (United States, France, Japan) come from Centro de Estudios Educativos y Sociales (CEES).
Note: Saving rates measured as a percentage of household income. The use of short-term (credit card) credit to finance consumption may inflate the estimated consumption, and thereby depress saving. Naturally, the opposite is true when the debt is paid-off.

(continued on next page)

BOX 2.2. *(continued)*

consumption. However, the extent to which these expenditures are actually used as saving vehicles is unobservable, and can vary across countries depending on the context. Therefore cross-country comparisons of alternative saving rates should be interpreted with caution.

Having said this, the evidence reported in figure B2.1 suggests that households in Latin America and the Caribbean spend higher shares of their disposable income on longer-term investments in human capital than households in Asia and in Advanced Economies. The result is a relatively larger increase in alternative saving rates when excluding health and education services from consumption compared to traditional saving rates (i.e., computed without discriminating by categories of consumption). This evidence suggests that traditional household saving rates in Latin America and the Caribbean may be dragged down by the relatively high share of consumption in health and education services by households in the region compared to households in both control groups. The same cannot be said in the case of durable goods; the share of these expenditures in total consumption (and therefore the alternative saving rates) is smaller in Latin America and the Caribbean than among the comparators.

---

[a] The household sector in national accounts typically includes households, unincorporated businesses and non-profit institutions serving households (NPISH). Household income is drawn from national labor statistics, in turn based on business and government payroll data; the overall income of unincorporated business may be inputted from extrapolating the average income of self-employed workers. Government accounts provide information on social contributions, benefits, transfers and tax payments that are required to compute disposable income. Household consumption is computed from retail sales figures compiled by national institutes of statistics, after deducting the portion of sales going to firms as intermediate consumption or investment.

[b] See Ravallion et al. (2003) for a measure in consumption estimates across data sources. For evidence specific to Latin America and the Caribbean, see Bebczuk et al. (2015), Hernani-Limarino, Jiménez, and Mena (2015), and Székely, Mendoza and Karver(2015).

[c] For example, Hurst, Li, and Pugsley (2014) find that the self-employed in the United States underreport their income by 30 percent and that this has important implications for the measurement of savings.

[d] Data for Latin America and the Caribbean is from Bebczuk et al. (2015), Székely, Mendoza and Karver (2015), and Hernani-Limarino Jiménez and Mena (2015). Latin American and Caribbean countries include Argentina, Bolivia, Brazil, Colombia, Ecuador, El Salvador, Guatemala, Mexico, Nicaragua, Panama, and Peru. The sample of advanced economies includes France, Japan, and the United States whereas the sample of Asian economies includes Sri Lanka, Taiwan, and Thailand.

share of the population with negative saving rates shrinks. This demographic dividend should, therefore, boost aggregate saving rates. This begs the question, how far along the demographic transition is Latin America and the Caribbean? And to what extent are the low relative saving rates driven by the demographic transition?

Figure 2.7 **Dependency Rates (Young and Old), by Region**

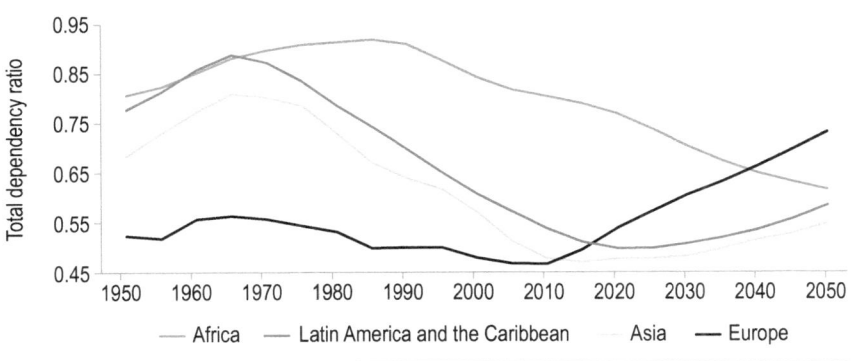

Source: Authors' calculations based on Cavallo, Sánchez, and Valenzuela (2016) and United Nations (2013).
Note: This figure shows the total dependency ratio (the ratio of the population aged 0–14 and older than 65 to the population aged 15–64) across four regions: Europe, Asia, Latin America and the Caribbean, and Africa. A ratio equal to 1 means there is a dependent person for every working age person. The greater the ratio, the more dependent people relative to the working age population.

Dependency rates have declined in all regions, except for Europe, since the 1960s (see Figure 2.7). In Asia, the decline has been rapid: between 1965 and 2010, the number of dependents for every 100 working-age adults fell from 81 to just 48. Interestingly, Latin America and the Caribbean followed a similar path. At the beginning of the demographic transition, the dependency rate was higher than in Asia, with approximately 89 dependents for every 100 working-age adults in 1965. In 2010, that number had dropped to 54. According to United Nations' projections, dependency rates in Asia and Latin America and the Caribbean will bottom out sometime between 2015 and 2020, signaling an end to the demographic dividend for both regions.

The synchronicity of the demographic transition in Asia and Latin America contrasts sharply with the divergence in their saving patterns. Based on this observation, Cavallo, Sánchez, and Valenzuela (2016) study the contribution of demographic factors to saving rates. Interestingly, demographic factors have had a significant impact on saving rates in Asia, but only a small impact in Latin America and the Caribbean.[11] That is, despite similar, favorable demographic transitions in both regions, and even after accounting for other saving determinants, saving rates did not increase as much in Latin America as they did in Asia.

Whatever factors prevented saving rates from rising in Latin America and the Caribbean despite the favorable demographics—a topic discussed in greater detail in Chapter 6—these empirical results confirm that the window of opportunity provided by the demographic dividend is closing fast. Moreover, countries like Guyana, Paraguay, Bolivia, Haiti, Belize, Honduras, Nicaragua, or Guatemala, among a few others where dependency rates have still not reached bottom (see Chapter 6 for a detailed list of where each country in the region lies along the demographic transition), should not count on shifting demographics per se to automatically boost saving rates. Instead, during this stage, they should actively promote private savings—both mandatory (see Chapter 7) and voluntary (see Chapter 9).

Too Old to Save?

People change their saving patterns over the course of their lifetime to meet their varying wants and needs. The expected saving pattern is for young households to borrow, working-age adult households to save, and older households to dissave once they reach retirement. In Latin America and the Caribbean, household saving rates increase with the age of the household head— but they do not drop after retirement! Saving rates increase for the vast majority of households' life cycle, reaching their peak at age bracket 55–59 to then stabilize around 15 percent after age 60 (see Figure 2.8). In contrast, in the United States, saving rates rise only until age 40–44 and then drop steadily thereafter.

Recent research confirms that saving rates remain relatively high even for households already at retirement age (Székely, Mendoza, and Karver, 2015; Tovar and Urrutia, 2014; Hernani-Limarino, Jiménez, and Mena, 2015). Unfortunately, people saving throughout their old age is not necessarily a good sign. Instead, it may reflect the distortions that high levels of labor informality, job insecurity, and low formal pension coverage generate on saving capacity during working-age years in Latin America. Working-age adults in the region simply do not save enough for retirement. This explains why older Latin Americans continue to work and save (more about this in Chapters 7 and 9).

Evidence from the Inter-American Development Bank's Base of the Pyramid (BoP) Survey (Box 2.3) shows that the savings behavior of households headed by people aged 55 to 65 is similar to that of households headed by younger people. Moreover, the proportion of older heads of household who work is 38 percent in Brazil, 48 percent

Figure 2.8 **Household Saving Rates by Age Group in Latin America and the Caribbean**

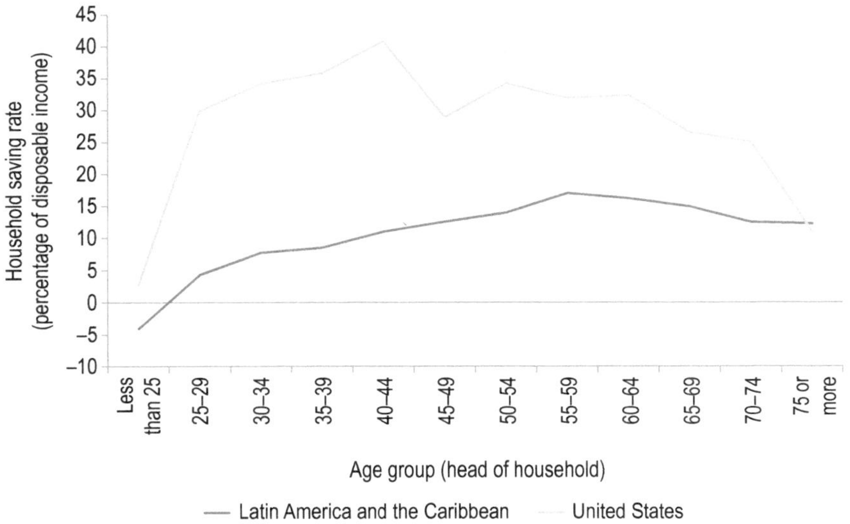

Source: Authors' calculations based on Gandelman (2015a).
Note: All estimates are based on the most recent data available in each country. The Latin American and Caribbean region is comprised of the simple average of: Argentina, Bahamas, Barbados, Bolivia, Brazil, Chile, Colombia, Costa Rica, Ecuador, Honduras, Mexico, Nicaragua, Panama, Paraguay, Peru, Trinidad and Tobago, and Uruguay.

in Mexico, and 81 percent in Peru. Older household heads earn nearly half of their households' monthly labor income and are more likely to be employed in the informal sector compared to younger household heads. Despite their active participation in the labor force, less than one-third of these households enjoys a pension plan through the head of household (21 percent in Peru, 23 percent in Mexico, and 36 percent in Brazil).

Both labor market distortions and limited retirement savings during working-age years force the elderly across Latin America and the Caribbean to keep working and saving beyond their retirement age. Moreover, this phenomenon is becoming more acute; with increases in life expectancy, people are living longer—and most of those extra years are in retirement. (Bloom, Canning, and Sevilla, 2001).

Higher Income, Greater Saving

People who earn more, save more (See Figure 2.9).[12] Rich households in the region save significantly more than poor households (as a share of

Figure 2.9 **Household Saving Rates by Income Deciles**

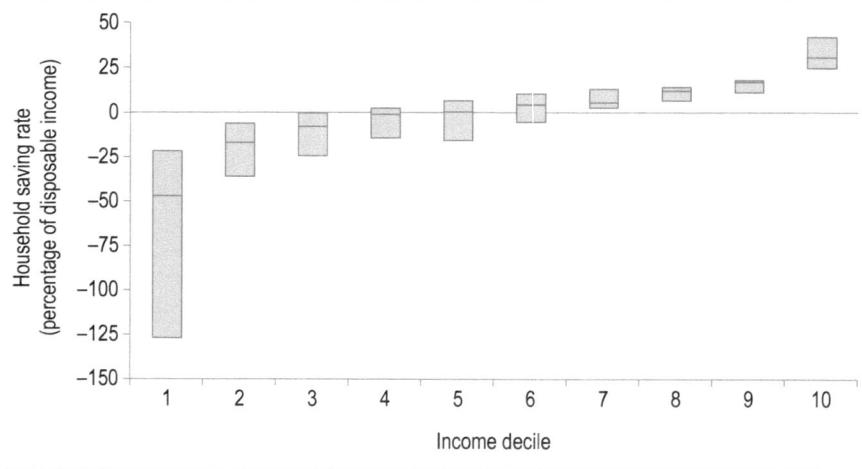

Source: Authors' calculations based on Gandelman (2015a).
Note: All estimates are based on the most recent data available in each country. The Latin American and Caribbean region is comprised of the simple average of: Argentina, Bahamas, Barbados, Bolivia, Brazil, Chile, Colombia, Costa Rica, Ecuador, Honduras, Mexico, Nicaragua, Panama, Paraguay, Peru, Trinidad and Tobago, and Uruguay.

their incomes) in 10 out of 14 countries with available data (Gandelman, 2015b).[13]

In most countries of the region, more than one-third (and sometimes half) of all households spend more than they earn, which means they display negative saving rates. These households tend to be relatively poor. However, negative saving rates do not seem to be financed by access to credit (Bebczuk et al., 2015), which suggests that these negative rates are attributable to income and consumption misreporting (see Box 2.2).[14]

But measurement-error notwithstanding, since highest income earners have higher saving rates than the relatively poor, it follows that saving by the wealthiest households accounts for the vast majority of aggregate household saving in the region.[15] Indeed, the median country in each country-specific income decile has a positive saving rate only in the top five deciles (see Figure 2.9). When considering all households with positive net saving rates, irrespective of their income level, an average of 53 percent of these total saving flows are generated by the top income decile alone (Bebczuk et al., 2015).

The bottom line is that household saving is unequally spread along the income distribution. Most of the household saving is done by the highest income earners. The lack of savings is thus a particularly acute problem for the poor.

Lower-Income Savers: Little to Show for their Efforts

Negative saving rates among lower-income households suggest that the relatively poor are net borrowers. Observing their saving habits through more specialized instruments (Box 2.3) tells a more complete

BOX 2.3. MEASURING HOUSEHOLD SAVING DIRECTLY

Specialized and in-depth instruments such as financial surveys help provide a more accurate characterization of households' saving behavior. The use of these instruments allows household saving stocks and regular saving deposits to be measured directly and at higher frequencies than household surveys.[a] In particular, the comparison of the money set aside for saving purposes and ac-cumulated saving stocks can be informative about the dynamics of saving at the household level, providing a better understanding of the observed saving rates. For instance, estimates of saving computed as residuals of income and consumption over the course of a year may hide a high turnover of savings at a higher time frequency.

However, the measures of saving derived from financial surveys are not comparable with the indirect measures computed as residuals from either national accounts or household surveys. Instead, financial surveys usually capture saving flows by directly asking households how much they set aside for saving purposes during a given period. Households that do not save will not report any flow into saving instruments; therefore, the cor-responding saving estimates are bounded from below at zero. Instead, household surveys and national accounts measure *net* saving flows over a given time period, which implies that estimated saving can be negative if consumption is financed by depleting saving stocks and/or credit during the relevant period.

Between late 2014 and early 2015, the Research Department and Oppor-tunities for the Majority divisions of the Inter-American Development Bank carried out extensive household surveys in the urban areas of Brazil, Mexi-co, and Peru.[b] These surveys were a hybrid between a traditional household survey and a financial survey. Targeted respondents were household heads (75 percent) or their spouses (25 percent) between the ages of 18 and 65. The main objective of these surveys was to identify consumption patterns and unmet demands of poor and middle-income households in several areas, including health, education, technology, housing, and financial services. The target population was the Base of the Pyramid, which consists of individuals

(continued on next page)

BOX 2.3. *(continued)*

living on US$10 or less per day per capita, at purchasing power parity (PPP) exchange rates.[c] Due to the nature of the sample restrictions, income data were collected. In addition, the survey collected information on socioeconomic, demographic, and behavioral profiles, with a special emphasis on financial practices, attitudes, and behavior, such as intertemporal and risk aversion preferences, saving patterns, and indebtedness behavior.

---

[a] Financial diaries are an extremely useful tool to measure cash flows and financial operations at the household level. However, the level of transaction detail, the frequency of the visits, and the logistics for reaching the poorest are constraints that impose very small sample sizes.

[b] The samples in all three countries are nationally representative at the urban level. The survey had a probabilistic, two (or three)-stage stratified sampling design where stratification was at the regional level in all three countries.

[c] See Ferreira et al. (2013) for more details on the definition of this per capita income cutoff.

and complex story: the poor constantly make saving deposits, although mostly into informal instruments. Even more importantly, these inflows into saving instruments represent a relatively important share of their monthly incomes.

The average household in the Base of the Pyramid Survey sample in Peru and Mexico sets aside 6 and 7 percent of its monthly income, respectively. In Brazil, the monthly deposit rate into saving vehicles is substantially lower at 1 percent of monthly income. Restricting the sample to households with positive deposits into saving instruments, monthly saving deposits are, on average, 12 percent of household income in Peru, 23 percent in Mexico, and 8 percent in Brazil. Despite these flows, the accumulated saving stocks (that is, the sum of net saving flows) are not very large, which means that these households regularly deplete their saving stocks. Average saving stocks are 83, 71, and 94 percent of monthly income in Mexico, Peru, and Brazil, respectively. In other words, the average household that saves in Mexico, for example, holds a stock of savings that is equivalent to approximately 3.6 months' worth of saving deposits.

For what do households use their savings? Figure 2.10 plots the percentage of households in each country that declare saving with a given purpose in mind, where multiple uses may coexist. In Mexico and Peru, over half the households save to acquire assets or make investments, while only one-quarter of households in Brazil save with this objective in mind. A large share of households also saves to cover daily expenses or

Figure 2.10 **Use of Savings among Households at the Base of the Pyramid**

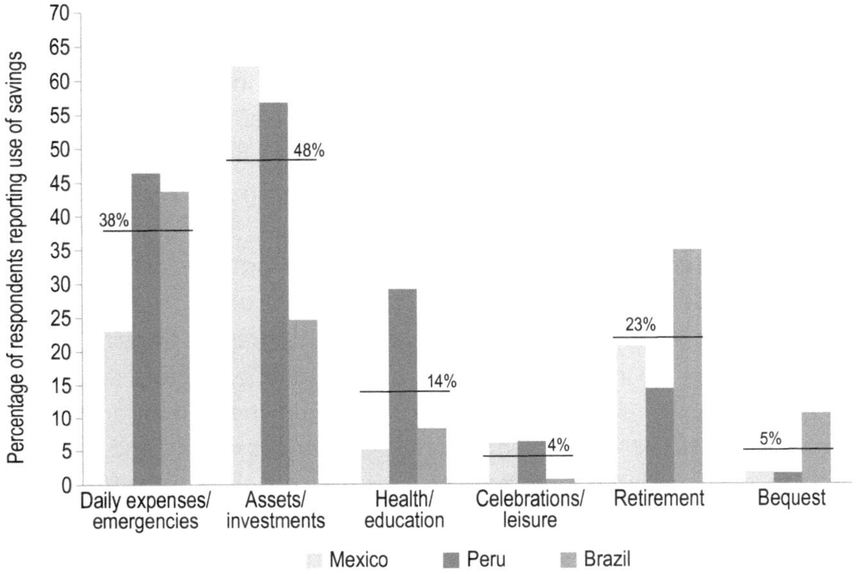

Source: Financial survey estimates are authors' calculations based on the Base of Pyramid (BoP) Survey.
Note: Percentages add up to more than 100 percent because multiple responses were allowed. Horizontal lines represent the average percentage for each use of savings across the three countries.

emergencies, which is consistent with a high turnover of savings in and out of saving vehicles. Relatively fewer responses included longer-term goals such as investments in health, education, or retirement.

In sum, poorer households move in and out of saving vehicles but do not accumulate large stocks of net savings over time. This pattern makes sense since these households use savings mainly to pay for short-term expenses or to finance investments that require small lump sums, rather than for long-term goals such as financing retirement. This behavior may reflect several factors including poorer households' limited choice of saving instruments and the limited reliability of those saving vehicles (see Chapter 11). Also, some households may find it hard to avoid temptations or resist social pressures within the household or from relatives and friends outside the household (see Chapter 9). Given the importance of savings for individual welfare, it is necessary to understand the reason (or combination of reasons) behind this pattern to improve the design of financial instruments to service the saving needs of poor households.

The Bottom Line

National saving rates are low in Latin America and the Caribbean compared to other regions. They are particularly low in the case of private saving which is paradoxically, the largest generator of savings in the economy. The relatively higher absorption of foreign saving has not filled the void; thus total saving (and therefore investment) in the region is comparatively lower.

Over the past few decades, low national saving rates in Latin America and the Caribbean have not reflected adverse demographic factors. In fact, the region has enjoyed a favorable demographic transition since the 1960s, yet saving rates have not increased as expected; the region did not generate savings (buffer stocks) when the dependency rates were falling. Now that the demographic dividend is ending and the population is aging, generating more savings will be both more difficult and more urgent.

This chapter reveals some saving distortions in the region. One of these is that people are forced to continue working and saving even beyond retirement age to compensate for a saving deficit during their more productive working age years. Latin Americans are living longer now, but old age brings them no rest as they must work and save to finance a longer life span.

The lack of adequate saving vehicles to channel household savings creates another slew of distortions. The majority of the net saving is generated by high-income households. However, in an ironic twist, relatively poorer households set aside a significant portion of their income each month for saving purposes. These savings are used mostly to meet their needs for fast cash or assets for their homes or businesses. Rarely do these savings make it into the financial system where they could be channeled to finance the longer-term investments that support individual well-being and national development.

Notes

[1] See Grigoli, Herman, and Schmidt-Hebbel (2014) for the most recent and comprehensive review on the implications of different consumption theories on saving behavior.

[2] For example, Coeurdacier, Guibaud, and Jin (2015) present a model in which demographic factors, the age profile, and heterogeneous income growth across generations interact with credit constraints, resulting in asymmetric saving patterns across countries.

[3] This book uses country groupings defined as follows, unless otherwise noted. *Advanced Economies:* Australia, Austria, Belgium, Canada, Cyprus, Czech Republic, Denmark, Estonia, Finland, France, Germany, Greece, Ireland, Israel, Italy, Japan, Latvia, Lithuania, Luxembourg, Malta, Netherlands, New Zealand, Norway, Portugal, San Marino, Slovak Republic, Slovenia, Spain, Sweden, Switzerland, United Kingdom and United States. *Emerging Asia:* China, Hong Kong, Indonesia, Malaysia, Republic of Korea , Singapore, Taiwan and Thailand. *Latin America and the Caribbean:* Argentina, Bahamas, Barbados, Belize, Bolivia, Brazil, Chile, Colombia, Costa Rica, Dominican Republic, Ecuador, El Salvador, Guatemala, Guyana, Haiti, Honduras, Jamaica, Mexico, Nicaragua, Panama, Paraguay, Peru, Suriname, Trinidad and Tobago, Uruguay and Venezuela. *Sub-Saharan Africa:* Angola, Benin, Botswana, Burkina Faso, Burundi, Cabo Verde, Cameroon, Central African Republic, Chad, Comoros, Democratic Republic of Congo, Republic of Congo, Côte d'Ivoire, Equatorial Guinea, Eritrea, Ethiopia, Gabon, The Gambia, Ghana, Guinea, Guinea-Bissau, Kenya, Lesotho, Liberia, Madagascar, Malawi, Mali, Mauritius, Mozambique, Namibia, Niger, Nigeria, Rwanda, Sao Tome and Principe, Senegal, Sierra Leone, South Africa, South Sudan, Swaziland, Tanzania, Togo, Uganda, Zambia and Zimbabwe.

[4] Estimated based on Becerra, Cavallo, and Noy (2015), who perform reduced form regression analysis in the tradition of Loayza, Schmidt-Hebbel, and Servén (1999) and Grigoli, Herman, and Schmidt-Hebbel (2014).

[5] The edges of the lines in the plot exclude outliers in statistical terms.

[6] The country groupings "Advanced Economies" and "Emerging Asia" categorize countries along two dimensions that tend to induce high national saving rates: high income levels and rapid growth rates, respectively (see Grigoli, Herman, and Schmidt-Hebbel, 2014). Therefore,

using these country groupings is bound to make saving rates in Latin America and the Caribbean look lower. Nevertheless, Latin America and the Caribbean, with its average saving rate of 17.5 percent from 1980 to 2014, exhibits lower national saving rates than other regional country groupings defined in the World Bank classification.

[7] LAC-7 is a group consisting of Argentina, Brazil, Chile, Colombia, Mexico, Peru, and Venezuela that jointly comprise over 90 percent of the regional GDP.

[8] In the case of Bebczuk and Cavallo (2016), the effective sample is 47 countries—eight of which are in Latin America and the Caribbean— over 1995–2013. In the case of Grigoli, Herman, and Schmidt-Hebbel (2015), the effective sample comprises 48 countries over 1981–2012.

[9] The average hides a significant degree of cross-country heterogeneity. For example, Székely, Mendoza, and Karver (2015) show that, in the case of Mexico, household saving accounts for 55 percent of domestic saving from the national accounts.

[10] See Bebczuk and Cavallo (2016) for a recent survey of the literature on the theoretical and empirical evidence on why households do not pierce the corporate veil.

[11] Cavallo, Sánchez, and Valenzuela (2016) show that dependency rates explain, on average, up to 22 percent of the variance of saving rates in Asia, and only 3 percent of the variance in Latin America and the Caribbean. This result contrasts with Grigoli, Herman, and Schmidt-Hebbel (2015), who find that demographic dependency is as important in Latin America and the Caribbean as elsewhere. Two differences explain the varying results. First, Grigoli, Herman, and Schmidt-Hebbel (2015) focus on private saving, while Cavallo, Sánchez, and Valenzuela (2016) focus on private plus public saving. Second, Grigoli, Herman, and Schmidt-Hebbel (2015) focus on "old age dependency," while Cavallo, Sánchez, and Valenzuela (2016) include young dependency and life expectancy as additional demographic variables, and thus their results relate to the three demographic factors.

[12] Many studies document that household saving rates rise with income. See Butelmann and Gallego (2000)—for Chile— and Grigoli, Herman, and Schmidt-Hebbel (2014) for the world. Bebczuk et al. (2015) and Gandelman (2015a) document the same fact for Latin America and the Caribbean.

[13] Gandelman (2015b) correlates saving rates and household lifetime income, while instrumenting the latter with the education level of the

head of household and spouse. The study uses a wealth index as a proxy for lifetime income as an additional identification strategy.

[14] In particular, they find that households with negative saving rates are headed by people with fewer years of schooling, lower labor formality rates, and a somewhat higher participation of government transfers and remittances in total income. All these factors could be linked to income underreporting. It may also be that excess consumption is financed with past saving stocks, but this is not possible to check with household survey data.

[15] For country-specific statistics, see Gandelman (2015a).

3 Financial Systems to Make Savings Count

In advanced economies, the vast majority of savings are intermediated through formal financial instruments. This intermediation can take one of three forms: direct financing, with individuals holding instruments issued directly by firms or the government; through institutional investors who then invest in those instruments; or through formal financial intermediaries such as banks. By contrast, in Latin America and the Caribbean, much of the savings of households does not go through the formal financial system. Some households—typically the less wealthy—keep savings in unregulated institutions, buy durables or other assets as a means to save, or simply stash their cash in the proverbial mattress. Others—typically more wealthy households—hold assets abroad or invest in real estate, bypassing the domestic financial system entirely.

Latin American and Caribbean financial systems lack depth and pose serious constraints to access credit.[1] Restricted credit is the other side of the coin of low savings in formal financial instruments or institutions. Indeed, as Levine's (2005) comprehensive review of finance and development makes clear, financial systems have five closely interrelated roles: to produce information ex ante about possible investments and allocate capital to them; to monitor investments and exert corporate governance after providing finance; to facilitate the trading, diversification and management of risk; to mobilize and pool savings; and to ease the exchange of goods and services.[2]

This chapter focuses on financial intermediation and mainly on the fourth role: to mobilize and pool savings. It asks why in Latin America and the Caribbean, the financial system has done a poor job in this role.

In Financial Systems, Small Is Not Beautiful

An efficient financial system should promote savings by providing easy and convenient access to appropriate savings instruments offered by high-quality, trustworthy institutions at reasonable cost. Clearly, there is no single optimal design for a financial system; many potential instruments and structures of financial systems may be equally efficient.[3] Comparing the very different financial systems of successful, advanced economies with different savings rates and deep financial systems confirms this point.

In some systems (such as the United States and the United Kingdom), direct financing through capital markets is relatively more important. Firms issue equities and bonds, which are bought by individuals or by institutional investors that pool the savings of individuals. In other countries, such as Germany and Japan, financial intermediaries, including banks, are relatively more important. They offer savings accounts and provide financing to firms. Banks play a critical role in allocating capital and in guiding the corporate governance of firms through representation on boards. Financial systems dominated by capital markets are often characterized as having "arms-length" financing because equity market valuations—and at the limit, hostile takeovers—play a disciplining role, as opposed to the more direct monitoring role played by financial institutions in systems dominated by banks.[4] However, in all advanced economies with deep financial systems, both direct financing and financial intermediaries exist; the question is not so much one or the other but the balance between the two and the precise and more subtle roles that each may play.[5]

In Latin America and the Caribbean, banks have tended to dominate the financial landscape, although capital markets have been growing. Most individuals do not buy equities or bonds directly, but rather hold them indirectly through mutual funds, pension funds, or insurance companies. The size of these institutional investors in the region has increased, and they are now very significant players in some countries.

Most financial savings in the region are held in banks and other financial institutions. On average, the deposits of banks exceed the total assets held by pension funds, mutual funds, and insurance companies combined in Latin America and the Caribbean (see Figure 3.1). The financial depth in the typical country in Latin America and the Caribbean lags far behind countries like the United States, with its expansive array

Figure 3.1 Financial System Deposits and Assets under Management of Different Institutional Investors

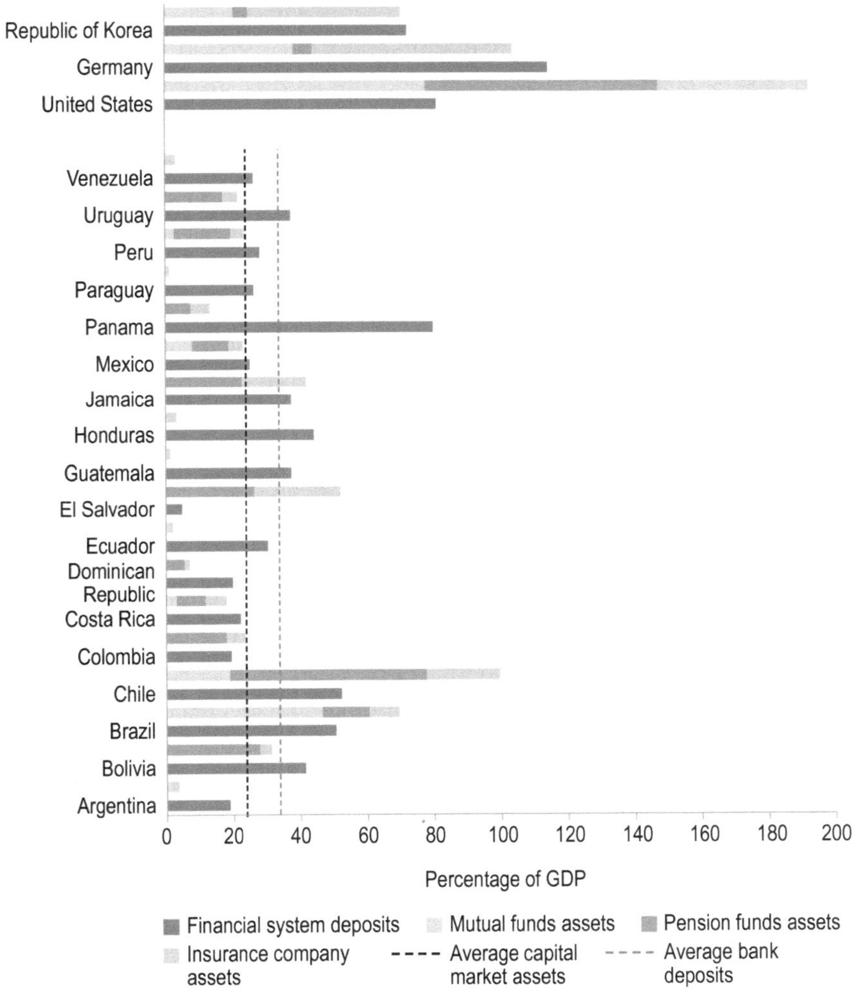

Source: Authors' elaboration based on data from Bebczuk (2015b).
Note: Data on assets rather than liabilities are used for mutual funds and pension funds, as these are the data available on a comparative basis. The figures have been adjusted for double-counting (as mutual funds, pension funds, and insurance companies may hold bank deposits, and banks may purchase mutual funds) as data sources allow, although it is possible that some may remain. For details, see Bebczuk (2015b).

of institutional investors, and Germany, where banks are relatively much larger, and even the Republic of Korea where banks and institutional investors are roughly on a par.

Countries vary considerably in the region in terms of the management of deposits and assets (see Figure 3.1). For example, in Brazil, the mutual fund industry has grown considerably and has assets under management approaching total banking sector deposits. In Chile, pension fund assets exceed bank deposits, and the sum of insurance company and mutual fund assets is close behind. Mexico has a large corporate bond market. These assets are typically held by pension funds and mutual funds, which together rival the amount held in bank deposits. And in Colombia, pension fund assets under management are almost comparable to the deposits of banks.

How are financial systems in the region likely to change as capital markets grow?[6] More capital market-based financial systems tend to promote transparency and information, which is generally considered a benefit. On the other hand, they may also promote greater instability. Writing in 2002 before the global financial crisis about a similar phenomenon in continental Europe, Rajan and Zingales (2003) warn about this trade-off. Still, Latin America and the Caribbean has experienced significant economic instability in its past, despite having a more bank-based financial system; indeed, as a result, the region has improved banking and capital market supervision and has been extremely conservative in its regulation of more exotic financial instruments. This approach surely helped the region survive the recent global financial crisis relatively well (Powell, 2015). It may also allow the region to transition to a more market-based system while maintaining financial stability.

A related question is whether as capital markets grow they will take over from intermediaries—or, in other words, whether capital markets are substitutes or complements to financial institutions.[7] Given the changing landscape and the diversity in the region, Latin America and the Caribbean provides fertile ground to analyze this question. A novel analysis suggests that for Latin America and the Caribbean—as for the rest of the world—banks and capital market institutional investors are complements, rather than substitutes.[8] What this means is that banks and capital markets have been growing together. Capital markets are not taking over from banks, although both grow more quickly in some countries than others. The region appears to be no different from the rest of the world in this regard.

For capital markets to grow, ultimately outside investors must feel comfortable either buying debt-type instruments or investing in equity issued by firms. In turn, this requires a set of conditions to be met.

Good information regarding firms' activities must be available. Financial accounts must be meaningful and transparent, which in turn means that auditors are doing their job and are being sanctioned if they don't. Rating agencies should be operating effectively; this saves individual investors the work of analyzing every firm, which would be prohibitively costly. Corporate governance should be effective so that outside equity or bond investors do not feel they will be taken advantage of by an inside group of equity holders.[9]

Latin America and the Caribbean typically scores rather poorly on these important aspects of what might be referred to as the plumbing that allows finance to flow freely from investors to users. This may be one reason why financial markets have remained small to date, and why financial intermediaries, particularly banks, continue to dominate. Indeed, one of the roles of financial intermediaries is precisely to "represent" small investors, given their likely lack of influence on firms.[10] Financial intermediaries may then play a very important role in increasing the quantity of financial savings. But in order to do this, they must build solid reputations so that investors feel comfortable entrusting them with what may be their life savings. They must also offer convenience and appropriate instruments with a reasonable return.

Despite recent growth, banking systems in the region remain relatively small compared to GDP, especially compared to other bank-dominated systems. Macroeconomic instability and weak creditor rights are frequently cited as underlying barriers to greater financial depth.[11] While the median banking system in the region has grown to have almost 40 percent of GDP in deposits, this remains much lower than the banking system of the median OECD and Southeast Asian economy. Moreover, as the region contains a number of smaller economies, the absolute size of financial systems in the region is considerably smaller than that of comparators. The median banking system in the OECD has some $300 billion in deposits compared to only $15 billion in deposits in Latin America and the Caribbean (Figure 3.2).

Large financial systems have two very important advantages. The first is economies of scale, which allow large banks to operate with low margins.[12] This can mean higher returns for savers and lower costs for borrowers—unless the rents are captured by bankers. The second advantage is that such systems can mobilize large amounts of financing for big projects; they can overcome problems of indivisibility. Large projects may require considerable financing, which may be a constraint

Figure 3.2 **Median Banking System, OECD and Latin American and Caribbean Countries**

a. Loans and Deposits (billions of US dollars)

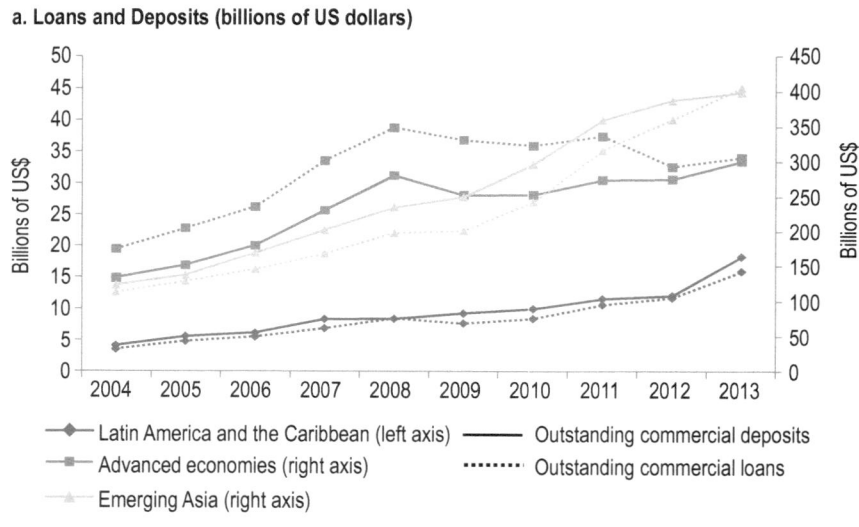

b. Loans and Deposits (percent of GDP)

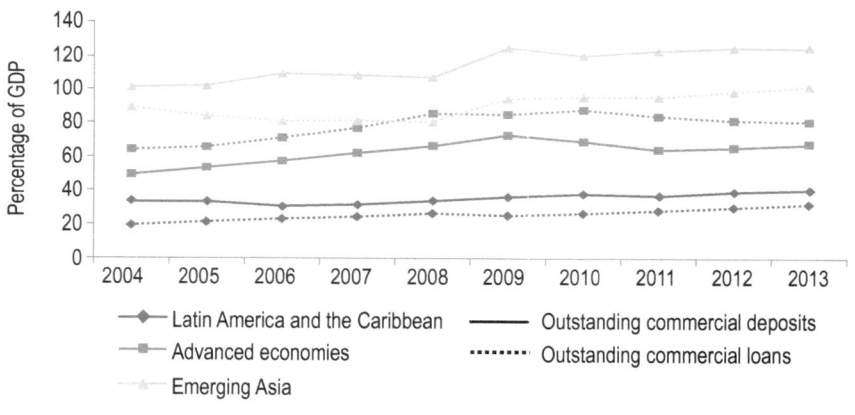

Source: Authors' elaboration based on data from Financial Access Survey, IMF.
Note: See endnote 3 of chapter 2 for the list of countries in each country group.

in some countries that lack large financial intermediaries.[13] The impact of scale on costs is considered in more depth in Chapter 11.

Formal vs. Informal Saving: Quality Counts

How financial intermediaries operate determines not only the quantity of savings, but also the quality. To increase the quality of savings, the intermediary should be fully integrated into the country's financial system. This ensures that the savings are allocated efficiently, which in turn allows them to offer better returns. Institutions should also be regulated appropriately and should have a high standard of corporate governance so that capital can be allocated efficiently.

The previous section focused on formal financial markets and formal financial intermediaries. But in Latin America and the Caribbean, savings through more informal mechanisms make up a sizable part of the financial assets of many households. On average, 48 percent of households in the region report some savings (Figure 3.3, panel a), and 45 percent say they have an account in a formal financial institution, but only 16 percent report saving in formal institutions (panel b), according to data collected by the World Bank's FINDEX dataset.[14] These averages put Latin America on the level of Sub-Saharan Africa (a region with significantly lower income per capita) and pale in comparison to Advanced Economies and Emerging Asia (see Figure 3.3).

Where does the rest of the savings go? A fraction is channeled through informal financial institutions. In fact, considering both formal and informal financial institutions, the composition of Latin America and the Caribbean's financial systems is complex. Most countries have a large number of small, cooperative-type financial institutions. On top of this, other types of institutions, including nongovernmental organizations (NGOs), provide financial services. Microfinance institutions have grown considerably in several countries of the region, and some of them also offer deposit-like instruments (Trujillo and Navajas, 2014). Typically, these smaller institutions operate only in a particular locality or region, and may not be highly integrated into countries' financial systems.[15] Since relatively poor households save using these alternatives, the aggregate amount of deposits in these institutions may be smaller than deposits at formal banks; however, they are very significant in terms of the number of accounts and the savings portfolios of those poorer households. If savings are highly dispersed—in either small formal or informal financial institutions—and not pooled, then they may not be allocated in the most efficient manner. In turn, the returns offered to savers may be low, reducing the total amount of savings.[16]

As panel a of Figure 3.4 shows, there are 604 commercial banks in 20 countries in the region, with deposits amounting to about 42 percent of GDP. Almost 2,000 non-bank regulated financial institutions hold about 2 percent of GDP in deposits, and around 4,000 non-regulated

Figure 3.3 **Financial Inclusion by Region**

a. Percentage of People Who Saved any Money

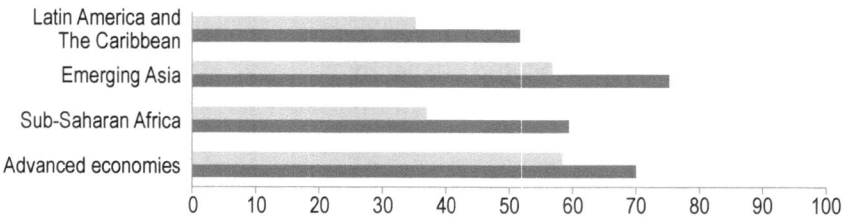

b. Percentage of People with Account in a Financial Institution

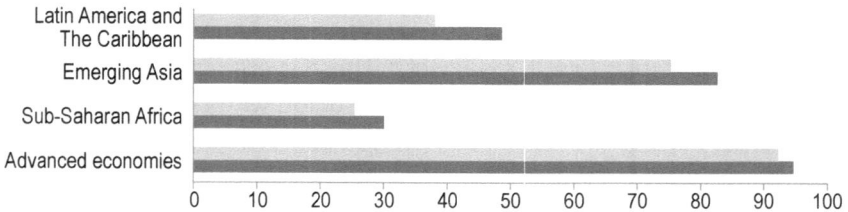

c. Percentage of People Saving in Financial Institutions

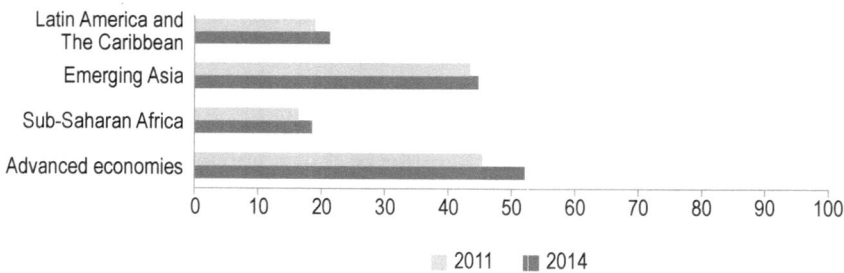

2011   2014

Source: World Bank, Global Financial Inclusion Database (FINDEX).
Note: All measures are simple country averages. Panel a, Save any money in the past year: Denotes the percentage of respondents who report saving or setting aside any money in the past 12 months (percent of respondents age 15+). Panel b, Account at a financial institution: Denotes the percentage of respondents who report having an account (by themselves or together with someone else) at a bank or another type of financial institution (see year-specific definitions for details) (percent of respondents, age 15+). Panel c, Saved at a financial institution: Denotes the percentage of respondents who report saving or setting aside any money at a bank or another type of financial institution in the past 12 months (see year-specific definitions for details) (percent of respondents, age 15+). See endnote 3 of Chapter 2 for the list of countries in each country group.

institutions hold a further 2.2 percent of GDP in deposits. Among the non-bank regulated financial institutions, 10 development banks and 14 investment banks have total deposits of 0.2 percent of GDP (panel

Figure 3.4 **Types of Financial Institutions: Number and Share of Savings as Percentage of GDP**

a. Regulated and Non-Regulated Institutions

b. Regulated Non-Banks and Non-Regulated Institutions

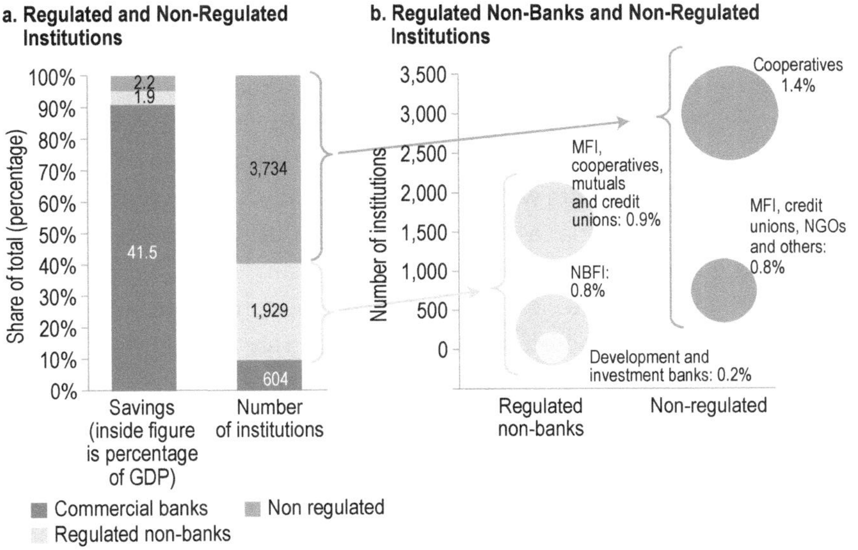

Source: Authors' calculations using data from Trujillo and Navajas (2014).
Notes:Panel a: Vertical axis shows percentage of total. Figures inside first column show savings as percentage of GDP, simple average across countries in the region. Figures inside second column show the total number of institutions. Panel b: Bubble size illustrates the average of savings as percent of GDP, simple average across countries.
MFI = Microfinancial Institutions.
NBFI = Non-Bank Financial Institutions. Include: Financial companies/corporations, mortgages institutions, trust companies, private financial fund in Bolivia, off-shore entities in Guatemala, SOFOMERs (Sociedades Financieras de Objeto Múltiple entidades reguladas) in Mexico, saving and lending society, rural financial Institutions, IFEs (Instituciones Financieras Externas) in Uruguay.
Non-Bank Regulated Institutions include: Development and investment banks, NBFI, MFI, cooperatives, mutuals and credit unions.
GDP series used: 2013 GDP in current US$ (Source: WDI).
Countries included: Argentina, Barbados, Belize, Bolivia, Brazil, Chile, Colombia, Costa Rica, Ecuador, El Salvador, Guatemala, Haiti, Honduras, Mexico, Nicaragua, Panama, Paraguay, Peru, Republica Dominicana and Uruguay. Bahamas and Venezuela excluded due to lack of complete data.

b). There are 116 microfinance institutions (MFIs); 1,413 cooperatives; 14 mutual funds; and 104 credit unions. Together, their deposits amount to about 1 percent of GDP, on average. The non-regulated institutions are mostly cooperatives (almost 3,000 of the 4,000 non-regulated institutions in the sample); their deposits amount to 1.4 percent of GDP. Deposits among the remaining non-regulated institutions account for 0.8 percent of GDP.

In addition, households may be saving in the form of non-financial assets, ranging from jewelry and consumer goods, such as refrigerators and cars, to houses and other property. They turn to these alternatives for a number of reasons. They may lack documentation to open an account; they may live far away from a financial institution; opening or servicing an account may be too expensive; or they may simply lack information or trust in financial institutions. In countries where people tend to mistrust the financial system—either because a history of relatively high inflation has eroded the real value of savings, or banking crises have wiped out financial savings—savers may seek to protect the real value of their savings by investing in assets with a better track record as a store of value.[17] In the case of Argentina, a substantial portion of savings is channeled through the real estate market (see Box 3.1).

Saving in real estate is more common among high-income households. As Chapter 2 noted, poor households rely heavily on informal saving strategies, which include keeping money at home or with family/friends, saving groups, providing loans to other individuals, buying and holding jewelry and other assets, and investing in family businesses. The use of these mechanisms is especially common among households that in turn are more likely to be excluded from formal financial systems. Again, while these forms of saving may not constitute a large part of total national savings, they can be an important component of the savings portfolio of individual households.

Poor and middle-income households in Brazil, Mexico, and Peru are more likely to make monthly deposits into informal saving instruments than use bank accounts or other formal instruments, according to data collected through targeted financial surveys (see Chapter 2).In Mexico and Peru, 20 percent and 33 percent of all surveyed households report saving through a variety of informal mechanisms, while 14 percent and 30 percent of them save using bank accounts, respectively. In Brazil, on the other hand, the saving rate is low irrespective of the instrument: only 4 percent of the surveyed households save informally, while 10 percent of them do so formally. Preliminary evidence from Colombia reveals a pattern similar to that in Mexico and Peru:[18] of the 16.5 percent of people who reported saving in 2013, only 25 percent saved through formal instruments.

Figure 3.5 shows how savings are distributed in Mexico, Peru, and Brazil by saving instrument and portfolio among those who save and hold positive savings stocks.[19] Several patterns are clear. First, the vast majority of surveyed households that save informally in these three countries do so mostly through family, friends, savings groups, or loans to others, and much less by buying assets for the home or business. Second,

BOX 3.1. ARGENTINA'S RESIDENTIAL REAL ESTATE SECTOR: A MAGNET FOR SAVINGS[a]

In the context of high macroeconomic volatility, residential real estate has been a popular investment for savers. After the financial crisis of 2001–02, in which the government and many private institutions restructured debts, and many financial contracts were switched from dollars to pesos, Argentines increasingly channeled their savings toward real estate.

As shown in Figure B3.1, from 1992 until 2000, term deposits at banks rose by an average of $7.6 billion per year, while from 2003 until 2012 they rose an average of only $2.2 billion per year, a 70 percent reduction. On the other hand, new savings channeled to real estate soared 78 percent (these figures are in constant US dollars of 2014). During the first period, for each dollar that went to real estate, about six dollars went to new term deposits. During the second period, for each dollar that went to real estate, only 99 cents went to new term deposits.

In the city of Buenos Aires, while saving flows into real estate were about 8.4 percent of total savings from 1992 to 2001, they rose to more than 13.3 percent of savings in the 2003–2012 period, a 57 percent rise in the ratio (see Figure B3.2).

Moreover, the real estate market absorbed 27 percent more square meters comparing the decade from 2003–2012 with that of 1992 to 2001. How did the real estate market react? Cruces (2016) finds that real rental rates fell signifi-

Figure B3.1 **Allocation of New Savings: Real Estate vs. Banks**

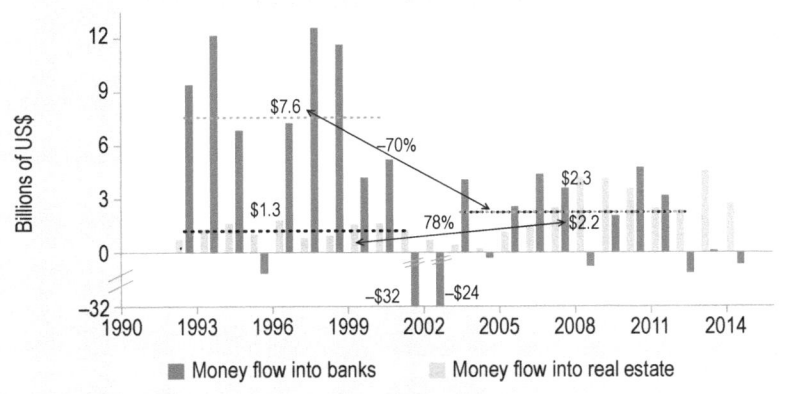

Source: Authors' elaboration based on Cruces (2016).
Note: This figure compares the flow of new savings channeled to real estate with that channeled to banks' term deposits. Flows into real estate only pertain to the City of Buenos Aires, while the increase in time deposits corresponds to the whole banking sector of the country. As a reference, the City of Buenos Aires accounted for about one-quarter of national GDP during both periods. All figures are in constant 2014 dollars.

(continued on next page)

BOX 3.1. *(continued)*

Figure B3.2 **Savings Channeled to Real Estate as a Fraction of City and National Savings**

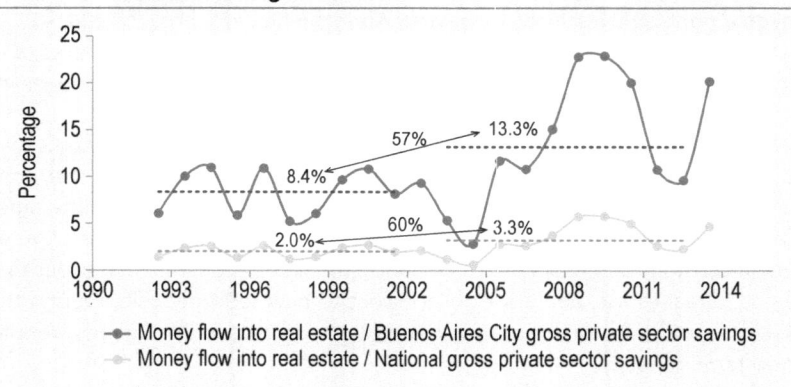

—•— Money flow into real estate / Buenos Aires City gross private sector savings
—•— Money flow into real estate / National gross private sector savings

Source: Authors' elaboration based on Cruces (2016).

cantly to adjust supply and demand: the net rental rates fell from an average of 7.1 percent from 1992 until 2001 to a low of 2.7 percent since 2003. At the end of the sample, the net rental yield was just 1.5 percent per annum.

The net rental yield on housing can be compared to the returns on alternative investments to estimate the efficiency loss (opportunity cost) from the money sunk in real estate. A reasonable range of return for infrastructure investment for example would be 5 to 15 percent (see Campos, Serebrisky, and Suárez-Alemán, 2015). Using this benchmark implies an efficiency loss of between $0.8 and $3 billion dollars per year. The higher end of this range amounts to a loss of 2.5 percent of Buenos Aires city's GDP per year. While it may make sense to channel so much savings to real estate from the individual investor's standpoint, it is inefficient for the society as a whole.[34]

---

[a] This box draws from Cruces (2016).

[b] There are multiple caveats that come with this exercise. For starters, it is assumed that the entire stock of new housing was offered for rental. This is not necessarily the case. If people build new homes to occupy them, or to sell then to new occupants, then that has a subjective value to the owner. This notwithstanding, clearly rental rates went down because the market could not absorb all the new stock of housing. The analysis suggests substantial amounts of resources obtain very low yields in the real estate sector, while financing for productive investments is in short supply.

households that save formally use saving accounts and employee paycheck accounts, but not other financial instruments that can provide higher long-term returns, such as fixed-term deposits and mutual funds (the total share of long-term saving instruments among households

Figure 3.5 **Portfolio of Savings among Low- and Middle-Income Households**

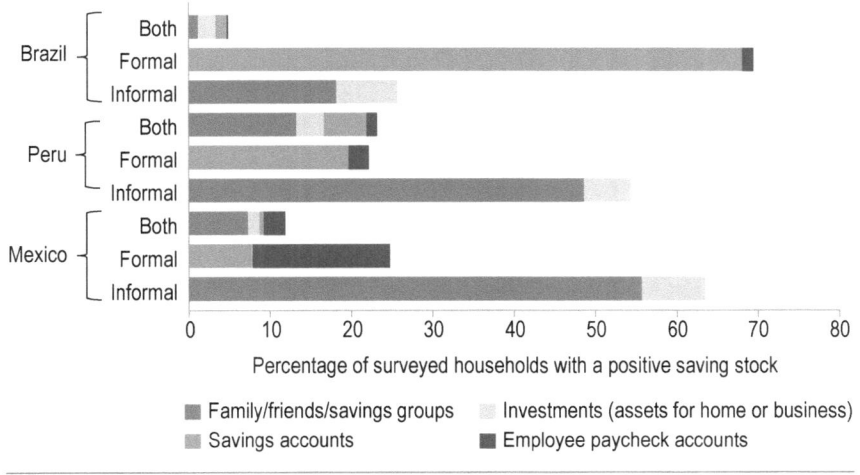

Source: Authors' calculations based on the Base of Pyramid (BoP) Survey.

saving formally is less than 0.5 percent). Third, households that save using both formal and informal instruments are the smallest group of savers in each country.[20] Moreover, the portfolios of those households that do use both types of instruments also tend to favor informal saving instruments.

The pattern of saving choices among households in Latin America is very different from a textbook model whereby households save, deposit those savings in banks or other financial intermediaries, which in turn allocate those savings to those in the economy that need the funds to invest. But how different is Latin America from other regions in this respect? In order to address this question, the flow of funds of households in a subset of countries in Latin America and in a comparator group of developing countries outside the region was tracked.

The flow of funds analysis separates the sources and uses of households' funds. Households receive funds from either "borrowing" or "saving." In turn, households use those funds to either "acquire financial assets" or "to invest directly;" for example buying physical (capital) goods for the household/family firm, or investing in a residential dwelling.[21]

A few interesting patterns emerge and are displayed in Figure 3.6. First, in terms of sources of funds, on average households in Latin America rely more on their own funds (savings) than on external funds

Figure 3.6 **Source and Use of Household Funds, Latin America vs. Comparators**

a. Household Financial Portfolios

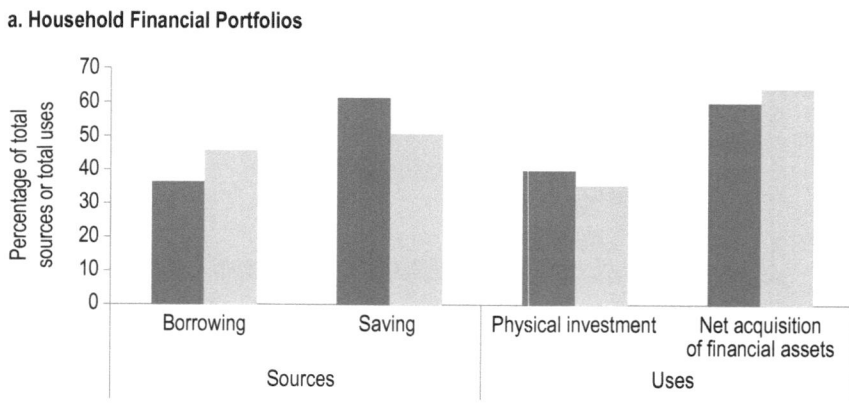

b. Net Acquisition of Financial Assets

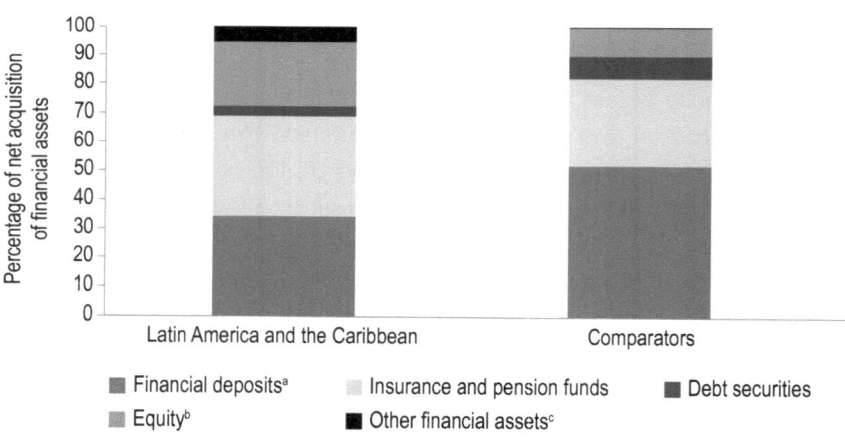

Source: Authors' calculations based on national accounts data from each country.
Notes: Computed as simple averages by country over the period 2005-2009.
[a] "Financial deposits" includes cash holding (for countries where deposits can be separated from cash holdings, the share of cash in the significantly smaller than deposits);
[b] "Equity" includes direct ownership of firms, equity securities and shares in mutual funds;
[c] "Other financial assets" is computed as a residual of "Net acquisition of financial assets" and the other sub-accounts.

(borrowing from banks or other sources). Roughly 60 percent of total available household funds come from their own savings compared to 50 percent among comparators (panel a). On the other hand, on average, households in Latin America invest approximately 40 percent of their funds directly in physical assets (mostly residential investments) and acquire financial assets with about 60 percent. Among the comparator group, the split is 35 to 65.

Second, within the category of "net acquisition of financial assets," the financial portfolios in Latin America tilt more toward instruments that are not necessarily intermediated by the formal financial system. Panel b shows the distribution of total net acquisition of financial assets. [22] In Latin America, average financial deposits account for approximately 34 percent of total purchases of financial assets, compared to more than 50 percent among the comparators. By contrast, "equity" accounts for 22 percent of the total net acquisition of financial assets in Latin America, compared to 10 percent in the comparator group. This category includes direct ownership of (family) firms, which is a non-intermediated financial asset, and which makes up the bulk of the account in those countries for which there are data. [23] Therefore, on top of allocating a smaller share of funds to purchasing financial assets compared to households in the comparator group, households in Latin America are much more likely to select financial instruments that are not formally intermediated.

The regional averages, however, hide much heterogeneity across countries. For example, in Chile, which has the deepest financial system in the region, 50 percent of funds are channeled into financial deposits and other financial instruments, while only 9 percent goes toward equity. In Ecuador, which has a smaller financial system relative to the size of its economy, only 25 percent of funds are channeled into financial instruments, and 32 percent go into equity assets. More funds appear to be intermediated in Chile than in other countries in the region, where funds tend to be used more for direct investments. Chile more closely resembles a country like the Republic of Korea in the comparator group. For the other four Latin American countries, a significantly smaller fraction is intermediated through financial deposits and other financial instruments.

Mexico provides an interesting country to analyze in more detail. National saving (as a percent of GDP) is reasonably high given income per capita, and household savings constitute some 50 percent of the national total. Most of that savings, however, is not intermediated through the formal financial system (Székely, Mendoza, and Karver, 2015) When "financial saving" is decomposed into financial deposits, acquisition of fixed assets, and the purchase of durable goods, deposits (both through formal and informal financial institutions) represents less than 10 percent of saving, while the purchase of durable goods represents nearly three-quarters of all saving. The household saving rate (defined as a residual between disposable incomes and consumption) increases from 8.1 to 21.7 percent when durable goods are considered a form of saving rather than consumption (that is, when consumption of durables is excluded from consumption).

A high share of savings that is not channeled through an integrated formal financial system suggests that resources are being poorly allocated. An interesting question is why these savings are not intermediated. If the reason is "lack of demand" for formal instruments, i.e., due to lack of access, poor information or mistrust in financial institutions, then the household may benefit considerably by improving access, financial literacy or trust (see Chapter 9 for more on information and trust).

This chapter focuses on the issue of lack of supply, or access. If many households live far from a formal financial institution, then factoring the costs of travel and time may encourage each individual household to save in an informal instrument even if that instrument pays little in terms of private returns. That informal saving instrument may have very little social return as well, as it may not lead to a very productive investment opportunity. In this case, if a sudden change in access occurs—for example, a local bank branch opens or mobile banking becomes available—then informal savers may switch instruments and the social return from the extra dollar of savings (the difference between the new return and the previous very low return) might be very high.

A complementary explanation for low intermediation relates to the high informality in labor markets in Latin America and the Caribbean. McKenzie and Woodruff (2006) find that in Mexico self-employed poor individuals receive above market rates of return for very small capital investments. Not surprisingly, these self-employed individuals tend to reinvest heavily in their own family business, buying goods such as refrigerators, trucks, or any other type of durable good that could simultaneously satisfy a consumption need for the household and serve as a capital good for their home business. [24] Unfortunately, McKenzie and Woodruff also find that with each additional investment, the marginal return declines steeply. Thus, these small capital investments may make sense for self-employed individuals or households but are an inefficient use of savings from an aggregate, economy-wide perspective. While no similar estimates of individual returns are available for other countries in the region, clearly Mexico is not the only country in the region with a large percentage of self-employed, informal entrepreneurs in the economy.

Informality in labor markets also creates a potential barrier to access formal financial instruments because labor income from informal sources is more volatile and is more likely to be paid out in cash. Evidence from surveys conducted in Brazil, Mexico, and Peru supports these patterns. A higher proportion of households working in the formal economy have access to formal saving instruments, while a higher proportion of informal workers save using informal instruments. In Mexico, 11 percent of households working in the informal labor market save formally compared to 34 percent of households working in the formal economy. In Peru, the gap is even larger: 16 percent versus 49 percent. In Brazil, this gap is negligible: 10 percent versus 11 percent.

Accounting for the Unbanked

Much has been written on the potential obstacles to accessing credit while the potential problems of accessing formal financial savings instruments have been less studied. The World Bank's 2014 *Global Financial Development Report* summarizes both sets of literature and analyzes the accompanying FINDEX dataset in order to determine the most important potential obstacles to greater financial savings, and hence to deeper financial intermediation. One interesting finding is the importance of cost and distance as significant deterrents to opening or using a bank account.[25]

Employing a cross-section of the 2011 FINDEX dataset, Rojas-Suárez, and Amado (2014) analyze similar issues, but specifically focus on Latin America to explain the region's "financial inclusion gap." They highlight three particular aspects: the quality of institutions, the level of income inequality at the macro level, and the level of education at the individual level.

Powell (2016) confirms the first set of results using the 2011 and 2014 FINDEX datasets. The variable "rule of law" (which is considered a proxy for the quality of institutions) and the country "Gini coefficient" (a measure of country inequality) are both significant in explaining the proportion of people that have an account in a financial institution. Stronger institutions and greater equality are associated with a higher percentage of individuals with accounts in financial institutions.

Figure 3.7 Percentage of Households with a Bank Account, Institutions and Inequality

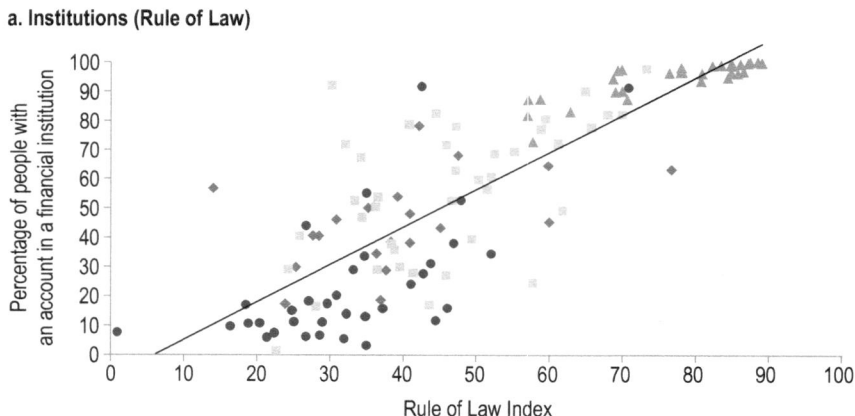

a. Institutions (Rule of Law)

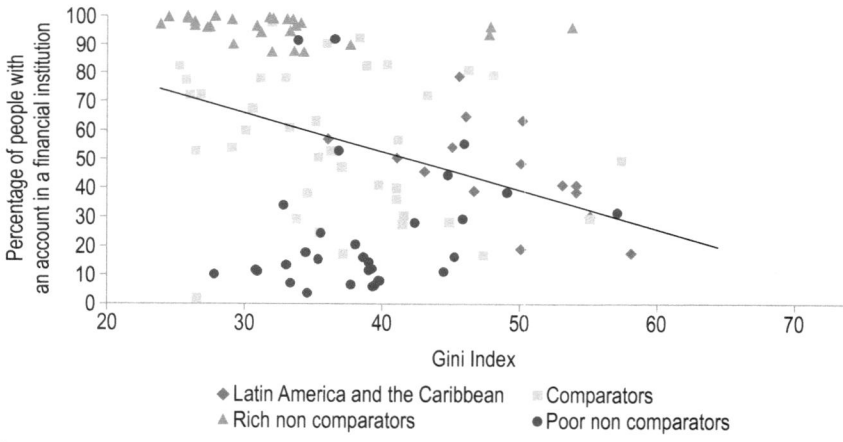

b. Inequality (Gini Coefficient)

◆ Latin America and the Caribbean   ■ Comparators
▲ Rich non comparators   ● Poor non comparators

Source: Authors' calculations using the Findex Macro Database (World Bank, 2014b).
Note: Latin America and the Caribbean: Argentina, Belize, Bolivia, Brazil, Chile, Colombia, Costa Rica, Dominican Republic, Ecuador, El Salvador, Guatemala, Haiti, Honduras, Jamaica, Mexico, Nicaragua, Panama, Paraguay, Peru, Trinidad and Tobago, Uruguay and Venezuela.
Comparators: Albania, Algeria, Angola, Armenia, Azerbaijan, Belarus, Bosnia and Herzegovina, Botswana, Bulgaria, China, P.R.: Mainland, Congo, Czech Republic, Djibouti, Estonia, Gabon, Georgia, Hungary, Indonesia, Iran Islamic Rep., Jordan, Kazakhstan, Latvia, Lebanon, Lithuania, Macedonia, FYR, Malaysia, Mauritius, Montenegro, Morocco, Philippines, Poland, Romania, Russian Federation, Saudi Arabia, Slovak Republic, South Africa, Sri Lanka, Swaziland, Syrian Arab Republic, Thailand, Tunisia, Turkey, Turkmenistan, Ukraine and Uzbekistan.
Rich non comparators: Australia, Austria, Bahrain, Kingdom of, Belgium, Canada, China, P.R.: Hong Kong, Cyprus, Denmark, Finland, France, Germany, Greece, Ireland, Israel, Italy, Japan, Korea, Kuwait, Luxembourg, Malta, Netherlands, New Zealand, Oman, Portugal, Qatar, Singapore, Slovenia, Spain, Sweden, United Arab Emirates, United Kingdom and United States.
Poor non comparators: Afghanistan, Bangladesh, Benin, Burundi, Cameroon, Central African Republic, Chad, Comoros, Democratic Republic of Congo, Ghana, Guinea, India, Iraq, Kenya, Kyrgyz Republic, Lao People's Democratic Republic, Lesotho, Liberia, Madagascar, Malawi, Mali, Mauritania, Mongolia, Nepal, Niger, Nigeria, Rwanda, Senegal, Sierra Leone, Somalia, Sudan, Taiwan Prov.of China, Tajikistan, Togo, Uganda, West Bank and Gaza, Yemen, Zambia and Zimbabwe.

Figure 3.7 plots the percentage of individuals with a bank account against rule of law and each country's Gini coefficient for Latin American and Caribbean countries, countries with similar levels of income (comparators) as well as richer (rich non-comparators) and poorer (poor non-comparators) countries. The relationship with rule of law is strong, although countries in Latin America and the Caribbean appear somewhat more dispersed than comparator countries. There is more overall dispersion in the case of inequality, although Latin America and the Caribbean countries appear to obey the relationship more strongly than some other country groups. For example, rich countries typically have a very high percentage of individuals with bank accounts irrespective of the level of inequality while, in the case of poorer countries, the opposite tends to be true. The negative relationship is then driven by Latin America and the Caribbean and comparator countries.

The FINDEX dataset also includes data at the individual level. Thus, whether a person has a bank account or not can be looked at as a function of individual as well as country level characteristics. Individual characteristics such as age, income, gender and the level of education are all significant determinants of whether an individual has a financial account (see Powell, 2016). Women are significantly less likely to have a formal financial account than men, while richer individuals are more likely to have one. The level of education turns out to be highly significant: individuals with secondary and tertiary education are much more likely to have an account.

Interestingly, the country's overall inequality is not significant. While income is an important determinant of whether a person has a bank account, the country's overall income inequality is not. However, when the Gini coefficient is interacted with income quintiles, from the poorest 20 percent of individuals to the richest 20 percent, the results change. The probability of an individual in a lower income quintile being banked depends greatly on the overall country Gini. Neither the Gini nor the income quintiles by themselves are significant. However, the interaction between the two variables is significant. Individuals of lower income quintiles tend not to be banked particularly when the country's income inequality is high (see Figure 3.8). The more unequal the society, the less likely lower income families are to be banked. Instead, for richer households, a country's income inequality has little bearing on their probability of being banked.

Figure 3.8 **Marginal Impact of Inequality for Different Income Groups**

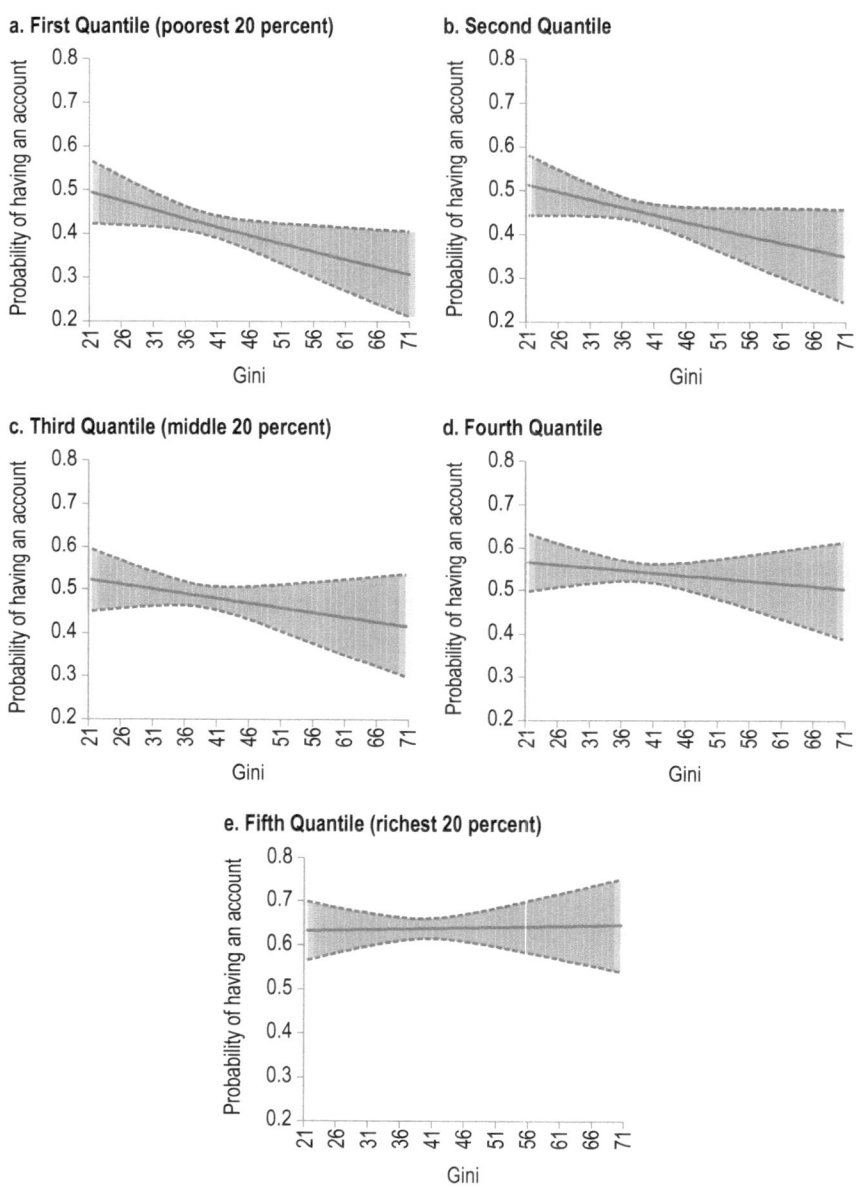

Source: Authors' calculations using 2011 data from the World Bank's Findex Micro Database.
Note: The figures illustrate that the probability of having a bank account falls sharply for lower income groups as inequality rises while inequality has little effect on rich households. The estimates known as margins plots stem from the estimates of a probit regression and use Findex microdata for the dependent variable (the probability of having an account in a financial institution, post office or microfinancial institution). The explanatory variable in each case is the country Gini coefficient (a measure of inequality) and a set of micro and macro controls.

This result is consistent with an explanation that factors in the behavior of banks and other financial institutions. If there is a fixed cost for using formal financial institutions for savings, then only people with sufficient resources will use those services. Banks will tend to open branches in communities where richer households will use banking services. If entry barriers to banking are high, the combination of fixed costs and economic inequality may limit the size of banking systems. The result is a financial system that remains relatively small and inefficient and caters largely to wealthier households. Regional inequalities may exacerbate this pattern. In a larger country, banks will naturally locate in areas where richer households reside. Financial institutions may steer clear of poorer areas, leaving poorer households to travel larger distances and face even higher costs in order to be banked. The location decision of banks, coupled with fixed and variable transport costs and economic inequality, leads to a banking sector focused on wealthier households of limited size and hence of higher costs, concentrated in specific geographic locations. A large share of poorer households are left with no banks nearby and are very likely unbanked.

The Link between Financial Access and Savings: The Case of Mexico

Typically, empirical work suggests that saving is determined by a set of country-level variables and individual or household characteristics. This type of analysis suggests that saving is low in the region due to macroeconomic uncertainty, weak institutions, or low household income, for example.[26] A drawback of this type of analysis is that it ignores the link between savings behavior and financial access. Without finer, within-country information, it is impossible to tease out the nature of the link between the two. It is generally assumed that financial access is driven by the same factors that also govern savings.

At the other extreme, a body of literature considers specific interventions that frequently involve improving access to financial services. In general, these studies find that such interventions may well result in greater use of financial services—both credit and saving instruments (see Chapter 9).

There is comparatively less literature on how financial presence (or access) affects saving behavior in an entire country.[27] There are two main reasons why such analyses have not been attempted. First, published household surveys typically do not include information on the location of the household. Second, good information on the precise location of different types of financial services also may not be available. Mexico does have the requisite information, however, and allows for an analysis not only of how financial access affects saving behavior, but also of how financial institutions may make location decisions. Moreover, Mexico is a large country with considerable heterogeneity and has enjoyed significant financial deepening (see Figure 3.9).

Mexico is thus an ideal country to consider the links between financial access and savings. Interestingly, the distribution of financial institutions by municipality is highly skewed. Some municipalities have many financial institutions but many municipalities have just one or none at all (see Figure 3.10).[28]

Naturally, there is a big divide between urban and rural areas. Many urban municipalities have numerous financial institutions, while many rural municipalities have none at all.[29] Moreover, access to a financial institution varies considerably depending on household income. Indeed, some 93 percent of households in the top decile have relatively easy access to a financial institution (defined as at least one institution in their locality), while those in lower income deciles do not. For example, only 28 percent of households in the lowest income decile have a financial institution nearby (see Figure 3.11).[30]

Figure 3.9 The Process of Financial Deepening in Mexico

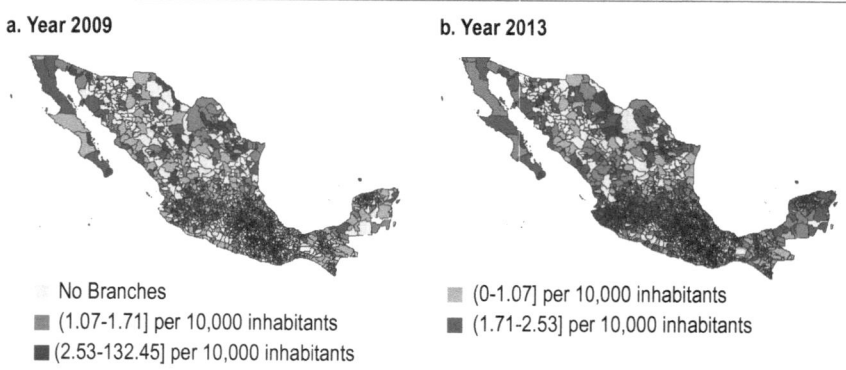

a. Year 2009

b. Year 2013

No Branches

(0-1.07] per 10,000 inhabitants

(1.07-1.71] per 10,000 inhabitants

(1.71-2.53] per 10,000 inhabitants

(2.53-132.45] per 10,000 inhabitants

Source: Authors' elaboration based on Powell and Székely (2015).
Note: Territorial shading illustrates the number of bank branches per 10,000 inhabitants at the municipal level in Mexico. The cut-off points were obtained by generating quartiles according to the 2013 distribution, excluding the municipalities that do not have a bank branch.

Figure 3.10 Financial Institutions per Inhabitant in Mexican Municipalities in 2012

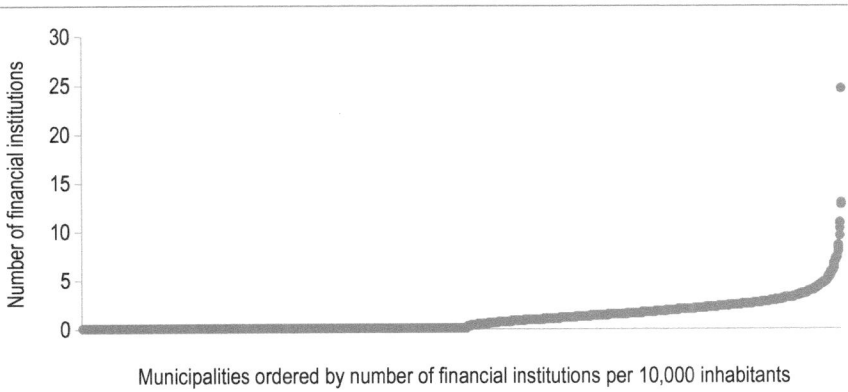

Source: Authors' elaboration based on Powell and Székely (2015).

Banks will naturally tend to open where they expect to find a market for their services. The number of financial institutions increases in munic-ipalities with fewer poorer households. Moreover, crime rates seem to be positively related with financial institution presence. One explanation may be that in high crime areas, it is more important to keep savings safe

Figure 3.11 Percentage of Households with Access to Financial Institutions by Income Decile, Mexico

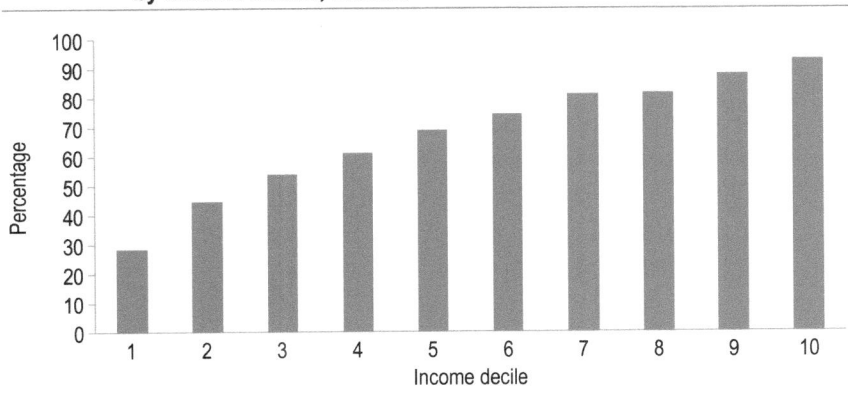

Source: Authors' elaboration based on Powell and Székely (2015).
Note: Includes 2012 data from the Encuesta Nacional de Ingresos y Gastos de los Hogares (ENIGH), 2013 data from the National Dictionary of Economic Units, and 2013 data from the National Banking Commission.

in a bank rather than at home. Municipal efficiency is also correlated with higher financial presence (see Powell and Székely, 2015).

Interestingly, the presence of a high school is associated with a larger bank presence. Not every municipality in Mexico has a high school. Municipalities are generally keen to obtain such an honor, which may be awarded by the state or federal authorities. One explanation for this relationship is that more people circulate in municipalities with high schools; parents transport their children back and forth to school, and teachers and other personnel come and go to work. Thus, placing a branch in an area with a school rather than one without a school brings greater convenience to a larger number of people. It reduces transaction costs, or what is referred to as "shoe-leather" costs. The decision as to where schools are located is not automatic; location decisions appear to be driven as much by politics as by any other factor. These considerations potentially make school location a useful variable to explain financial presence that is not directly related to savings.[31]

How does financial presence affect savings decisions? To research this question, several years of household surveys and information regarding financial presence were matched at the municipality level. A difficulty is that banks will locate where they think households will use their services. Hence, the measures of financial presence are not used directly. Rather what is used is the estimated financial presence using the preferred proxy: namely, high school presence. As the location of high schools is unrelated per se to savings behavior directly but is a good predictor of bank presence, it appears to be a valid instrument for this analysis.[32] The main result is that financial savings do indeed increase with financial presence where financial presence is estimated using high school presence as a proxy (see Powell and Székely, 2015).

In theory, the effect could go either way. With financial institutions close by, households might save less, as they might then have more opportunities to borrow in case of a negative shock. However, the results suggest that the lower costs of greater proximity to a financial institution outweigh this potential effect.

The Missing Link

Ideally, people save, deposit their savings in financial institutions, which in turn allocate those savings to productive investments in the economy that fuel overall growth and development. Financial intermediaries are, therefore, the crucial link between savers and investors. Unfortunately, in Latin America and the Caribbean, financial intermediation is the missing link, the break in the chain between savings and investment that determines the quality of saving in the region. Increasing access and use of financial institutions are keys to deepening the financial system and ensuring that Latin America and the Caribbean generate not only more, but better, saving.

Notes

1. For an in-depth analysis of credit constraints, see IDB (2004). For a more recent treatment, see Didier and Schmukler (2014).

2. This definition of the roles of financial systems borrows from Levine (2005), who followed the earlier work of Nobel prize-winner Robert Merton in constructing this list.

3. For discussion on this point, see Allen and Gale (2000).

4. For information about how corporate governance differs around the globe, see OECD (2015b). For a discussion of comparative financial systems and the link to corporate governance, see Mayer (1998) and Allen and Gale (2000). For an account of how the global financial crisis has prompted new interest in finance and corporate governance issues, see Hopt (2011).

5. For a discussion of the alternative disciplining roles of banks and capital markets, see Mayer (1996) and Franks, Mayer, and Renneboog (2001).

6. Rajan and Zingales (2003) provide an interesting discussion on a similar phenomenon in continental Europe.

7. For a review of the literature, see Levine (2005).

8. In a panel regression analysis, bank deposits were regressed on the assets under management of capital market institutions (pension funds, insurance companies, and mutual funds) with both time and country fixed effects. If the coefficient on the assets under management of capital market institutions is positive and significant, then the hypothesis that they are substitutes to banks may be rejected. This was indeed the result. The hypothesis that Latin American and Caribbean countries may differ from comparator countries was also rejected.

9. Many of these issues are discussed in more depth in OECD (2015b).

10. See in particular Dewatripont and Tirole (1994), who argue that small investors would have little chance in disciplining firms, but banks that pool such investors may attempt to play that role. They also argue that financial regulation is needed to discipline banks, and refer to this as the "representation hypothesis" rationale for financial regulation.

11. See IDB (2004); Chong and Pagés (2010); Didier and Schmukler (2014).

12. Berger and Mester (1997) find significant scale economies in U.S. banking. Anderson and Jõeveer (2012) also argue in favor of scale

economies, and employ a novel approach considering the rents accru-
ing to shareholders versus bankers. Other studies find less evidence for
scale economies in banking. For a set of papers on this issue, see Feldman (2010, Mester (2010), and DeYoung (2010). Economies of scale are
normally considered on the basis of individual institutions; this raises
the question of competition. A small number of larger banks may be
efficient in reducing fixed costs, but then each may have extensive
market power. A larger number of banks may promote competition,
but may lead to an inefficient repetition of fixed costs.

[13] In the late 1800s, Bagehot (1873, 3–4) argued that a major difference
between England and poorer countries was that in England, the financial system could mobilize resources for "immense works."

[14] The World Bank's FINDEX dataset is available at http://datatopics.
worldbank.org/financialinclusion/.

[15] Of course, there are exceptions. The Unit Trust Corporation of Trinidad and Tobago is a cooperative, is highly integrated into the financial
system, and has assets of close to 10 percent of the country's GDP.
Creditcoop of Argentina is also a cooperative and is highly integrated
into the country's financial system; it is regulated and supervised by
the central bank and the superintendence of financial and exchange
entities as a regular commercial bank.

[16] See Sirri and Tufano (1995); Acemoglu and Zilibotti (1997).

[17] See Aizenman, Cavallo, and Noy (2015).

[18] Evidence for Colombia comes from ongoing background work by
Camacho and Hofstetter employing the ELCA household surveys
(Universidad de los Andes) and complementary data sources.

[19] The figure considers the main saving instrument for each household,
defined as the one with the highest stock.

[20] For the most part, surveyed households in these countries (which are
low- and middle-income households) save either formally or informally, but not both ways.

[21] Data were collected for five countries in Latin America (Brazil, Chile,
Colombia, Ecuador, and Mexico) and seven other countries (the Czech
Republic, Hungary, the Republic of Korea, the Philippines, Poland, South
Africa, and Thailand). The analysis can be performed only for those
countries that have sufficiently disaggregated national account data. In
particular, a detailed breakdown of the capital and financial accounts
by institutional sector (households, government, corporations, foreign)
is required. These 12 countries satisfied these requirements.

[22] Household funds that are intermediated formally include "financial deposits" (including cash holdings), "funds allocated to insurance and pension funds," and "debt security holdings." Household funds that are not intermediated or are savings parked in informal instruments include "direct ownership of firms" (which comprises shares and other equity holdings) and the residual category, "acquisition of other financial assets."

[23] The other subcomponents of "equity" are purchases of equity in firms listed on the stock market, and purchases of shares through mutual funds. It is not likely that either one of these two explains the difference between Latin America and the comparator group. First, households participate little in the stock market in Latin America. On average, only 1 percent of the population in a select group of countries in the region owns shares of publicly listed companies directly, while among four countries in Emerging Asia, the ratio is 20 percent (see Grout, Megginson, and Zalewska, 2009). Second, for a subset of countries for which data are available, there is no difference in the households' investments in mutual funds between countries in the two groups. In Brazil, Chile, and Colombia, households use 4.6 percent of total funds to purchase mutual funds, while comparator countries use 4.5 percent.

[24] National accounts may record activities like purchasing a durable good like a refrigerator or a truck as consumption; thus some of these activities may not be included as savings, even though such activities are a form of savings, from the standpoint of the individual.

[25] After "not enough money" and "family member already has an account," cost and distance were the most common reasons respondents gave for not having a bank account, with 23 percent and 20 percent giving those replies, respectively (World Bank, 2014a, Figure 1.14).

[26] For a recent empirical analysis along these lines, see Grigoli, Herman and Schmidt-Hebbel (2015).

[27] Aportela (1999) and Ruiz (2013) both consider the expansion of (different) specific financial institutions in Mexico and the impact on households' financial decisions. For further discussion, see Chapter 11.

[28] A point of access here is a bank branch, a correspondent bank location, or an automatic teller machine (ATM).

[29] Powell and Székely (2015) provide further statistics regarding the location of financial institutions, correspondent banks, and ATMs.

[30] A locality is a subdivision of a municipality. There are more than 2,400 municipalities in Mexico and over 190,000 localities.

[31] In other words, it may be a useful "instrument" in an "instrumental variables" analysis.

[32] A further "matching methodology" was also pursued as a robustness test, and the same results were found to hold. For further details and for further robustness tests, see Powell and Székely (2015).

4 More and Better Saving for Productive Investment

Why save more? One good reason is to invest more. Economies that save more can take advantage of investment opportunities and thus grow faster. Investing to improve access to education and health, for example, can boost growth by increasing people's productivity and income. Investing in plants and machinery is critical to maintain, expand, and incorporate technological progress in countries' productive structures.

Among all investment types, investment in infrastructure is one of the most crucial for growth. Infrastructure (transport, telecommunications, energy, and water and sanitation) complements other forms of capital and labor. If properly planned and built, it can eliminate bottlenecks that reduce growth potential. What differentiates infrastructure from other forms of capital is the need for long-term financing to pay for it. This financing should be in local currency as much as possible, which is precisely the type of financing that national saving provides. The challenge going forward for Latin America and the Caribbean is how to develop the proper instruments to channel national saving to infrastructure. This chapter also explores the region's options to enhance infrastructure as an asset class and make it an attractive investment opportunity for institutional investors.

Investment and National Saving: Low, Lower, Lowest

Investment has the potential to impact growth positively in both the short and long term. In the short to medium term, investment generates growth by boosting aggregate demand. In the long term, investment's growth effect works via aggregate supply and the productive apparatus;

BOX 4.1. DEFINITION OF GROSS FIXED CAPITAL FORMATION

The variable used in national accounts to measure investment is Gross Fixed Capital Formation (GFCF). GFCF is a component of a country's gross domestic product (GDP), together with consumption, government spending, and net exports. It includes land improvements (fences, ditches, drains); plant machinery and equipment purchases; and the construction of roads, railways, and other infrastructure. It also includes schools, offices, hospitals, private residential dwellings, and commercial and industrial buildings.[a]

---

[a] The precise definition of Gross Fixed Capital Formation is provided in the World Bank's World Development Indicators (2015b).

higher investment triggers technological changes, induces higher productive capacity, and fosters resource reallocation toward higher productivity sectors (Jiménez and Manuelito, 2013).

If investment is such an important determinant of economic growth, then it's crucial to ask whether Latin America and the Caribbean is investing enough. If comparisons with other regions are any indication, the answer is no. Latin America and the Caribbean has systematically invested less over time than other regions.

When countries are grouped by income level, the evolution of investment follows two distinct paths (Figure 4.1). Up to 2000, low-and-middle and high-income countries invested a similar share of GDP, around 23 percent.[1]

Figure 4.11 Private Investment in Infrastructure, 1990–2012

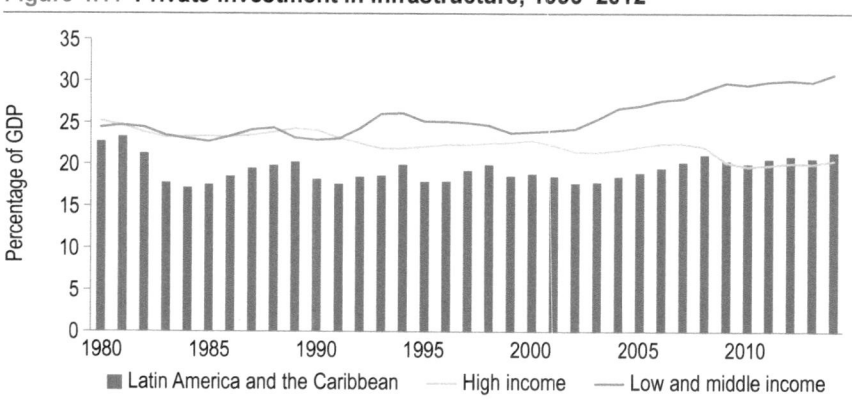

■ Latin America and the Caribbean ——— High income ——— Low and middle income

Source: Authors' calculations based on Serebrisky, Margot, and others (2015).

However, after 2000, low-and-middle-income countries began to invest an increasing share of GDP, while gross fixed capital formation (GFCF) among high-income countries began to decline. Since most countries in Latin America and the Caribbean are low-and-middle-income countries, the region should follow the pattern of increasing investment. Instead, average GFCF in the region between 2000 and 2014 was 20 percent—much lower than the 25 percent average for low-and-middle-income countries in the same period.

Apparently, 25 percent is a sort of magic number when it comes to investment. According to the Commission on Growth and Development, 25 percent is the minimum investment level compatible with long-term growth.[2] Its 2008 report on growth analyzed 13 economies[3] that grew an average 7 percent a year or more for at least 25 years between 1950 and 2005. The diverse sample of countries included economies on four continents, big and small countries, some rich in natural resources, and others that were not. All 13 success stories experienced investment rates above 25 percent of GDP during the periods of high growth—hence the conclusion that a 25 percent of GDP investment rate is the minimum necessary level compatible with sustained economic growth.

Unfortunately, Latin America is far from the 25 percent benchmark recommended by the Commission. With the exception of Haiti, which only reached the threshold thanks to extensive external assistance, no other country in Latin America and the Caribbean has come close to the 25 percent benchmark (Figure 4.2). The regional average between 1980 and 2014 was just 20 percent.

Investment in Latin America is not only low; a breakdown of investment by region confirms that between 1980 and 2014, Latin America and the Caribbean had the lowest GFCF flows of any region (Figure 4.3). The comparison with Emerging Asia is the most striking, with an investment gap equivalent to 10 percent of Latin America's annual GDP between 1980 and 2013. Sub-Saharan Africa invested 1.7 percent of GDP more than Latin America and the Caribbean during the period.

While Latin America and the Caribbean has recorded low GFCF in recent decades, it has enjoyed a few episodes of high GFCF. A review of 770 country-year observations in 25 countries in the region between 1980 and 2013 identified 70 cases of high investment (defined to be higher than the threshold 25 percent of GDP), or 9 percent of the observations. Thus, Latin American and Caribbean countries can achieve high levels of investment, even in a context of low averages. These cases,

Figure 4.2 **Average Investment, National Saving, and Foreign Saving Rates, 1980–2014**

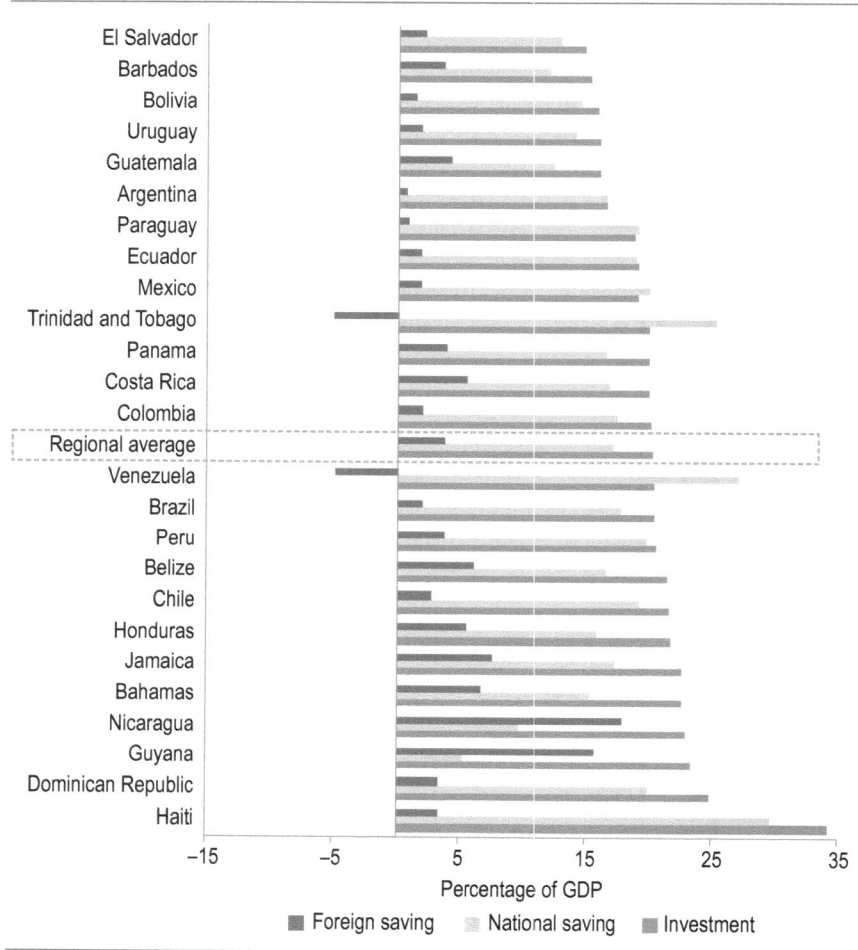

Source: Authors' calculations based on World Economic Outlook database (IMF, 2015).

however, are concentrated in a few countries (most of them in the Bahamas, Honduras, Jamaica, and Trinidad and Tobago) scattered across different years and likely related to reconstruction after natural disasters. The challenge for the region is to extend these successful experiences to more countries and sustain high investment rates for consecutive years.

Investment in Latin America and the Caribbean is not only relatively lower than in other regions, it is also more volatile. While volatility patterns vary by country, they generally consist of scattered investment

Figure 4.3 **Gross Fixed Capital Formation by Region, 1980–2014**

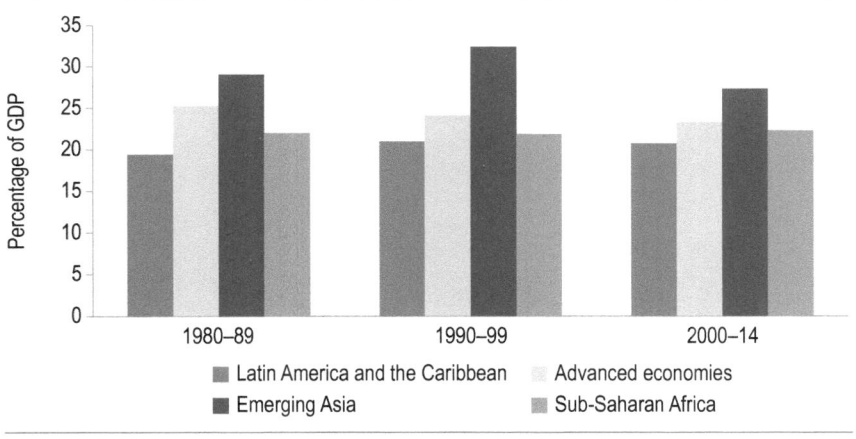

Source: Authors' calculations based on World Economic Outlook database (IMF, 2015).

peaks followed by years of low investment rates. Using the coefficient of variation (the ratio between the standard deviation and the mean of series) to measure volatility, China, the advanced economies, and Emerging Asia (excluding China) have the lowest volatility.[4] Interestingly, the countries with the most stable series of investment (China and the rest of Emerging Asia) also have the highest levels of investment, while Sub-Saharan Africa—the most volatile region—along with Latin America and the Caribbean, are the regions that invest the least.

So who is to blame for this low level of investment in Latin America and the Caribbean? Is it the public sector, the private sector, or a more systemic problem of the economic environment that leads to low levels of investment by both the public and private sectors? Unfortunately for Latin America and the Caribbean, the answer is that both public and private investment are low compared to other regions and country groupings (Figure 4.4).

While private investment is the main component of total investment in Latin America and the Caribbean, as it is in all regions, private investment in Latin America and the Caribbean is lower than in the rest of the world; the only exception is Sub-Saharan Africa. Public investment is also low by international standards. Given that the difference has persisted over time, Latin America and the Caribbean is opening an investment gap with the world. What is worrisome is that this gap has been present since the 1980s and there are no signs of it getting any smaller.

Figure 4.4 **Average Gross Fixed Capital Formation by Region, 2000–2014**

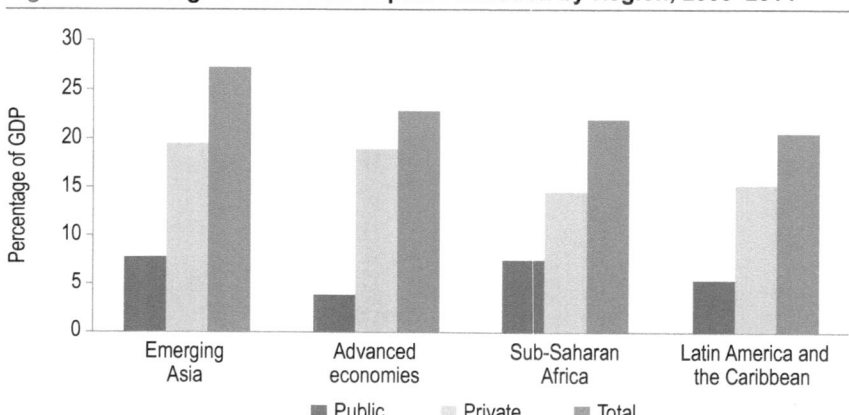

Source: Authors' calculations based on IMF (2015).

Financing Investment: No Place Like Home

National and foreign saving are the only options economies have to finance investment. A quick glance at the evolution of investment and national saving in Latin America and the Caribbean shows that as low as investment has been, it has still been higher than national saving since 1980, with the exception of only one year (Figure 4.5). The experience of other regions is very different. Indeed, national saving is higher than investment in the economies that invest the most: Emerging Asia.[5] In contrast, Latin America and the Caribbean has relied on foreign saving to finance its investment. On average, the region had to "import" saving in amounts equivalent to 3.5 percent of GDP.

Without increasing national saving, Latin American and Caribbean countries would need to boost foreign saving from the current 3.5 percent of GDP to 8 percent to catch up with the critical 25 percent of GDP investment level needed for growth rates above 5 percent. That's double the current foreign saving rates! Even economies with access to foreign financing would find it difficult to finance a gap between the domestic investment and national saving rates much above 5 percent of GDP (Corbo, 1998). Data confirm this hypothesis for almost every country in Latin America and the Caribbean: with the exception of Nicaragua and Guyana, no country in the region was capable of sustaining foreign saving rates above 8 percent of GDP for prolonged periods of time.[6]

Figure 4.5 **National Saving and Investment in Latin America and the Caribbean and Emerging Asia, 1980–2014**

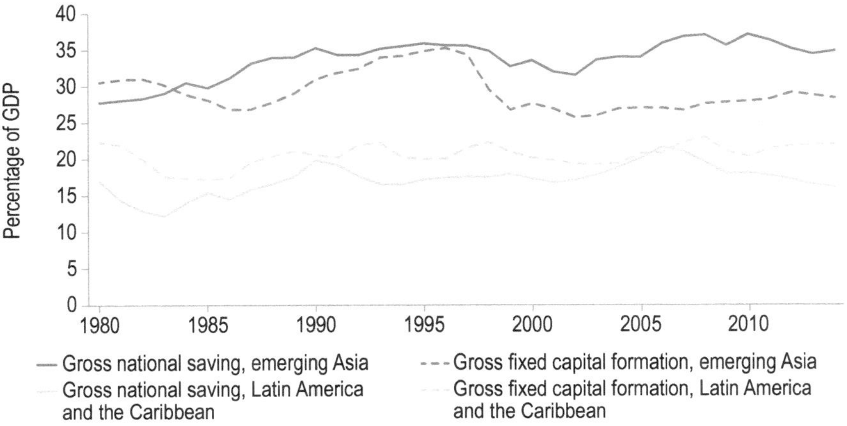

— Gross national saving, emerging Asia
   Gross national saving, Latin America
   and the Caribbean

--- Gross fixed capital formation, emerging Asia
    Gross fixed capital formation, Latin America
    and the Caribbean

Source: Authors' calculations based on World Economic Outlook database (IMF, 2015).

A dramatic increase in foreign saving, while possible, might not be desirable. Relying on foreign saving to finance domestic investment is risky, for various reasons. In the first place, national transaction costs that affect expected returns, perceived riskiness of assets in foreign currencies, and information asymmetries induce home bias in investing. Local investors tend to invest in local assets (either in national firms or foreign firms with local presence) much more than they invest in foreign markets (Coeurdacier and Rey, 2013; Ke, Ng, and Wang, 2010). Second, foreign capital flows tend to be volatile and prone to sudden stops (Calvo, Izquierdo, and Loo-Kung, 2006), so relying less on foreign saving reduces vulnerability to crises provoked by turbulent international financial markets. Moreover, it is difficult to maintain large current account deficits (of the magnitude required to close the investment gap with foreign saving alone) for prolonged periods of time without abrupt reversals, or external indebtedness problems (Powell, 2013).[7]

In a fully integrated world economy, the origin of saving is irrelevant, as profitable domestic investment opportunities would find financing, either locally or from the rest of the world. In this ideal world, national saving need not correlate strongly with domestic investment. But can the data confirm the decoupling of investment and the source of saving? A paper by Feldstein and Horioka (1980) finds otherwise. For a sample of 16 member-countries of the Organisation for Economic Co-operation and Development (OECD) from 1960 to 1974, increases in national saving were matched by practically equal increases in domestic investment.[8] Feldstein and Horioka (1980) conclude that international capital is not perfectly mobile; hence, an economy in need of increasing investment must rely on additional domestic capital (saving) to finance it. Research on Latin America and the Caribbean confirms the close link between investment and national saving. In the period 1980–2012, for every 1 percentage point increase in national saving, domestic investment increased by almost 0.4 percentage points (Cavallo and Pedemonte, 2015).

While Feldstein and Horioka's study is centered on flows—domestic investment *rates* and national and foreign saving *rates*—the same results hold when examining stocks—domestic capital stock and the stock of national savings. In developing countries, more than 90 percent of the stock of capital is self-financed—which means that foreign savings have not provided a materially sufficient source for financing domestic capital. This result was obtained by calculating self-financing ratios (SFR): the stock of tangible capital financed by past national saving, relative to the actual stock of capital (Aizenman, Pinto, and Radziwill, 2007). Aizenman, Pinto, and Radziwill define the SFR as the ratio of discounted past national saving and discounted past domestic investment. Intuitively, the self-financing ratios capture the proportion of the current domestic capital stock that is financed with past local savings. An SFR of 1 would correspond to an economy in which the entire stock of domestic capital is self-financed. A self-financing ratio below 1 indicates reliance on foreign saving. An SFR above 1 describes an economy that is a net exporter of capital, and contributes to finance capital in the rest of the world.

Recent SFR calculations for 1980 to 2011 using data from the International Monetary Fund's World Economic Outlook (WEO) database show that, as of 2011, while SFR are above 80 percent in all regions of the world, in Latin America and the Caribbean, they are 96 percent, a value that confirms the results of Aizenman, Pinto, and Radziwill (2007). As expected, Asian economies have the highest ratios, surpassing 1 (Figure 4.6). Overall, for advanced economies and all other country groupings, the SFR are very close to 1,[9] indicating that most domestic capital stock is supported by past national saving. Importantly, SFR are growing in all regions, and especially in developing regions. Between 1980 and 2010, Latin American and Caribbean countries increased their SFR from 81 percent to 96 percent, Sub-Saharan African countries raised theirs from 69 percent to 79 percent, and the region that invests the

Figure 4.6 **Self-Financing Ratios by Region, 1980–2011**

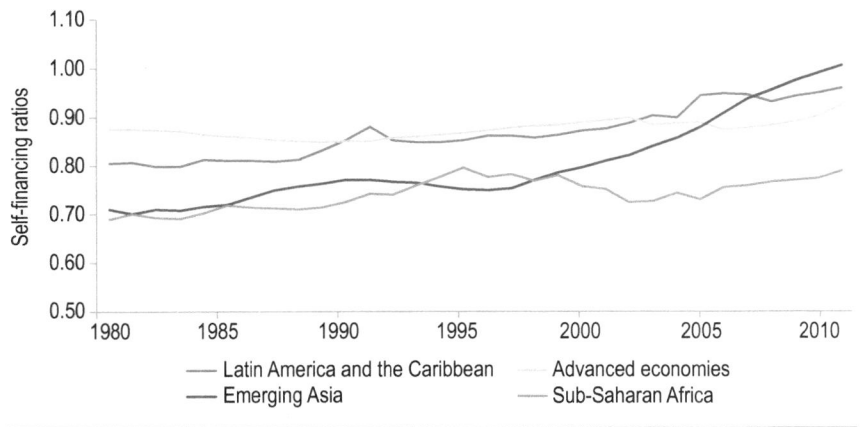

Source: Authors' calculations based on data for years 1960–2011 from World Development Indicators database, based on methodology from Aizenman, Pinto and Radziwill (2007), extended on Cavallo, Fernández-Arias, and Marzani (2016).

most, Emerging Asia, also increased its SFR the most: from 71 percent to 106 percent. These trends confirm that countries rely mostly on national saving to finance domestic capital stocks. The message is clear: there's no place like home as a source of saving for investment.

For Policy, Which Comes First: Saving or Investment?

The existence of a high positive correlation between national saving rates and domestic investment rates is one of the most robust and stable regularities observed in the data across countries and decades (Baxter and Crucini,1993). However, correlation does not mean causation. Does national saving drive investment, or vice versa? Is investment in Latin America and the Caribbean low because of the lack of national saving, or is national saving low because of low investment rates? There are arguments that support both points of view (see Serebrisky, Margot, et al., 2015).

Chapter 10 describes how episodes of important increases in total factor productivity generate expectations of higher returns on investment and thus incentivize subsequent increases in savings to take advantage of the enhanced return opportunities. This argument suggests that in an economy, saving increases endogenously when better investment opportunities exist. However, even if such a favorable environment sparks a sharp increase in investment demand, for that investment to materialize, the domestic saving rate must also rise. In this context, policies that mobilize saving will help bring about higher investment rates in the economy (Corbo, 1998).

The argument in Chapter 10 does not invalidate the exogenous components of saving and the evidence that increases in saving tend to precede higher levels of investment. Empirical evidence for the world and for Latin America and the Caribbean shows that national saving precedes investment, but investment does not anticipate future saving.[10] A 10 percent increase in past national saving raises current investment by 1 percent, while an increase in past investment has no significant effect on current saving. This is true regardless of indirect channels through which investment and saving could affect each other. For example, current investment might generate growth, which in turn increases future savings. The data show that saving drives investment even considering the indirect effect through growth, but the reverse is not true. However, there are episodes (particular countries, or certain years) in which causality runs in both directions. For example, in LAC-7 (Argentina, Brazil, Chile, Colombia, Mexico, Peru, and Venezuela), past saving increases current investment and past investment drives current saving (Serebrisky, Margot, et al., 2015).

Bidirectional effects do not invalidate the main premise: national saving in Latin America and the Caribbean must increase if the region is to foster investment. However, higher saving is only a necessary condition to increase investment, not a sufficient one: in some recent examples in Latin America and the Caribbean, investment did not catch up with significant increments in national saving.[11]

Moving forward, the most important policy recommendation is that policies to promote national saving and policies to promote investment should be consistent (Cavallo and Pedemonte, 2015). If pro-savings policies unintentionally discourage investment, then those policies will likely fail. This is not merely an abstract debate; some popular pro-savings policies, such as tax breaks to encourage local saving, have backfired. For example, in 1989, Mexico lowered the tax rate for distributed dividends to facilitate the flow of profits from companies to shareholders, which could then be channeled toward investments in other firms. However, this reform was implemented at a time when the relative prices of consumption goods and real estate were distorted. Thus, shareholders channeled the additional income to purchase consumer goods and real estate rather than toward financing investments in other firms. Corporate saving diminished because the lower retained earnings and household saving did not cover the difference. As a result, private saving declined from 12 percent of GDP in 1989 to an average of 8 percent for the period 1991–93 (see Calderón-Madrid, 1998).

Investment in Infrastructure: First among Equals?

Why is it important to analyze investment in infrastructure in a book about saving? Among investment alternatives, infrastructure is unique: it has characteristics of a public good, and the role of the public sector is vital to make it as productive as possible; it requires long-term financing; Latin America and the Caribbean invests too little and does not always allocate funding to the best infrastructure projects; and the region has proven incapable of channeling a significant share of private savings to infrastructure. No other component of investment more accurately reflects Latin America and the Caribbean's dual need to save more and to save better. The region must save more to increase investment in infrastructure and save better, channeling more savings to an asset class that is highly productive.

A Catalyst for Productivity and Growth

Infrastructure encompasses transport, energy, water and sanitation, and telecommunication assets. It is a component of the capital stock of a country and serves as an enabler to the supply and demand of services or, more technically, as an input in the production function. It is virtually impossible to think of the production process in modern societies or the demand for basic services such as education or health without the existence of reliable roads, water, and electricity services. Thus, infrastructure impacts growth by improving productivity, reducing production costs, facilitating human capital accumulation by easing access to educational facilities, helping diversify the productive structure, and creating employment through demand for the goods and services used to provide it.

Recent empirical research shows a positive correlation between growth and infrastructure investment in Latin America. Calderón and Servén (2010) find that comparing 1991–95 and 2001–05, the accumulation of infrastructure stock contributed 1.1 annual percentage points to economic growth in this region. Standard & Poor's (2015) find that three years after an increase in infrastructure investment of 1 percent of GDP, the GDP of Brazil would jump 2.5 percent, Argentina 1.8 percent and Mexico 1.3 percent. [12]

How much infrastructure investment does Latin America and the Caribbean need? This is probably the most frequently asked question in the infrastructure public policy arena in the region. Clearly motivated by the plummeting volumes of infrastructure investment since the late 1980s (Figure 4.7), this question has inspired several academic and policy publications to try to quantify the region's infrastructure gap (Calderón and Servén 2003; Kohli and Basil, 2011; Perrotti and Sánchez, 2011).

The most common ways of measuring an infrastructure gap include determining the infrastructure a country or region needs to meet a target growth rate, to achieve a specific objective such as a coverage rate (for example, 100 percent access to water and sanitation), or to achieve an infrastructure stock similar to a country or group of countries. Regardless of the definition of the gap and the methodologies used, the results are the same: Latin America and the Caribbean needs to invest at least 5 percent of GDP in infrastructure for a prolonged period of time. Assuming the estimates are right, the region requires additional investment in infrastructure in the range of 2 to 2.5 percent of GDP per year, or the equivalent of US$120 billion to US$150 billion (based on the region's GDP in 2013).

Figure 4.7 Evolution of Infrastructure Investment, 1980–2013

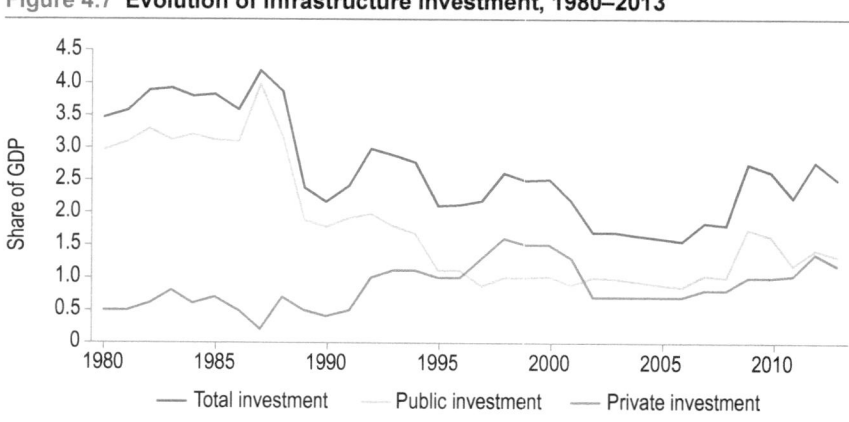

Total investment — Public investment — Private investment

Source: Authors' calculations based on Calderón and Servén (2010), CAF (2013), and ECLAC (2014a).
Note: The figure includes data for Brazil, Chile, Colombia, Mexico, and Peru, the countries for which data from the 1980s are available.

Investment in infrastructure in the region averaged 2.4 percent of GDP from 1992 to 2013, while investment in other regions and countries was significantly higher during the same period: 8.5 percent in China, 5 percent in Japan and India, and around 4 percent in other industrialized countries.[13] Moreover, Latin America and the Caribbean's infrastructure investment is 0.8 percent of GDP lower than in the United States and the European Union, regions with a much more developed capital stock that require relatively more maintenance investment than new infrastructure capacity (McKinsey Global Institute, 2013).

Investment in infrastructure is low across Latin America and the Caribbean and has taken its toll on the quality of the region's infrastructure services. Only one small country (Nicaragua) surpassed the 5 percent of GDP threshold between 2008 and 2013. None of the largest economies (Argentina, Brazil, Chile, or Mexico) invested more than 3 percent of GDP—much less than what is needed to close the infrastructure gap (Figure 4.8). The World Economic Forum's survey of infrastructure quality perceptions—the most cited and used worldwide— is conclusive:

Figure 4.8 Investment in Infrastructure by Country 2008–13 (annual average)

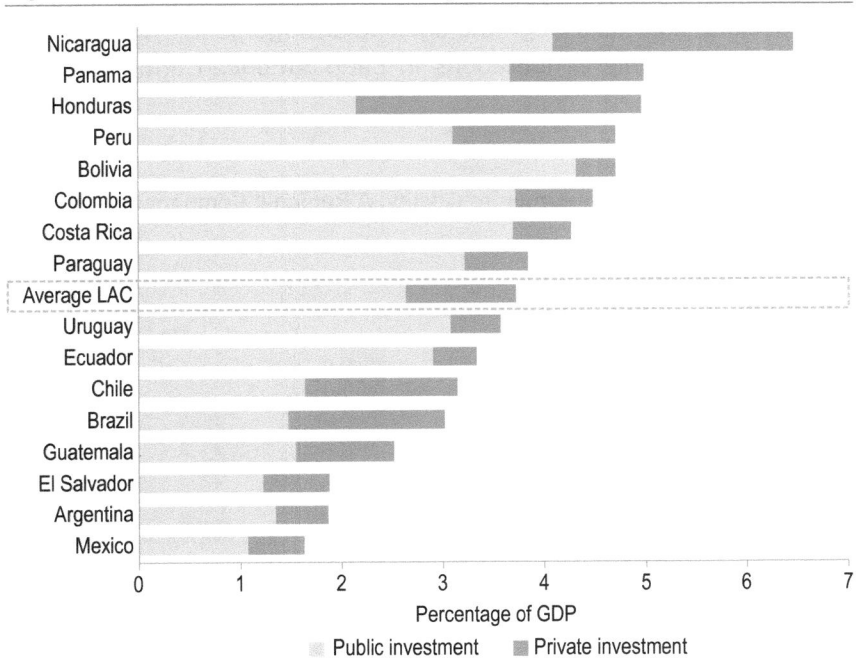

Source: Authors' calculations based on CAF (2013) and ECLAC (2014a).

the quality of infrastructure in Latin America and the Caribbean is lagging behind, particularly when compared with advanced economies and Emerging Asia. Even more worrisome is the comparison with Sub-Saharan Africa, which is reducing its quality gap. In Latin America and the Caribbean, quality increased slightly between 2006 and 2014, but Sub-Saharan Africa improved much more. If the trend continues, Latin America and the Caribbean will be the region with the lowest perception of infrastructure quality.[14]

Public or Private Investment: Both Is Best

Infrastructure requires rigorous planning because it creates both positive externalities (network effects), as well as negative ones (mainly in the environmental and social realms). It also requires proper supervision to make sure services comply with adequate quality standards. These activities must be performed by the public sector. However, the public sector need not provide infrastructure services directly. In many countries, infrastructure services are provided by private firms through a variety of arrangements, such as management contracts or concessions, that commonly fall under the umbrella term "public-private partnerships" (although the specific arrangements have different legal and economic connotations in Latin American and Caribbean countries).

Figure 4.9 Perceived Infrastructure Quality: A Regional Comparison, 2006–15

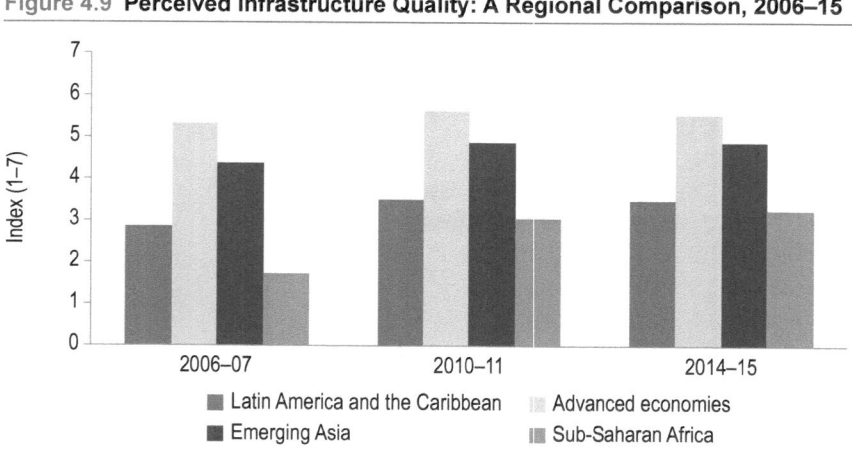

Source: Authors' calculations, based on World Economic Forum (2006, 2010, 2014).
Note: The perception index is based on a scale from 1 (worst) to seven (best).

Despite falling from its 1980s peak (see Figure 4.7), public investment in infrastructure is higher than private investment in all countries in Latin America and the Caribbean. The decline in public investment was the consequence of two factors: less fiscal space following the macroeconomic adjustment policies in the 1990s that reduced public spending, and a concurrent belief that opening infrastructure services to private ownership and operations would compensate for lower public investment in infrastructure (Fay and Morrison 2007). Unfortunately, the role of private investment in infrastructure has increased, but not enough to replace public investment.

From 1990 to 2013, the region accumulated US$680 billion in private investment, exceeding Emerging Asia (US$503 billion) and Sub-Saharan Africa (US$130 billion). Even though the level of private investment increased from the early 1990s, reaching 1.5 percent of GDP in some years, it never achieved expected levels, leaving the region with much lower total investment levels as a percent of GDP than in the 1980s.

Undoubtedly, Latin America and the Caribbean needs more investment in infrastructure and, given the size of the infrastructure gap, both public and private investment will have to increase. But is there room to increase both public and private investment? The answer is a qualified yes, if actions and policies specific to each sector are adopted.

Public investment in infrastructure, expressed as a percentage of total public investment, fell during the 1990s and remained at 30 percent until the mid-2000s. Starting in 2005, the composition of public investment changed, and the share devoted to infrastructure rose from 30 percent to 50 percent. Public investment in infrastructure as a share of total public expenditure increased as well from 2005 onward, but only managed to reach the level of the 1990s (Figure 4.10).[15] The challenge for Latin America and the Caribbean is to sustain the increase in public infrastructure investment. Unfortunately, if history is any guide, prospects are not favorable to ramp up infrastructure investment permanently.

When fiscal conditions deteriorate, infrastructure investment is among the main budgetary items to be axed. In times of crisis or recession, cuts in public capital expenditures—particularly infrastructure investment—are proportionally much higher than cuts in current expenditures or new tax revenue.[16] Carranza, Daude, and Melguizo (2014) argue that between 1987 and 1992—a period of financial and fiscal crises in Latin America and the Caribbean—one-third of the improvement in fiscal accounts came at the expense of lower infrastructure investment:

Figure 4.10 **Public Investment in Infrastructure, 1990–2012**

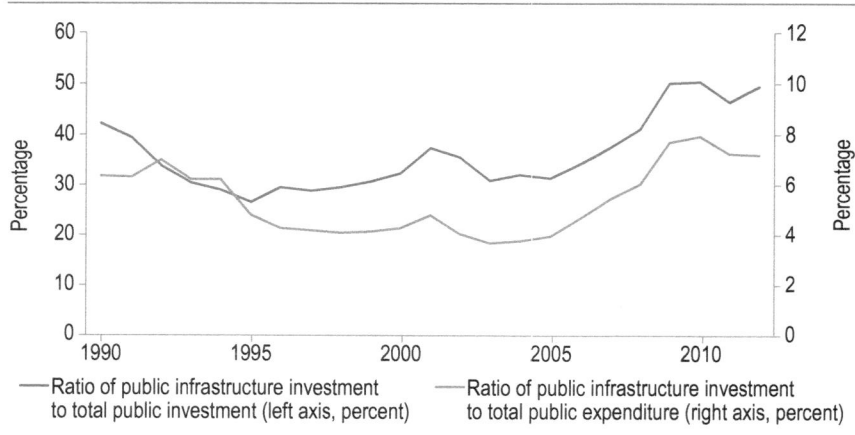

—Ratio of public infrastructure investment
to total public investment (left axis, percent)

—Ratio of public infrastructure investment
to total public expenditure (right axis, percent)

Source: Authors' calculations based on Serebrisky, Margot, and others (2015).

public deficits shrank by 6 percent of GDP, and public investment in infrastructure diminished, on average, by 2 percent of GDP—equivalent to reducing public infrastructure investment by more than 60 percent. Evidence for the first half of 2015 for subnational governments in Brazil indicates that the slowdown in economic growth forced states to reduce their investment in infrastructure by 46 percent.[17]

What can be done to increase public investment in infrastructure on a sustainable basis and thus help close the infrastructure gap? Unavoidably, public saving must increase. But how can it increase? One option is to create more fiscal space through additional revenues (such as general tax financing) and channel it to infrastructure. Another option is to change the composition of public expenditure, reducing current expenditures in favor of capital (infrastructure) investment. Other necessary policies include i) increasing user fees in sectors where tariffs are lower than cost recovery levels; ii) implementing charges to capture value that results from new infrastructure; and iii) boosting the efficiency of public investment in infrastructure by streamlining the project cycle of infrastructure delivery from planning to procurement, better supervising works, and raising the quality of regulation of infrastructure services.

The key policy message is that to increase public investment in infrastructure, public saving needs to increase. Public saving does not need to come via additional taxation or budget cuts. Switching from current to capital expenditures and improving expenditure efficiency can boost public saving and generate additional resources for public investment (see Chapter 8).

The Other Half

The public sector cannot do it alone. The way forward for the region is to generate the conditions required to substantially increase private investment in infrastructure. How much does private investment need to increase? The answer depends on the future behavior of public investment. Assuming, just as an exercise, it reaches an optimistic level of 2 percent of GDP, private investment would need to triple (from 1 percent to 3 percent of GDP) to reach the threshold of 5 percent of GDP required to close the infrastructure gap. Just by looking at the evolution of private investment in infrastructure compared with total private investment and national private saving (Figure 4.11), it is clear that private investment in infrastructure has room to grow—at least to match the values observed in the late 1990s.

Boosting private investment in infrastructure requires simultaneous action on two fronts: strengthening regulatory and institutional capacity to generate a well prepared pipeline of projects; and developing infrastructure as an asset class to channel private savings to

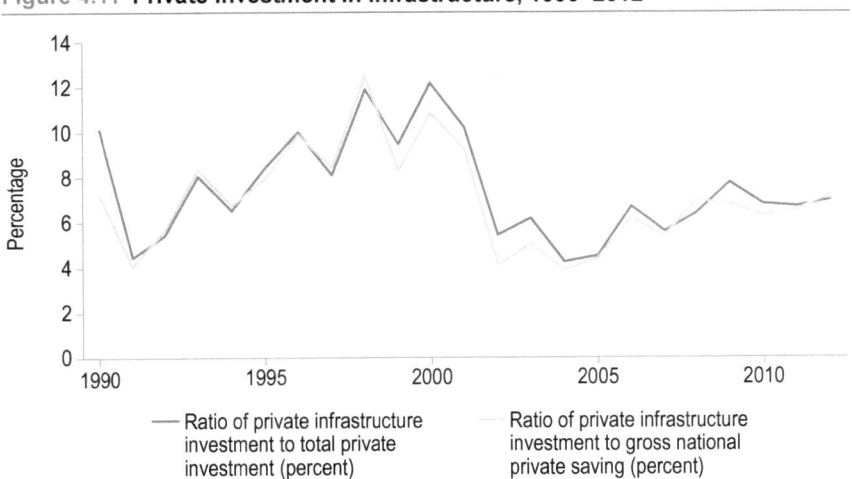

Figure 4.11 **Private Investment in Infrastructure, 1990–2012**

Source: Authors' calculations based on Serebrisky, Margot, and others (2015).

infrastructure. An important body of knowledge addresses the specifics of how to design and implement projects with private participation or public-private partnerships.[18] The available studies concentrate almost exclusively at the project level, focusing on the project's characteristics (sector, investment commitments, sponsors, finance structuring) and its performance (productivity, quality of services). However, there is a notable lack of evidence on what the region must do to promote infrastructure as an asset class. Surprisingly, there is no regional macro-level analysis of the financing sources used to pay for infrastructure. That is, regardless of who builds and operates the assets, the question of where the financing comes from (whether national or foreign savings) remains unanswered.

The following sections analyze the private infrastructure financing market in Latin America and the Caribbean in depth and lay out an agenda to make infrastructure a more appealing asset, particularly to institutional investors, which administer an increasing amount of private savings.

Understanding the Infrastructure Financing Market

Infrastructure assets are different from all other assets (industrial buildings, machinery equipment, schools) that make up the definition of Gross Fixed Capital Formation. They involve significant upfront construction costs, imply high initial risks due to unexpected construction costs followed by uncertain demand, generate revenues only after the largest expenditure (construction costs) has been made, and cannot be reconverted to alternative uses. Given these particular characteristics, the only feasible way to pay for most infrastructure assets is with long-term financing.

Foreign saving to finance infrastructure is possible, but not likely in the region. Even in recent years, with positive growth prospects and foreign direct investment (FDI) reaching 3 percent of GDP, only 10 percent of that amount has gone to infrastructure, and almost all of that has been concentrated in Chile and Brazil (Powell, 2013). Given this history of FDI flows to infrastructure, foreign saving is clearly not a game changer for infrastructure financing in Latin America and the Caribbean.

But volume isn't the only problem with FDI. Local currency provides other clear advantages as a source of long-term financing. In Latin

America and the Caribbean, where capital markets are not sufficiently developed, hedging opportunities are not usually available; thus external financing is difficult to secure for infrastructure projects, whose assets have no alternative use. In addition, there is a mismatch between the income, in local currency, obtained from infrastructure and the payment of debt obligations in external currency. This currency mismatch has been a source of instability and renegotiation of long-term contracts for infrastructure services. Another reason why long-term financing in local currency should be available is that international investors usually require the active participation of local investors as co-financiers in infrastructure projects. All evidence suggests that national saving in sufficient quantity and good quality (channeled with the appropriate instruments to accommodate the specific needs of infrastructure) will be necessary to close the prevailing infrastructure gap in Latin America and the Caribbean.

A rash of policy reports by multilateral development banks, the Group of Twenty (G-20), think tanks, and academics, sparked by the decline in available financing for infrastructure and budget cuts in several countries following the financial crises of 2008–09, came to an additional conclusion: greater private sector participation in infrastructure is the only way to maintain and improve the stock and quality of infrastructure services.[19] The reports shared another worrisome finding: there is an alarming lack of information about *who* is included in the definition of private sector, *what* the role of each private sector actor is, and *which* vehicles they prefer for channeling infrastructure investments. Not surprisingly, the lack of information is more acute in developing regions, and Latin America and the Caribbean is no exception.

Private infrastructure financing takes one of two forms: investors may choose to invest directly in infrastructure projects by committing equity or, by lending to specific projects or infrastructure companies (through bonds, loans, and funding from foreign governments and international financial institutions) (Figure 4.12). Investments can be allocated through *listed vehicles* (such as publicly traded stocks of infrastructure companies, publicly traded government or corporate bonds, and investments in listed infrastructure funds) or *unlisted vehicles* (such as equity or debt transactions made through private markets, or investments in unlisted infrastructure funds).

The relative importance of each channel in the infrastructure financing market varies greatly across countries. The preferred investment

Figure 4.12 **Infrastructure Financing Market**

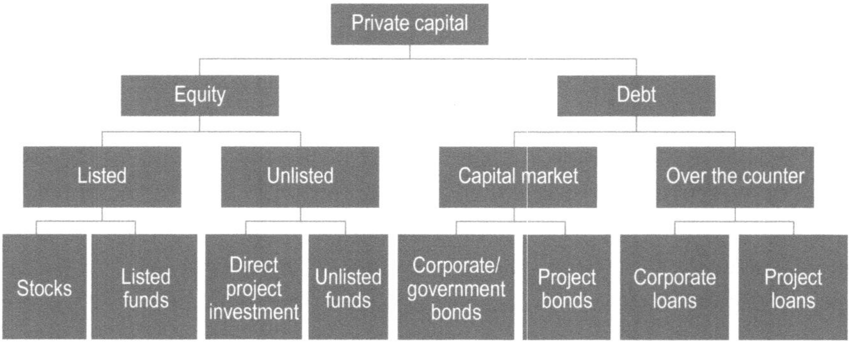

Source: Authors' calculations, adapted from Inderst (2013) and Inderst and Stewart (2014).

vehicles are normally determined by the degree of development of domestic capital markets, the regulatory and governance frameworks, and investors' capacity and knowledge (Estache, Serebrisky, and Wren-Lewis, 2015). Different agents or instruments generally fund different phases of the project cycle: banks are usually better prepared to assume the risks involved in complex infrastructure operations and to address information asymmetries, particularly in the early stages of the project design, while long-term bond issuances and financing from institutional investors are more viable alternatives to extend and consolidate investment financing later in the project life (Ehlers, 2014; Canuto, 2014). That is why equity and bank loans are more common during the construction phase, when risks are higher, while project bonds are normally used during the operational phases, when projects can generate reliable cash flows and risks are lower.

How is private infrastructure being financed in Latin America and the Caribbean? A natural way to answer this question would be to fill in the boxes in Figure 4.12. However, limitations in data translate into only partial information. No publicly available source details the composition of the Latin American and Caribbean infrastructure finance market. To fill this gap, Serebrisky, Suárez-Alemán, et al., (2015) examined the typology of active investors in the region's infrastructure financing market.[20] The study relied on a sample of 377 infrastructure projects implemented in Latin America and the Caribbean between 2004 and 2014, obtained from the *Infrastructure Journal* database, totaling over US$56 billion.[21,22]

Debt Stands Out

Latin America and the Caribbean's infrastructure has traditionally been financed with lending, as shown in Figure 4.13. Although equity gained ground at the end of the last decade due to the financial crises, debt rapidly recovered thereafter. On average, debt accounted for 67 percent of the private financing for infrastructure between 2004 and 2014. Debt "over the counter"[23] (which includes bank loans to infrastructure projects) accounts for almost all debt financing and highlights the lack of depth of capital markets in Latin America and the Caribbean.

Unfortunately, available data are insufficient to disentangle the components of equity financing. The scarce data available suggest that the most common form of equity investment in infrastructure is through unlisted options and mainly by making direct equity contributions to projects. Thus, most of the equity investment in the region is done directly, instead of relying on the stock market or on funds operated by third parties (listed or unlisted).

The composition of financing vehicles and its evolution over time are very similar in Latin America and the Caribbean and worldwide (figures 4.14 and 4.15). Latin America and the Caribbean recovered before, and more quickly, from the financial crises, although the recovery has

Figure 4.13 Evolution of Equity and Debt Shares in Private Infrastructure Financing, 2004–14

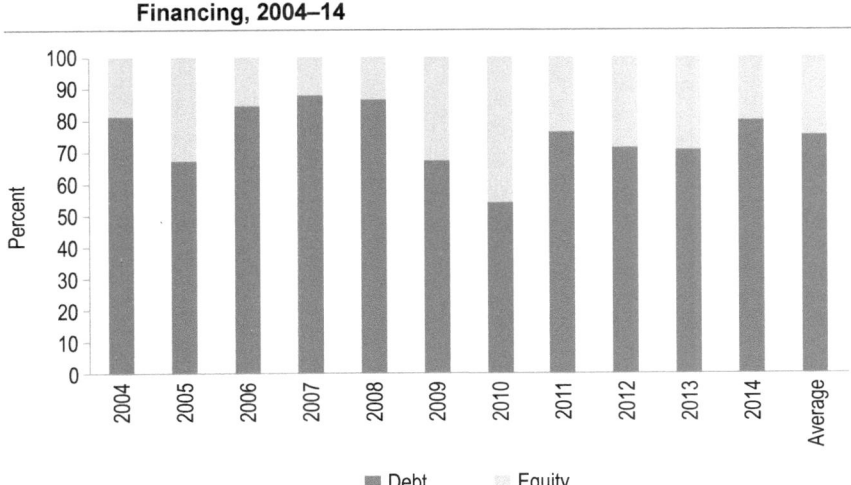

Source: Authors' calculations based on Serebrisky, Suárez-Alemán, and others (2015), based on *Infrastructure Journal* database.

Figure 4.14 **Private Infrastructure Financing by Type of Instrument, 2004–14**

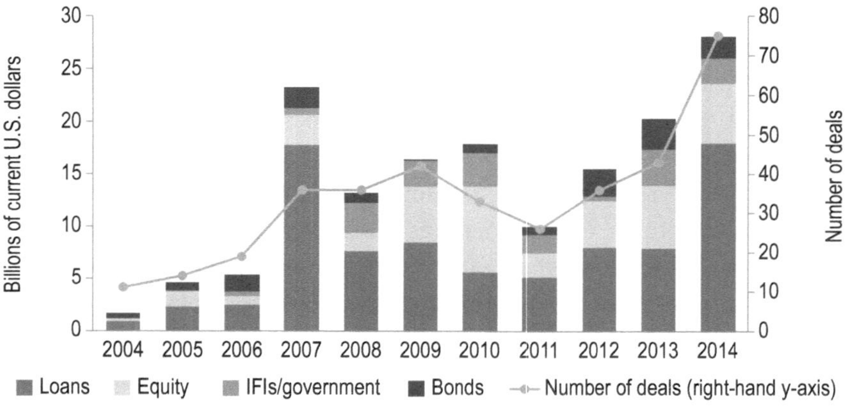

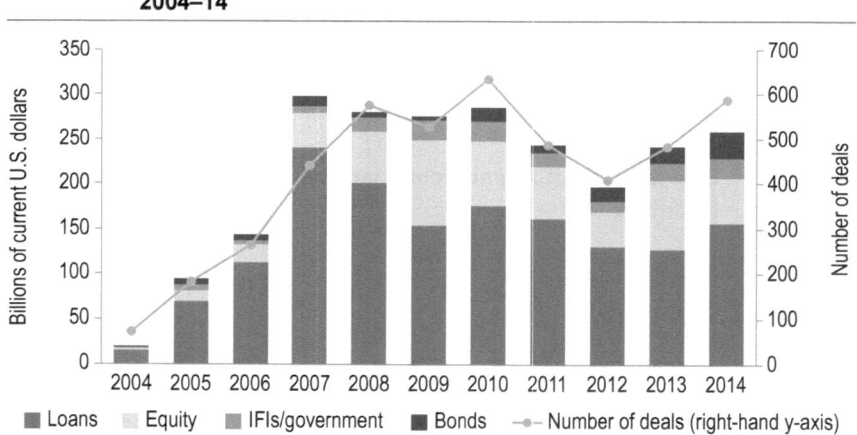

Loans ░ **Equity** ▓ **IFIs/government** ■ **Bonds** ─●─ Number of deals (right-hand y-axis)

Source: Authors' calculations based on Serebrisky, Suárez-Alemán, and others (2015), based on *Infrastructure Journal* database.
Note: IFIs = international finance institutions.

Figure 4.15 **Worldwide Private Infrastructure Financing by Type of Instrument, 2004–14**

Loans ░ **Equity** ▓ **IFIs/government** ■ **Bonds** ─●─ Number of deals (right-hand y-axis)

Source: Authors' calculations based on Serebrisky, Suárez-Alemán, and others (2015), based on *Infrastructure Journal* database.
Note: IFIs = international financial institutions.

been weak; it was not until 2014 that total private financing in Latin America and the Caribbean surpassed its 2007 levels. The shares of debt and equity are similar in Latin America and the Caribbean and worldwide. The remarkable, although expected, fact is that bank loans

Table 4.1 Private Financing Suppliers in Infrastructure Projects, 2005–14

Ranking	Type of agent	Share (percent)
1	Commercial bank	50.55
2	National or state bank	13.65
3	Developer/eng. procurement or const. firm	9.12
4	Private company	8.83
5	Multilateral (or) development bank	7.34
6	Investment bank	3.28
7	Export credit agency	2.05
8	Investment or infrastructure fund	1.90
9	Government agency/public authority	1.88
10	Pension fund	1.11
11	Sovereign fund	0.24
12	Insurance company	0.04

Source: Authors' calculations based on Serebrisky, Suárez-Alemán, and others (2015), based on *Infrastructure Journal* database.
Note: the classification shown is the one used by the *Infrastructure Journal* database. Eng. Procurement or const. = engineering procurement or construction firm.

have contracted sharply, a direct consequence of more stringent reserve requirements.

Who supplies the financing in this debt-heavy market? Several capital providers participate in the private infrastructure finance market (Table 4.1). Commercial banks hold the largest share of private infrastructure financing in Latin America and the Caribbean, by far: one out of two infrastructure projects were financed by commercial banks during the period studied.[24] Table 4.1 confirms several interesting facts about private infrastructure financing in the region. First, national development banks play an important role, with a 13.65 percent share.[25] Second, multilateral development banks' share is low, consistent with previous estimates both for sovereign and nonsovereign lending (Powell, 2013). The participation of institutional investors (such as pension funds, insurance companies, and investment funds) is negligible (less than 2 percent) in the private financing of infrastructure in Latin America and the Caribbean.

Infrastructure as an Asset Class

In the language of this book, developing infrastructure as an asset class would be a tool to save better, as it provides a mechanism to match private saving with assets that enhance productivity. Infrastructure may be thought of as an asset class in its own right, rather than a sub-class derived from real estate. Though it resembles real estate, it differs in some fundamental ways. In all cases, infrastructure involves assets with a long lifespan that create recurring, stable returns and are usually indexed by inflation. Compared to real estate, infrastructure is less exposed to economic cycles, has more predictable cash flows (enabling higher leverage), and has legal and sometimes economic barriers to entry (giving stability to returns if economic regulation is adequate). However, as of 2014, not even the most sophisticated investors considered infrastructure an asset class. A recent survey concluded that more than 40 percent of investors still do not categorize infrastructure as an asset in their portfolios (J.P.Mprgan Asset Management and Af2i, 2014).

Despite unmet and fast-growing demand for infrastructure services, the high transaction costs, political and governance risks, and policy and regulatory barriers found in most countries in the region make risk-adjusted investment returns too low to attract private investment. The pipeline of well-prepared projects is small; appropriate financial instruments of sufficient liquidity (such as project bonds) to mobilize local investors are lacking; daunting inconsistencies persist in contracts, con-cessions, bidding documents, and critical underlying cost recovery; and cash flow challenges plague sectors that need private investment. Thus, it is imperative to strengthen institutional capacity in the public sector along the entire infrastructure project cycle. Better technical capacity in the public sector, coupled with less political interference that alters the economic condition of providing infrastructure services (through arbitrary changes in tariffs and investment programs), would reduce uncertainty and, therefore, the cost of capital faced by private investors. According to a recent study, 87 percent of investors in Latin America and the Carib-bean consider institutional weaknesses a major drawback to increase infrastructure investment, compared with 41 percent in Europe and the Middle East, and just 31 percent in Asia and the Pacific (BlackRock, 2015).

Institutional Investors: An Untapped Source of Financing

Institutional investors, particularly pension funds, insurance companies, and mutual funds, are becoming more important players in financial markets. In the member-countries of the OECD alone, these institutional investors held over US$70 trillion in 2012. Most of the attention to attract long-term financing to infrastructure focuses on insurance companies and pension funds. In OECD countries, these long-term investors held US\$45 trillion in assets in 2012 (US\$24 trillion by insurance companies and US\$21 trillion by pension funds). In Latin America and the Caribbean, the amount was just over US\$ 1 trillion, or approximately 20 percent of GDP (Della Croce and Yermo, 2013).

Pension funds and their portfolio allocation in infrastructure have attracted much more policy and data-based analysis than insurance companies. Despite the increasing attention, information on the allocation of pension funds to infrastructure is very difficult to obtain, in part because infrastructure is usually not considered an asset class of its own. The OECD is leading an effort to fill the data gap. The first attempt to compare pension fund allocation in infrastructure was by a survey carried out in 2014. Pension funds in Australia and Canada have been the leaders in direct investment in infrastructure, allocating 5 percent of total assets to this sector.[26]

While pension funds in Latin America administer an increasing pool of funds, allocations to infrastructure are low. The countries with the largest portfolios of pension funds under management in the region—measured as a percentage of GDP—are Chile (63 percent), Mexico (48 percent), Peru (18 percent), Colombia (16 percent), and Brazil (11 percent). Although the numbers vary according to different sources, the share these funds allocate to infrastructure is relatively minor. Funds in Brazil invest 2 percent in infrastructure; funds in Mexico invest 1 percent; while funds in Chile invest only 0.2 percent (Della Croce and Gatti, 2014). The average allocation to infrastructure of the five countries is 2.6 percent, according to Alonso, Arellano, and Tuesta (2015). Serebrisky, Suárez-Alemán, et al., (2015) calculates a regional average allocation of 1.1 percent between 2005 and 2014.

The current allocation of pension funds in Latin America and the Caribbean—in the range of 1 to 2 percent of total assets under management—is clearly not enough to boost infrastructure investment. But how much exposure to infrastructure would be reasonable for pension funds in Latin America and the Caribbean? Two alternative scenarios are assessed. At the low end is a hypothesis of 3 percent of funds' investment portfolios, which represents the minimum level to contribute in a meaningful way to increase investments in infrastructure. The high-end scenario posits a 7 percent allocation of funds' investment portfolios, which corresponds to the highest exposure to infrastructure by pension funds in the world (observed in Australia and Canada).

A first stab at estimating the impact on infrastructure investment focuses on *stocks* of assets under management and calculates the additional total investment in infrastructure that would result from allocating a percentage of the accumulated stock of pension fund assets under management. Suppose pension funds increase their *stock* exposure to infrastructure by investing 3 percent (or 7 percent) of their assets under management in infrastructure projects. Infrastructure investment would rise significantly in Chile and Mexico. It would also rise—but not enough to have a notable impact—in Brazil, Colombia, and Peru (see Figure 4.16) because of the smaller size of accumulated assets under management in those economies. In Chile, infrastructure investment could rise between 2 percent and 4 percent of GDP (depending on the hypothesis used); this could double the current investment rate. In Mexico, a change of portfolio allocation by pension funds could more than double the current infrastructure investment rate, from less than 2 percent of GDP to nearly 5 percent of GDP.[27]

The preceding exercise uses the *stock* of assets under management to increase investment in infrastructure. This can be done only once. It is a one-shot deal. Once pension funds reach the hypothesized 3 percent (or 7 percent) exposure to infrastructure, no more funds are available to finance

Figure 4.16 Impact on Infrastructure Investment of a One-Shot Increase in Pension Fund Assets under Management

■ Total (public + private) investment in infrastructure (average, 2008–13)
▨ Pension funds invest 3 percent of portfolio in infrastructure
■ Pension funds invest 7 percent of portfolio in infrastructure

Source: Authors' calculations based on IMF statistics and the following country sources: Superintendência Nacional de Previdência Complementar (Brazil); Superintendencia de Pensiones (Chile); Superintendencia Financiera de Colombia (Colombia); Comisión Nacional del Sistema de Ahorro para el Retiro (Mexico) and Superintendencia de Banca, Seguros y AFP (Peru).

Figure 4.17 **Impact on Infrastructure Investment of Flow Increases in Pension Fund Assets under Management (AUM)**

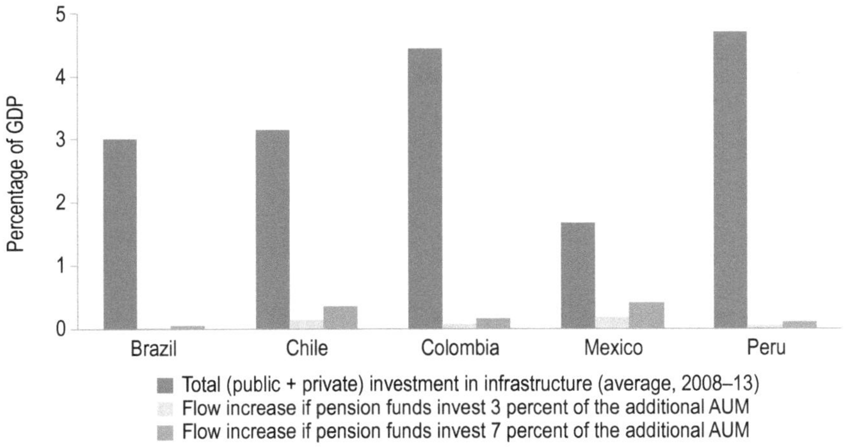

Total (public + private) investment in infrastructure (average, 2008–13)
Flow increase if pension funds invest 3 percent of the additional AUM
Flow increase if pension funds invest 7 percent of the additional AUM

Source: Authors' calculations based on IMF statistics and the following country sources: Superintendência Nacional de Previdência Complementar (Brazil); Superintendencia de Pensiones (Chile); Superintendencia Financiera de Colombia (Colombia); Comision Nacional del Sistema de Ahorro para el Retiro (Mexico); Superintendencia de Banca, Seguros y AFP (Peru).
Note: AUM = assets under management.

additional investments in infrastructure. In order to increase the infrastructure investment rates over time —not just once, but for many years—it is necessary to increase investments using *flows*, rather than stocks.

What does this mean for pension funds? Pension funds could invest in infrastructure using the additional funds they receive from (net) new contributors to the system and their capital gains. These figures can be obtained by computing the variation in assets under management from one year to the next. Flows, however, are not as big as stocks. Pension fund assets under management tend to grow from year to year (except during years of financial turmoil, like 2008). Between 2007 and 2014, assets under management grew on average around 5 percent of GDP annually in Chile and Mexico, 2 percent in Colombia and Peru, and less than 1 percent in Brazil. Investing 7 percent of these increments in infrastructure generates an annual increase in total investments in infrastructure of 0.35 percent of GDP in Chile and 0.4 percent of GDP in Mexico, the countries where investment would grow the most. In all other countries, pension fund contributions to (annual) increases in total infrastructure investment would not reach 0.2 percent of GDP (see Figure 4.17 and Table 4.2).

Table 4.2 **Potential Additional Investments in Infrastructure Using Flows of Pension Fund Assets under Management (percentage of GDP)**

Country	Total (public + private) investment (average, 2008–2013)	Additional investment if pension funds invest:	
		3 percent of increase in AUM	7 percent of increase in AUM
Brazil	3.01	0.02	0.06
Chile	3.14	0.15	0.35
Colombia	4.45	0.07	0.16
Mexico	1.68	0.18	0.41
Peru	4.70	0.05	0.11

Source: Authors' calculations.
Note: AUM = assets under management.

While the additional investment in infrastructure from savings administered by pension funds is sizable in some countries, it's hardly a game changer. Investing 7 percent of the additional assets under management can increase investment in infrastructure by no more than 0.4 percent of GDP in the most optimistic scenario. Table 4.2 shows that infrastructure investment rates increase less than 0.2 percent of GDP in most cases. From this point of view, pension funds may not be the panacea to increase infrastructure investments. The additional investments generated from pension funds would do little to close the prevailing infrastructure gap in Latin America and the Caribbean.

Pension funds may not close the infrastructure gap, but they can still help increase investments in infrastructure. To do so, however, requires an important set of actions beyond the purview of pension funds or their regulators. To begin with, the political risks associated with unstable macroeconomic and regulatory environments must be reduced. Other actions involve reforming regulations that restrict the share of assets under management that pension funds can invest in infrastructure. Removing other barriers will require close collaboration between financial regulators and pension funds in the following areas:

- Asset valuation: Some countries require pension funds to report daily variations in their account balances. Direct investment in infrastructure involves instruments that are not liquid and thus require an ad hoc valuation formula to comply with valuation of the portfolio on a daily basis.

- Transparency and risks: Because infrastructure assets are seldom transacted in markets, it is difficult for supervisors (superintendents of pension funds) to monitor accurate valuations of the infrastructure asset. Given limited information and resources, it is also difficult for supervisors to assess the performance risks of infrastructure assets.
- Liquidity: Even understanding that infrastructure assets are held over long periods, a superintendent needs to guarantee liquidity of the whole portfolio (this is particularly relevant in countries where constraints for members to change pension funds are low). Thus, there are no incentives to foster the growth of assets, like infrastructure, that are illiquid.

Despite the need to attract private financing to improve Latin America and the Caribbean's infrastructure, the fundamentals of an infrastructure project should not be changed to guarantee investors a rate of return higher than comparable projects. In other words, favorable conditions to attract institutional investors should be created and maintained, but they should not come as excessive costs through higher average prices, or larger subsidies for both operational and capital expenditures.

Pension funds offer the potential to raise private financing in infrastructure. However, they are just one of the building blocks to help finance the construction of the infrastructure needed to support a productive economy. While not negligible, the potential of pension funds is, in fact, limited and highlights the need to tap all available private saving sources (including insurance and other institutional investors) and channel them to infrastructure investment.

Building a Better Investment Strategy

Investment in Latin America and the Caribbean should increase to levels compatible with high, sustainable, long-run GDP growth rates. Ideally, investment should be close to 25 percent of GDP. Latin America and the Caribbean is far from that level, languishing below 20 percent on average in the last 30 years.

If the region hopes to significantly increase investment, it will have to be financed through national saving. Foreign saving is no match for national saving when it comes to financing domestic investment. Of course, greater national saving is a necessary condition to increase investment, but it is not sufficient. In order for the additional saving to have the maximum impact, it must be channeled to the most productive investment alternatives in an efficient manner.

Enter infrastructure. One of the most productive uses for national saving is infrastructure. Efficient, quality investment in infrastructure reduces bottlenecks, which enhances growth prospects. Unfortunately, Latin American and Caribbean countries are not investing enough in infrastructure; in fact, investment as a percent of GDP is lower today than 30 years ago. The infrastructure gap in Latin America and the Caribbean is widening with respect to other developing regions and advanced economies. Local long-term financing—precisely the type provided by national saving—is required to expand the region's infrastructure. Foreign saving is at most a complement to national saving to finance infrastructure.

Lifting infrastructure investment in Latin America and the Caribbean demands an increase in both public and private investment. The public sector will continue to play a very important role because many infrastructure projects have characteristics of public goods. At the same time, the private sector can raise its profile by increasing the efficiency of infrastructure service operations and helping finance infrastructure projects during tight fiscal times, thereby easing the burden on the public sector.

Of course, the private sector is not a monolith. It consists of different agents with different expertise and different attitudes toward risk and uncertainty, who use different vehicles at different stages to invest in infrastructure. The key is to develop infrastructure as an asset class, allowing the expansion of existing vehicles, or the creation of new ones, to attract the most suitable agents at each stage of the project's life cycle. A step in this direction is to attract institutional investors like pension funds and insurance companies that have available resources, and match them to projects that meet their need for long-term returns and low volatility for their investments. This would open up the possibility of increasing the current share of private investment in infrastructure while helping channel future growth of national saving to infrastructure.

Notes

1   Countries are classified using the country income classification of the World Bank database. Low-income economies are defined as those with a Gross National Income (GNI) per capita—calculated using the World Bank Atlas method—of US$1,045 or less in 2013. Middle-income economies have a GNI per capita of more than US$1,045 but less than US$12,746. High-income economies have a GNI per capita of US$12,746 or more. Lower-middle-income and upper-middle-income economies are separated at a GNI per capita of US$4,125.

2   The Commission on Growth and Development is a group sponsored by four government organizations from Australia, the Netherlands, Sweden, and the United Kingdom, plus the William and Flora Hewlett Foundation and the World Bank Group. It consists of 19 policy, government, and business leaders, mostly from the developing world, and two Nobel Laureate economists.

3   The countries are Botswana, Brazil, China, Hong Kong, Indonesia, Japan, Rep. of Korea, Malaysia, Malta, Oman, Singapore, Taiwan, and Thailand.

4   The ranking of regions, from the least to the most volatile according to the coefficient of variation, is China (0.18), Advanced Economies (0.21); Emerging Asia (except China) (0.23); Latin America and the Caribbean (0.26); and Sub-Saharan Africa (0.45).

5   Emerging Asia includes China, Hong Kong, India, Indonesia, Republic of Korea, Malaysia, Singapore and Thailand.

6   Nicaragua's foreign saving rate is 15 percent of GDP and Guyana's rate is 10 percent. Other countries have rates close to 8 percent—including the Bahamas (7.2 percent), Belize (6.2 percent), and Jamaica (7.4 percent)—but most of these countries have high rates of remittances. The largest economies of the region had foreign saving rates lower than 3 percent of GDP between 1980 and 2014.

7   For a detailed explanation of macroeconomic vulnerabilities caused by excessive reliance on foreign saving, see chapter 5.

8   Feldstein and Horioka (1980) estimate an econometric model of investment using national saving as a regressor. They find that for every increase of 1 percent of GDP in national saving, domestic investment increases 0.94 percent.

[9] The only possible exception is Sub-Saharan Africa, but even in this region the SFR indicates that most of the domestic stock of capital has been financed with national savings.

[10] Attanasio, Picci, and Scorcu (2000) use data for 123 countries from around the world from 1961 to 1994. Serebrisky, Margot, et al., (2015) is based on Attanasio, Picci, and Scorcu (2000), but uses expanded data from 1980 to 2013. The update of Attanasio and his co-authors gains relevance because the time period is associated with increasing financial integration.

[11] Bolivia is an interesting case in which investment is lagging behind saving, creating a sizable gap (Jemio and Nina, 2016).

[12] The theoretical work on the contribution of infrastructure to productivity and growth began in the 1970s with Arrow and Kurz (1970), which was the first study to include public capital as an input in the economy's aggregate production function. The empirical research started later with Aschauer (1989), and several papers followed. A comprehensive review of the theoretical and empirical literature on the impact of infrastructure on productivity and growth can be found in Infrastructure Canada (2007).

[13] This group includes Australia, Canada, Croatia, Iceland, Lichtenstein, New Zealand, Norway, Republic of Korea, Singapore, Switzerland, and Taiwan.

[14] Efficiency gains in the provision of infrastructure services have been documented for Latin America and the Caribbean in the last two decades; for details, see Serebrisky (2014). However, these gains have not been able to compensate for the low levels of investment, resulting in the relative deterioration of perception of quality of Latin America and the Caribbean compared to other regions.

[15] Data are for Argentina, Brazil, Chile, Colombia, Mexico, and Peru because complete time series for other Latin American and Caribbean countries are available only from the mid-2000s.

[16] See, for example, Calderón and Servén (2004) from the World Bank; de Mello and Mulder (2006); Lora (2007); CAF (2009); Carranza, Daude, and Melguizo (2014).

[17] See http://app.folha.uol.com.br/#noticia/563261.

[18] See EIU (2014) for a recent study specific to Latin America and the Caribbean that surveyed the enabling environment for public-private partnerships in infrastructure.

[19] See, for example, World Bank (2011); Inderst (2013); Della Croce and Yermo (2013).

[20] The sample covers the traditional economic infrastructure sectors: water and sanitation (6.45 percent of total projects): potable water, sanitation services, and flood defenses; power (50.9 percent): generation, transmission, and distribution of electricity (including renewables); transmission and distribution of natural gas; telecommunications (4.7 percent): fixed and mobile telecommunications, satellite and internet connectivity, and multimedia services; transportation (37.9 percent): roads, urban mass transit, rail, ports, airports, and river transport. Social infrastructure or the production of tradable goods like oil and petrochemicals are not covered.

[21] The sample is geographically distributed as follows: Brazil (28 percent of projects); Mexico (26.66 percent); Chile (12.92 percent); Peru (7.88 percent); Panama (5.32 percent); Uruguay (3.82 percent); Honduras (2.82 percent); Colombia (2.14 percent); Jamaica (1.86 percent); Costa Rica (1.5 percent); Nicaragua (1.34 percent); Argentina (1.34 percent); and others (4.4 percent, consisting of Bahamas, Dominican Republic, Trinidad and Tobago, Belize, Bolivia, Ecuador, and Guatemala).

[22] The World Bank Private Participation in Infrastructure database (PPI) also gathers information for infrastructure projects. It represents the most exhaustive database worldwide in terms of number of projects and investment; it provides information on more than 6,000 infrastructure projects dating from 1984 to 2013. PPI, however, does not break down projects by financing sources. The *Infrastructure Journal* database is the most comprehensive source that provides this breakdown.

[23] The term "over the counter" refers to off-exchange transactions that take place directly between two parties without the supervision of an exchange, such as the New York Stock Exchange.

[24] The top commercial banks funding infrastructure in the region are Santander (5.61 percent of total projects amount), Citigroup (3.25 percent), HSBC (3.2 percent),and BBVA (3.14 percent).

[25] This share is biased by Brazil, where BNDES, the largest national development bank, accounts for 35 percent of private infrastructure financing in that country.

[26] From an investor perspective, pension funds with a separate allocation to infrastructure gain direct exposure to the characteristics of

the infrastructure asset (including their long-term, stable, and infla-tion-linked nature). Direct exposure is gained mainly through unlisted equity instruments (direct investment in projects and infrastructure funds) and project bonds, while indirect exposure is normally associ-ated with listed equity and corporate debt.

[27] The result is obtained by adding the current infrastructure investment rate of 1.8 percent of GDP and the additional 1.5 percent to 3 percent of GDP that would come from new investments in infrastructure by pension funds.

5 Saving for Stability

Countries invest in physical capital in order to grow. In principle, domestic investment can be financed with either national or foreign financing. However, foreign financing is not a good substitute for national financing. To begin with, it may not be available. Moreover, it is generally more expensive or more uncertain, or both. Consequently, the scarcity of national saving to finance good investment opportunities is a constraint to growth.

Besides investment, foreign financing is also a poor substitute for national financing in terms of macroeconomic stability. National and foreign savings are different in that absorbing capital inflows risks destabilizing external accounts, which can lead to costly macroeconomic crises.[1] Crisis-related volatility—which unfortunately has plagued many Latin American and Caribbean countries—in turn discourages saving in domestic assets because the real value of savings usually falls in the aftermath of financial crises. It also discourages foreign investors from committing resources to the domestic economy, which jacks up the cost premium for external capital. This sets in motion a vicious circle of low national saving, higher demand for foreign saving (which is less forthcoming), increased sovereign risk, macroeconomic crises, and so on. Mobilizing national saving would thus help break the circle and set in motion the opposite, and positive, dynamic.

Foreign Financing: A Different Animal

Foreign and national financing are simply not the same. If foreign and national financing were two sides of the same coin, countries could substitute one for the other with ease. A world with such perfect financial integration across countries would look entirely different. National savers would prefer to stash most of their wealth in foreign assets in order to hedge the fluctuations of their domestic sources of income. This financial incentive for portfolio diversification would lead to domestic investment being mainly funded by foreign financing. But this imaginary world doesn't exist. In the real world, foreign saving is small relative to the volume of domestic investment, and the financing of the domestic capital stock in each country is predominantly national.[2]

The underlying reason for this poor substitution is that foreign financing is simply a different animal. It carries an additional risk pre-mium—the so-called country risk spread—because each sovereign state retains jurisdiction to rule in favor of nationals. Even with relatively lit-tle foreign exposure, when a country's economic prospects deteriorate, the risk premium may spike and eventually become prohibitive. This is hardly surprising: foreigners tend to know less about local conditions and may be more vulnerable than domestic investors to, for exam-ple, the risk of expropriation. Why would foreigners want to invest in countries where locals are not eager to save more, in the absence of a premium to entice them?

In the absence of country risk spread, the supply of foreign financ-ing would be totally elastic at the international interest rate. Any shortfall of national financing could be seamlessly replaced by additional foreign financing, thereby keeping investment unchanged.[3] However, because there is a foreign risk premium, national financing is cheaper and it there-fore supports more investment.[4]

National savings may also attract better foreign financing. Aghion, Comin, and Howitt (2006) explain how national financing is a form of collateral that entices foreign savers to participate in domestic invest-ment. They need that collateral as an incentive to invest because they know less about local conditions than local investors. Their lack of knowl-edge is a so-called agency problem. Without the collateral in the form of national financing, foreign financing of local projects would be slim indeed; as a result, investment would be even more constrained.

Because foreign financing is different, domestic investment and national saving are highly correlated across countries (see Feldstein and Horioka [1980] and Chapter 4).[5] The "home bias" captured by Feldstein-Horioka–type estimates around the world is also verified in Latin America and the Caribbean (Cavallo and Pedemonte, 2015). A positive correlation between domestic investment and national saving is the natural consequence of de facto imperfect financial integration across countries, where shocks to national saving would directly impact investment because they would not be completely offset by foreign saving. Foreign saving can help fill gaps in investment, but it cannot cure weak national saving.

For all these reasons, strong national saving is important for strong investment. This chapter goes beyond this point and will show that foreign saving is not only a poor substitute for national saving for investment purposes but also in terms of macroeconomic risk. In contrast to national saving, foreign saving contributes to the risk of an external crisis, that is, a crisis in the balance of payments. Low national saving not only constrains real investment but may also create financial vulnerabilities associated with external crises.

Risky Business: Absorbing Foreign Saving

Countries in Latin America and the Caribbean exhibit low national saving rates and absorb more foreign savings (as a share of their national product), on average, than those, for example, in East Asia (see Chapter 2). There are reasons to suspect that foreign savings may contribute to building up risks that may evolve into macroeconomic crises, and the ensuing volatility associated with these crises.

First, foreign financing may be unreliable because its availability and financial terms depend on changing international circumstances that are beyond the control of national authorities. Capital flows to Latin America and the Caribbean are influenced by external factors (the so-called "push factors").[6] For example, events such as the U.S. Federal Reserve Board's decision to raise interest rates may significantly impede capital inflows to the region.

Second, foreign financiers may be especially anxious because they rightly fear that under economic stress, national policies may discriminate against foreign liabilities or even expropriate them as a quick way to favor national welfare—especially if foreign liabilities become too large relative to the size of the domestic economy. In those contexts, foreign investors may understandably want to limit their exposure to a country and, if they decide to run the risk, favor capital flows that are short term, liquid, and easier to repatriate. This behavior, in turn, would lead to procyclical capital flows during crisis periods that undermine macroeconomic stability.

Third, to attract foreign financing, investments must offer high returns in foreign currency, which requires the host country to be capable of generating foreign exchange. Again, foreign and national savings are different. In most cases, external debt contracts are stipulated in foreign currency and need to be serviced correspondingly. The inability to issue foreign debt in local currency at reasonable terms—the so-called "original sin" of emerging economies—still dogs the region and hampers financial integration (see Levy Yeyati and Zúñiga, 2015). More generally, regardless of the specifics of the foreign liability contract, in the final analysis, foreigners care about the real value of their holdings in terms of their purchasing power in their own countries. For example, U.S. holders of equity assets, either of national or foreign companies, care about the dollar value of their shares. This means that foreigners care about the potential conversion of domestic assets into foreign currency. In the absence of disposable foreign assets, the ability of a country to generate foreign exchange may be limited. In fact, transforming domestic resources into foreign exchange by increasing net exports is a disruptive and costly process, especially if it has to be done quickly.

Unreliable foreign savings and difficult balance of payments adjustments make for an explosive mix, which can often end in a macroeconomic crisis. Therefore, while more foreign savings helps in filling the gap left by limited national saving and relieving the constraint on domestic investment, it carries serious financial risks (Rancière, Tornell, and Westerman, 2006). In a worst case scenario, the macroeconomic risks of accumulating too many foreign liabilities over time may incur not only direct crisis costs, but may raise the cost of capital and ultimately depress investment.[7]

By contrast, by reducing reliance on foreign saving, stronger national saving is positive on both counts: it not only helps raise investment but also lowers macroeconomic risks. Each factor reinforces the other, thereby contributing to faster and less volatile growth.

Can the market be trusted to adequately balance foreign savings with macroeconomic risk? Possibly not. Firms that turn to foreign financing may not adequately weigh their needs against the collective harm of contributing to mounting aggregate foreign financing that may upset macroeconomic equilibrium. By raising macroeconomic risk, each addition to foreign liabilities compromises the net returns of aggregate investment without facing any disincentive to do so at the firm level.[8] Furthermore, the true measure of macroeconomic risk may actually exceed what is reflected in financial market pricing (such as sovereign spreads or yields on credit-default swaps): much of the cost of crises is often ultimately borne by workers and other third parties (including tax-payers) not involved in the financial transactions. The bottom line is that the market may fail to find the right trade-off between economic risk and return on foreign saving. If so, this market failure provides a rationale for public policy to promote national saving.[9]

Does the use of foreign saving increase crisis risk in practice? Coun-tries vary widely in their rates of absorbing foreign saving over time and, therefore, in their net foreign liabilities positions—that is, the sum of for-eign liabilities minus foreign assets (Lane and Milesi-Ferretti, 2007). This is because the net foreign liabilities position of a country is the sum of its accumulated foreign saving, appropriately priced and depreciated over time. Catão and Milesi-Ferretti (2014) show that a country's ratio of net foreign liabilities to GDP performs well as a predictor of external crises.[10] Their definition of external crisis includes major episodes that affect the domestic economy, for example, sovereign debt defaults and resched-uling events, as well as events associated with significant support by the International Monetary Fund (IMF).[11] These crises, in turn, are usually associated with a drop in output and other economic, social, and politi-cal costs.[12]

Figure 5.1 shows the proportion of countries in Latin America and the Caribbean, and in the rest of the world, that entered into an exter-nal crisis in a given year.[13] In the early 1980s, most countries in Latin

Figure 5.1 Proportion of Countries Entering into External Crisis

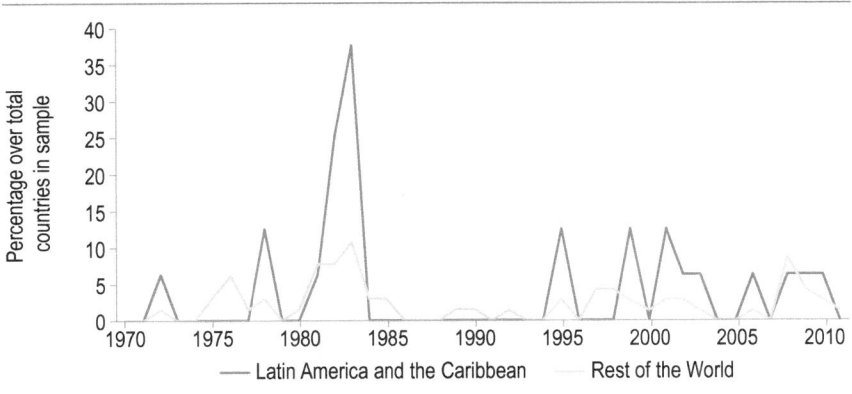

Source: Authors' calculations based on the definition of "external crisis" in Catão and Milesi-Ferretti (2014).
Note: The figure shows the proportion of countries in Latin America and the Caribbean, and in the rest of the world, entering an external crisis in a given year. The data shows some bunching over time; that is, external crises affect multiple countries at the same time.

Figure 5.2 **Net Foreign Liabilities Positions**

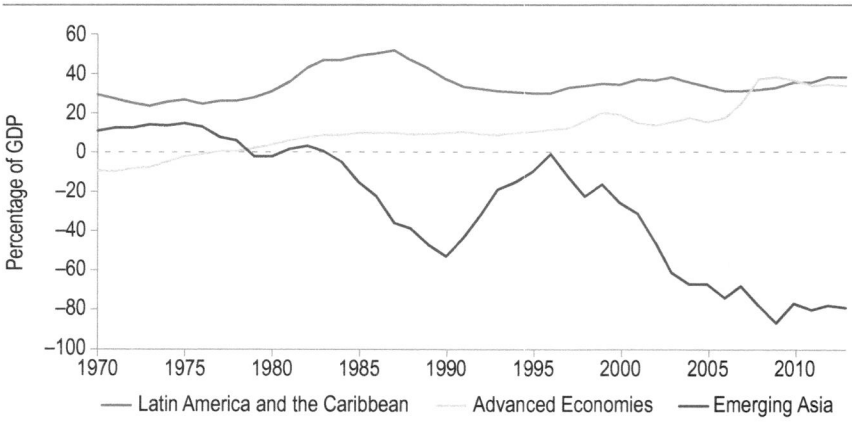

Simple Average by Country Group

— Latin America and the Caribbean   Advanced Economies   — Emerging Asia

Source: Authors' calculations based on External Wealth of Nations database.
Note: Figure shows the simple average of Net Foreign Liabilities (as a percent of GDP) for select country groupings. See endnote 3 in chapter 2 for the list of countries in each country group.

America and the Caribbean suffered an external crisis. Other volatile periods included the mid-1990s (the "Tequila Crisis," which originated in Mexico and spread throughout the region); the late 1990s through the early 2000s (the aftermath of the Asian and Russian financial crises of 1997 and 1998); and the period following the global financial crisis of 2008. Compared to the rest of the world, Latin America and the Caribbean is clearly a region of high risk.[14]

According to Catão and Milesi-Ferretti (2014), the high risk in this region can in turn be traced to its large net foreign liabilities position (measured as share of GDP). Figure 5.2 shows that the typical Latin American and Caribbean country has a larger net foreign liabilities position (relative to GDP) than the typical country in other regions. The contrast is striking vis-à-vis Emerging Asia, where the typical country is a large net creditor.

The pattern of high net foreign liabilities is especially relevant for the smaller countries in the region, many of which are located in Central American and Caribbean (see Figure 5.3). Net foreign liabilities (as a share of GDP) have been increasing over the last decade in the typical country in the group of smaller countries. By contrast, the same ratio has been declining for the typical country in the group of largest economies in the region (the so-called "LAC-7" of Argentina, Brazil, Chile, Colombia, Mexico, Peru, and Venezuela).

Figure 5.3 **Net Foreign Liabilities Positions in Latin America and the Caribbean**
Simple Average by Country Group

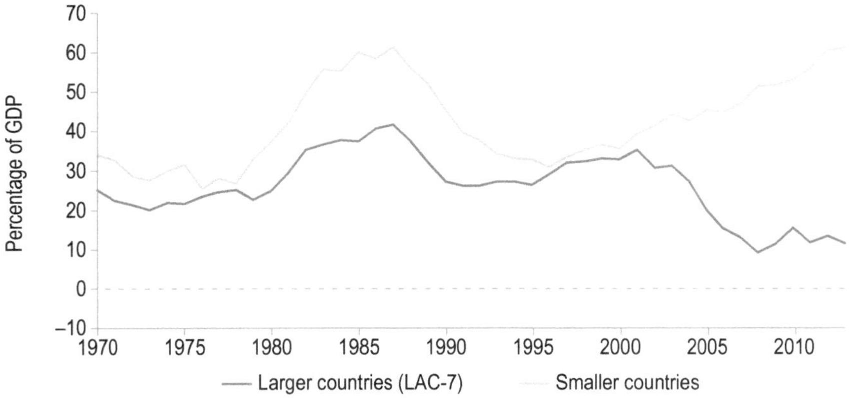

Source: Authors' calculations based on External Wealth of Nations database.
Note: The figure shows the simple average of Net Foreign Liabilities (as a percent of GDP) for select country groupings. LAC-7 includes Argentina, Brazil, Chile, Colombia, Mexico, Peru, and Venezuela. Together, they account for more than 90 percent of the regional GDP. Smaller countries are the rest of the countries in the region not included in LAC-7, most of them in Central America and the Caribbean.

Can the risks of crisis be reduced by financing domestic investment with national savings instead of foreign savings? In other words, is national saving better in terms of associated macroeconomic risks? Cavallo, Fernández-Arias, and Marzani (2016) expanded Catão and Milesi-Ferretti's statistical analysis to include the so-called *self-financed capital stock* (i.e., the sum of accumulated national saving, appropriately depreciated over time) as an additional explanatory variable for external crises in the regressions. The self-financed capital stock provides a stock measure of the portion of domestic investment that is covered by national saving; it is the domestic capital stock for which financing did not rely on foreign saving. By construction, the self-financed capital stock is the "national" counterpart to the net foreign liability position of a country.[15] Therefore, introducing the self-financed capital stock simultaneously with the net foreign liability (both measured as ratios of GDP) in the regressions allows for assessing the relative contribution of each to building up external risks.

The results confirm that net foreign liabilities (which is accumulated foreign saving) remain a significant predictor of external crises, while the self-financed capital stock carries much less risk, or no risk at all.[16] Changing the composition of investment financing in favor of national saving would reduce the risk of external crises. In fact, given the large difference in the estimated risk coefficients, increasing national savings would lessen risk even if foreign savings are reduced only marginally.[17] National saving is thus a safer source of investment financing.

Not All Foreign Saving Is Created Equal

Economists refer to foreign saving as the *net* flow of capital into a country. Therefore, countries running current account deficits (where investment exceeds national saving) are net importers of saving, while countries running current account surpluses are net exporters of saving. Yet the *net* flow itself is a combination of two elements: "gross capital inflows" to the reporting economy from foreign savers minus "gross capital outflows" from the reporting economy by national savers. The latter is national saving that is used to acquire foreign assets. Specifically, whenever a resident purchases a foreign asset, that transaction—all else equal—reduces foreign saving in the country where the transaction originated. If this is not made up by a gross capital inflow (that is, a financial transaction in the opposite direction), less aggregate financing will be available for domestic investment. What implications—if any—do these two-way financial transactions have on external crisis risk? Is it only the *net* foreign liabilities (the absorption of capital inflows *net* of capital outflows) that really matter for macroeconomic risk? Or, instead, do gross inflows and outflows contribute differently to risk?

The arguments concerning poor substitutability between financing sources focus on the weaker position of foreigners with respect to nationals and the potential difficulties in generating the foreign exchange that foreigners care about. This argument demands looking at gross—rather than net—positions, differentiating *gross liabilities* (which result from the accumulation of capital inflows from foreigners) from *gross assets* (which result from the accumulation of capital outflows from nationals).[18]

Gross foreign liabilities are likely to be risky because they require a premium to leave the home country and may be unreliable (volatile) as a source of financing. How about gross foreign assets? National saving used to purchase foreign assets—sometimes referred to as capital flight—is presumed to be inconsequential for risk because these assets are placed outside the domestic economy. However, they can also be a safety net for nationals if they can be used to stabilize shocks when foreign financing dries up. In particular, residents can repatriate accumulated foreign assets to offset a sudden stop in gross capital inflows.[19]

Figure 5.4 **Gross Foreign Assets and Liabilities around the World**
Simple Average by Country Group

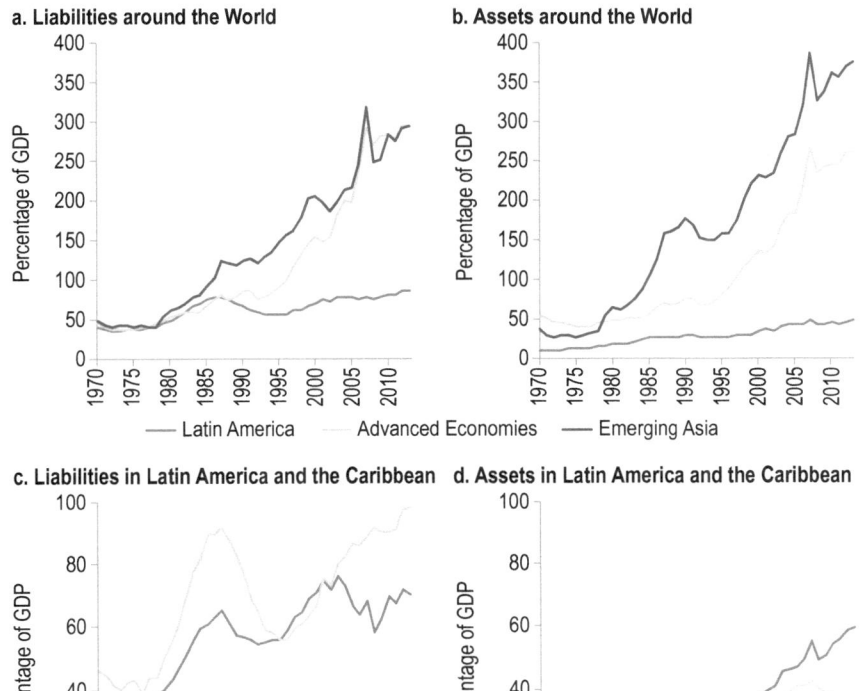

a. Liabilities around the World

b. Assets around the World

c. Liabilities in Latin America and the Caribbean

d. Assets in Latin America and the Caribbean

— Latin America   Advanced Economies   — Emerging Asia

— Larger countries (LAC-7)   Smaller countries

Source: Authors' calculations based on the External Wealth of Nations database.
Note: The figure shows the simple average of gross foreign liabilities and assets (as percentage of GDP) for select country groupings. See endnote 3 in chapter 2 and note on figure 5.3. for the list of countries in each country group.

At the same time, capital flight would contribute to risk by indirectly reducing available funding and creating the need to absorb more gross capital inflows to finance any given domestic investment. The net effect would depend on whether the protective effect of foreign assets more than offsets the risk effect of higher foreign liabilities.

Over the last decade or so, both gross capital inflows and outflows have increased significantly. Figure 5.4 tracks the resulting gross foreign liabilities and assets in the typical country in select regions of the world. In Advanced Economies and in Emerging Asia, gross foreign assets and liabilities have risen remarkably to approximately 300 percent of GDP. In Latin America and the Caribbean, the trend is similar but well below the other two groups of countries.

These trends of increasing gross assets and liabilities are likely the result of deeper financial integration, which has facilitated cross-border financial transactions to diversify portfolios and share international risks.[20] The corollary of this process is that, in many countries, including in Latin American and the Caribbean, net foreign liabilities are now underpinned by more substantial gross external assets and liabilities (see Figure 5.5).

To analyze the implications of *gross* positions for the risk of external crises, the effect of foreign liabilities and assets were examined separately using the same empirical model as in the preceding section (see Cavallo, Fernández-Arias, and Marzani, 2016). The net foreign liabilities were replaced by the gross components (i.e., total foreign liabilities and total foreign assets respectively, both as ratios of GDP) in the regressions;[21] the other explanatory variables (including the self-financed capital stock) were left unchanged. The results confirm that gross foreign liabilities increase the probability of crisis. At the same time, foreign

Figure 5.5 Gross Foreign Assets and Liabilities

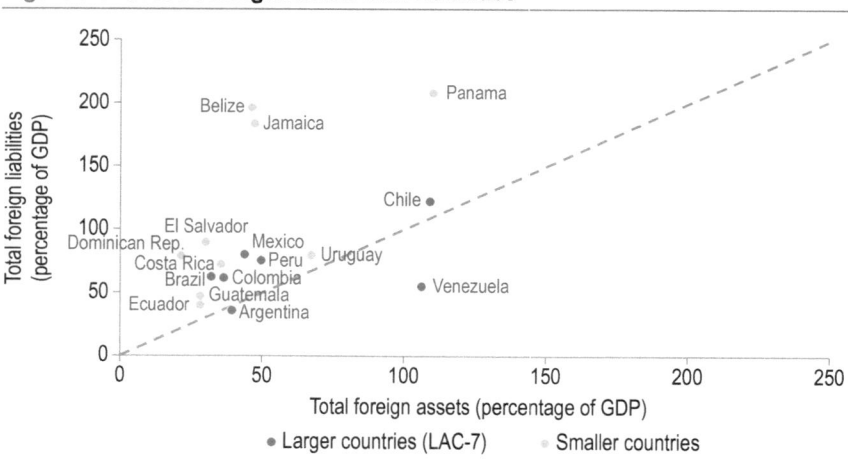

● Larger countries (LAC-7) ● Smaller countries

Source: Authors' calculations based on External Wealth of Nations database.
Note: The figure shows the simple average of total foreign assets and liabilities (as a percent of GDP) for select country groupings in 2013. At the 45° line, total foreign assets equal total foreign liabilities: that is, net foreign liabilities (NFL) equal zero. Dots above the 45° line depict countries with NFL > 0. Dots below the 45° line depict countries with NFL<0.

assets appear to *reduce* the risk of crisis, suggesting that foreign assets do serve as insurance because they can be repatriated. This last finding contradicts the popular view that what really matters for risk is gross foreign liabilities and that capital outflows are irrelevant. Of course, higher capital outflows can be expected to go hand in hand with additional capital inflows needed to satisfy domestic investment demand—a natural consequence of better international financial integration that allows inflows and outflows to grow in tandem (see Borio and Disyatat, 2011). So it is important to gauge the *extent* to which the protection afforded by foreign assets mitigates the risk brought by foreign liabilities. Based on the coefficient estimates on foreign assets and liabilities respectively, a dollar of foreign assets appears to more than offset the risk generated by a dollar of foreign liabilities.[22] Thus, the net position of foreign liabilities is not sufficient to predict the risk of external crises. The underlying gross positions are also important: a given net position is less risky if it is supported by deeper financial integration (i.e., more gross foreign assets and liabilities).

Finally, it is important to note that in the expanded regressions, the self-financed capital stock (i.e., the accumulated national saving) continues to carry little or no risk. This in turn implies that more national saving in order to lower the dependence on foreign saving for investment would reduce macroeconomic risk. If the absorption of less foreign saving takes the form of fewer foreign liabilities, some of the risk would be removed. If it takes the form of more foreign assets, some of the risk would be mitigated. All told, stronger national saving is the key to increasing investment at minimum risk.

Different Risks for Different Financial Flows

Different types of foreign financial flows may pose different risks to the domestic economy. If so, assessing macroeconomic risk by looking at aggregates, even if discriminating between gross foreign assets and liabilities, paints a misleading picture. In particular, countries with riskier types of foreign liabilities would underestimate the macroeconomic risk of foreign financing.

Liabilities are often differentiated by characteristics such as the international risk sharing they provide and how volatile they are. A pecking order of foreign liabilities might consider short-term debt in foreign currency the riskiest and foreign direct investment the safest.[23] The key point is that different types of capital inflows may impact country solvency differently (both the ability and willingness to honor foreign claims) and the liquidity the country needs for macroeconomic stability. There is much less research on how different types of foreign assets may help prevent macroeconomic crises or cure their effects. However, it stands to reason that how easy it is to repatriate assets and how effectively they can be channeled by the financial system to address the sources of financial stress are key for their insurance value.[24]

Distinguishing foreign assets and liabilities by type may be relevant for both the risk potential of foreign liabilities and the safety value of foreign assets because portfolio composition varies across countries. In order to study the countries' risk profile in a more granular fashion, the same empirical model of the preceding sections was used. In this case, however, gross foreign liabilities and assets were decomposed into their main components. For this purpose, total foreign liabilities are disaggregated into three types of stocks: debt, portfolio equity investment, and direct equity investment. In the case of total foreign assets, the decomposition also includes foreign exchange reserves held by the public sector as a separate category on top of this three way classification.

The results show that the type of financial flow matters. On the liabilities side, the finding is that external crisis risk rises as the composition of gross foreign liabilities tilts toward debt instruments. Statistical evidence suggests that equity instruments (both portfolio and direct investment) are relatively low risk compared to debt. In particular, foreign direct investment is less risky than debt.[25] Still, in the expanded regressions, the risk associated with self-financed capital stock remains negligible compared to the risk associated with foreign debt liabilities.

On the assets side, foreign assets that can be more easily sold (portfolio equity assets, reserve assets, and debt assets) reduce the risk of external crises. By contrast, foreign direct investment (FDI), the least liquid of the four, has no such insurance value. Once again, the types of asset that are more easily repatriated carry an insurance value. In particular, reserve assets, which are designed to protect external equilibrium, appear in fact to be useful to prevent crises.

Thus, the risks associated with net foreign liabilities vary with the financial characteristics of international financing—mainly the debt/equity divide of foreign liabilities and the degree of liquidity of foreign assets. Therefore, fully assessing the risks of using foreign saving to supplement national saving requires taking into account the composition of the resulting portfolio of foreign assets and liabilities. Put differently, what is gained in stability by strengthening national saving depends on how the portfolio of net foreign saving would shrink.

Given these differential risk features, it is reassuring that the composition of assets and liabilities in Latin America and the Caribbean has been changing for the better since the 1990s (Figures 5.6 and 5.7). The most remarkable trend in the region is the increase in the share of equity among foreign liabilities, especially foreign direct investment, and the corresponding decline in the share of debt. On the foreign assets side,

Figure 5.6 Composition of Gross Foreign Liabilities
Simple Average by Country Group

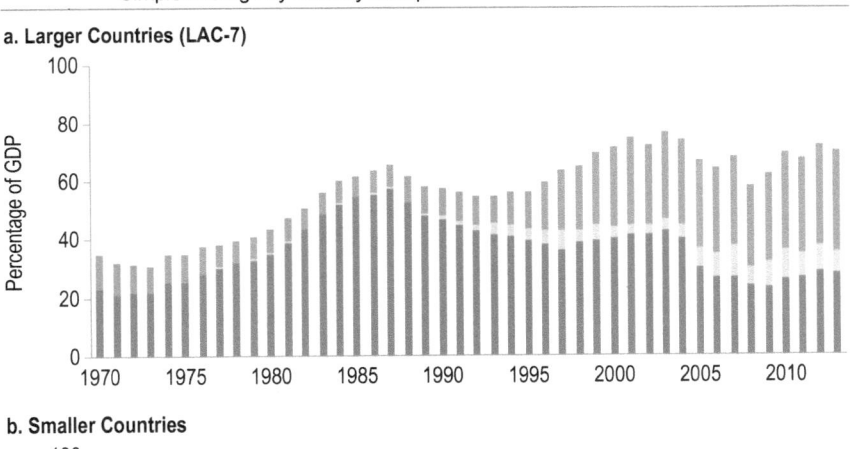

a. Larger Countries (LAC-7)

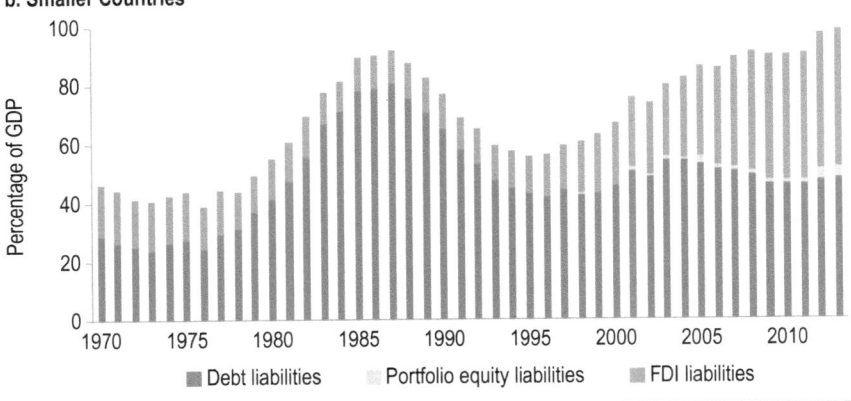

b. Smaller Countries

■ Debt liabilities   Portfolio equity liabilities   ■ FDI liabilities

Source: Authors' calculations based on External Wealth of Nations database.
Note: The figure shows the composition of foreign liabilities by instrument. Simple averages by country group are presented. Financial derivatives, which are small in Latin America and the Caribbean, are not shown in this decomposition. FDI = foreign direct investment. For country groupings see note on Figure 5.3.

Figure 5.7 **Composition of Gross Foreign Assets**
Simple Average by Country Group

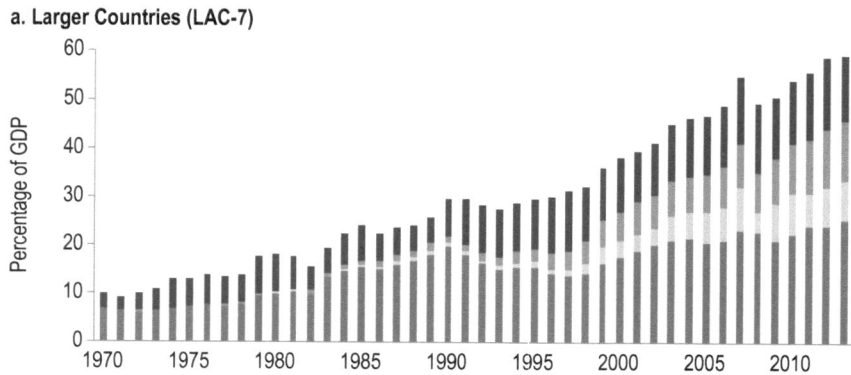

a. Larger Countries (LAC-7)

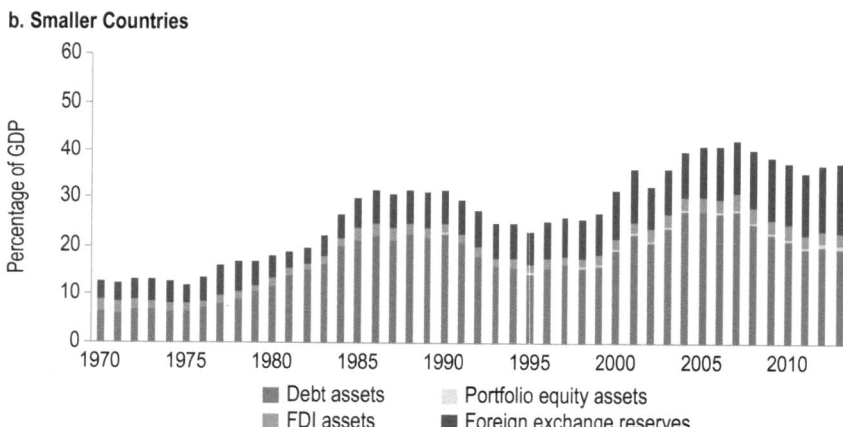

b. Smaller Countries

■ Debt assets   ▨ Portfolio equity assets
■ FDI assets   ■ Foreign exchange reserves

Source: Authors' calculations based on External Wealth of Nations database.
Note: The figure shows the composition of foreign liabilities by instrument. Simple averages by country group are presented. Financial derivatives, which are small in Latin America and the Caribbean, are not shown in this decomposition. FDI = foreign direct investment. For country groupings see note on Figure 5.3.

reserve assets have increased significantly among both large and small countries in the region while portfolio and direct equity investment assets have also risen considerably among the larger countries.

Cavallo, Fernández-Arias, and Marzani (2016) use the model described earlier to obtain a risk profile of foreign savings that depends on the portfolio composition of foreign assets and liabilities in a country's balance sheet. Their External Portfolio Vulnerability Index (EPVI) sums up how each country's portfolio item contributes to the risk of an external crisis and is normalized such that values higher than 1 indicate

Figure 5.8 **External Portfolio Vulnerability Index (EPVI)**
Simple Average by Country Group

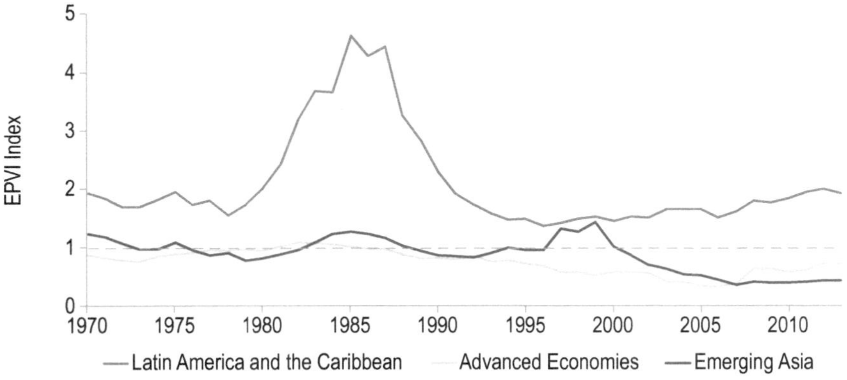

— Latin America and the Caribbean   Advanced Economies   — Emerging Asia

Source: Authors' elaboration based on Cavallo, Fernández-Arias, and Marzani (2016).
Note: The External Portfolio Vulnerability Index (EPVI) is the exponential of the linear combination of the observed values of the variables related to the external portfolio (gross foreign assets and liabilities) with the estimated coefficients in the probit regression acting as coefficients. Values of the EPVI higher than 1 indicate the portfolio by itself increases the probability of an external crisis. The figure presents the simple average by region. See endnote 3 in Chapter 2 for the list of countries in each country group.

that the external portfolio is a risk factor (it increases the probability of an external crisis) and values lower than 1 mean that the portfolio is a risk mitigating factor (it reduces the probability of an external crisis). [26]

In Latin America and the Caribbean, the external portfolio in the 1980s was clearly very risky (see Figure 5.8). From the end of that decade to the mid-1990s, the index declined rapidly. However, since then, it has been creeping up again as net foreign liabilities have been rising, on average. The EPVI for the typical country in the region is still above the neutral level, meaning that on average the portfolio of foreign liabilities and assets is still a risk factor for external crisis. In sharp contrast, in Emerging Asia, countries' external portfolios help reduce the risks of external crisis.

The bottom line is that the gradual shift to safer foreign assets and liabilities has helped lower the risk posed by the external portfolio. However, despite this improvement, the risk associated with the external portfolio in Latin America and the Caribbean has been on the rise for several years and remains high by international standards. As discussed earlier, stronger national saving would help reduce the risk (assuming that investment increases less than national saving, as the evidence indicates), either by lowering demand for foreign liabilities or by facilitating the accumulation of foreign assets. Therefore, countries in which liabilities are riskier and assets are safer would benefit the most from stronger national saving. As foreign portfolios become safer, the effectiveness of stronger national saving crucially depends on whether the offset foreign saving takes the form of less liabilities or more assets. On the margin, risk reduction is maximized when additional national savings are channeled to strengthen foreign assets. In that case, a safer composition of the external portfolio strengthens the case for more national saving as a means to reduce risk.

Financial Integration Is No Cure

Better financial integration can facilitate the flow of financial capital across countries. Consequently, it can alleviate the negative impact of a national saving shortfall and sustain higher domestic investment with a low cost of capital. [27] However, if financial integration ushers in too much foreign financing (particularly risky forms), it can also jack up the risk of external crises. [28] In turn, if costly crises occur more frequently, financial integration could even deter investment down the road. Moreover, open capital accounts may conceivably reduce, rather than expand, the pool of national saving available for domestic investment. In countries where domestic conditions do not nurture national saving—such as inflationary environments, or institutional environments that offer little protection of property rights—savers may choose to place their saving abroad, thereby reducing the pool of national saving for financing domestic investment. Opening capital accounts without providing the correct incentives for local savers can facilitate capital flight, further constraining domestic investment in countries with little access to foreign financing.

The first sign that Latin America and the Caribbean should not pin too much hope on international financial integration as a cure-all is the evolution of the so-called "self-financing ratio" of the domestic capital stock, which does not appear to be declining over time (See Figure 5.9). The self-financing ratio is the ratio of the self-financed capital stock (i.e., the accumulated national saving, appropriately discounted) to the total domestic capital stock (see Aizenman, Pinto, and Radziwill, 2007). The flipside of the high importance of national saving as the main source for investment financing is the low importance of foreign saving in building capital stock. True, some national savings do not finance domestic investment but leak abroad as capital outflows, meaning the amount of

Figure 5.9 **Self-Financing Ratio**
Simple Average

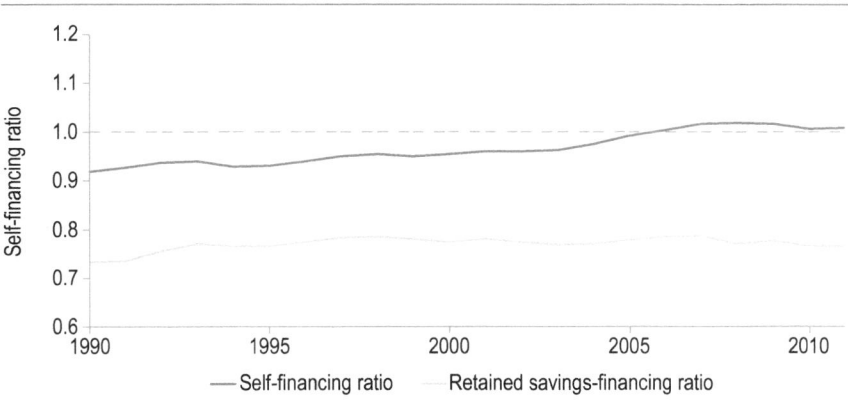

Source: Authors' calculations based on data from World Bank World Development Indicators database based on methodology developed by Aizenman, Pinto and Radziwill (2007), extended on Cavallo, Fernández-Arias and Marzani (2016).
Note: The figure shows the regional simple average for the self-financing ratio (SFR), and a version of the SFR in which gross outflows are deducted from gross national saving in the numerator of the formula. This is the so-called retained savings-financing ratio.

investment financed from abroad is larger than what (net) foreign saving suggests. Nevertheless, even if all the capital outflows are subtracted, which yields a lower bound for national financing, the high importance of accumulated national saving does not appear to be declining over time (Figure 5.9).

To calculate the possible impact of increased financial integration on domestic investment, Cavallo, Fernández-Arias, and Marzani (2016) extend the basic Feldstein and Horioka (1980) framework relating domestic investment to national saving to also include how this relationship is affected by financial integration.[29] They find that financial integration appears to benefit investment the most when national saving is weak.[30] However, at the average national saving rates in Latin American and Caribbean countries today (less than 20 percent of GDP), the investment impact of financial integration is practically nil. Moreover, if greater financial integration is not matched with appropriate policies and regulations to control exposure to macroeconomic risk and these risks escalate, then the net result of the trade-off between more investment and higher risk could even be negative.

The steady advance of financial integration over the past 20 years in the region, coupled with the equally steady increase in the index of macroeconomic risk shown in Figure 5.8, is a warning sign. Clearly, more financial integration is beneficial when soundly managed. Even then, however, it is far from a cure. Stronger national saving remains the key to faster and sustainable growth.

Safety First

Clearly, national and foreign saving are not good substitutes. If national saving falls short of investment needs, at best, foreign saving will fill only part of the gap. Furthermore, the inflow of foreign saving comes with a price tag: it can raise the likelihood of external crises and overall macro-economic risks. In turn, crises can further deter investment and growth. National saving does not. It is safer, and with no strings attached. Sound policies that promote national saving support faster and more sustainable growth.

Higher national saving reduces the need for importing saving from abroad. This is particularly important for most countries in Latin America and the Caribbean, for whom higher levels of foreign saving represent a crisis risk factor that is again on the rise. A slower accumulation of foreign liabilities would reduce risks, particularly in countries with a riskier composition of liabilities. Even if some national saving moves abroad (in the form of capital outflows), external assets would protect against external crises, especially in countries that invest in safer instruments.

Safety is a virtue, particularly for a region that has been wracked by volatility and macroeconomic crises for the last half century. These gyrations have taken their toll on development and must be controlled if the region is to grow and prosper. National saving is safe and supports stability—a critical factor in an environment conducive to equitable and sustainable development.

Notes

[1] This chapter draws heavily on Cavallo, Fernández-Arias, and Marzani (2016).

[2] Aizenman, Pinto, and Radziwill (2007) show that accumulated national saving represented some 90 percent of the total stock of domestic capital across emerging countries during the 1990's. Similar estimations in Cavallo, Fernández-Arias, and Marzani (2016) confirm the overwhelming importance of national savings in Latin America: the portion of the capital stock that can be accounted by national savings has ranged on average from 90 percent to 105 percent during the past few decades. These measures overestimate the importance of national saving because not all such saving is applied to domestic investment financing. Nevertheless, if capital outflows are fully deducted from national savings to arrive at a lower bound for national financing, the self-financed portion of the capital stock is still predominant (averaging between 70 percent and 80 percent in the last few decades).

[3] Even then, as argued by de la Torre and Ize (2015), the absorption of foreign savings would hurt growth by reducing net exports, which is found to be associated with high productivity and growth. In this case, stronger national savings would support growth even under perfect financial integration.

[4] The level of investment is not all that counts. Shortcomings in national saving may constrain not only the level of domestic investment but also its quality. Savings that are not efficiently allocated due to domestic distortions lead to the financing of low return investments, which would be reflected in lower aggregate total factor productivity.

[5] "National saving" (the unconsumed part of national income) differs from "domestic saving" (the unconsumed part of gross domestic output). The difference between the two is international factor payments. In terms of national accounting, national saving is equal to Investment + current account deficit (foreign saving). Domestic saving is equal to Investment + Trade Balance.

[6] For a summary of the discussion on the role of global factors versus domestic factors in driving capital flows to emerging markets, see Calvo, Leiderman, and Reinhart (1996).

[7] For example, in Latin America and the Caribbean in the 1980s, the unyielding external debt overhang acted as an implicit tax on

investment (the fruits of growth would increase countries' capacity to pay and then be captured by external creditors). Perhaps more importantly, it also created deep uncertainty over how the burden of the ultimate costs would be distributed across different economic agents (see Cavallo, Fernández-Arias, and Powell, 2014).

[8] See Jeanne and Korinek (2010) and Fernández-Arias, and Lombardo (1998).

[9] The study of macroeconomic risks resulting from the absorption of foreign savings opens a policy agenda on how to address these market externalities, including the regulation of the rate of absorption and policies discriminating among types of capital inflows and outflows. The analysis of these financial policy implications is beyond the scope of this chapter.

[10] Catão and Milesi-Ferretti (2014) do the statistical analysis using a probit regression model for panel data. On the left-hand side of their regressions is the external crisis indicator variable (a dichotomous variable that takes value zero if there is no crisis, and 1 when there is a crisis), while on the right-hand side (explanatory variables) is the net foreign liabilities (NFL) as a ratio of GDP. The risk of crisis increases sharply as NFL exceeds 50 percent of GDP and whenever the NFL/GDP ratio rises some 20 percentage points above the country-specific historical mean. The implication is that foreign liabilities are risky and should be kept under control.

[11] IMF support is defined as IMF loans at least twice as large as the respective country's quota in the IMF, when all net disbursements are computed from the program's inception to end.

[12] In general, economic studies on the negative effect of macroeconomic crises on productivity and growth underscore the adverse effects of short-run macroeconomic instability and output volatility on long-term growth. Crises increase uncertainty, drive away investment, produce social tensions, and permanently reduce productivity and output. See, for example, Ramey and Ramey (1995); Cerra and Saxena (2008); and Blyde, Daude, and Fernández-Arias (2010).

[13] The sample consists of 71 countries (including 42 emerging economies, of which 16 are from Latin America and the Caribbean) for the period 1970–2011.

[14] The bunching of the crises around specific dates—a phenomenon documented by Calvo, Izquierdo, and Mejía (2004) in their work on Sudden

Stops—suggests that the prevalence of crises is, to some extent, due to factors that are beyond the control of national authorities.

[15] The concept of self-financed capital stock is based on the self-financing ratio introduced by Aizenman, Pinto, and Radziwill (2007). In background work for this book it was measured using three alternative metrics (see Cavallo, Fernández-Arias, and Marzani, 2016).

[16] Like in Catão and Milesi-Ferretti (2014) the sample consists of a maximum of 71 countries with annual data for the period 1970–2011. This exercise is based on a slightly smaller sample limited by the availability of information needed to conduct the more detailed statistical analysis used in this chapter. For methodology and extensive robustness checks, see Cavallo, Fernández-Arias, and Marzani (2016).

[17] As discussed in Chapters 1 and 2, the correlation between foreign and national savings across countries is consistently negative. The Feldstein-Horioka regressions imply that, despite imperfections in financial integration, increased national saving substantially crowds out foreign saving.

[18] See Borio and Disyatat (2011) for a discussion about the role of gross versus net capital flows and the links to external financing.

[19] See Cavallo et al., (2015) for an analysis of the implications of two-way gross capital flows for the stability of net flows.

[20] See Committee on International Economic Policy and Reform (2012).

[21] The data on gross foreign assets and liabilities comes from External Wealth of Nations database.

[22] Statistical tests were run to gauge the extent of risk offsetting. In all the specifications the hypothesis of full offset was rejected to favor more than full offset at the 5 percent confidence level. For details, see Cavallo, Fernández-Arias, and Marzani (2016).

[23] Fernández-Arias and Hausmann (2001). For a recent survey, see Levy Yeyati and Zúñiga (2015).

[24] See Cavallo, Fernández-Arias, and Marzani (2016) for a fuller discussion.

[25] Hansen and Wagner (2015) confirm and go beyond this result. They show that FDI liabilities are a particularly safer form of capital inflows when they are substantially based on the retained earnings of multinational corporations. It turns out that retained earnings used to finance domestic investment behave as national saving, and both are components of what the authors call "local savings." From the point of

view of macroeconomic financial risks, it is as if these companies were in part owned by nationals.

[26] The EPVI refers only to the contribution of a country's external portfolio to overall risk. Overall risk also depends on the other factors included in the statistical exercise.

[27] Of course, financial integration can have other benefits. For example, fewer impediments to cross-border financing can widen the scope for risk diversification. This discussion focuses on only one of the many benefits of financial integration: the investment response.

[28] In addition, financial integration may facilitate capital flight, which would deepen macroeconomic instability in certain circumstances.

[29] Financial integration is captured through two standard measures used in the literature: a) the Chinn-Ito index measuring de-jure financial openness (i.e., lack of formal restrictions to the movement of capital flows across countries); and b) the Lane and Milesi-Ferretti (2007) index of de-facto financial openness (i.e., the sum of foreign assets and liabilities as a share of GDP), which encompasses de-jure considerations concerning financial openness as well as easier financial conditions in the supply of foreign savings.

[30] This assumes that national saving remains constant as financial integration deepens. This assumption of no crowding out may be optimistic to the extent that financial integration brings lower domestic interest rates.

6 Running Out of Time: The Demographics of Saving

When it comes to consumption and saving, there are two groups of people: those who produce resources actively in the labor market, and those who depend on what others produce because they are either too young or too old to work. For the world as a whole, the ratio of potential dependents to producers has been declining since 1965—mostly because fertility rates have dropped more quickly than life expectancy has increased. However, this shift in the age structure of society—the so-called demographic dividend—is ending (Figure 6.1.)[1]

The steady decline of the dependency ratio worldwide since 1965 stopped in 2010 (United Nations, 2015). From now on, the gains of having fewer young people to care for will be outweighed by the burden of having to attend to a growing elderly population.[2]

Nowhere in the world will these demographic changes be as intense as in Latin America and the Caribbean. For the past five decades, the region's decline in the dependency ratio has been the steepest in the world. In 1965, for each 100 individuals of working age (15 to 65 years old) in the region, there were 90 young and old dependents; today there are fewer than 50. In a way, this has been a gift. A greater number of people have been contributing to production, savings, and growth. However, the gift is really a loan that will have to be repaid in the decades to come. As the low fertility rates that triggered the demographic dividend play out, countries will age, and they will age rapidly. The demographic dividend is projected to end in 2020. From 2020 to 2100, the number of dependents will increase by 35.5—again the largest increase of any region (Figure 6.1). In 2085, Latin America and the Caribbean will surpass Europe as the region with the highest share of elderly per working age population (ECLAC, 2014b).

Providing for the elderly is an enormous task that the region is not ready to undertake. Aging will put more pressure on already scarce

Figure 6.1 **Extension of the Demographic Dividend**

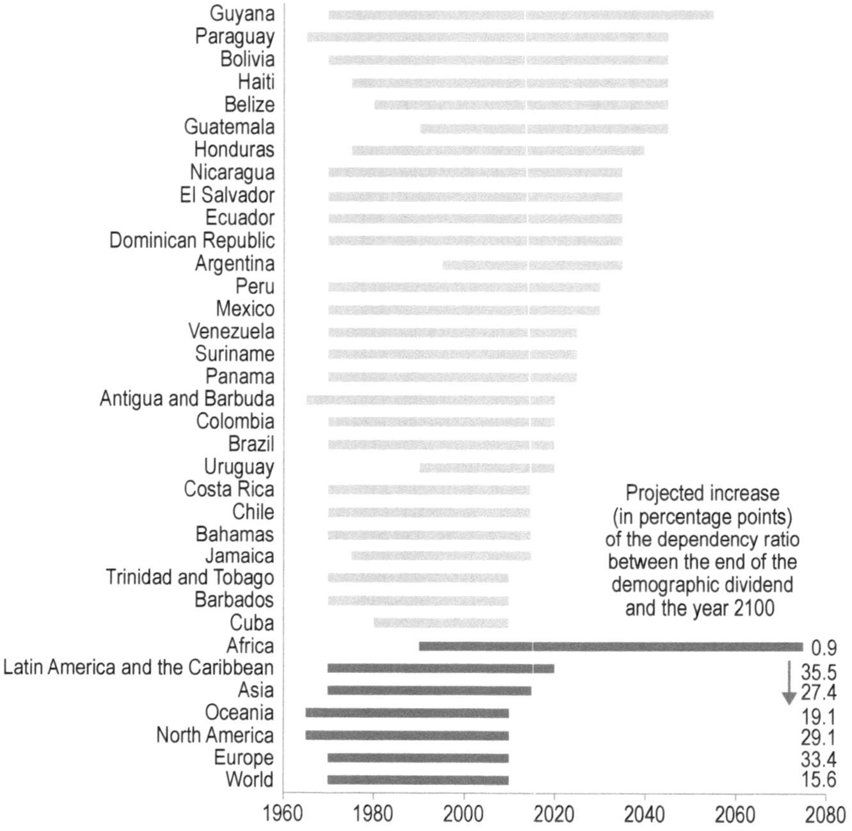

Source: Authors' calculations based on United Nations (2015).
Note: The bars depict the period in which the total dependency ratio (Population <15 + Population >65/Population 15–64) is falling.

funds to finance development. The future of an aging society is a challenge that requires action sooner rather than later. However, conveying the need for swift action to policymakers is difficult because the region is still enjoying the demographic dividend. Demographic trends fueled an important part of the region's recent economic performance.[3]

Not all the news is bad. Demographics will still provide room for maneuver for several years—in some countries more than in others. For countries like Belize, Bolivia, Guatemala, Guyana, Haiti, and Paraguay, the demographic dividend will last two to three more decades (Figure 6.1). For countries like Bahamas, Barbados, Chile, Costa Rica, Cuba, Jamaica, and Trinidad and Tobago, the demographic dividend is all but gone.

Figure 6.2 **Age Profile in Latin America and the Caribbean**

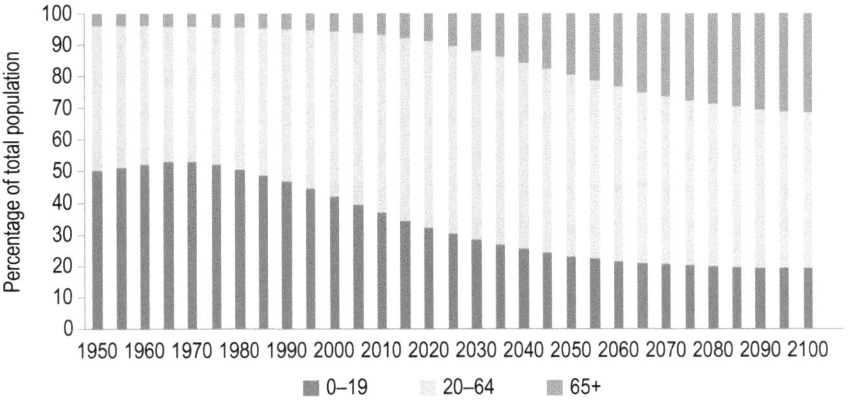

Source: Authors' calculations based on United Nations (2015).

However, even for these countries, the dependency ratios, while increasing, will remain relatively low by historical standards for several years (United Nations, 2015). In addition, the region has other unexploited dividends that can extend the demographic dividend, at least temporarily. One of them is the increase in the participation of women in labor market. Female participation rates are still low, compared to more advanced countries (Morton et al., 2014). Another is to decrease the large share of youngsters who are neither participating in the labor market nor studying. Some 22 percent of the region's youth were idle in 2013 (Alaimo et al., 2015). Furthermore, reducing the large share of the labor force who do not work in the formal sector—and thus do not pay taxes or contribute to pensions—could help to boost savings and growth (Bosch, Melguizo, and Pagés, 2013; Levy, 2008; Hsieh and Klenow, 2014).

Governments, households, and firms must address the challenge of population aging by combining efforts. This chapter argues that improving savings in general and pension systems in particular, are necessary steps to ensure that longer lives will mean better lives.

More Elderly with More Needs

During the past 40 years, the age profile of the population and dependency ratios in Latin America and the Caribbean have changed dramatically. Figure 6.2 shows how this profile has evolved and how it is likely to continue. The change in the share of the population over 65 years

old is especially striking, from a very small portion 50 years ago to a significant percentage in the future. At the same time, fertility has fallen from
5.9 births per 1,000 women in 1950–55 to 2.15 in 2010–15, and is projected
to decline even further to 1.78 in 2045–50. Around 2050, life expectancy
and fertility rates in Latin America and the Caribbean are expected to con-
verge to the levels of more advanced countries (United Nations, 2015).

Not only will the number of older people be greater, but so too will
the portion of the very old with higher needs. While less than 2 percent of the population in Latin America and the Caribbean is older than
85, by the end of the century, that share will increase to more than 8
percent. The need for care of the elderly over the age of 85 increases
significantly, despite technological advances. The share of adults that
need help with functional activities of daily life (FADL) or instrumental
activities of daily life (IADL)[4] increases between two to five times after
the age of 80, surveys conducted in Latin American cities in 2002 indicate (Table 6.1). Other sources suggest the same pattern. For instance,
a survey conducted in Chile in 2009 showed that 12.8 percent of the
elderly aged 60–64 were dependent in some way, while this percentage increased to more than 65 percent at ages 85 or over (SENAMA,
2009). This situation is similar in more advanced countries with better
health systems. In countries like Italy, Germany, and Spain, the increase
in the case of FADL is from nearly 10 percent at ages 60–64 to more
than 30 percent for those over 75 years old. In the case of IADL, dependence at older ages is three times higher than for those between 65 and

Table 6.1 **Elderly with Limitations Who Receive Help with Daily Activities (Percentage)**

	Buenos Aires, Argentina	Bridgetown, Barbados	São Paulo, Brazil	Santiago, Chile	Havana, Cuba	Mexico City, Mexico	Montevideo, Uruguay
FADL							
65–80	4.0	4.6	7.7	10.2	6.7	6.4	3.8
80 +	18.8	17.8	21.9	33.8	23.2	24.4	13.8
IADL							
65–80	11.2	14.7	31.1	23.1	20.7	25.3	9.9
80 +	29.1	36.8	59.6	55.1	50.7	51.8	35.4

Source: Authors' calculations based on the Health, Well-being and Aging Survey (CDE and others, 2002).
Note: FADL = functional activities of daily living; IADL = instrumental activities of daily living.

74, reaching almost 40 percent in countries like Italy and Spain. Therefore, even if overall health conditions in Latin America and the Caribbean
improve, dependency rates of the very elderly will still likely increase as
life expectancy rises. Compounding the problem, as societies age, more
people need care, but fewer caregivers are available, given the drop in
fertility (WHO, 2015).

In a world where more people are both elderly and dependent, two
main challenges loom for future generations: providing health care and
income support (pensions) for the elderly. Combined, these challenges
could prove burdensome.

Taking care of the elderly is substantially more expensive than taking care of the young. Evidence from both OECD member-states and
Latin American and Caribbean countries shows that people spend a
substantial portion of their medical expenses in the last decade of life,
and that the percentage of people at this stage is increasing as the
population ages. Health care spending in per capita terms is between
four and ten times higher for an 80 year-old than for a 3 year-old (see
Figure 6.3).

The shift in population composition will substantially increase health
care costs. Currently, the elderly consume 17 percent of total health expenditures in Latin America and the Caribbean (even though they make up
less than 8 percent of the population): this share is projected to rise to over

Figure 6.3 **Public and Private Consumption of Health Care over a Lifetime**

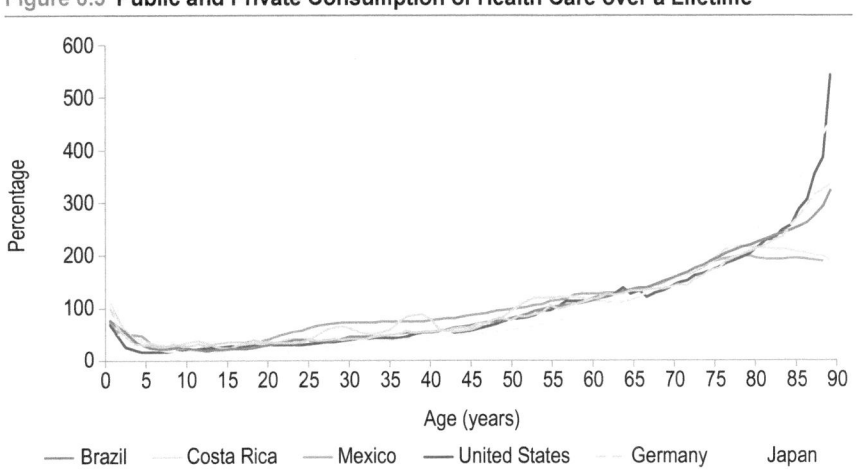

Source: Authors' calculations based on National Transfer Accounts Database, http://www.ntac-
counts.org.
Note: Per capita health care consumption as a percentage of lifetime average health care consumption.

50 percent in 2070 (United Nations, 2015). Today, families finance much of the health care needs of the elderly, but as the size of families shrinks, it will be harder to cope with higher costs. Thus, countries will have to find resources to finance curative and palliative services. Preventive services are another way to control costs and improve the health of the elderly. The role of chronic diseases on the costs of health care, and the prevalence of these conditions at old age, have been well documented. Future health expenditures due to the change in the age structure will depend on actions taken to prevent the impact of chronic disease (see Saad, 2011).

The other major challenge for Latin America and the Caribbean will be how to finance pensions, particularly because, despite relatively young populations, governments are already spending substantially more on the old than on the young. Indeed, total spending on education in Brazil and Uruguay accounted for 5.3 percent and 3.8 percent of GDP in 2009, respectively, and total spending on social security and pensions reached 13.8 percent and 11.7 percent on the same year for these 2 countries. In per capita terms, current public benefits for the young are significantly lower than for the elderly. For instance, on average for the region, public expenditure on social security and pensions per person older than 65, amounted to more than five times the level of expenditure on education per child under 20 in 2015 (ECLAC, 2015a).

Population aging will increase the pensions' financing challenge as well. One way to quantify the magnitude of this challenge is to calculate what would be the future level of spending on pensions taking into account the projected demographic changes. If by 2100 the region keeps spending the same amount per person over 65 (as a share of GDP) on pensions as it is spending now, total expenditure would have to increase five-fold on average. Some countries, including Argentina, Bolivia, Brazil, Panama, and Venezuela, might need to spend more than 20 percent of GDP on pensions (Figure 6.4). This amount of spending on pensions alone would probably crowd out other expenditures. If nothing is done, then the region might end up spending less on other productivity-enhancing investments just when boosting productivity would be critical for growth in the region in the face of aging.

Countries need to understand that more resources will inevitably be required to address the necessities of an aging population. How much will be needed in the future depends greatly on the package of benefits promised to the elderly, and on when they would start receiving those transfers. More developed countries, which are at a further advanced

Figure 6.4 Current and Future Public Spending on Pensions

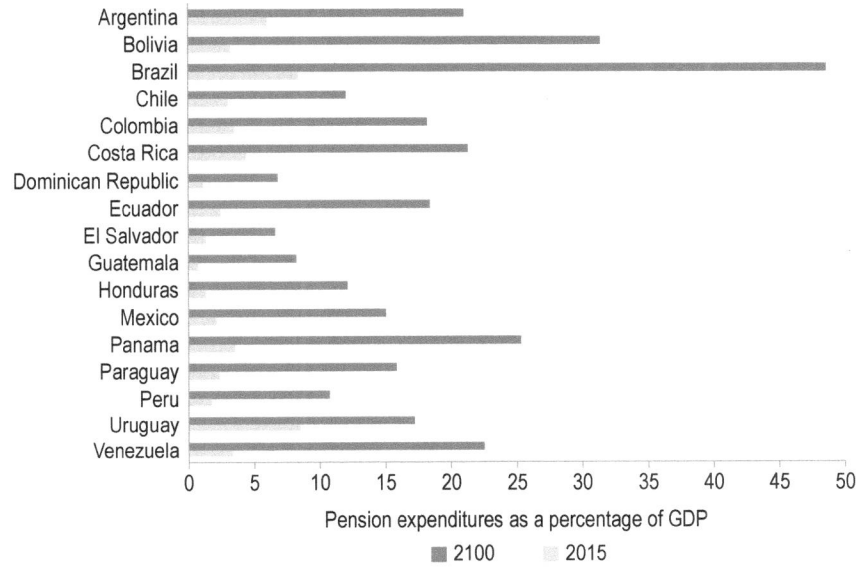

Source: Authors' calculations based on ECLAC (2015b) and CELADE (2015).
Note: Pension spending in 2015 is calculated by multiplying the average pension by the share of pension recipients according to household surveys (see Chapter 7 for details). Pension expenditures in 2100 are calculated leaving expenditure per capita (as a share of GDP) constant at 2015 levels multiplied by the growth factor of people over 65 between 2015 and 2100.

stage in the demographic transition, should be a reference for the region to prepare adequately for the challenge that aging presents. Providing adequate conditions for the elderly to decide how long to work is an important component of old-age policies. Pensions are a critical element in this equation (Chapter 7).

Facing the Challenge: More and Better Savings

To meet the needs of the elderly, countries can pursue essentially two strategies. One is to "promise" the elderly that societies will take care of them (in exchange for contributions made during the working years, as part of family arrangements, or as a citizen's right). The other is to set resources aside (i.e., saving) when countries are young and use them as they age.[5] Pension arrangements broadly follow these two strategies (see Box 6.1). It is important to understand that aging will pose important challenges to both strategies.

Fulfilling Promises

Promising a pension in the future in exchange for contributions today is how most pension systems in the world operate. Most mandatory pension systems have at least a component that is a defined-benefit system (PAYG/DB), either unfunded or usually only partially funded. In these systems, the contributions of current workers' pay for the pensions that were promised in the past to other workers (see Box 6.1).

Fulfilling that promise in periods of rapid demographic change is a challenge. As the proportion of the elderly increases, more and more resources are required from the shrinking pool of working populations in the form of pension contributions, taxes, or intra-family transfers. The kind of promises a country can afford is largely driven by demographic trends (see Box 6.2). As these trends change, so do the implicit rates of return that a pay-as-you-go (PAYG/DB) system can offer in a sustainable way, given a certain level of contributions and a certain retirement age.

BOX 6.1. PENSION SYSTEMS: DEFINING THE CONCEPTS

Types of pension systems
Defined-benefit systems (DB). The pension level is determined by a rule based on the number of contributions and the employee's salary in the final years of work. The benefits rule may be set according to the final salary payment or a longer period (such as the final five or ten years of contributions). This rule is usually not actuarially fair, and entails subsidies within or across generations. This type of system can be funded or not; it is usually partially funded.

Defined-contribution system (DC). The pension is determined by the value of the assets accumulated by an individual over his or her working life. The benefits may be withdrawn all at once, scheduled for programmed withdrawals, or used to purchase an annuity, which would provide monthly income for the remainder of the individual's life. The formula is actuarially fair. There are no subsidies across or within generations, unless there is a guaranteed minimum pension. Usually these systems are funded, but not necessarily. When the system is not funded, it is called a notional defined contribution system.

Noncontributory pension (NCP) or Social Pensions (SP). The pension benefits do not come from any type of contribution made by the individual. They may be granted universally, as in Bolivia, or targeted as a poverty prevention device. This system can also be funded, partially funded, or not funded.

(continued on next page)

For most Latin American and Caribbean countries with PAYG/DB pension systems, the promised benefits are significantly higher than what these countries can afford. On average, in 2015 given current contribution rates, retirement ages, system rules, and demographics, the pensions that could be financed correspond to around 37 percent of the worker's final salary (the variation across countries is substantial). By contrast, the average PAYG/DB system promised pensions equivalent to 67 percent of the worker's final salary. The demographic transition will make that promise even more difficult to fulfill. By 2100, the pension that can be financed by future contributors will be only 15 percent of the final salary for the same set of parameters (see Box 6.2).

In addition to the high fiscal burden, these promised benefits will likely be paid to a relatively small share of future retirees. This is so because pension coverage is very low in the region. The tension between increasing coverage and maintaining a sustainable system will be a key challenge to fulfilling past promises. Increasing coverage without

BOX 6.1. *(continued)*

Funding
Fully funded. Pension benefits are paid from the assets accumulated through the pension plan. Therefore, pension fund liabilities are fully matched by assets.

Partially funded. Pension benefits are paid both from the accumulated assets and current contributions from workers or general taxes collected by the state. Therefore, liabilities are partially matched by assets.

Unfunded. Pension benefits are paid from contributions or general taxes collected by the state. These systems are typically called pay-as-you-go (PAYG).

Although in theory the combination of systems and funding schemes can vary (see Barr and Diamond, 2006), the region's defined-benefit systems are either unfunded or partially funded. This situation requires a transfer of workers' assets across generations, from those of working age who make contributions to elderly adults who contributed in the past and are now collecting a pension. Fiscal risks for these systems will be greater as demographic pressures mount. Noncontributory pensions (NCP) are an extreme example of a defined-benefit system in which no one contributes directly; instead, they must be funded through general revenues or reserves, or a combination.

Defined-contribution (DC) systems are generally fully funded. Therefore, each generation's pension is financed by its own savings.

BOX 6.2. FUNDING TO COPE WITH DEMOGRAPHIC SHIFTS

Demography will transform how much citizens can expect from their pension contributions if systems are to be affordable. This calculation is not easy and depends on the unknown evolution of many variables over long periods of time. However, understanding the balance between what countries promise their elderly and what they ask in the form of contributions and retirement age, is crucial for a proper strategy to cope with demographic shifts.

Demographic forces have a different impact depending on the type of pension system. In systems with PAYG pillars, the expected rate of return for pension financing is the rate of growth of aggregate taxable salaries (Samuelson, 1958; Aaron, 1966). This is the rate at which wages increase times the increase in the size of the contributor's base. Hence, as the contribution's base decreases, so does the average pension that can be paid without relying on other funding sources.

Fully funded capitalization systems will also be affected by demographic changes. As Attanasio et al. (2015) show, in an aging world, interest rates will be lower, decreasing the returns to pension savings. Furthermore, if the retirement age remains constant as longevity increases, those savings will generate lower pensions.

This box estimates the pension based on the last salary (replacement rate) that the average worker should expect under: (i) a sustainable PAYG system; and (ii) a fully funded system, and compares them with what countries are actually promising (Figures B6.1 and B6.2). There are three main messages.

1. Countries are making unrealistic promises
For most Latin American and Caribbean countries that have a pay-as-you-go/defined-benefit (PAYG/DB) pension pillar, promised benefits are significantly higher than what these countries can afford in a sustainable way. This implies that in order to meet those promises, countries will probably have to draw resources from elsewhere outside the pension system and trade-offs will arise between competing development needs.

The mismatch between promises and what can be afforded occurs because benefits are generous with respect to the contribution rate (which is calculated as a percentage of a worker's salary) and retirement age in the country. For example, in Honduras, whose contribution rate is only 3 percent of the salary, retirees are entitled to a pension that could be between 65 percent and 70 percent of the final salary (although with a relatively low pension ceiling). In Jamaica and Haiti, which also have contribution rates of 3 percent, retirees can receive benefits in the range of 30 percent of their final salary. While this is significantly lower, it is still very generous given the level of contributions paid. For PAYG/DB pillars in countries like Belize, Mexico, Costa Rica, Venezuela, and Ecuador with contributions between 6 and 8.7 percent of salary, promised replacement rates are over 60 percent with respect to the final salary. In Mexico, for a contribution rate of 6.3 percent of salary, some

(continued on next page)

BOX 6.2. *(continued)*

Figure B6.1 **Promised and Affordable Replacement Rates in PAYG/DB and FF Systems for Retirees in 2010–15 and 2095–2100**

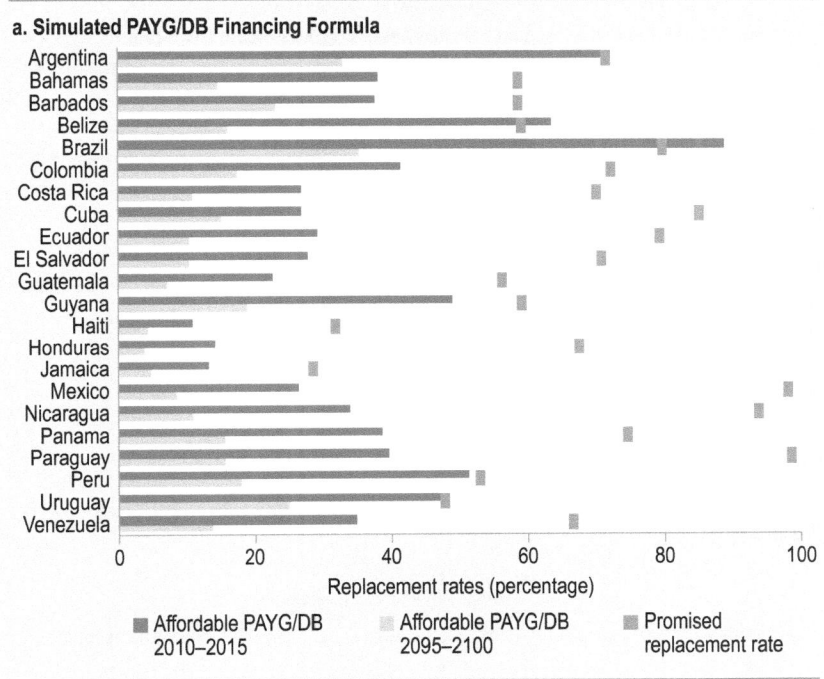

a. Simulated PAYG/DB Financing Formula

beneficiaries are entitled to a pension close to 100 percent of their final salary.[a] Nicaragua and Paraguay, which have somewhat higher contribution rates, have committed to pensions close to the level of the worker's final salary. But, as shown in panel a, this might still be unaffordable with the prevalent contribution rates (11 percent and 13 percent, respectively) and current retirement age (60 years) in those countries.

The non-affordability problem becomes aggravated as the population ages. Simulations show that in all cases, the affordable replacement rates over the 2095–2100 period are significantly below the affordable replacement rates in the present. For promised benefits to be affordable, huge increases in contribution rates would be needed (or retirement ages should be incremented substantially). For instance, in Nicaragua and Paraguay, where the current contribution rate is 11 percent and 13 percent, respectively, and promised benefits are over 90 percent of the final salary at age 60, contributions would need to be around 25 percent in 2010-15 and soar to over 70 percent in 2100, in order for benefits to be paid without generating an actuarial deficit.

(continued on next page)

BOX 6.2. *(continued)*

Figure B6.1   **Promised and Affordable Replacement Rates in PAYG/DB and FF Systems for Retirees in 2010–15 and 2095–2100** *(continued)*

b. Simulated Fully Funded Financing Formula Assuming 3.5 Percent Real Return

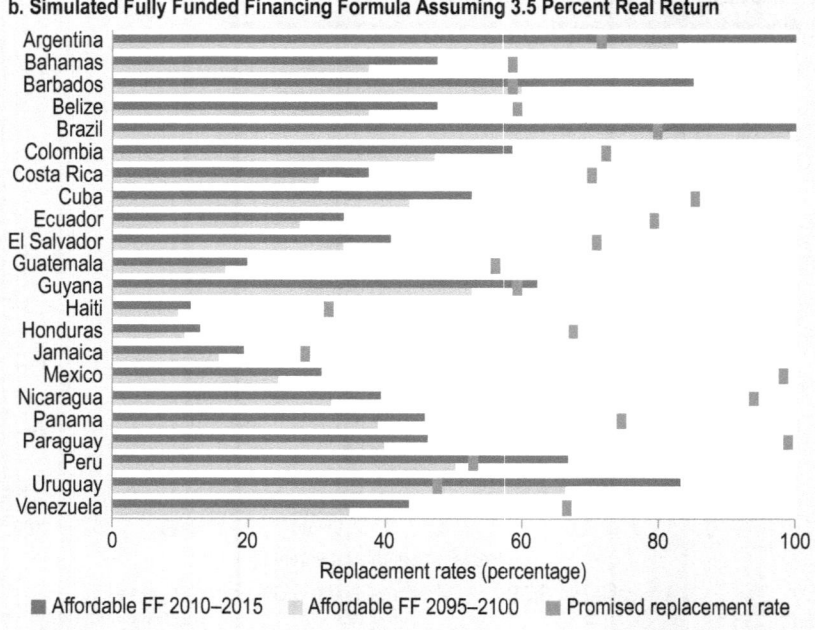

Replacement rates (percentage)

■ Affordable FF 2010–2015   ▨ Affordable FF 2095–2100   ■ Promised replacement rate

Source: Authors' calculations based on system's design parameters and their own assumptions.
Note: PAYG = pay as you go, DB = defined benefit, FF = fully funded.

2. Moving to funding might help but pensions will probably remain lower than promised

Suppose now, that the system was fully funded; i.e., that the same worker accumulated contributions in an individual account and was paid the same promised pension at retirement. Of course, the affordability of the promised pension (assumed to be the same amount as in the preceding example) will now hinge on the returns on the accumulated assets. To assess the level of affordable replacement rates, the exercise assumes a constant real rate of return of 3.5 percent on accumulated assets. Panel b of Figure B6.1 illustrates the affordable replacement rates now and in 2095–2100, taking into account how demographic changes impact affordable benefits under fully funded systems.

Overall, as panel b shows, compared to the unfunded PAYG/DB, the level of affordable benefits is generally higher and the impact of aging is generally smaller for fully funded schemes (assuming a 3.5 percent return). Moving toward funding could help increase savings and also the capacity of

(continued on next page)

BOX 6.2. *(continued)*

countries to finance adequate benefits for future retirees for relatively low interest rates. Nevertheless, pensions might still need to be lower than currently promised benefits in some countries and/or parameters might need to be changed.

These exercises may overestimate the benefits of funding as they may not take into account the indirect impact of declining real returns on savings as the population ages. In simulations by Attanasio et al. (2015), the world's interest rate declines from 4 percent in 2010 to 1.5 percent by 2100. If this were the case, increasing funding would provide less benefit. On the flip side, if savings are well invested and thus generate higher productivity growth, then the benefits of funding pensions would be higher.

3. Some countries will benefit more from funding than others.
In relation to present time affordability, Panel b shows that for some countries with relatively young populations, including Belize and Guatemala, affordable replacement rates under fully funded arrangements are lower than under unfunded PAYG/DB. For other countries—for example, the Bahamas, Ecuador, Haiti, Mexico, Nicaragua, Panama, Paraguay, and Venezuela—funding helps to increase affordability, but by less than 20 percent vis-à-vis the affordability of the unfunded PAYG/DB. Finally, for countries with a more advanced demographic transition, such as Argentina, Brazil, and Uruguay, the benefits of funding in terms of increasing affordability are very large vis-à-vis the PAYG/DB systems. Nevertheless, it is important to consider that funding implies important transition costs, given that rights to retired workers must be preserved.

------

[a] This system has been replaced by a fully funded system, and therefore this extremely high level of benefits is transitory.

increasing contributions (for example through noncontributory pensions) might make it difficult to sustain the system in some countries. On the other hand, low coverage directs benefits to relatively high-income people (who tend to be the ones that are covered), resulting in high inequality.

Families face similar challenges. The way families take care of elderly relatives resembles a PAYG/DB system. The young take care of the old with their own resources, not in exchange for previous payments but because of family altruism. This arrangement will also be tested in the future. Smaller families will find it more difficult to take care of a greater number of elderly.

Saving for the Future

Saving for the future is a reasonable way to prepare for the demographic change, but it is not without problems. Putting resources aside, investing them, and using them when needed is a good strategy from the individual point of view. Intuitively, the more countries save, the less they will need of current transfers from the working generation. However, what may be optimal from the point of view of the individual may not be optimal in the context of global aging. Indeed, if a large proportion of the population saves during their active years and then sells those assets to the next generation (which will consist of fewer people because of the demographic transition) the prices of those assets will decline, and hence the ability of this up-and-coming group to finance its future will be at risk. One of the key findings in Attanasio et al. (2015) is that future returns on saving (i.e., interest rates) in an aging world will be lower. Indeed, a situation in which there is "too much saving" can lead to an inefficiently high level of capital (Diamond, 1965). However, this is definitely not the case in Latin America and the Caribbean in the present, where more saving is needed to finance productive investment (see Chapter 4). Even if interest rates decline in the future as the population ages, the affordable level of pension might still be higher for countries that built savings buffers (see Box 6.2).

A crucial point to understand is that there is no unique way of saving for the future. Countries that have chosen PAYG/DB pension systems can and should save by reforming the parameters of PAYG/DB systems (i.e., retirement age, contribution rates, and salary replacement rates) that threaten their sustainability. Setting aside resources, either public or private, while demographics still permit, to fund future pensions in preparation for the demographic transition is another way of saving.

Transitioning from PAYG/DB to fully funded defined-contribution systems with individual accounts is yet another way to increase saving. That was the route taken in many countries in the 1990s. However, this is not a magic solution. It must take into account the transition costs of meeting the obligations of past promises. As discussed in Chapter 7, these transition costs have proven to be very large for many countries.[6] In addition, mandatory contributions to individual accounts may not necessarily increase private saving if they displace saving through non-pension vehicles (Attanasio and Rohwedder, 2003; Attanasio and Brugiavini, 2003). In all, the evidence shows that for countries that switched from PAYG/DB to defined-contribution systems, the resources channeled to individual accounts were not fully offset by a decrease in non-pension saving, and thus aggregate saving increased (see Bebczuk [2015a] for a recent survey of the literature and new results). Even so, funding (saving) entails other problems related to risk sharing and pension adequacy that are present in defined-contribution systems. These issues are addressed in more detail in Chapter 7.

More—and Better—Savings to Enhance Growth

Not only does the region need more savings, but it also needs better savings. Being prepared for the future entails both an increase in savings, which will alleviate the burden on future generations, and an improvement in the efficiency with which those savings are used, which will boost productivity, and therefore the returns to those savings (see Chapter 10). Savings can help a society and individuals prepare for the future in at least two ways. First, savings that are channeled into productive investments with higher returns can help overcome the demographic transition. Of course, this requires well-functioning financial markets to intermediate savings (see Chapter 11). Second, if savings lead to higher aggregate productivity growth, they support whatever strategy a country has chosen to take care of the elderly. For example, if pension design entails benefits based on intergenerational promises (as PAYG/DB systems), higher productivity leading to larger output can help meet those promises, even as the share of dependents increases with population aging.[7] If, instead, accumulated assets back pensions (as in defined-contribution systems), a smaller cohort of workers with higher wages can support the demand for assets and mitigate a drop in rates of return. Any policy that promotes productivity growth can thus help alleviate the ill effects of an aging society (See Box 6.3).

How Is the Region Preparing for the Future?

Despite better macroeconomic management and pension reforms in recent decades, the region is ill prepared to confront the challenges of the demographic transition. Participation in formal pension plans is low; thus, so is pension coverage. Other forms of saving are not playing a significant role in providing income security for the elderly. And, given that families are shrinking in size, financing old age in this way will be difficult.

BOX 6.3. PRODUCTIVITY IN AN AGING WORLD

Predicting what will happen with the saving rate as societies age is a complex exercise. There are several forces at play. The most direct impact of demographic changes on overall saving rates is through the age structure of the population. Simply put, the working-age population is doing the saving in countries, while elderly people consume. When the balance shifts toward an aging society, aggregate savings decrease; this would be the first order direct impact.

However, as the demographic transition continues, other forces come into play. Smaller families mean fewer dependents to take care of, which frees up resources for saving. Moreover, as life expectancies increase, rational individuals will save more, as they foresee longer retirement periods.

Therefore, individual responses to changes in family size and life span (El Mekkaoui de Freitas and Oliveira Martins, 2014) could totally or partially offset the effect of the change in the age structure of the population (Heller, 1989).

Attanasio et al. (2015) build and simulate a model to understand the quantitative impact of these forces in a context in which demographic trends around the world are not synchronized and capital can flow across regions. Under a benchmark scenario in an open economy, the saving rate of Latin America and the Caribbean should increase in the next two decades. The effect of having more consumers than savers would be offset by an increase in savings associated with smaller families and stronger saving motives for retirement as life expectancy increases. After that, savings in Latin America and the Caribbean would decline gradually as longevity stabilizes and the first order effect takes over.

Models like this one help explain how different forces interact in the demographic transition and affect savings. For instance, in an exercise that isolates the impact of fertility, the model shows that the driving force for the decrease in future savings, under the benchmark scenario, is lower fertility. Indeed, if fertility is assumed to be constant instead of decreasing, then saving rates should be 6 percentage points higher than in the benchmark scenario by 2100. Essentially, more working-age people would generate more saving.

The model can also help explain how productivity growth can contribute to the saving rate. Total factor productivity (TFP) is what the economy is capable of producing beyond the use of labor and capital. Attanasio et al. (2015)

Pension Systems: Not an Option Today

Coverage of mandatory contributory pension system is low. Today only 45 percent of workers are contributing to a pension system, many of them irregularly. This share has been roughly constant over the last two decades (Figure 6.5). If the contribution patterns do not change

BOX 6.3. *(continued)*

Figure B6.2 **Saving Rates for Open Economy**

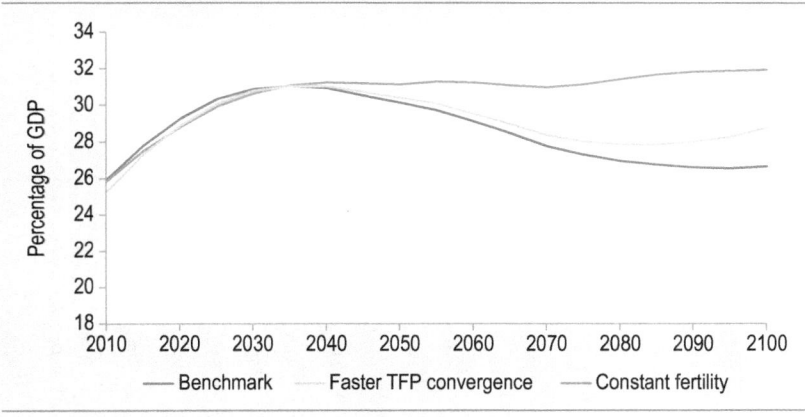

Source: Authors' calculations based on Attanasio et al. (2015).

model the benchmark scenario to assume that Latin America and the Caribbean converges to the productivity of more developed countries by 2150, with
a growth rate of 1.5 percent from then on. This implies that TFP grows by 1.41
percent per year from 2010 to 2150 in Latin America and the Caribbean to
achieve the same level and growth rate as high-income countries.

To assess the importance of productivity on savings and future growth,
the model explores a scenario of rapid convergence, in which it is assumed
that the TFP level and growth in Latin America and the Caribbean will reach
the levels of high-income countries by 2100, instead of 2150. TFP is assumed
to grow 1.51 percent annually from 2010 to 2100. In this case, an additional 0.1
percent of productivity growth from 2010 to 2100 can moderate the fall in
saving rates due to lower fertility by about one-third (2 percentage points).
Bearing in mind all the caveats of this stylized exercise, these results illustrate
that not only does the amount of saving matter to be able to cover the needs
of the future population, but also how countries invest those savings is important.

dramatically, coverage will be very limited for the next few generations
as well. Between 60 and 80 million people over 65 will not have contributed for a pension in 2050 (Bosch, Melguizo, and Pagés, 2013).

Coverage is not only low, but highly inequitable as well (Figure 6.6).
In virtually every country in the region, the poorest households are not,

Figure 6.5 **Share of Workers Contributing to Pensions, 1993–2013**
Population aged 15–64

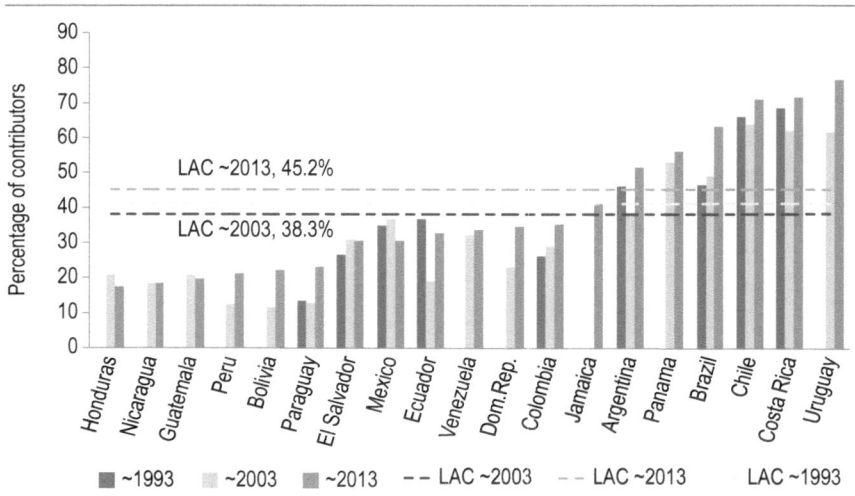

Source: Authors' calculations based on the IDB's Labor Markets and Social Security Indicators System database.
Note: Data circa 2013.

Figure 6.6 **Share of Workers Contributing to Pensions, by Daily Income, circa 2013**

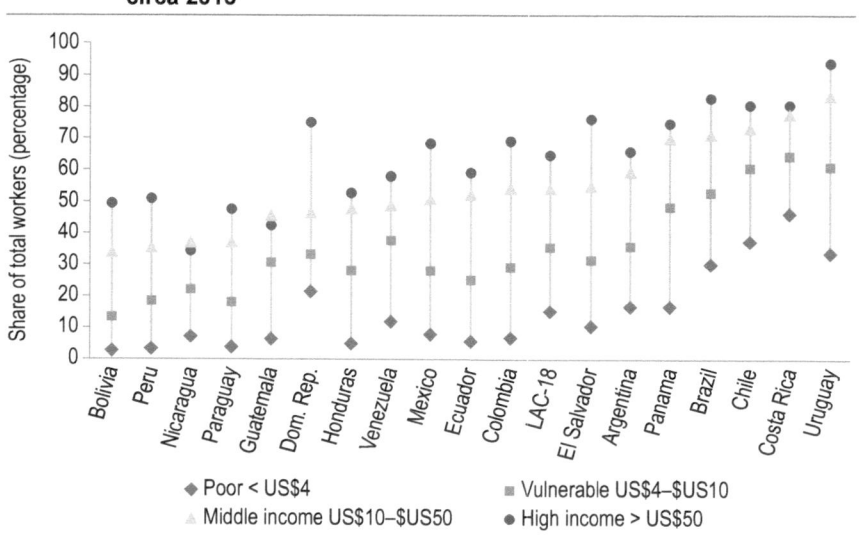

Source: Authors' calculations based on the IDB's Labor Markets and Social Security Indicators System database.
Note: Income classification as of 2005 in purchasing power parity (PPP) terms.

and will not be, covered by mandatory pension systems. On average, only 15 percent of the workers with incomes below US$4 a day in purchasing power parity terms (the standard moderate poverty line used in the region) contribute to pensions. Even the new emerging middle class is largely left out of pension coverage (Ferreira et al., 2013). On average, only 53 percent of all middle-income workers (defined as those earning between US$10 and US$50 a day in 2005 purchasing power parity terms) currently contribute to pensions.

Furthermore, many of those who contribute at a given moment in time will not become eligible for an adequate pension. Contribution densities (the share of active working life during which workers contribute to a pension system) are very low. In Chile, one of the countries with higher coverage, only 59 percent of men and 30 percent of women aged 25 to 60 have contribution densities over 50 percent (Berstein et al., 2006). In Mexico, El Salvador, and Peru, only between 20 to 30 percent of men and 10 to 20 percent of women contribute during more than 50 percent of their active lives (Bosch, Melguizo, and Pagés, 2013).

On the other hand, the pension rules that still exist in many pension systems remain relatively generous; this will generate a regressive redistribution of resources from low- to high-income households who are the ones that are covered (see Chapter 7). Furthermore, in some countries pension systems could become a source of fiscal deficits (public dissaving) that could threaten their sustainability.

Every country in the region faces the same challenges with varying degrees of intensity according to the country's pension system structure. Regardless of the pension arrangement (i.e., whether it be PAYG/DB or Defined Contributions), a common trait is low active coverage. This pattern suggests that coverage has little to do with the actual pension system and more to do with the overall functioning of labor markets.

Plan B: Household Savings in Other Assets

Households could be preparing themselves for the future in a different way. They could be bypassing mandatory pension systems (working informally), but compensating with savings in other assets. However, little household savings is occurring outside the pension system, particularly among lower-income households—precisely those most often on the margin of the pension system. Workers, and their families, who do not contribute to

Figure 6.7 **Share of Workers Who Report Savings in the Previous Year**

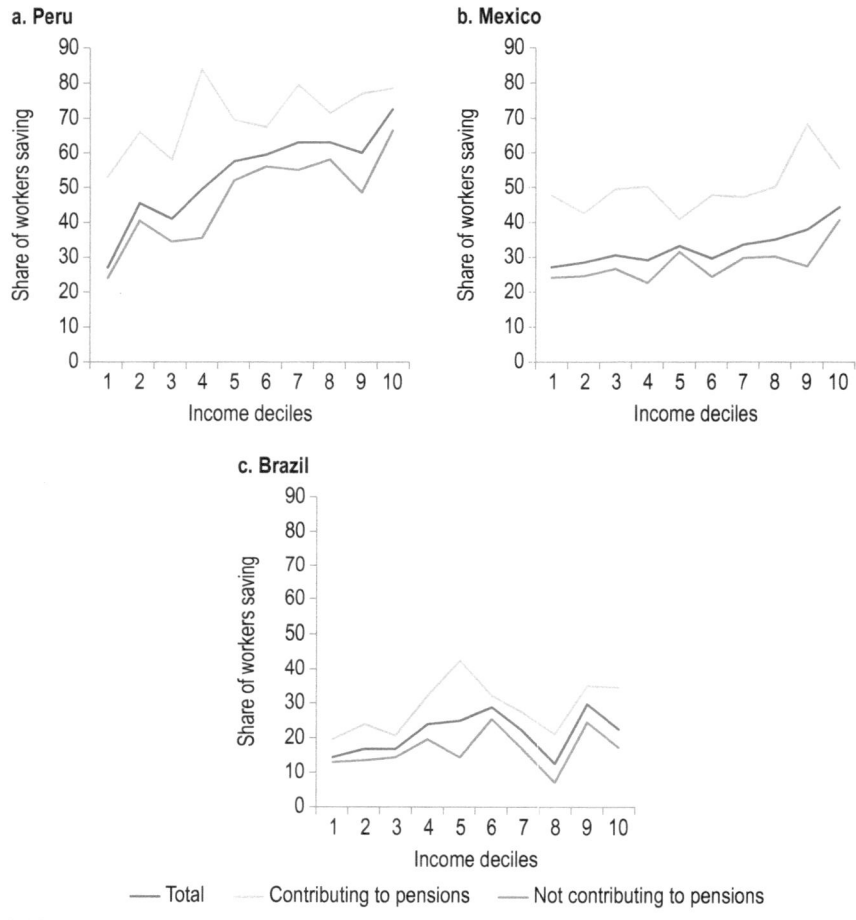

Source: Authors' calculations based on the Base of Pyramid (BoP) Survey.
Note: The survey excludes the richest 30 percent of the households in each country. The decile distribution maps the poorest 70 percent of the households.

pensions, do not save more than workers who contribute. On the contrary, surveys in Brazil, Mexico, and Peru show that informal workers (who do not contribute to pensions) save less at every income level (see Figure 6.7). Furthermore, not only do informal workers save less at every income level they largely do so through informal means (see Chapter 3).

These patterns are occurring during a generally favorable time to save in demographic terms. Since the society is still relatively young in Latin America and the Caribbean, savings should be high. However, saving rates do not always respond to movements in demographics. Asia is the only major region in the world to substantially increase savings during the demographic dividend (Cavallo, Sánchez, and Valenzuela, 2016). The decline in the dependency ratio can explain 22 percent of the saving increases between 1963 and 2012 in Asia, but only 3 percent in Latin America and the Caribbean during the same period.

Why doesn't Latin America and the Caribbean seem to be taking advantage of good demographics to increase saving? There are multiple reasons. Despite the last decade of growth, the region is still relatively poor and unequal. Many individuals and families cannot cover basic needs. A relatively large segment of the population earns too little to accumulate substantial savings in general, much less for a potential retirement, be it through formal pension contributions or through non-pension instruments. According to social protection surveys in Mexico and Peru (IDB, 2008), approximately 30 percent of those who do not contribute give insufficient income as the main reason (see Figure 6.8). This situation could explain the high correlation between a country's per capita income and the percentage of formal workers (Loayza, Oviedo, and Servén, 2005) as well as the relationship between an individual's income level and the probability that he or she will save for retirement (see Figure 6.6). It could also explain why the demographic dividend has had little effect on saving patterns in the region.

Figure 6.8 **Why Don't Workers Contribute to Pensions?**

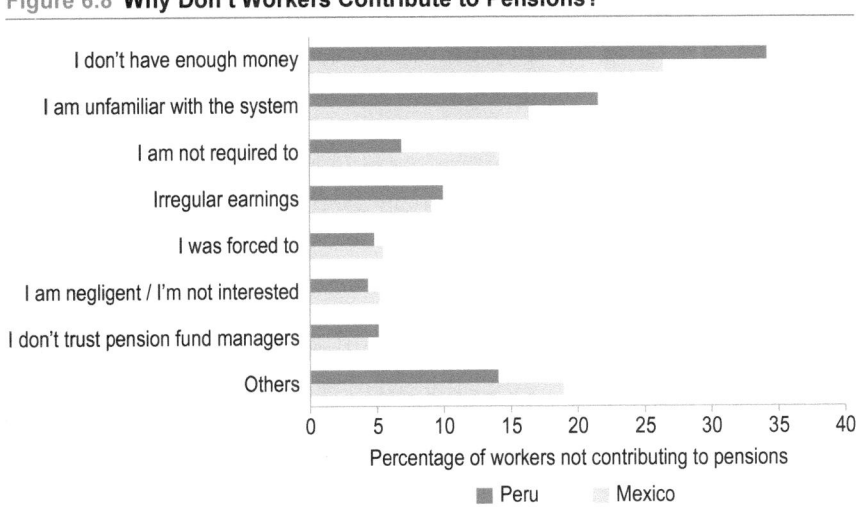

Source: Authors' calculations based on the Social Protection Survey in Mexico City and Metropolitan Lima, Peru (IDB, 2008).

While for low-income workers saving for retirement may not be feasible, it is less clear why the middle class in Latin America and the Caribbean is not saving enough. Income restriction should be less of an issue. However, all potential savers confront several barriers to generating savings for retirement outside mandatory pension systems. Chapter 9 explores two likely explanations. The first is a general lack of trust in the financial system and low effective returns to financial savings. Second, proactive savings behavior (particularly long-term savings) may be undermined by behavioral biases, including present bias, discount factors, myopia, agency problems within the household, and pure irrationality.[8] Given these limitations, relying on saving outside a mandatory pension system almost guarantees that resources to finance pensions will be insufficient.

The Last Resort: Taking Care of Grandma

Many Latin American and Caribbean citizens who do not contribute to mandatory pension systems hope they will be able to support themselves by remaining in the labor market. Labor income is an important source of income in old age, at least between ages 60 and 80 (Figure 6.9). A large majority of informal workers in the region rely on working until a very advanced age (Bosch, Melguizo, and Pagés, 2013). However, labor supply patterns in the region suggest that very few people are willing or able to work past 80. Only 17 percent of men and 6 percent of women are working by the time they turn 80. Unless labor support patterns change dramatically, labor income will not be a reliable source of funding for old age.

The other source of support for the elderly outside pension systems is the family. Families have traditionally been the most reliable safety net for the elderly.[9] In 2013, around 57 percent of adults 65 and older were living with working-age family members (not including spouses). However, families are unlikely to be a reliable source of support as aging continues. The average woman in 1950 in Latin America and the Caribbean had six children. In 2015, the average woman had just enough children to maintain the population level (around 2.1). The implications of this dramatic shift are just emerging. From 2000 to 2013, household surveys reveal that the average size of households shared by adults 65 and older and working-age population decreased by 9 percent (from 4.4 to 4 members), mimicking an overall trend of smaller households

Figure 6.9 **Sources of Income in Old Age**

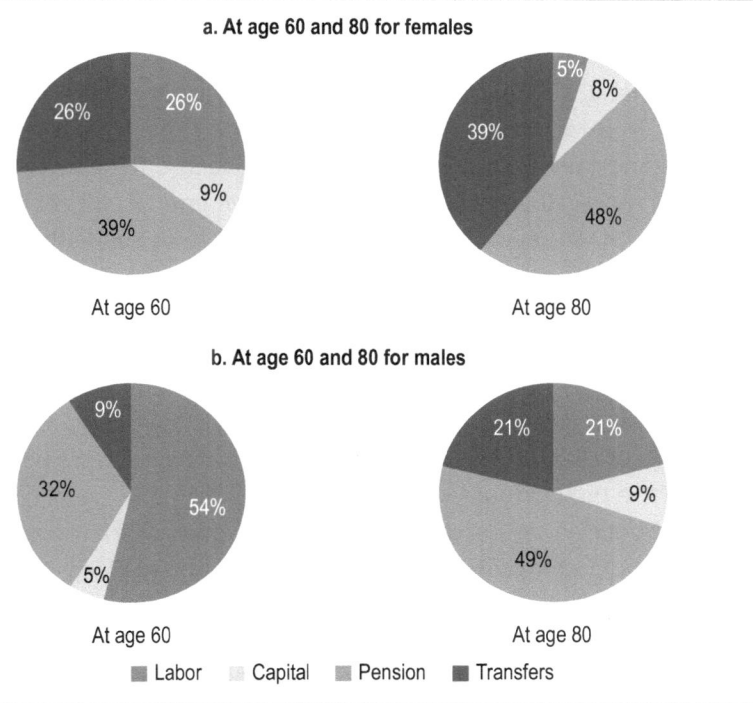

Source: Authors' elaboration based on Saad (2011).

in the region. In just 13 years, the average household in Latin America and the Caribbean decreased by 12 percent (from 4.9 to 4.3 members). Several demographic, cultural, and economic trends may be behind this decline, but one thing is certain; families are getting smaller. Maintaining the elderly will be more difficult without rapid economic growth. Smaller families will have fewer descendants to take care of elderly parents. Meanwhile, parents have children at a later age. Thus, working-age parents may have to take care of their children, parents, and grandparents. Women, who are traditionally the main caregivers of the elderly, will likely suffer the most from these changes in family structure.

Act Today, for a Better Tomorrow

Aging is a reality that countries will have to face in the future, but the future is approaching rapidly. Longer lives are certainly good news; however, longer lives will not be better lives if there is no appropriate financing. Latin American and Caribbean countries, like all regions around the world, will have to face this challenge.

The dramatic transformation in the age profile in the region and the changes that it will bring are difficult for both citizens and policymakers to grasp. In principle, individuals could predict the changes in demographics and take the appropriate steps to secure their future income by saving more. However, people do not save enough for retirement in the region. Many must contend with immediate needs. Others do not foresee their future needs or think they will be able to work until a very advanced age. Indeed, this is the main reason pension systems around the world have compulsory social arrangements. However, compulsory arrangements by and large have failed to prepare the countries of the region for the demographic change. While policymakers clearly recognize the challenge, the problem seems too far away and beyond the scope of the typical four-year mandate.

What policies can secure the necessary resources for the aging population without compromising other competing needs? Saving more for the future could play a central role, but only if it addresses the fundamental challenges of an aged society. Saving per se will not necessarily secure the funds needed to take care of large numbers of elderly in the future. A large generation followed by a small one implies that savings might have lower returns and higher volatility. Savings not only need to be higher, they must be mobilized in a way that enhances productivity and generates economic growth. This is the only way that countries will be able to afford the ever-increasing costs of an aging society.

Although the window of opportunity is closing on the demographic dividend, Latin America and the Caribbean has significant room to grow in the coming years. Well-designed pension systems that are better prepared to cope with aging will be crucial to meeting this challenge. How to reform these systems to increase coverage in sustainable ways while at the same time dealing with an aging population will be covered in the next chapter.

Increasing savings and funding the pension systems now could boost the economy and prepare for the graying of the region. The current age composition in the region supports these steps. Seizing this opportunity in Latin America and the Caribbean in the decades to come will be vital to secure the region's future.

Notes

[1] The demographic dividend is defined by the United Nations Population Fund (UNFPA) as "the economic growth potential that can result
from shifts in a population's age structure, mainly when the share of
the working-age population (15 to 64) is larger than the non-working-
age share of the population (14 and younger, and 65 and older)."

[2] For a global perspective of the aging phenomenon, see Lee and
Mason (2011b).

[3] Between 1993 and 2013, around 60 percent of the GDP per capita
growth in the region was due to increases in employment because of
population growth, while the other 40 percent was due to increases in
output per worker (Alaimo et al., 2015).

[4] FADL include activities such as walking, eating, dressing, and toilet-
ing. IADL include activities such as shopping, answering the phone,
preparing food, housekeeping, and the ability to handle finances.

[5] This analogy and the text in section draws on Barr (2002) and Barr
and Diamond (2009).

[6] Something that is not observable is the path that countries that
switched from PAYG/DB to fully funded private accounts might have
followed if they continued unreformed. In this sense, systems with
escalating costs and potential pressures to increase benefits or relax
access to benefits could have ended up with large deficits and consequently important dissaving.

[7] However, it is important to understand how those "pension" promises
are made (see Chapter 7).

[8] For evidence of insufficient savings for retirement in the United Kingdom, see Banks, Blundell, and Tanner (1998).

[9] For a discussion of how transfers across generations may act as a substitute for savings in the absence of well-functioning private annuity
markets, see Kotlikoff and Spivak (1981) and Kotlikoff (1988).

7 Saving for the Future: Pension Systems

Pension systems in Latin America and the Caribbean are broken. To begin with, they cover less than half the population. Moreover, flaws in structure and financing make some of them unsustainable, even for this limited beneficiary population. The approaching end of the demographic dividend only magnifies these problems. Since pensions are the main vehicle through which households save for retirement, the pension crisis is effectively a saving crisis.

As populations in Latin America and the Caribbean age, many countries face a steep road ahead to provide economic security for a growing number of retired adults. The design and performance of pension systems will be crucial to ensure that enough resources are provided to the elderly, without compromising growth and the prospects of future generations.

Policymakers around the world are struggling with this trade-off between generations. Latin America and the Caribbean faces particular challenges, ranging from high inequality, low coverage, and lack of pension adequacy (Bosch, Melguizo, and Pagés, 2013) to fiscal sustainability (Gill, Packard, and Yermo, 2005).

Preparing Latin American and Caribbean countries will require not only more and better savings, but also important changes in the way individuals and countries think about work life and retirement. This will not be easy. Pension systems are deeply embedded in the architecture of the welfare state and even the constitutional design of some countries. There are intense ideological divides as to which system best provides pensions, how to finance them, how much risk individuals should assume, and how much income redistribution to lower-income people is needed within and across generations.

Unfortunately, in most Latin American and Caribbean countries, systems are not ready to face the demographic transition and need to be thoroughly rethought to ensure that the great majority of elderly have an adequate pension in the future without compromising other development objectives. When it comes to saving for the future, pensions are at the center of the debate.

Newer Systems for Older Populations

Over the past three decades, reforms have led to a variety of pension systems in the region. Most countries in the region have a defined-benefit system, usually PAYG (only some partially funded). Nine countries have defined-contribution systems, which usually coexist with some defined-benefit pillar. Despite these reforms, one thing is clear: contributory pension systems will not provide income security to most Latin American and Caribbean citizens in their old age. Only 45 percent of workers in the region contribute to a pension system, many of them irregularly (see Chapter 6). This is particularly true among the self-employed, low-income workers, young workers, and women. Therefore, coverage through these systems is and will remain limited without further reforms.

How benefits are determined and financed seems to have little impact on the participation of workers in the system. Regardless of the type of system, social security coverage is low (Bosch, Melguizo, and Pagés, 2013). Low coverage is rooted in the fact that most systems were designed to cover only salaried employees, leaving the self-employed outside the system. Moreover, many firms do not register their employees. Preparing pension systems for the future will require expanding coverage. However, other challenges need to be addressed as well—some of them before extending coverage. These range from building up savings to ensure the systems' long-term sustainability to improving public information about pensions and how they work. Some issues will be more acute under one pension system than another, and countries will have to respond differently, depending on how pensions are determined and financed. Consequently, the characteristics of the system will matter.

PAYG/Defined-Benefit Systems: Promises, Promises

All pension systems in the world were initially designed as defined-benefit systems—either partially funded or fully unfunded, pay-as-you-go schemes (referred to here as PAYG/DB). This has important implications for national savings. From the perspective of workers, this arrangement looks very much like savings. The government takes part of their salary (around 15 percent, on average, in the region), and puts it away, preventing the worker from using those resources for consumption. However, that money is immediately spent to pay for current pensions, so governments are not saving in a pure PAYG system. Moreover, workers are not saving at all; they are just buying the promise of a future pension.

PAYG/DB systems generally offer contributors some positive features. They provide insurance against changes in returns (the pension does not depend on the return of any specific asset), and against longevity (the pension provides an annuity until the end of the beneficiary's life). In a solvent PAYG/DB system, the return to the "saving" implied by participation in the system is the same as the growth rate of the wage bill.

Two additional characteristics of these systems are particularly important and determine most of the challenges they will face in the future. First, for their long-term sustainability, they depend dramatically on the ratio of contributors to pensioners (as pensions are financed with current contributions). Thus, in an aging world, the parameters that determine benefits in PAYG systems must be changed periodically and sustainability must be monitored. Unfortunately, few systems do this, which partially transfers these risks back to individuals at some point. Second, there is substantial implicit redistribution within the system, since the benefit rules do not perfectly match contributions with benefits. Understanding this redistribution is crucial to evaluating the performance of these systems. For instance, since longevity is largely linked to wealth, any pension system could be considered regressive, as relatively rich individuals enjoy longer lives (National Academies of Sciences, Engineering, and Medicine, 2015). In Latin America and the Caribbean the effect is magnified because high-income workers are most likely to qualify for the generous rules offered by DB pension systems. Main challenges for PAYG/DB systems include aspects related to sustainability, adequacy, and redistribution, as well as institutional arrangements.

Sustainability

The region spends a lot on pensions, despite low coverage and a relatively young population (see Box 7.1). Although measuring pension spending is not as easy and transparent as it should be, the orders of

BOX 7.1. HOW MUCH IS SPENT ON PENSIONS TODAY?

This chapter reports several measures of pension spending. Methodology and coverage vary across studies. As can be seen in Figure B7.1, although there is some disparity among sources, the orders of magnitude are clear. High-coverage countries like Argentina, Brazil, and Uruguay spend more than 6 percent of GDP on pensions, while Central American countries with relatively young populations and low coverage spend between 1 and 2 percent of GDP.

Pension spending may very well be the largest single expenditure line in the budgets of many governments around the world. On average, it represents 18 percent of government expenditure in OECD countries (OECD, 2015a).

It is remarkably difficult to figure out how much many Latin American and Caribbean countries spend on pensions. It is even more difficult to predict how much these countries will have to spend on pensions in the future. This report draws on primary data (administrative records and government

Figure B7.1 **Pension Expenditure as a Share of GDP**

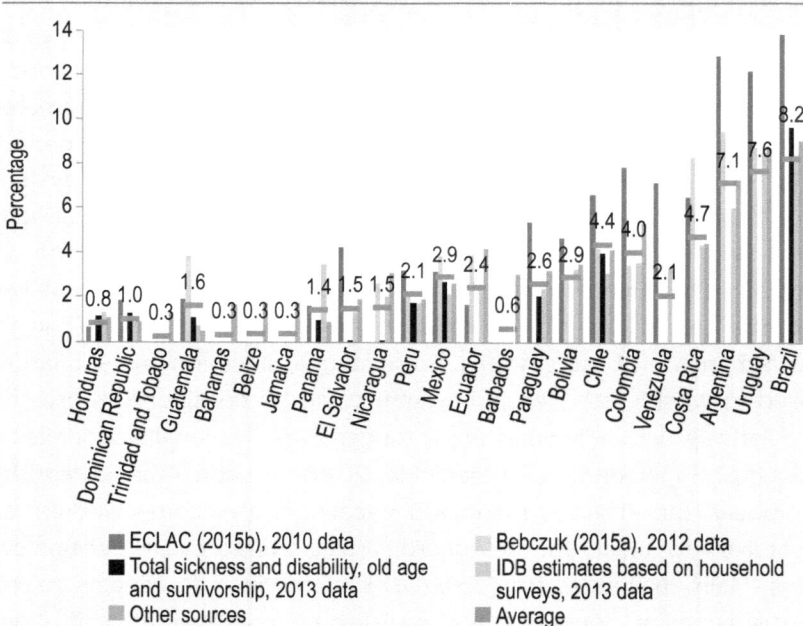

Source: Authors' elaboration based on ECLAC (2015b); Bebczuk (2015a); IDB's fiscal database; household surveys; and other sources, including fiscal sector and country economists of the Inter-American Development Bank and Lustig, Pessino, and Scott (2014). Specific country sources include, for Argentina, Lustig and Pessino (2013); for Bolivia, Paz Arauco et al. (2014); for Brazil, Higgins and Pereira (2014); for Chile, Ruiz-Tagle and Contreras (2014); for Colombia, Meléndez (2014); for Costa Rica, Sauma and Trejos (2014); for Ecuador, Llerena Pinto et al. (2015); for El Salvador, Beneke, Lustig, and Oliva (2015); for Guatemala, Cabrera, Lustig, and Morán (2015); for Mexico, Scott (2014); for Peru, Jaramillo (2014); for Uruguay, Bucheli and others (2014).

(continued on next page)

BOX 7.1. *(continued)*

budgets) and secondary data (household surveys) to grasp the fiscal burden countries face in meeting their pension commitments.

Why is it so difficult to obtain reliable information on the amount countries in the region spend on pensions? First, pension regimes within countries are often quite fragmented. Some countries have different regimes for public and private employees. Some countries have occupational regimes for teachers, the military, and public servants. Peru has 14 different pension regimes. Large federal countries like Brazil and Mexico not only have public federal systems, but also systems for state public employees, and even (in the case of Brazil) municipal governments. Second, data are not centralized in most countries. The labor histories of many workers are still recorded with paper-based systems or are undocumented. Contributors often must provide documents or witnesses to certify the contributions they have made during their entire active working age. Third and more importantly, few countries have an accountability mandate that forces them to make spending on pensions more transparent and easier to scrutinize. Few legal and institutional settings systematically require countries to publish information on pension spending in a centralized manner, accounting for all the special regimes and subnational governments. It is even rarer to find information about the actuarial long-term financial situation of pension funds. This type of calculation requires information that might not be available or sufficiently well organized.

magnitude of pension spending in the region are on par with, if not greater than, pension spending in high-spending, advanced European countries such as France, Greece, Italy, and Spain.

Argentina and Uruguay, which have relatively high coverage (and a relatively older population by Latin American and Caribbean standards), spend about the same as France, Greece, Italy, and Spain, and spend significantly more than low-spending OECD countries such as Canada, the United Kingdom, and the United States (Figure 7.1). Because current demographics vary widely (Figure 7.1, panel a), these levels are perhaps better illustrated by comparing what OECD countries were spending when their demographics resembled those of Argentina and Uruguay (Figure 7.1, panel b). Back in 1980 (the earliest year for which comparable data on pension spending are available), France and Italy had similar demographics to Uruguay today and were spending slightly more than Uruguay is spending today. Similarly, Argentina's demographics and spending resembled Spain's in 1980, and pension expenditures were almost identical.[1]

Figure 7.1   **Pension Spending and Aging in Select Latin American and Caribbean and OECD Countries, 2011–13**

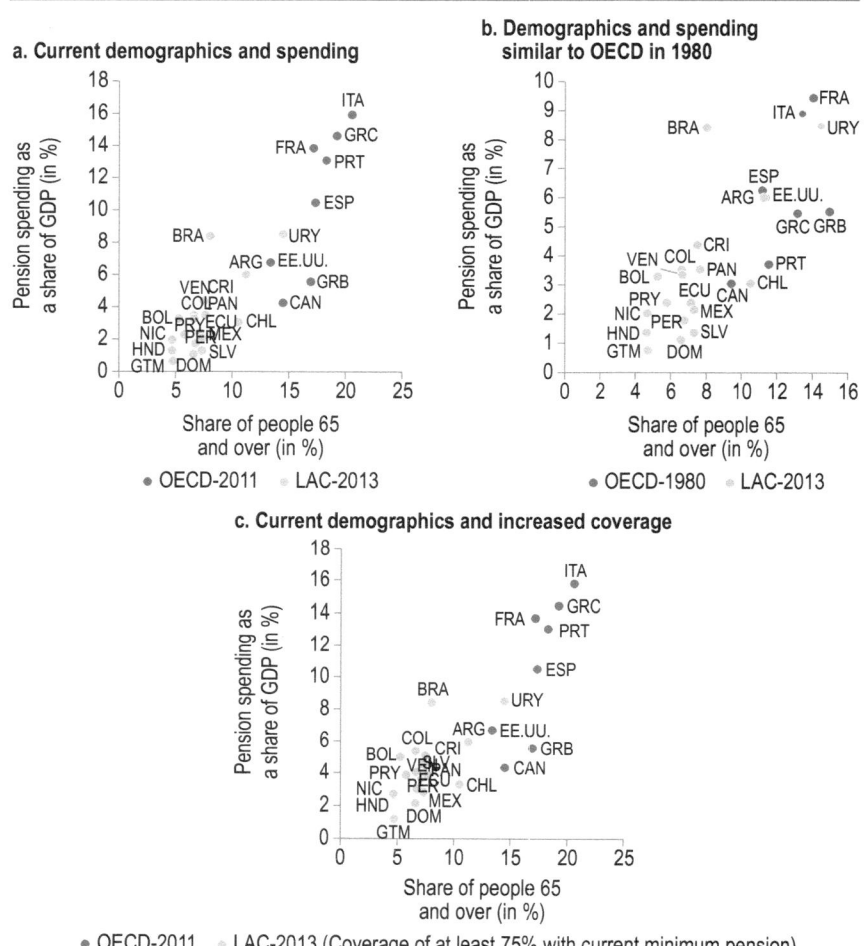

Source: Authors' calculations based on the IDB's Labor Markets and Social Security System Indicators database, OECD (2014b), CELADE (2015), and United Nations (2015).
Note: Pension spending in Latin America and the Caribbean is calculated by multiplying average pensions by the share of pension recipients using household surveys.

Brazil deserves special mention. In 2015, some 8 percent of its population was aged 65 and over. Yet its spending on pensions was similar to what France and Italy were spending in the 1980s, and they were much older at that time (with 14 percent of the population 65 and older). Estimates by Clements et al. (2011) suggest that, if unreformed, Brazil will be spending 16 percent of GDP on pensions in 2050.[2]

Pension spending is lower in most other countries in the region, thanks more to lack of coverage than adequate sustainability. Most countries spend between 1.5 and 4 percent of GDP on pensions. If countries enjoyed relatively higher coverage, the fiscal picture would look very different. A simple simulation in which countries achieve 75 percent coverage providing the minimum mandated pension to those who do not have a pension today, would significantly elevate costs and put many countries on the spending level of countries like Canada, the United Kingdom, and the United States, (low-spending OECD countries) with much younger populations (Figure 7.1, panel c).

This spending is not backed up by contributions and, in some cases, such large expenditures go to a very small portion of the elderly population. Despite the relative youth of countries, some PAYG/DB systems cannot cover pension spending with contributions and must fund them with additional government revenue (Figure 7.2). Pension imbalances in Argentina and Brazil already absorb more than 1 percent of GDP. Countries that reformed their systems partially or totally like Colombia, El Salvador, or the Dominican Republic during the 1980s and 1990s face significant deficits during their transition periods.

Figure 7.2 Difference between Contributions and Benefits in Select PAYG/DB Systems

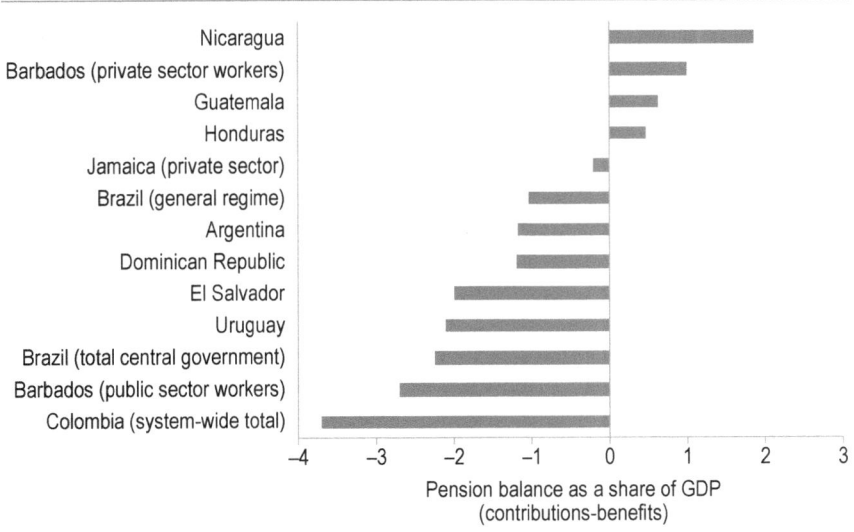

Source: Authors' calculations; Colombia (Bosch et al., 2015), Barbados public sector workers (Eckler, 2014), Brazil, Uruguay, Dominican Republic, Honduras, Guatemala (IDB's fiscal database), for Brazil general regime (Ministry of Social Security, Brazil), Jamaica private sector (Hall, 2014).

BOX 7.2. MANDATORY INDEPENDENT ACTUARIAL REVIEWS

Long-term commitments of PAYG/DB plans should be followed closely; thus sustainability should be adequately monitored. Given the impact of demographic changes on liabilities, actuarial studies are required. This type of assessment considers the parameters of the model, projections of contributions and pension payments, and the evolution of any reserves. In terms of contributions, the number of workers depends significantly on the number of working-age people in the future, labor market participation, and wage growth. In terms of pension payments, a critical variable is the number of people who retire and how long they will live. Projections also depend on future rates of return for any reserves.

While these studies are very important, technical robust analysis is not always possible because of lack of information. One very important piece of information is life expectancy, with projections of mortality for the long term. Many countries use life expectancy tables based on other countries, like Chile or the United States. Another important source of information needed to project the growth of the system is the history of contributions, which is not always complete.

In Jamaica, an actuarial analysis is required by law every five years. The last actuarial study was finished in March 2013. The National Insurance Scheme in Jamaica is a PAYG/DB system that is partially funded. According to the 2013 study, reserves in the base scenario will be depleted by 2033. The study proposes specific measures to extend sustainability. The government is considering alternatives to proactively improve the system's long-term financial stance.

In Barbados, an actuarial analysis is required every three years. This review has helped bring about adjustments in the parameters of the pension system. For instance, in 2002, to address medium-term sustainability problems, contribution rates were increased to 20 percent of wages and the retirement age was increased to 67 by 2018 (it is currently 66). Despite these reforms, the 2008 actuarial review projects that contributions will be sufficient to cover all expenditures only up to 2022, and that the fund will be completely depleted by 2068.

In Caribbean countries like Barbados and Jamaica, the public PAYG/DB pension systems for private sector workers are more in balance, but actuarial reviews (see Box 7.2) point to upcoming deficits that will require substantial reforms. Public sector schemes in Barbados, although already reformed, still absorb almost 3 percentage points of GDP directly from general revenues. Other relatively younger countries with very low coverage, such as Honduras and Nicaragua, still pay out less to beneficiaries than what they collect in their mandatory pension systems.

These pension imbalances also illustrate a critical characteristic of PAYG/DB systems: the parameters that are supposed to balance contributions and benefits adjust very slowly to changes in demographics. In principle, minor imbalances in PAYG/DB systems could be fixed by fine-tuning parameters such as retirement ages or contribution rates. However, changing these parameters tends to be very unpopular and is rarely done unless a fiscal crisis is imminent, or they can be made very slowly.

Without reforms, these imbalances of PAYG systems will worsen in the decades to come, increasing fiscal pressure, drawing down future government resources (dissaving), and shrinking resources available for other important areas like education or infrastructure. Not only are these systems an inadequate saving mechanism for individuals, the pressure they place on government finances compromises public saving as well. The countries that switched to defined contribution systems will eventually reduce their deficits, but in the short term these imbalances are exacerbated and budget pressures will persist for many decades.[3]

Adequacy and Redistribution

Some of the sustainability problems stem from the generosity of benefits for those covered by the system. In general, in Latin America and the Caribbean the rules determining pensions in the PAYG/DB systems are very generous compared even to richer countries, especially for workers who have contributed for many years. This does not necessarily mean that pensions are high for all retirees.

The generosity of the system is determined by how much a beneficiary (and a beneficiary's dependents) will receive compared to how much they contributed. These two seemingly easy concepts are not easy to quantify and are influenced by parameters such as retirement age, contribution rates, the benefit rule, the survivors benefit, and other less-obvious factors such as wage growth or the interest rate assumed (see Berstein, Bosch, and Oliveri, 2016). Around one-half of the average pension in PAYG/DB systems in the region is not financed by contributions and will have to be subsidized by the government if parameters of the system remain unchanged. In some countries, up to 75 percent of the pension is subsidized. This subsidy must be financed by general revenues.

However, most of the generous benefits implicit in PAYG/DB systems are currently accrued by higher-income pensioners. This is a direct consequence of the inequality in coverage. Perversely, benefit rules, combined with low coverage, sometimes result in redistribution from low-income workers to high-income workers. If rules stipulate that retirees who did not contribute a minimum number of years (vesting period) are not entitled to a pension, in many cases workers who did not contribute or contributed to the system for just a few years do not receive a pension benefit (Berstein and Puente, 2015). For instance, in Colombia's PAYG/DB pillar, around 65 percent of workers that have contributed to pensions will not qualify for a pension (Bosch et al., 2015). Thus, their contributions are paying for, or "subsidizing," benefits that will flow to high-income workers. Some 80 percent of all subsidies in Colombia's PAYG system flow to the richest 20 percent (Lasso, 2006).

Institutional Arrangements

Despite the large amount of public resources that PAYG/DB systems require, transparency and sustainability monitoring are limited. For some countries it is difficult to know exactly how much is being spent on pensions, because of the multiplicity of systems and subnational levels. Furthermore, lack of data or the inability to process it, makes it difficult for many countries to foresee or estimate future liabilities. Very few countries have a clear protocol to undertake sustainability monitoring or the capability to implement it. This, in turn, impairs the policy debate and hampers efforts to fashion an agenda for reform. Some countries are taking advantage of sustainability monitoring and are making progress in implementing parametric reforms to their systems; at the same time, they are raising public awareness by communicating the financial stance of pension systems.

Transparency and governance are relatively weak in the region. Souto and Musalem (2012) developed a Transparency and Governance Index (TGI) for National Public Pension Funds and ranked 83 countries, including 14 Latin American and Caribbean countries.[4] No country in the region was in the top 10; the highest-ranked countries were Mexico and Costa Rica, with 22 out of 33 points. Weak governance is an important issue, as it can impair the investment performance of pension funds (Yang and Mitchell, 2008; Hess, 2005). Policymakers always face short-term demands; strong institutions must be able to withstand such pressure and prepare societies for the eventuality of increasing longevity.

Recommendations

Lack of coverage is the main challenge faced by pension systems. This will increase pressure to relax access to benefits (Bosch and Oliveri, 2015) or establish noncontributory pensions (discussed later in this chapter) to alleviate poverty in old age. Under this scenario, increasing coverage while monitoring the sustainability of PAYG/DB systems would become even more critical.

Three general principles guide possible reforms:

- *Rethink fundamental parameters to adapt to the demographic change.*
  To deal with the demographic transition, PAYG/DB systems need to adjust their fundamental parameters. How and when will be a matter of preference and political will, but inevitably these reforms will have to address benefit rules, retirement ages, and contribution rates. Systems that adjust sooner rather than later could distribute the impact of longevity in a more equitable way across generations. Given high levels of labor informality, raising contribution rates does not seem as viable an option as in developed countries. Automatic adjustments to demographic changes (for instance, indexation of retirement to longevity every five years) are preferable to swift reforms. A number of OECD countries, including Spain, have followed this path. Others have established a so-called Notional Defined Contribution arrangement, in which benefits depend on the entire working life, interest rates, and longevity, as in the case of Italy (OECD, 2014).
- *Build reserves whenever possible.*
  Public, defined benefit systems can save for the future (fund the system). Actuarial studies need to determine the level of assets required to assure that future liabilities would be covered. Regulators of defined benefit systems usually require minimum levels of funding, which in some cases is 100 percent, as in the Netherlands (IOPS, 2012). Building reserves imposes a challenge in terms of how they are invested. Accumulated savings should be aimed at increasing growth and productivity. Adequate regulation, sound investment policies, and good governance are needed to pursue long-term objectives. Appropriate management of assets and liabilities should be the main

driver of decisions. Countries like Norway (Government Pension Fund) and Chile (Pension Reserves Fund) created special funds to finance their PAYG systems. Adequate governance is crucial for such arrangements.

- *Improve information and increase public awareness.*
  Reforms will be better informed and implemented if information is available and the consequences of action or inaction are explicit. Improving data collection and dissemination, periodic independent actuarial analysis, continuous policy debate, public awareness campaigns, and transparency are requisites to implement reforms.

Defined Contribution Systems: A Work in Progress

Faced with the fiscal imbalances of the PAYG/DB systems, many countries switched to defined contribution systems pioneered by Chile in 1981 and followed by eight other countries in the 1990s (World Bank, 1994). In contrast to the PAYG/DB systems, in fully funded defined contribution (FF/DC) systems, workers' contributions are saved in an account and invested. Unlike PAYG/DB systems, these are real savings that are invested. Nevertheless, as mentioned earlier, transition from one system to another risks exacerbating some preexisting imbalances for a long period of time.

With the transition to DC systems, some challenges remained while new ones emerged. First, coverage did not improve. In the transition to DC systems, the hope was that coverage rates would increase. These expectations did not materialize, in large part because nothing intrinsically changed in the labor market (the cause of low coverage). The main challenge for FF/DC remains increasing coverage.

A second significant challenge for FF/DC systems relates to the provision of longevity insurance. In a DC arrangement the retiree can withdraw all funds at once, schedule withdrawals for the retirement period, or purchase an annuity. The only way the retiree is insured against outliving his savings (one of the main objectives of pension systems) is by purchasing an annuity, something that less than half of pensioners in these systems are doing today.

Third, a crucial challenge for these systems is to assure efficiency in terms of returns and costs, which in many cases depends on competition among providers. Given the lack of knowledge and engagement by participants, competition among providers does not necessarily resolve the problem.

A number of countries that launched defined contribution systems in the 1990s have returned to the PAYG/DB systems, both within and beyond the region (Holzmann, 2013). Fiscal challenges in some countries that were phasing in transition costs paved the way for these reversals. Defined contribution systems were advertised to people as a means of receiving higher pensions with lower contribution rates. The fact that people were not receiving benefits in line with their expectations also eroded support for continuing the reforms.

Still other important pending issues include financing the cost of transition; encouraging better investments, increasing returns, and lowering operation costs; enhancing the offer of retirement products and insurance arrangements; building financial literacy, legitimacy, and confidence; and appropriate regulation and supervision.

Transition Costs

While the 1990s reforms will be helpful in the long-term sustainability of countries, they entail large transition costs that could last for decades. The short-term fiscal situation is particularly worrisome for these countries. In transitioning to a defined contribution system with individual accounts, these countries lost all or a significant part of contributions to the old PAYG/DB system, while still facing significant pension outlays. Chile, Colombia, the Dominican Republic, and El Salvador still dedicate between 1 and 4 percentage points of GDP to pay for the system in transition. In particular Chile, which reformed its PAYG system more than 30 years ago, is still spending three percentage points of GDP per year on this transition. An actuarial assessment of possible transition costs should be part of any reform effort.

Investments, Returns, and Costs

Pensions in defined contribution systems depend on investment returns and management cost. A 1 percent return over 40 years translates into a 20 percent increase in pension payments. Therefore, the quality of investments is critical because of the direct impact of returns on pension financing (Davis, 2002). There is also an indirect impact through the effect that institutional investors, such as pension funds, can have on economic performance. This positive impact would depend not only on *how much* of these pension funds are invested, but also on *how* these resources are invested.

Thus, investment regulation and pension fund supervision are important and have an impact on the performance of managers. Indeed, pension funds could be an essential source of long-term financing that could enhance countries' productivity. Since pension fund investment needs to be well protected and oriented to financing future pensions, structuring financial products that would enhance development in the region could be a winning strategy (see Chapter 4).

On the other hand, funds could be invested in government bonds to finance current government spending and would thus have little impact on aggregate savings and growth promotion. On average, almost 50 percent of pension funds in the region are invested in government bonds; this level is as high as 80 percent in countries like El Salvador (Figure 7.3). Investment restrictions might affect the efficiency of investment and lower returns for a given risk level. Restrictions on variable income and foreign investment during the first years of the 1980s reform in Chile suppressed pension fund earnings by 10 percent, compared to a scenario with no restrictions (Berstein and Chumacero, 2006). There is certainly a role for regulation in aligning the incentives of pension fund

Figure 7.3 Investment Portfolio of Private Funds

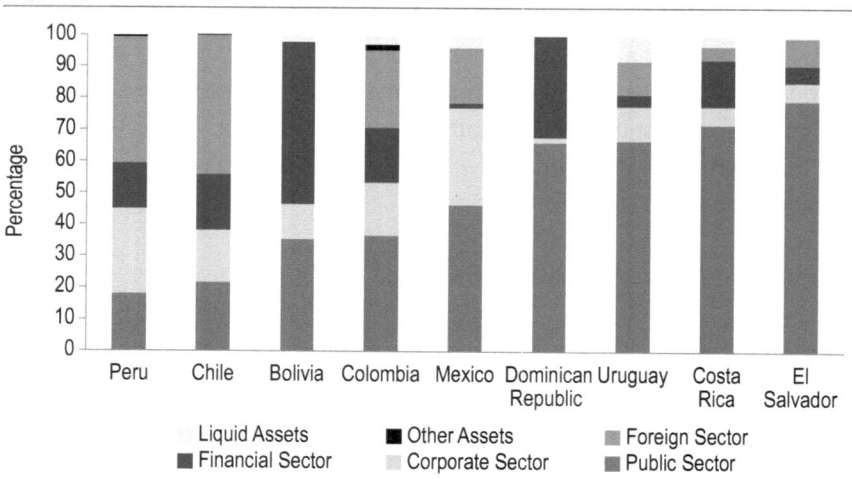

Source: Authors' calculations based on Federación Internacional de Administradoras de Fondos de Pensiones (FIAP) statistics (FIAP, 2015).

managers with the long-term objectives of pension funds; however, regulators must consider the cost embedded in any restrictions.

Even though the pension portfolios of most Latin American and Caribbean countries with FF/DC pension systems are not well diversified, rates of return have been high compared to other regions. However, volatility has also been high, especially during the past few years (Figure 7.4). Real returns from 2004 to 2014 were positive, on average, despite significant losses during and following the 2008 crisis. Peru had the highest real return (8.51 percent), and Bolivia had the lowest (1.81 percent), followed closely by El Salvador (1.83 percent). The unweighted average for these nine countries was close to 5 percent. Among OECD countries, Chile and Mexico are above the average with the seventh and ninth highest real rate of return from 2004 to 2014 (OECD, 2015c). Colombia and the Dominican Republic exceeded all OECD countries.

As pension funds increase and represent a significant share of GDP, investments must be further diversified. As strict quantitative investment restrictions are relaxed, it will become more important to adopt a "prudent person" approach for regulation, implementing best practices in terms of corporate governance, so that the responsibilities in making investment decisions would be adequately defined and decision-making processes established and supported (OECD, 2009). Moreover, the potentially

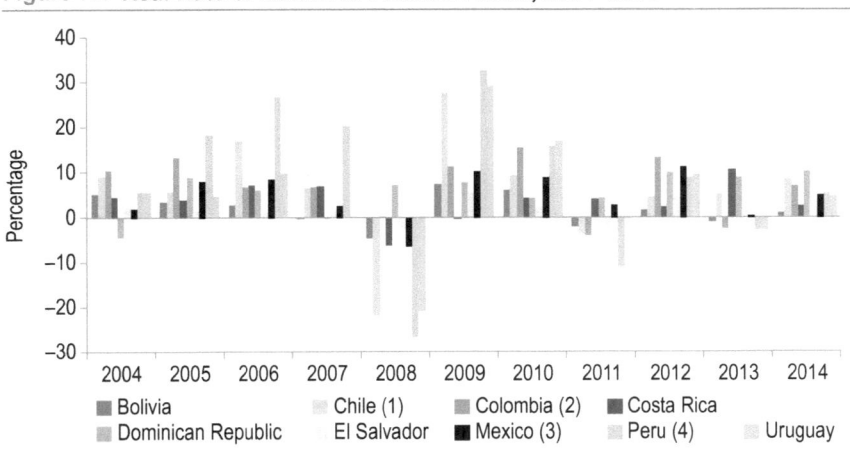

Figure 7.4 **Real Rate of Return of Pension Funds, 2004–2014**

Source: Authors' calculations based on Federación Internacional de Administradoras de Fondos de Pensiones (FIAP, 2015).
Notes: (1) For Chile, Fund C. (2) For Colombia, Moderate Fund. (3) For Mexico, Weighted Average of SB1, SB2, SB3 and SB4. (4) For Peru, Balanced Fund.

significant volatility in pension fund portfolios, which may pay off in terms of returns, might affect contributors who are close to retirement. Different funds with a life cycle approach to investments could provide better protection for future retirees (Berstein, Fuentes, and Villatoro, 2013). This strategy has been followed by Chile, Colombia, Mexico, and Peru.

Management costs could also absorb significant resources. Thus, increasing efficiency could be important. Different pension arrangements have different types and amounts of costs. Under privately managed pension systems, some measure of the costs is possible, but even in this case, costs are difficult to compare across countries. Differences include the terms of the services provided by each country, the fee structure, the explicit and implicit charges, and pension system maturities.

Despite these considerations, Ionescu and Robles (2014) calculate charge ratios—the percentage paid in fees over the working life, at the end of a 20- or 40-year period—for 37 countries. Overall, charges are significant in all Latin American and Caribbean countries, averaging 18 percent for the region.[5] Nevertheless, the average charge ratios for countries outside the region is higher: 23 percent, for a 40-year horizon. Costs are relevant, but they vary significantly across countries. Given the impact of costs on pensions, an effort should be made to promote efficiency.

Various countries in the region have tried to increase competition and reduce costs. Chile and Peru have successfully incorporated a bidding process that assigns workers that enter the labor market to the lower fee pension fund manager. In Chile, the three bidding processes have brought the average charge ratio down almost 30 percent, from 16.4 percent in 2009 to 11.6 percent as of December 2015. Other countries, including Colombia, Costa Rica, the Dominican Republic, and El Salvador, have adopted fee ceilings. In these countries the amount effectively charged by managers is equivalent to or very close to the cap. Setting caps at an appropriate level is difficult for regulators since it limits competition and can end up being too high or too low.

Retirement Products and Insurance Arrangements

Despite relatively high average returns, one of the main problems of DC systems is that they are not providing actual pensions for a large number of workers. Part of the explanation resides in the very low savings of many workers who move in and out of the labor market and cannot make any contributions for long periods (see Chapter 6). If these workers are not entitled to a minimum pension or other subsidy, they must take their savings as a lump sum, as do 82 percent of the workers who reach retirement age in Colombia (Bosch et al., 2015), or in monthly installments until their funding is exhausted, as in Chile.

Even where savings for a pension are sufficient, FF/DC pension systems generally offer a choice at retirement between a phased withdrawal and an annuity. Thus, in effect, many pensioners do not have longevity insurance (Bodie, 1990).[6] For those that can choose a pension product, only 60 percent of the pensioners in Peru, 51 percent in Chile, and 11 percent in Colombia are insured against longevity risk (Berstein, Morales, and Puente, 2015). For phased withdrawal products offered in DC systems in the region, the pension is computed as self-insurance; the amount withdrawn is expected to last for the rest of the retiree's life. Eventually, if savings are not sufficient, and if the person lives longer than expected, or returns are lower than assumed, the person might end up depleting all of her savings before passing away. By contrast, annuities are insurance products that pool idiosyncratic risk. The amount of the pension is fixed for life; beneficiaries receive a certain amount independent of how long they live or how interest rates fluctuate, or even how inflation varies in some cases. An insurance company covers these risks for a premium (Milevsky, 2013).

In spite of these desirable properties of annuities, they present important challenges across the world. In general, annuity markets are small and annuities are expensive. Asymmetric information can lead to high costs, which in turn implies that only high-risk individuals would buy the product and boost the costs even higher (Finkelstein and Poterba, 2004). PAYG/DB schemes avoid this problem because the entity promoting the plan assumes the longevity risk. Nonetheless, in systems with full compulsory annuitization, incentives to contribute could be lower since contributors are less likely to get back what they contributed during their working life (Milevsky, 2015). Partial or deferred annuitization could attain the goal of longevity insurance in a more effective way (OECD, 2012; Berstein, Morales, and Puente, 2015).

Another feature that distinguishes FF/DC systems is that a contributor will always receive the actuarial accumulated balance as a pension or a lump sum, if the balance is too small. This differs from PAYG/DB systems, in which a person who contributed for few periods, or did not comply with other requirements, does not receive a benefit, or receives only a refund of the amount contributed adjusted for inflation.

A drawback of these lump sum payments is that they do not provide for longevity insurance, but can seem attractive because they seem large compared to the lifetime pension payment. Even if the pension implies a significant subsidy (because of the minimum pension guarantees in some DC schemes), some people are willing to choose a lump sum.[7]

Increased longevity will affect DC systems, particularly the level of pensions and how they are financed. Increased life expectancy is certainly good news, but it has significantly reduced a main source of pension financing in the past: mortality credits, which are the unspent funds when someone passes away. The probability of reaching the retirement age—which continues to be 60 in many countries—is more than 90 percent or higher in many countries. Thus, most people will require a retirement benefit and receive payment for more years than in the early 1930s. After age 80 or 85, the likelihood of living one more year declines and continues to decline at a rapid pace as the person ages (See Box 7.3). Therefore, for ages beyond this threshold, risk pooling continues to be an important source of financing for benefits, as it was for ages 60 and over in the 1930s. Therefore, savings are required to finance a very likely retirement event, and at that stage, having insurance for the very long term becomes valuable. Taking advantage of old age mortality credits could

BOX 7.3. FINANCING PENSIONS: MORTALITY CREDITS

In the early 1930s, when retirement programs such as the U.S. social security system were launched, the probability of reaching 60 years old, the normal retirement age in many countries at that time, was extremely low. Life expectancy at birth in European countries was around 60 years old, and it was significantly lower in Latin America and the Caribbean. Therefore, when pension systems started around the world, the schemes resembled an insurance product. Every worker paid an insurance premium during his or her working life. In the unlikely event that he or she reached the retirement age, the benefit would substitute for the labor income she had paid into the system until she passed away. The average retirement period for the few that reached the retirement age of 60 was 13 or 14 years. Thus, contributions paid by numerous workers could finance pensions for a small number of retirees. An important source of funds was mortality credits: contributions paid by members who died before they could collect all that they had paid into the system. This is what usually happens with insurance. The insurer will cover a risk, but the insurer does not end up paying a benefit to everyone who paid a premium. This is the essence of risk-pooling arrangements, and it is an efficient way of covering a risk.

(continued on next page)

BOX 7.3. *(continued)*

Figure B7.2 **Sources of Funding for a Life Annuity in Chile for Retirees Aged 65–105**

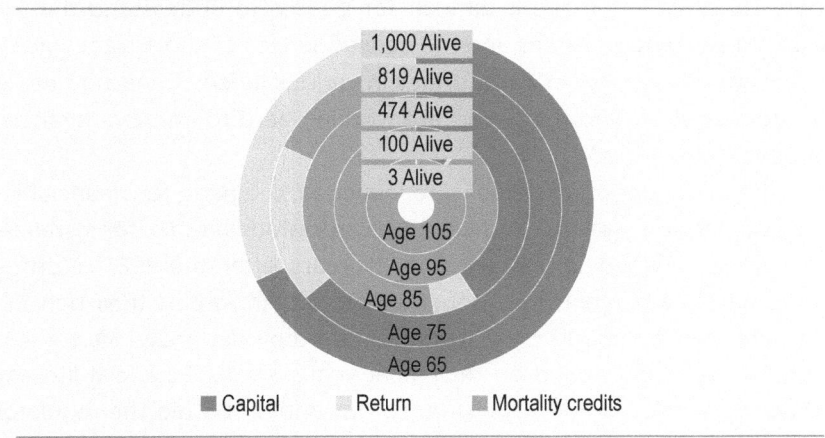

1,000 Alive
819 Alive
474 Alive
100 Alive
3 Alive

Age 105
Age 95
Age 85
Age 75
Age 65

■ Capital   Return   ■ Mortality credits

Source: Authors' calculations.

Mortality credits are a source of financing pensions, given the decreasing probability of living as a person ages. Those who survive longer benefit from the resources of those who passed away. This is basically risk pooling and taking advantage of the unknown event of who will survive longer. Figure B7.2 shows an annuity payment in Chile that starts at age 65, and the associated sources of financing over time. Mortality credits became the most significant source after age 85. In this example, the mortality credits from the 1,000 people alive at age 65 would finance the pensions of the 3 of them who survive to age 105 at the same level as they received at age 65, because they are using the resources of the ones who did not survive.

still be an important source of financing pensions, mainly at advanced old age. This is the insurance component, at least for the very old.

In all, for DC systems increased longevity will imply that a larger share of the pension will have to be financed through savings (accumulation and returns) rather than through mortality credits. If the contribution rate and retirement age remain unchanged, pensions will be lower.

Financial Literacy, Legitimacy, and Confidence

A lack of financial knowledge in the region is hurting confidence in pension systems. In general, people do not expect to live as long as projected by life expectancies, and therefore do not necessarily foresee the need for sufficient savings. In addition, many people in the region believe that the state should ultimately be responsible for funding pensions. These beliefs make it difficult for people to understand the full costs of providing pensions and the consequences of short-term volatility on returns. Supervisory authorities in various jurisdictions, not just in the region but around the world, are working hard to improve financial literacy (see IOPS, 2011).

When DC pension systems were launched, the need for financial literacy on pensions was not sufficiently appreciated. In Chile, for instance, a survey conducted in 2002—some 21 years after the 1981 reform—found that 78.4 percent of respondents did not know how their pension was determined. Among those who claimed they did know, 34 percent thought that it depended on their final year's salary. Financial literacy did not vary much among age groups. Not until 2005 did the regulator require pension fund managers to send pension projections to members, so that they would be better informed and take timely action to improve their pensions. Even in 2009, almost 30 years after the reform, the Social Protection survey showed that most workers did not know how much they contributed to their pensions. Almost 75 percent of those with primary education and 50 percent with higher education did not know the pension contribution rates. Of those who said they knew, fewer than 10 percent in any educational level gave the correct answer for the contribution rate.

Efforts have been made to promote financial knowledge in Chile, Costa Rica, the Dominican Republic, and Mexico, among other countries. In Chile, shortly after fund managers began sending saving projections, individuals began saving more (see Fajnzylber, Plaza, and Reyes, 2009; Miranda Pinto, 2013). Mexico has established a five-year (2013–18) Financial and Pensions Education Strategy. The pension regulator in Mexico—Comisión Nacional del Sistema de Ahorro para el Retiro (CONSAR)—redesigned the periodic statement of pension balances to make it easier to understand, launched a new Web site and, as in Chile, started issuing individualized pension projections. Costa Rica and the Dominican Republic are taking similar steps.

The lack of public understanding and contributor involvement prevents competition from playing the role it should to promote market discipline. Many contributors are not sensitive to differences in prices or returns between pension fund managers, which could have a huge impact on their return. Indeed, most people do not even know how much they are charged. In Chile, the first private system in the region, 93 percent of members in 2002 were not aware of the fee charged.[8] Under this scenario, sales agents play a critical role. Berstein and Cabrita (2007) found that workers do not switch on their own to lower-cost managers but do so if advised by a sales agent. This imposes additional overhead in this industry.

Appropriate Regulation and Supervision

In an FF/DC system, individuals' decisions have an impact on their final pension. Good decision making requires adequate information and tools, but also regulation that mitigates risks. Since these systems are managed by the private sector, one of the main roles of the government is to build confidence in the system through adequate regulation and supervision to mitigate excessive risk taking.

In systems where individuals can choose their own investments, the alternatives from which workers can choose might imply that significant risks could be taken. For instance, Chile has five different funds. In the riskiest fund, Fund A, up to 80 percent can be invested in equity; in the most conservative fund, Fund E, up to 5 percent can be invested in equity. There are three funds between these extremes (Funds B, C, and D) that gradually reduce exposure to equity with age from 60 percent to 20 percent, following a life cycle approach as a default strategy. These act as default choices. Fund A is not available to workers who are close to retirement, and Funds A and B are not allowed once participants have retired. However, there are no restrictions on switching between funds; therefore, contributors close to retirement might switch from Fund E to B, back and forth, as they try to stop shortfalls and maximize return; this could also increase their risk just when they cannot afford losses.

Colombia, Mexico, and Peru also offer a choice of funds, but with fewer alternatives and more restrictions on switching. Each country has a different default. Which is the proper default? How many alternatives should be offered? How much freedom should be given to individuals? These are all issues that FF/DC systems need to address.

Whatever the regulatory setup, supervision needs to be efficient and effective. A risk-based supervisory approach allows resources to be allocated effectively, prevents problems that would impact beneficiaries, and proactively improves the performance of the pension industry. Supervisors from different jurisdictions in OECD and non-OECD countries have agreed to ten principles to guide the proper supervision of pension funds. These are common to different pension systems and apply to both private and public systems (IOPS, 2010).

Recommendations

Moving from PAYG/DB to FF/DC does not necessarily increase either coverage or savings. In Latin America and the Caribbean, insufficient coverage remains a huge issue. Additional measures need to be taken to afford aging in the long run. Some general recommendations to enhance FF/DC schemes follow.

- *Find ways to increase returns and reduce administrative costs.*
  Regulation needs to be dynamic and consider reforms to capital markets that allow pension funds to be invested in ways that boost growth in the country. Enhanced corporate governance to assure solid investment decisions is also important; this might strengthen the overall financial sector. As pension systems mature, investment abroad offers countries an alternative to achieve appropriate diversification. Countries in the region have tried to control costs; the impact of these efforts must be assessed, and further innovations may be required.
- *Rethink parameters and retirement products.*
  As people live longer, the level of pensions will decrease if the retirement age remains fixed. Hence, either retirement savings or retirement ages should be raised. Parametric reforms are also needed to insure the adequacy of pensions. Retirement products must be consistent with the main goal of a pension system, which is to provide income security during retirement. In some cases, the contributory and noncontributory pillars may need to be combined to deliver sustainable protection. For contributors who have saved enough, lump sums and phased withdrawals do not provide long-term longevity protection and do not take advantage of mortality credits as a source of financing. Therefore, annuity markets need to be developed and other longevity insurance arrangements could be explored to combine savings and insurance to support old age effectively.
- *Provide sound information and financial education for participants.*

Information and education are important tools for workers to manage their future pensions. Pension fund managers should advise contributors during their working life, while they have time and opportunity to add to and improve the returns on their retirement savings. Managers must act in the best interest of their customers and communicate with them on a timely basis.

- *Enhance regulation and supervision to mitigate risks and promote adequate pensions.*
  Regulation and supervision should be enhanced and constantly reviewed. Regulation should address the alternatives and choices available in FF/DC systems. Proper defaults should be put in place for those pension fund participants who do not want or do not have the knowledge to make decisions. The default strategy for investment that considers a life cycle with less risk exposure as the worker ages has shown to be appropriate (Berstein, Fuentes, and Villatoro, 2013). Defaults might also consider a specific retirement product at the time of retirement or other decisions that must be taken during a member's lifetime.

  Pension supervisory authorities should be guided by the Principles on Private Pension Supervision (IOPS, 2010). Best practices need to be considered and implemented. It is critical to prevent events that might damage confidence in pension systems. Unfortunately, issues are bound to arise, so supervisors must have the power to take proper action when needed, including levying sanctions on pension fund managers.

- *Promote voluntary savings.*
  The way systems are designed can significantly affect results. Automatic enrollment has been shown to be effective in New Zealand, the United Kingdom, and the United States. These mechanisms could help workers contribute less during periods when money is very tight. Many African countries are using mobile phone technology to facilitate voluntary contributions. Aspects of these experiences may be applicable to Latin America and the Caribbean.

When All Else Fails: Noncontributory Pensions

Reforming current mandatory pension systems will not be enough. Greater participation in pension systems is imperative to prepare for the demographic transition. However, if coverage is to be adequate, noncontributory pensions may inevitably be part of the answer. They must be carefully designed so as not to threaten the sustainability of benefits.

Why do so few people in the region contribute to pension systems? The consensus points to a combination of at least four factors.[9] First, jobs are not productive enough to pay for the entire package of formal benefits (which must cover not only pensions, but also health care, regulations, firing costs, and the like). Second, workers do not value pension contributions and try to avoid them. Third, firms try to avoid paying contributions since enforcement is lax. Fourth, a significant share of workers in the region are self-employed (around one-third of the labor force in the region, and as much as 70 percent in some countries); for the self-employed, pension contributions are either voluntary or unenforceable.[10]

In response to the failure of contributory pension systems to provide adequate coverage, so-called noncontributory pensions have become increasingly popular. This type of pension is not based on contributions but on eligibility criteria such as age, income, or area of residence. It is financed mostly by general taxation (although some countries like Colombia finance these pensions through solidarity contributions).

Noncontributory pensions are equivalent to a PAYG/DB system without direct contributions from the beneficiary. Thus, they will also be subject to the pressures of the demographic transition and the fiscal sustainability considerations discussed in previous sections.

This type of arrangement is not new. Most advanced countries provide some kind of pension assistance to alleviate poverty in old age, regardless of whether people contribute to the system. In the region, their importance is growing as they have become the main tool to expand coverage in the last two decades. Today, noncontributory pensions account for one-third of pension coverage in the region. In several countries, more people receive noncontributory pensions than contributory pensions (Figure 7.5).

Perhaps the most important challenge is how to finance these pensions without generating larger distortions in mandatory contribution systems. Currently, the design and extension of these systems vary considerably in the region. Some countries, such as Bolivia, have chosen universal programs. Others have set up relatively modest means-tested programs targeted at the very poor. The generosity of benefits also

Figure 7.5 **Contributory and Noncontributory Coverage in 19 Latin American and Caribbean Countries, circa 2013**

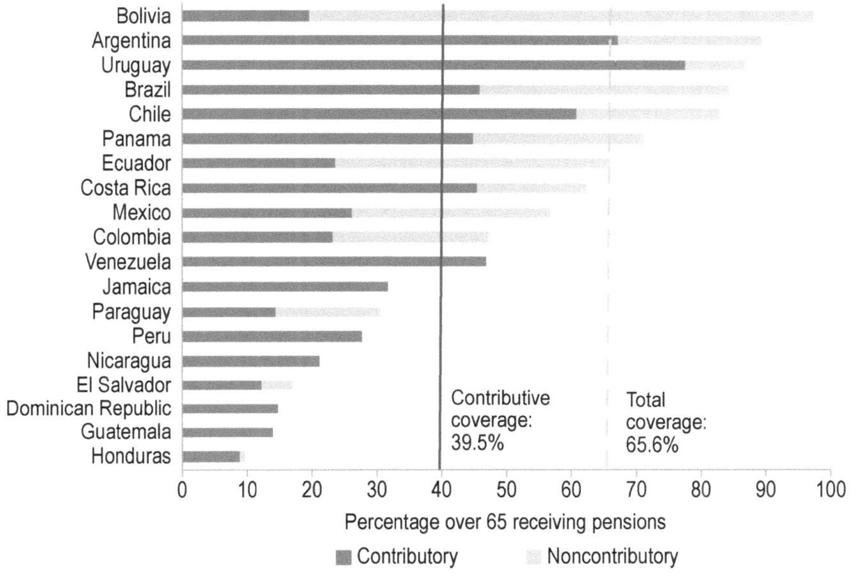

Contributive coverage: 39.5%

Total coverage: 65.6%

Percentage over 65 receiving pensions

■ Contributory   ▨ Noncontributory

Source: Authors' calculations based on the IDB's Labor Markets and Social Security Indicators database.
Note: The division between contributory and noncontributory pensions in Argentina, Brazil, and Uruguay was obtained by dividing the number of beneficiaries of these programs by the number of adults over 65. This could be an imperfect measure in countries where the beneficiary can begin drawing a pension at a younger age.

varies significantly, ranging from very low (between 5 percent and 7 percent of income per capita) in Colombia, Mexico, Panama, and Peru to generous programs (around 30 percent of income per capita) in Argentina, Brazil, Paraguay, and Trinidad and Tobago.

The choice of design will be crucial to insure coverage and fiscal sustainability. Today, the noncontributory pensions with the highest coverage cost between 0.7 percent and 1 percent of GDP. This cost will more than double by 2050 if generosity and coverage remain constant, just to account for changes in demographics. If programs were to provide benefits to adults aged 60+ at the average level of the region (17 percent of income per capita, which is just above the poverty line pension in many countries) the cost by 2050 would be between 2 percent and 3 percent of GDP (Figure 7.6). These pensions are absolutely necessary to increase coverage. But in an aging world, they will absorb ever more precious resources. Countries must rethink ways of financing them.

Figure 7.6 Current and Future Fiscal Costs of Noncontributory Pensions in Latin America and the Caribbean, 2015–50

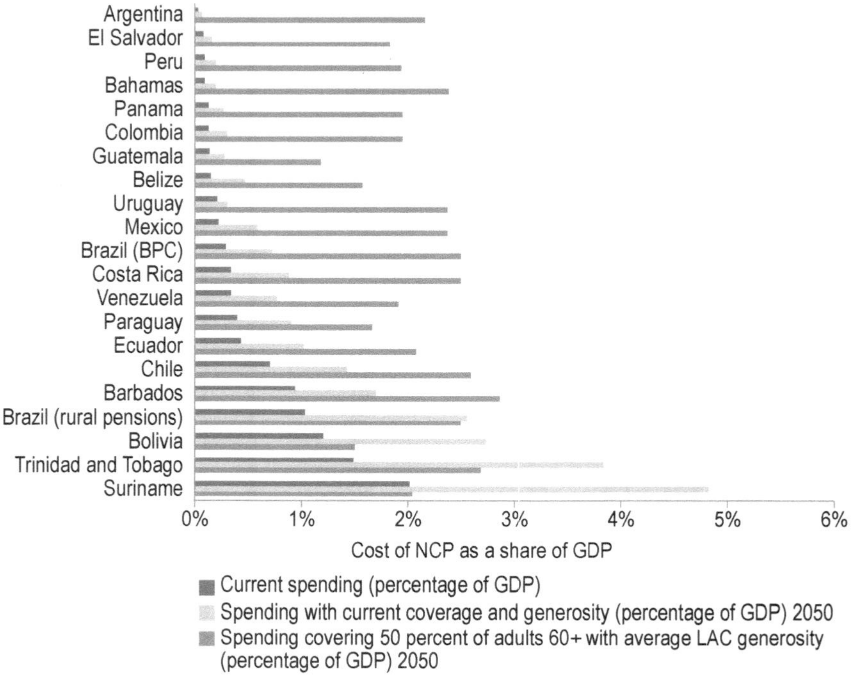
Argentina
El Salvador
Peru
Bahamas
Panama
Colombia
Guatemala
Belize
Uruguay
Mexico
Brazil (BPC)
Costa Rica
Venezuela
Paraguay
Ecuador
Chile
Barbados
Brazil (rural pensions)
Bolivia
Trinidad and Tobago
Suriname
0%
1%
2%
3%
4%
5%
6%
Cost of NCP as a share of GDP
Current spending (percentage of GDP)
Spending with current coverage and generosity (percentage of GDP) 2050
Spending covering 50 percent of adults 60+ with average LAC generosity (percentage of GDP) 2050

Source: Authors' elaboration based on HelpAge International (2015) and authors' calculations.

It is also important to take into account the possible effects of noncontributory pensions on incentives to save. Household decisions are changing with the arrival of noncontributory pensions. The emergence of these pensions has yielded some very relevant insights into how individuals and households react to changes in benefits (see Box 7.4). Noncontributory pensions decrease the participation rates of beneficiaries in contributory systems and, in some cases, their savings. They also reduce the transfers that beneficiary households receive from other households. Juárez (2009) finds that for every peso the government allocates to an elderly adult in Mexico City, private transfers drop by 87 cents.

Recommendations

Increasing participation in mandatory pension systems will require an integrated approach that addresses the many causes of labor informality.

BOX 7.4. HOUSEHOLD SAVING AND NONCONTRIBUTORY PENSIONS

In the last decade, the most radical reform in the world of pensions in Latin America has been a relatively silent one. Noncontributory pension programs (NCPs) now provide coverage to more than 25 percent of the elderly. These programs have greatly improved the well-being of elderly adults in some cases (Galiani, Gertler, and Bando, 2014). However, there is concern that providing NCP might reduce the need for precautionary savings, and thus alter incentives to work longer or contribute to pensions, even as they induce increases in consumption and alter saving decisions, very much like minimum pensions (Jiménez-Martín, 2014). By now, there is ample evidence that NCP facilitate retirement in the region (Bosch, Melguizo, and Pagés, 2013) but in some instances, contributions to the mandatory system have declined (Bosch and Oliveri, 2015).

The impact of NCP on savings is much less studied and the evidence is mixed. In Argentina and Mexico, beneficiaries of NCP saved less (between 3 and 4 percent) after noncontributory pensions were expanded (González-Rozada and Ruffo, 2015). However, in Bolivia, some specific population groups (i.e. men versus women) increased household savings (Hernani-Limarino and Mena, 2015). In Mexico, no significant effect was found when federal and state noncontributory pension programs were considered (Alonso, Amuedo-Dorante, and Juárez, 2015).

However, increasing coverage without addressing the issues described in previous sections could worsen problems of adequacy, redistribution, and sustainability.

Noncontributory pensions will be an essential tool to prevent old-age poverty and redistribute resources to the most needy in the region. They are necessary to increase coverage and reduce inequities in the pension system. However, they are not the solution in the face of demographic change, particularly if they are aimed at something more than poverty reduction (Holzmann and Hinz, 2005). The design and implementation of noncontributory pensions can be improved in three basic areas: institutions, incentives, and financing.

- *Institutions*
  Build appropriate institutions and fully integrate them into the pension system. In some cases, this would require rethinking the institutions that manage the delivery of funds and monitor the fiscal sustainability of the systems, as well as adjusting the generosity of benefits and the eligibility age to address poverty alleviation and make them fiscally sustainable.

- *Incentives*
  Contributory and noncontributory pensions should serve a common purpose and interaction between them should be explicitly considered, mainly in terms of incentives. Competition between them should be avoided, for instance by allowing noncontributory pensions to be combined with contributory benefits so that they complement each other. Conditioning the eligibility of noncontributory pensions only on those who do not have contributory pensions is likely to generate further distortions in the pension system.
- *Financing*
  Appropriate ways to finance the system must be found. Noncontributory pensions are largely financed through general taxation. As expenses grow in the future, additional sources of funding will be needed.

Pensions Count

The pension deficit is essentially a savings deficit—already. Pension coverage is too low, households are not saving enough for retirement, and some of those who are already retired are not receiving adequate pensions. As the region advances in its demographic transition, the situation is bound to become worse. Substantial reforms are needed and must be informed by a thorough reflection on the key objectives of pension systems and how to better finance them. Countries with PAYG/DB systems need to build up saving funds (accumulating excess contributions) while the number of retirees is still low compared to the working-age population, and put in place the mechanisms to adapt to the demographic transition. Sometimes, this will imply tough decisions about retirement conditions. In countries that have switched—or are planning to switch—to fully funded, defined-contribution systems based on individual accounts, a number of remaining issues put into doubt the ability of these systems to provide adequate pensions. Insuring participants against risks, increasing returns, and improving confidence in these systems are all paramount. Of course, coverage is and will be one of the key concerns in all systems. The importance of pension systems will only increase in an aging world. Proper design, implemented in a timely fashion, could make the difference.

Increasing pension saving is a necessary step to resolve the region's saving deficit, but it is not enough. As the population greys, it will be necessary to defy demographic forces and increase returns to be able to provide more with less. With pensions, as with other forms of saving, the region needs more *and* better saving. In the case of pensions, "better" means that the accumulated savings must be invested well, providing the highest possible returns to retirees and enhancing productivity and growth. This is not an easy task, but it is an important one. It is the responsibility of regulators and other policymakers to provide adequate regulation and supervision to encourage better pension saving.

Notes

1   This exercise uses pension spending derived from household surveys.
2   By 2100, pensions could escalate to almost 50 percent of GDP if Brazil maintains the same per capita spending on pensions.
3   See Bosch et al. (2015) for the case of Colombia.
4   The TGI is composed of two sub-indices, namely the Transparency Index (TI) and the Governance Index (GI). The former includes five elements: Web site, annual report, communication, information completeness, and name of responsible person. The latter comprises six elements: governing body, selection and appointment, external control, investment committee, market experts, and code of conduct (see Musalem and Souto [2009] for a detailed description of each of these components). Data used are from 2007.
5   Fees on total final assets represent a larger part of the fund when the fee structure is an annual percentage of the fund and a longer period is considered. This is because when the pension fund manager charges the same annual fee over assets and accumulated assets are larger, the total amount becomes very significant. These fees could reasonably be expected to fall over time. This analysis assumes they are constant.
6   Longevity risk covers a worker/insured who lives longer than expected and runs the risk of exhausting accumulated funds.
7   Bosch et al. (2015) describe this situation in Colombia.
8   Subsecretaría de Previsión Social [Undersecretariat of Social Security] (2002).
9   See Rofman and Oliveri (2012); Bosch, Melguizo, and Pagés (2013).
10 For further analysis, see Bosch, Melguizo, and Pagés (2013) and Alaimo et al. (2015).

8 A Better Way for Government to Save

Increasing national saving requires everyone to pitch in, including the government. Traditionally, policies to boost public saving have focused on either raising taxes or cutting spending—or both. However, in Latin America and the Caribbean today, that two-pronged strategy is largely a nonstarter. Plummeting commodity prices, rising interest rates, and a prolonged global recession have translated into deteriorating fiscal and external accounts and low, or no, growth for much of the region. To ask people and firms to contribute more in taxes and receive less in public services would be salt in the wounds of these ailing economies. There are, however, other ways for government to save. Essentially, the idea is for government to spend better in order to save more.

Governments, like individuals, save by postponing consumption. Public saving is the part of national saving that is under the direct control of governments. The contribution of public saving to total saving varies by country and by region. In Latin America and the Caribbean, the public sector contributes about 15 percent to total national saving—approximately 3 percentage points of GDP—on average. This is roughly midway between Emerging Asia, where public saving is about 23 percent of national saving (8 percent of GDP), and Advanced Economies, where public saving is approximately 7 percent of national saving (1.5 percent of GDP) (see Chapter 2).

Public saving is total government revenue minus its consumption. Importantly, not all government spending is consumption. Government expenditures can be divided into current expenditures and capital expenditures. Current expenditures include the wage bill of public employees, current transfers made by the government (for example, to pay for social programs and subsidies), and government spending to provide public services such as education, health, and security. Current expenditures are government consumption. Instead, capital expenditures (public investment) are the real resources that governments use to build up the stock of capital in a country: for example, investments in infrastructure. Capital expenditures are part of a country's investment, rather than a country's consumption. Therefore, they are part of public saving (government revenue that is not used for current consumption).

Increasing public saving in the region is necessary to strengthen fiscal sustainability and to support long-term growth. Lower growth in industrial countries and falling commodity prices have dealt a blow to economic performance in the region, causing structural fiscal deficits to rise since 2009. In many countries, public saving must be increased to guarantee fiscal solvency.

There are three ways of generating public saving: by increasing government revenue, by reducing current expenditures, or by increasing capital expenditures. When it comes to increasing government revenue, the policy options are limited, especially in Latin America and the Caribbean. Governments everywhere derive most of their revenue from taxes. In Latin America, raising taxes to increase public saving is not an easy option in many countries, either because tax pressure is already high or because many countries have already undertaken tax reforms, making it politically difficult to increase taxes.[1]

In addition to the practical difficulties of raising taxes, tax policies can have significant implications for saving that go beyond increasing government revenue (see Box 8.1). In particular, taxes can distort private saving incentives. Thus, while they may add to government coffers, they may have little effect on total saving if they depress household and firm saving. The guiding principle for tax policy as it relates to saving is to design a tax system that avoids harming the saving incentives of individuals and firms, which are the largest sources of saving in the economy (see Chapter 1).

Actions to control government spending offer more space to increase public saving. Of course, cutting expenditures is not easy or popular in most contexts. However, this chapter focuses on two powerful levers that governments have at their disposal to increase public saving without necessarily cutting expenditures across the board. The first is to switch expenditures from current to capital expenditures. The second is to increase the efficiency of current spending.

BOX 8.1. THE EFFECT OF TAXES ON SAVING

Taxes have a direct negative impact on private saving because they reduce the disposable income of households and firms that pay taxes. At the same time, taxes have a direct positive impact on public saving because they are the main source of government revenue. Compared to other regions, Latin America and the Caribbean has a relatively high average tax burden on complying taxpayers, but relatively low average tax revenue (as a share of GDP).[a] This is the worst possible combination for saving: a tax system that imposes very high tax rates (thereby distorting private saving decisions) and collects very little revenue (thereby adding little to public revenues and potentially not adding to public saving). This anomaly is compounded by the types of taxes paid and who pays those taxes in the region.

Taxes affect private saving decisions and the composition of savings through a variety of channels. Income taxes discourage private saving by taxing both the income from which saving is derived, as well as the return to accumulated savings (interest and dividends). By contrast, indirect taxes (for example, the Value-Added-Tax) are less damaging to personal saving because they do not distort the rate of return to saving—provided tax rates remain constant over time.

The Latin American and Caribbean region derives a higher share of its tax revenue from "saving friendly" indirect taxes than from "saving foe" direct taxes on income. The contribution of indirect taxes to total revenues in Latin America and the Caribbean (46 percent of total revenue) and Emerging Asia (49 percent of total revenue) is higher than in Advanced Economies (35.5 percent of total revenue). The contribution of pure direct taxes in Latin America (29 percent of revenue) is lower than in both Emerging Asia and Advanced Economies (39 and 37 percent of total revenue, respectively) (Figure B8.1).

However, in practice who pays income taxes, and hence the structure of direct taxes, matters for saving. On this aspect, Latin America penalizes saving more than other regions. Latin America and the Caribbean and Emerging Asia derive a relatively high share of revenues from corporate income taxes (CIT) rather than from personal income taxes (PIT) (Figure B8.2). The higher reliance on corporate income taxes penalizes saving. Firms generate the largest share of private saving in the economy (see Chapter 2); thus, taxing firms' profits is taxing the main source of savings directly. There is more robust empirical evidence that changes in corporate taxes affect business saving than there is that personal income taxes hurt household saving.[b] In Chile, for example, reforms that lowered corporate income taxation in the mid-1980s triggered a 12 percentage point increase in private saving between 1985 and 2012 (see Cerda et al., 2015).

[a] The "average" country hides diversity among countries. Some countries, such as Guatemala and Mexico, have a low tax effort, while others, like Argentina, Brazil and Uruguay have a high tax effort close to Advanced Economies.

[b] See Callen and Thimann (1997); Djankov et al. (2010); Corbacho, Fretes Cibils, and Lora (2013); Cerda et al. (2015).

(continued on next page)

BOX 8.1. *(continued)*

Figure B8.1 **Tax Revenue as Percentage of GDP by Indirect, Direct and Other Direct Taxes, 2012**

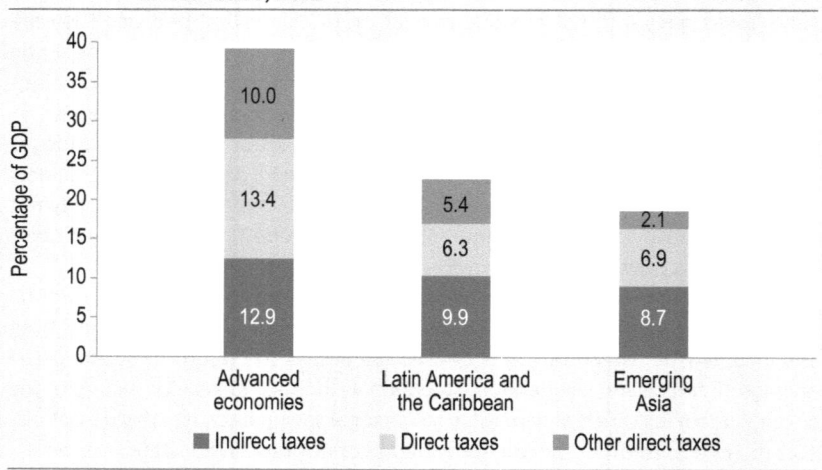

Source: IDB-CIAT Tax Database and WEO, IMF.
Note: Other direct taxes includes payroll taxes, trade taxes, property taxes and financial transactions taxes.

Moreover, CIT tax rates in Latin America and the Caribbean (at about 26 percent) are higher than in Emerging Asia (21 percent) and Advanced Economies (about 24 percent). However, CIT tax revenue, as a share of GDP, is lower in Latin America than in the other two regions (Figure B8.2). This reflects high tax evasion (high informality and weak enforcement) and a smaller tax base (more tax exemptions and large tax expenditures) in Latin America compared to other regions.[c] The combination of high CIT tax rates, with high evasion and a small tax base, results in a higher tax burden for tax compliers. Therefore, the effective corporate tax rate in Latin America and the Caribbean (18.3 percent of profits) is higher than in both Emerging Asia (14.1 percent) and Advanced Economies (15.5 percent) (World Bank and PwC, 2015). When considering all taxes on profits (turnover taxes, financial transaction taxes, and payroll taxes on employers), the burden of taxation for a typical *formal* firm in Latin America reaches about 51 percent of profits, compared to 28 percent in Emerging Asia and about 41 percent in Advanced Economies.[d]

Hence, while the ratio of revenue derived from direct taxes to GDP in Latin America is low by international standards, effective rates for compliers are

---

[c] Tax expenditures from the corporate income tax amount to about 0.9 percent of GDP on average, more than one-quarter of actual corporate tax collection, but they have been quite ineffective in incentivizing investment. Tax evasion on average, amounts to about 52 percent of potential tax collection in Latin America. (Corbacho, Fretes Cibils, and Lora, 2013).

[d] This effective tax rate is for one type of firm described in the Doing Business database (World Bank and PwC, 2015).

Figure B8.2 **Income Tax Revenue by Corporate Income Tax and Personal Income Tax, 2012**

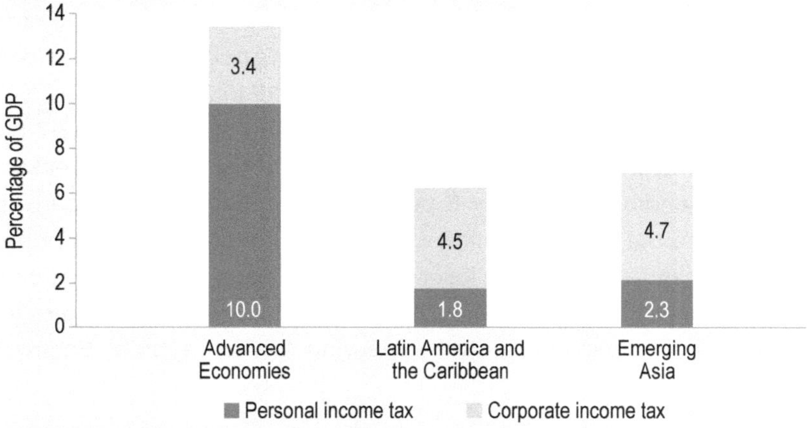

Source: IDB-CIAT Tax database and IMF (2015).

high. This has significant negative implications for private saving for two reasons. First, the relatively high tax burden on compliers (formal firms) reduces their saving capacity. Second, the tax structure that penalizes formal firms encourages informality (as firms try to evade high tax burdens) and thereby distorts the efficient allocation of economic resources, lowers productivity growth, and reduces the returns to saving and investment.[e]

Finally, tax systems can affect not only how much people and firms save, but also how they save. The structure of incentives embedded in tax systems across the region generates distortions. For example, the effective capital gains tax rate on housing is 23.3 percent in Emerging Asia, 17.9 percent in Advanced Economies, and only 12.2 percent in Latin America.[f] And while most Latin American countries tax dividends and financial returns (interest), they do not tax the imputed rents of owner-occupied housing. Hence, financial savings end up paying the highest effective tax rate.[g] This may discourage financial savings in favor of alternative saving vehicles such as housing—thereby reinforcing other distortions that increase the already high propensity of some people in Latin American and the Caribbean to save through housing, to the detriment of financial saving instruments.[h]

---

[e] See Pagés (2010).
[f] Authors' elaboration on the basis of Global Property Guide Research, Contributing Accounting Firms. http://www.globalpropertyguide.com/faq/guide-taxes.
[g] See IMF (2009).
[h] See Cruces (2016) and Piazzesi and Schneider (2012).

Current vs. Capital Expenditures: Fix the Mix

Starting from very low levels, Latin America slowly but surely increased public savings from as little as 1 percent of GDP in 1989 to almost 6 percent of GDP in 2007 as policymakers recognized the urgent need for fiscal consolidation (see Figure 8.1). Since 2009, public saving has been on a declining path, reaching 2.8 percent of GDP in 2014.

Total government expenditure from 2007 to 2014 jumped 3.7 percentage points of GDP. More than 90 percent of that increase went into current expenditure, and only 8 percent was devoted to public investment (Figure 8.2). Thus, public investment—a fundamental component of public saving—was the big loser in terms of expenditure allocation.[2]

As a consequence of these policies, public investment in the region has paled in comparison to other emerging markets such as Emerging

Figure 8.1 Public Saving in Latin America and the Caribbean

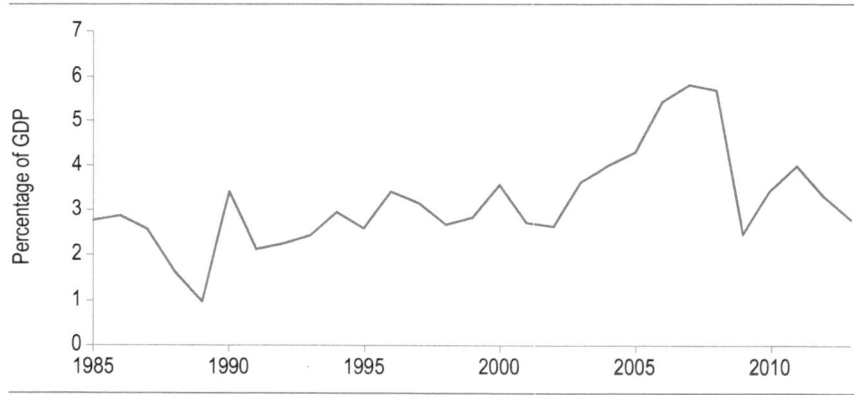

Source: Authors' calculations based on World Economic Outlook database (IMF, 2015).

Figure 8.2 Composition of Average Increase in Primary Public Spending, 2007–14 (percentage of GDP)

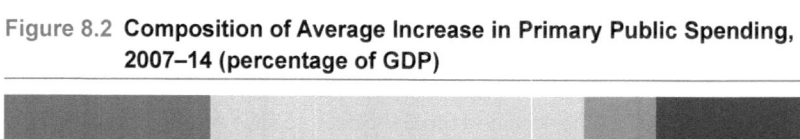

3.7

0.9   1.7   0.3   0.7

■ Wages and salaries   Subsidies and transfers   ■ Investment   ■ Other current   ● Total

Source: Authors' calculations based on national budget data.

Asia. Despite a slight uptick in public investment as a share of GDP in the 2000s, public investment in Latin America and the Caribbean represents only 60 percent of the level of public investment in Emerging Asian economies (Figure 8.3).

Public investment is not only relatively low, but its share in total government expenditure has been declining. Figure 8.4 shows the evolution of current expenditure vis-à-vis capital expenditure from 1995 to 2014. Current expenditure has climbed steadily, while capital expenditure

Figure 8.3 Public Investment Behavior in Latin America and the Caribbean vs. Emerging Asia

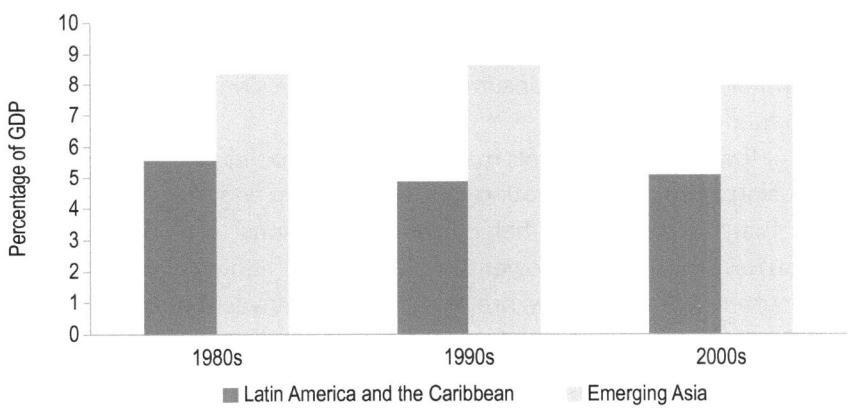

Source: Authors' calculations based on national budget data.

Figure 8.4 Evolution of Current and Capital Expenditure, Latin America and the Caribbean Average

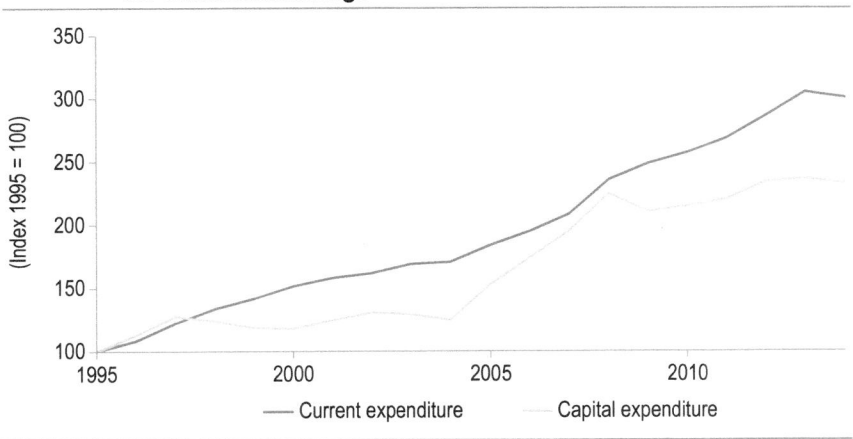

Source: Authors' calculations based on national budget data.

has had its ups and downs, increasing sharply from 2004 to 2008, but leveling off thereafter. While current expenditure has almost tripled throughout this period, capital expenditure has only doubled. As a result, public investment decreased to only 17 percent of primary government expenditure by 2014, down from almost 23 percent in 1995. Fiscal belt tightening in the region in 2015 and 2016 as a result of worsening external conditions has accentuated the trend as several governments chose to cut back on capital expenditures (saving) instead of current expenditures (consumption).[3]

Several factors may account for the low level of investment compared to current spending in Latin America and the Caribbean. First, many countries may have mistakenly viewed the favorable external factors of the early 2000s as permanent, and thus channeled a larger share of windfall revenues to consumption (by increasing current expenditures) than to saving.

But low investment levels may also reflect a political economy problem. Using a probabilistic voting model, Izquierdo and Kawamura (2015) show that, to the extent that current generations (the "old," in their model) have more voting power than future generations (or the "young"), then current spending may prevail over public investment, even if low investment hurts long-term growth. The stronger the electoral power of the old, the weaker will be the incentives for public investment, in favor of generous current-period spending (transfers). In other words, since future generations do not vote today on their preferred spending allocation, current generations that need resources now—or do not give priority to the needs of their offspring—may shift expenditure allocation away from capital expenditure.[4] This description reflects the situation in Latin America and the Caribbean, where surveys show that people do not save enough for retirement because they expect somebody else (or the government) to provide for their retirement needs (see Chapter 6).

Another reason for the bias toward current expenditure over investment lies in government's response to the economic cycle. Best practice would suggest increasing capital expenditure in bad times and reducing it in good times: that is, using capital expenditure to spend countercyclically. However, if governments must adjust their budgets in bad times—thereby precluding countercyclical policies and forcing expenditure cuts—they may find it easier to cut public investment than salaries or transfers that might risk political turmoil. But once capital expenditure has been reduced in a downturn, governments should remember to increase public investment in good times. Typically, this has not been the case in Latin America and the Caribbean.

Ardánaz and Izquierdo (2016) evaluate the procyclicality of current and capital expenditures in Latin America and test whether the two types of spending respond differently to changes in the business cycle.[5] If real expenditure were to grow at a constant rate—say, the long-term growth rate of real output—it should not be affected by cyclical fluctuations. However, the authors find that current and capital expenditures react to the business cycle in different ways. Current expenditures grow in good times, but do not fall back in bad times. The opposite holds for real capital expenditures, which shrink in bad times, but do not rebound in good times. These estimated impacts and their relevance are described in Figure 8.5, panel a, which clearly illustrates this asymmetric response. The implications are serious: current expenditures tend to increase as a share of total expenditure, confirming the bias in favor of current expenditure and against capital expenditure—and, by extension, against public saving.

Figure 8.5 Sensitivity of Spending to Output Gaps

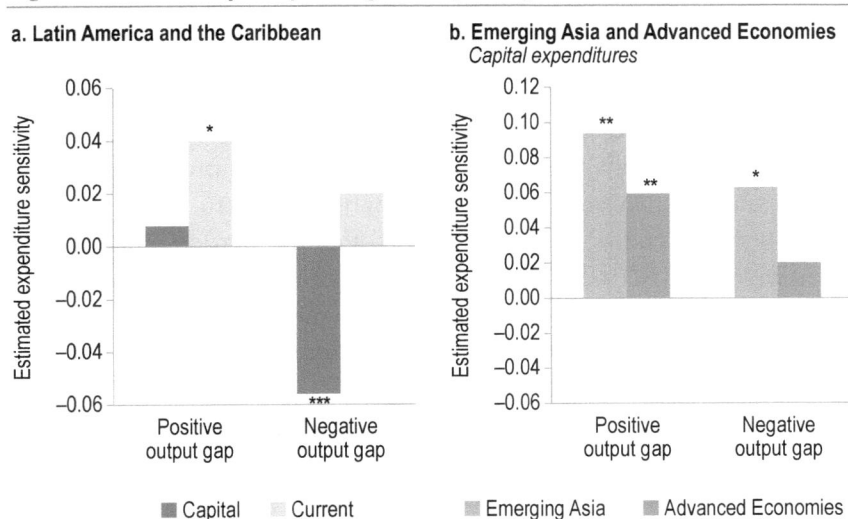

Source: Authors' calculations based on national budget data.

Note: Authors' estimates based on Ardánaz and Izquierdo (2016). Ardánaz and Izquierdo run regressions of the type $\Delta g = a + b*$Positive Cycle $+ c*$Negative Cycle $+ \varepsilon$, where Δg is the change in real expenditure, Positive Cycle is the value of the cyclical component of output when it is positive, and Negative Cycle is the value of the cyclical component when it is negative. The value reported on the y-axis is the estimated coefficient measuring expenditure sensitivity to cyclical component. Label y-axis: ***$p<0.01$, **$p<0.05$, * $p<0.1$.

Latin America contrasts starkly to Emerging Asia and Advanced Economies (Figure 8.5, panel b), where capital expenditures do not react negatively at all in bad times; if anything, East Asian countries expand their capital spending during trying times. Thus, the bias against capital spending is more marked in Latin America and the Caribbean than in other regions. Governments in the region should adjust their spending policies to remedy this bias. The key is to design and implement fiscal policy rules that reduce discretion in the allocation of public spending over the business cycle and help overcome the bias against capital expenditures that is currently built into spending behaviors. Mending the mix between current and capital expenditures can increase saving without affecting the overall level of spending.

Efficiency: A Path to Saving

Governments can also boost public saving by increasing capital expenditures directly. In fact, increasing public investment enhances productivity in the private sector and, therefore, propels growth in the region (see Chapter 4). How can governments make room in their budgets to increase capital expenditures? One way is by switching expenditures, as described above. Another way is to borrow from abroad. However, this option is restricted, particularly in a less favorable external environment. Moreover, external borrowing carries its own set of risks (see Chapter 5). Another way is to adjust current expenditures.

Adjusting current expenditures can be a painful process; however, understanding their composition and identifying inefficiencies in public expenditure can be very useful to reduce the burden. This process is known as "smart" adjustment. Instead of cutting expenditures across the board—as has been done many times in the past—it is better to dissect the budget sector by sector and sort out inefficiencies. But how can inefficiencies be identified?

A key tool for reducing inefficiencies is appropriate targeting of current expenditure. Typically, expenditures will target a particular group, be it energy subsidies for low-income families or social programs for the poor. However, in practice many recipients of these subsidies are not part of the targeted population. For example, an electricity subsidy for consumption on the first 150 KWh for the entire population in a country may very well reach low-income households that consume less than 150 KWh, but will also subsidize higher-income households on those first 150

KWh. The receipt of the subsidy by the higher-income household would be considered leakage, and an inefficiency because people outside the target group are receiving the subsidy. Or consider an exemption on the value added tax on food, also called a tax expenditure. Typically, this measure aims to make food more affordable to low-income households. However, this tax expenditure also benefits higher-income households that should not be receiving the benefit and, thus, constitutes an inefficiency. Or think of a conditional cash transfer program focused on poor families: in many cases, beneficiaries of these programs may include families that are sufficiently well-off to finance whatever the transfer is supporting; in such case the transfer would be poorly targeted and a source of inefficiency.

A key element to define up front when identifying leakage is the population to be targeted. In this discussion, the targeted population is the poor, defined as those individuals whose income lies below the national poverty line.[6]

The leakage concept can be easily applied to sectors in the public budget that work with targeted populations, as is the case of electricity subsidies, social programs, or tax expenditures. However, two key areas of government expenditure that account for a significant portion of the budget—health and education—aim at universal coverage. For these areas of expenditure, leakage is not an issue. Therefore, defining inefficiency in those sectors is much more challenging.

For these sectors, benchmarking provides a means of determining inefficiency. Countries that are good at providing those services—that is, that achieve good results with the lowest amount of inputs—serve as benchmarks against which other countries can be compared.[7] However, this approach inevitably raises caveats because other factors—many of them difficult to measure consistently—may affect the results.[8]

Inefficiencies in expenditure stem not only from input numbers (i.e. the number of teachers or doctors), but also from their cost. For example, if for a given job qualification, wages are much higher in the public sector than the private sector, then there is room for improvement. Both the usage of inputs and wage differentials in the public and private sectors provide indications of inefficiency in universal coverage sectors such as education and health.

The next section analyses five sectors for inefficiencies: energy, social programs, tax expenditures, education, and health. These five sectors amount to roughly half of primary expenditure for the average Latin

American country. Admirably, the region has worked hard to boost welfare by increasing the provision of these important services. However, the efficiency and targeting of these services is important if they are to realize their full potential.

Energy

In the case of energy subsidies for low-income families, governments often set prices at a level that does not cover operating costs. Bolivia's Tarifa Dignidad and Brazil's Tarifa Social Baixa Renda provide good examples. Using household expenditure surveys, it is possible to assess how many beneficiaries of the subsidy were initially targeted by the program. For instance, in the case of price subsidies to low-income households for the use of electricity below 150 KWh, any household consuming more than that amount, or whose income is above the poverty line, should not receive the subsidy. Figure 8.6, based on household survey micro data for a representative country, illustrates this point clearly: all points below the poverty line and to the left of the 150 KWh line are households that should be targeted by the subsidy policy. However, many households that are not poor, but that consume less than 150 KWh, receive the subsidy. This group constitutes what is typically called "inclusion error," or leakage. Aggregating subsidies provided to these households yields a measure of the leakage in electricity subsidies.

When policies are generalized so that all households receive a subsidy—such as fixing the retail price of gasoline below the cost of producing it—then leakage can be estimated as the cost of this policy to the public institution covering the shortfall. However, the entire shortfall does not constitute leakage, as part of it will reach poor households. Expenditure surveys can help estimate the share of a fuel subsidy (on gasoline, for example) that goes to households above the poverty line. The size of the leakage is the product of this share and the total amount of the shortfall spent by the government agency.[9] A similar approach can be applied to other energy subsidies, including those for fuel oil, natural gas, and liquefied petroleum gas.[10]

Table 8.1 shows government subsidies to the energy sector in each of 18 Latin American countries with available information as of 2013 (no data is available for Venezuela, which is the largest energy producer in the region and offers large subsidies to domestic consumption of gasoline). Although they vary widely across countries, on average, energy subsidies eat up close to 1 percent of GDP, ranging from countries with high subsidies, such as Bolivia (3.3 percent of GDP) and Argentina (2.1 percent of GDP), to countries with no subsidies, such as Chile and Peru. The point is that more than two-thirds of these subsidies leak out to nonpoor households that are not part of the targeted population. The magnitude of this inefficiency—and therefore the margin for improvement—is huge.

Figure 8.6 Example of Leakage (Inclusion Error) in Electricity Subsidies in Nicaragua

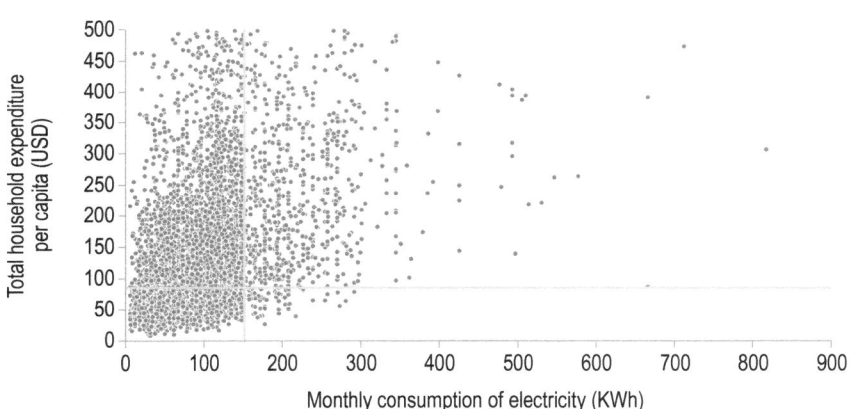

Subsidy Targeting: Inclusion and Exclusion Errors (percentage)

Fee intervals (kWh)	Households in each interval (percentage)	Interval consumption (MWh annual)	Deciles 1–4 (percentage)	Deciles 5–10 (percentage)
0–25	5%	0.8	0.5	0.3
26–50	23%	8.8	5.3	3.5
51–100	33%	23.9	10.7	13.2
101–150	26%	32.1	7.6	24.5
151–500	12%	27.7	1.6	26.0
501–1000	1%	4.7	0.0	4.7
+1000	0%	2.0	0.0	2.0
Total	100%	100	25.7	74.3
Inclusion error (MWh)		63.3%		
Exclusion error (MWh)		2.5%		

Source: Authors' calculations based on Izquierdo, Loo-Kung, and Navajas (2013).

Table 8.1 **Energy Subsidies and Leakages, 2013 (percentage of GDP)**

Country	Total subsidies	Residential subsidies	Rest of subsidies	Residential leakages[a]	Rest of leakages[a]	Total leakages[a]
Bolivia	3.29	0.91	2.37	0.76	1.92	2.68
Argentina	2.06	0.85	1.21	0.79	1.15	1.94
Honduras	1.85	0.90	0.95	0.55	0.71	1.25
El Salvador	1.75	1.39	0.36	0.91	0.30	1.21
Domican Republic	1.38	0.65	0.73	0.43	0.62	1.05
Mexico	1.29	0.53	0.77	0.33	0.49	0.82
Nicaragua	1.11	0.86	0.25	0.60	0.21	0.81
Panama	0.81	0.51	0.30	0.47	0.30	0.77
Brazil	0.80	0.24	0.56	0.21	0.50	0.71
Colombia	0.37	0.27	0.10	0.19	0.08	0.27
Guatemala	0.33	0.33	0.00	0.22	0.00	0.22
Uruguay	0.12	0.02	0.09	0.02	0.09	0.11
Paraguay	0.05	0.04	0.01	0.02	0.01	0.04
Peru	0.00	0.00	0.00	0.00	0.00	0.00
Belize	0.00	0.00	0.00	0.00	0.00	0.00
Costa Rica	0.00	0.00	0.00	0.00	0.00	0.00
Chile	0.00	0.00	0.00	0.00	0.00	0.00
Jamaica	0.00	0.00	0.00	0.00	0.00	0.00
Average	0.85	0.42	0.43	0.31	0.35	0.66

Source: FIEL and IDB based on official fiscal, energy, and household survey data.
[a] Leakages to non-poor households.

This analysis was carried out with information up to year-end 2013. With energy prices plummeting (and the structure of subsidies largely unchanged), the size of subsidies across the different energy subsectors (gasoline, fuel oil, natural gas, and liquefied petroleum gas) may be lower. The sensitivity of prices in these subsectors with respect to international oil prices varies country by country, and may or may not be large depending on the specific case. The price of oil has fallen by as much as 50 percent on average between 2013 and 2015; thus, the total cost of leakage may have declined. However, this decline does not make waste in energy subsidies any less important: since energy prices may go up again, leakage is likely to catch up with previous levels if the current subsidy structure remains intact.

Social Programs

Expenditures on social programs, defined as spending to guarantee a basic level of economic and social welfare, can be analyzed in a similar way. Unlike contributory pension payments, transfers for social programs do not require individuals to contribute anything to receive benefits (hence, these transfers are "noncontributory"). The target population typically consists of individuals, families, communities, or groups that are considered vulnerable and require special attention, such as the poor, children, or the elderly.[11]

The two main social program expenditures are conditional cash transfers (CCTs) and noncontributory pensions (NCPs). Both are considered monetary transfer programs. The major objective of CCTs is to reduce the intergenerational transmission of poverty by investing in human capital. They provide transfers to families with children below 18 years of age and/or pregnant women—usually on a monthly basis—subject to their compliance with particular requirements, such as school enrollment and health checkups. These programs, pioneered in the early 1990s by Progresa in Mexico and Bolsa Escola in Brazil, have become popular throughout Latin America.

Noncontributory pensions are a more recent phenomenon that has grown significantly in several Latin American countries since 2000 to deal with the many individuals who reach retirement age without enough formal contributions to any pension system (see Chapter 7). This situation weighs heavily in the decisions of younger individuals to participate in formal labor markets and save long term, because noncontributory pensions can provide incentives for informality and may lower saving. This chapter will examine only the targeting aspect of NCPs.

Table 8.2 shows the evolution of social program expenditures from 2003 to 2013. Spending increased continuously in most countries and in some countries, it more than tripled. Overall, this trend has been a positive development because it has helped reduce poverty and inequality in the region.

However, not all spending on social programs has been properly targeted to the poor. Table 8.3 shows the estimated leakage for

Table 8.2 **Social Programs Expenditure (percentage of GDP)**

Country	2003–06	2007–10	2011–13
Argentina	1.1	2.3	3.6
Paraguay	0.1	1.1	1.9
Uruguay	0.9	1.8	1.7
Bolivia	1.3	1.6	1.6
Costa Rica	0.9	1.1	1.4
Brazil	0.8	1.0	1.2
Honduras	0.6	0.9	1.1
Chile	0.5	0.7	1.1
Belize	n.a.	n.a.	1.0
Colombia	0.7	0.9	1.0
El Salvador	0.4	0.5	0.8
Guatemala	0.5	0.7	0.7
Dominican Republic	1.3	1.1	0.7
Mexico	0.3	0.7	0.7
Nicaragua	0.9	0.7	0.6
Jamaica	0.3	0.5	0.5
Panama	0.0	0.2	0.5
Peru	0.6	0.5	0.5
Average	0.7	1.0	1.1

Source: FIEL and IDB based on national budget data.
n.a. = Data not available.

monetary transfer programs—conditional cash transfers and noncontributory pensions—as well as other social programs as a share of GDP. Although on average they represent only one-half of 1 percent of GDP, countries vary substantially. Leakage tends to be smaller in Central American countries, averaging 0.3 percent of GDP. For these countries, social spending is lower and populations are relatively poorer, leaving less margin for error. However, leakage is much higher for South American countries, averaging 0.8 percent of GDP. Once again, the striking feature about expenditures on social programs is how high leakage is as a share of total expenditures: 45 percent, on average, for the region (52 percent in South American countries, and 35 percent in Central America). Although leakage is high, its share of total subsidies is not as high as in other sectors, such as energy or tax expenditures, which lack a clear targeting strategy and are, therefore, more prone to leakage.

Table 8.3 **Indicators of Leakages in Social Programs (percentage of GDP)**

Country	In monetary transfer programs	In other programs	Total leakages	Leakages as percentage of social program expenditures
Argentina	1.9	0.1	2.0	56.2
Paraguay	0.2	0.9	1.1	58.2
Uruguay	0.7	0.4	1.1	62.4
Bolivia	0.7	0.1	0.8	50.9
Chile	0.6	0.1	0.7	65.2
Brazil	0.4	0.2	0.6	51.8
Costa Rica	0.3	0.3	0.6	42.1
Colombia	0.1	0.4	0.5	50.6
Belize	0.0	0.4	0.4	39.0
El Salvador	0.1	0.3	0.4	46.3
Jamaica	0.2	0.2	0.4	66.6
Dominican Republic	0.1	0.2	0.3	44.3
Panama	0.2	0.1	0.2	48.0
Mexico	0.1	0.1	0.2	28.9
Nicaragua	0.0	0.2	0.2	31.7
Guatemala	0.1	0.1	0.2	24.3
Peru	0.1	0.0	0.2	35.1
Honduras	0.1	0.0	0.1	8.2
Average	0.3	0.2	0.6	45.0

Source: FIEL and IDB based on household surveys and national budget data.

Tax Expenditures

Instead of transferring resources directly to needy households through budgetary spending, governments often offer tax relief, and thus transfer resources indirectly through tax exemptions. With the aim of protecting the poor, many goods and services that weigh heavily in the consumption basket of the poor—including foodstuffs, medicines, and rents—are exempted from taxes. This policy is one of the most prone to leakage, as most of the foregone tax collection goes to better-off individuals, who typically spend more in the aggregate than do the poor.

The value added tax (VAT) is the main tax used for this purpose. Most countries in Latin America offer either VAT reductions or exemptions for food, medicine, and rent, irrespective of income. Most countries also produce estimates of tax expenditures, which serve as a benchmark to calculate leakage.[12] Household surveys and specific studies on tax expenditures in the region are then used to estimate how much the nonpoor consume in food, medicine, and rent. These two pieces of information allow for estimating the leakage in tax expenditures.[13]

On average, total tax expenditures amount to 2.3 percent of GDP (see Table 8.4). Of this total, tax spending on food, medicine, and housing account for almost 1 percent of GDP. Nearly three-quarters of tax expenditure on these items benefits nonpoor households: equivalent to 0.73 percent of GDP. In some countries, leakage is as high as 1.8 percent of GDP. Overall, tax expenditures are probably the most regressive item in the subsidy agenda.

Table 8.4 **Tax Expenditure in VAT on Food, Medicine and Housing, and Associated Leakages (percentage of GDP)**

Country	Total tax expenditure on VAT	Tax expenditure on food, medicine, and housing	Leakage	Leakage (share of tax expenditure)
Nicaragua	4.5	2.3	1.8	75.3
Dominican Republic	3.2	2.2	1.5	65.6
Costa Rica	3.4	2.0	1.8	87.2
Colombia	4.9	1.3	1.1	84.6
Mexico	1.5	1.2	0.6	52.7
Uruguay	2.2	1.1	0.9	82.5
Panama	2.3	0.8	0.7	81.2
Guatemala	1.4	0.8	0.4	52.0
Jamaica	3.5	0.8	0.7	88.8
Brazil	3.0	0.7	0.6	91.7
Peru	1.3	0.4	0.4	85.2
Argentina	1.0	0.4	0.4	90.1
El Salvador	1.0	0.5	0.3	65.3
Chile	0.8	0.2	0.2	78.3
Bolivia	0.0	0.0	0.0	n.a.
Belize	n.a.	n.a.	n.a.	n.a.
Honduras	3.6	n.a.	n.a.	n.a.
Paraguay	n.a.	n.a.	n.a.	n.a.
Average	2.3	1.0	0.7	77.2

Source: FIEL and IDB estimates based on national data and other studies.
n.a. = Data not available.

Education and Health

Estimating spending inefficiencies in areas that offer universal cover-age such as health and education call for a different methodology and raises several questions. For example, should the focus be on searching for best practice countries that provide the best possible education with the lowest number of teachers per student? Or should inefficiencies be estimated in relation to each country's success in achieving the desired results for the sector? The latter may be more appealing, but requires an in-depth knowledge at the country level about the particular strat-egy for the sector—and even then, the strategy may be loosely defined in many countries, or may not be ambitious enough. Moreover, coun-try comparisons may be very difficult. For these reasons, this analysis uses the first approach, in which all countries are compared against a benchmark considered the best performer in each sector. Of course, this methodology has its own drawbacks. It assumes that the technology used by the best performer is replicable by other countries—an issue up for debate among practitioners in this area.

The first step is to identify a benchmark country. A tool often used to obtain this benchmark is Data Envelopment Analysis (DEA), which assumes a production frontier based on cross-country data on inputs and their corresponding outputs.[14] With this frontier as reference, the country that produces the best results with the lowest amount of asso-ciated input is identified.

The discussion that follows assumes that workers in the sector—whether teachers in the education sector or doctors and nurses in the health sector—are the main production factor generating the results in that sector: say, test scores in education or life expectancy in health. Of course, other factors may affect results, such as diet or smoking, in the case of health. However, studies in health care, for example, indicate that expenditure in the sector is a main factor driving results in terms of life expectancy.[15] Since the wage bill comprises the largest share of expen-diture, the analysis will focus on both components of the wage bill—the number of workers and wages—to identify inefficiencies.

Despite the support provided by DEA studies to follow this route, the inefficiency analyses below represent only a first pass at the extremely difficult exercise of capturing inefficiencies in sectors with universal cov-erage. A full analysis should control for other idiosyncratic factors that affect outcome variables which, given the scope of this study and data availability restrictions, will not be taken into account. However, these caveats do not make the analysis any less relevant: to date, no comparative analysis of inefficiencies in these sectors is available for Latin American countries. Estimations below should be useful to start a discussion about efficiency management in two important sectors, including the production of additional performance and quality indicators to allow a more detailed estimate of outstanding inefficiencies.

Education

International benchmarks are often used in education. A common benchmark is PISA (the Program for International Student Assessment), a triennial international survey that aims to evaluate education systems worldwide by testing the skills and knowledge of 15-year-old students. Figure 8.7 shows the secondary-students-per-teacher ratio contrasted against average PISA scores for a group of OECD countries.[16]

In this high performing group of countries, the Republic of Korea stands out as the country with the highest score for one of the lowest input (teachers). With Korea as the benchmark country, student to teacher ratios, at both the primary and secondary school level, are contrasted with those of Latin American countries with available data to determine a roadmap for improving the efficiency of spending on education. In the typical

Figure 8.7 Average Math, Reading, and Science PISA Performance vs. Students per Teacher Ratio, OECD Countries, 2012

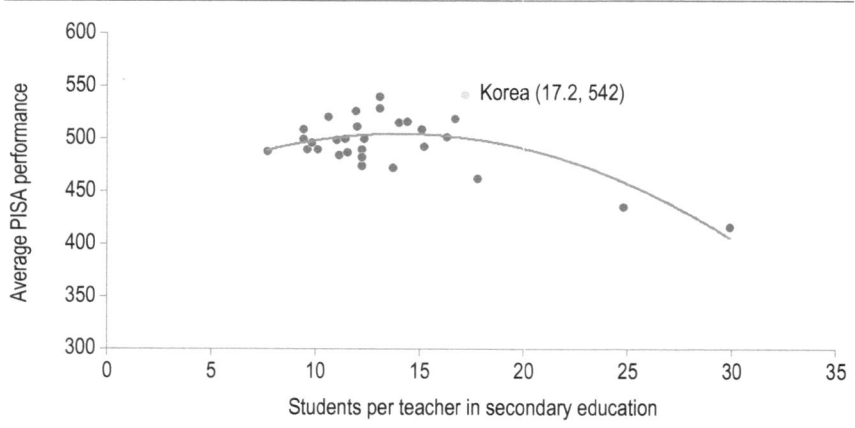

Source: Authors' calculations based on OECD.
Note: PISA = Programme for international student assessment.

case, this entails reducing the number of teachers while investing heavily in teacher training to reach OECD standards: a major undertaking.[17]

The second factor affecting efficiency in this sector is the teacher wage bill. This is a thorny issue since salaries should reflect productivity, which is difficult to measure. A shortcut is to compare teacher wages in public schools against those in private schools to determine their competitiveness. Another option is to fit a curve depicting the relationship between public teacher wages relative to per capita GDP in that country against GDP per capita levels. Large deviations from this relationship can be viewed as evidence of excessive pay (when above the curve) or insufficient pay (when below the curve). Figure 8.8 displays the behavior of this relationship for a group of OECD and Latin American countries. Countries well above fitted values (outliers) indicate countries where savings could be achieved.

Considering both the worker and wage tools defined above provides an approximation to assess the current wage bill against a hypothetical efficient wage bill. The efficient wage bill covers a workforce of teachers consistent with the students per teacher ratios defined by the benchmark, and wages that fall within acceptable levels of the wage to GDP per capita ratio. Differences between the current wage bill and the efficient wage bill are considered a proxy for inefficiency, and thus an indication of potential savings in expenditures of the sector.[18]

This analysis is based on data for 13 countries in the region: Belize, Brazil, Chile, Colombia, Costa Rica, Dominican Republic, El Salvador,

Figure 8.8 Relative Primary Teacher Wages vs. GDP per Capita, 2011

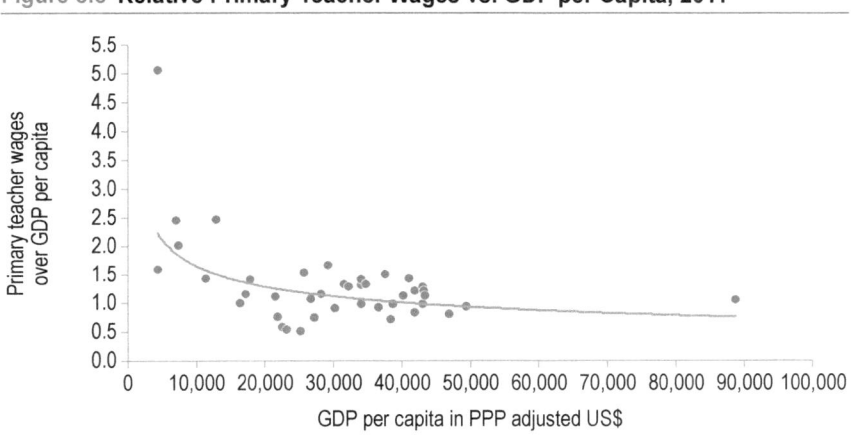

Source: OECD (2011) for OECD countries, and IDB for Latin American countries.

Guatemala, Honduras, Nicaragua, Panama, Peru, and Uruguay. Within this group, the average savings from bringing the wage bill in education down to efficient levels amount to 0.7 percent of GDP. However, countries vary considerably. Most of these savings stem from wage differentials rather than inefficiencies in student per teacher ratios. The numbers are only indicative, given the caveats of the methodologies used to generate them, and the importance of preserving incentives to attract qualified teachers and reward performance. Nevertheless, the discrepancies point to the need to evaluate the wage bill in education.

Health

The health sector is assessed in a similar fashion. Figure 8.9 shows the Data Envelopment Analysis (DEA) and the associated frontier obtained by comparing life expectancy against the number of health professionals employed by the sector. The efficiency frontier is shown by countries that have a red data point. Most countries in the upper part of the frontier have a life expectancy in the neighborhood of 80 years. However, many more health professionals are needed to obtain only marginal increases in life expectancy beyond 80 years. Studies by the World Health Organization (WHO) recommend a figure of 22.8 health staff (doctors and nurses) per 10,000 inhabitants for public sector systems (WHO, 2006).

Figure 8.9 Health Professionals per 10,000 Inhabitants vs. Life Expectancy at Birth

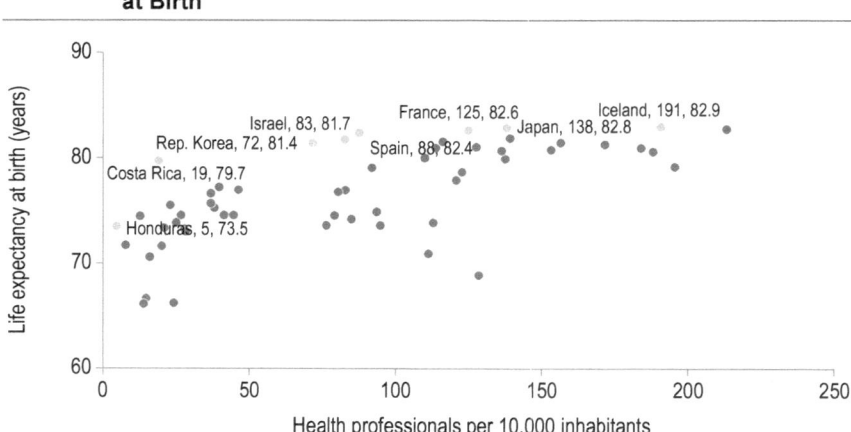

Source: Authors' elaboration based on World Health Organization.

Figure 8.10 Health Professionals Relative Wage vs GDP per Capita, 2011

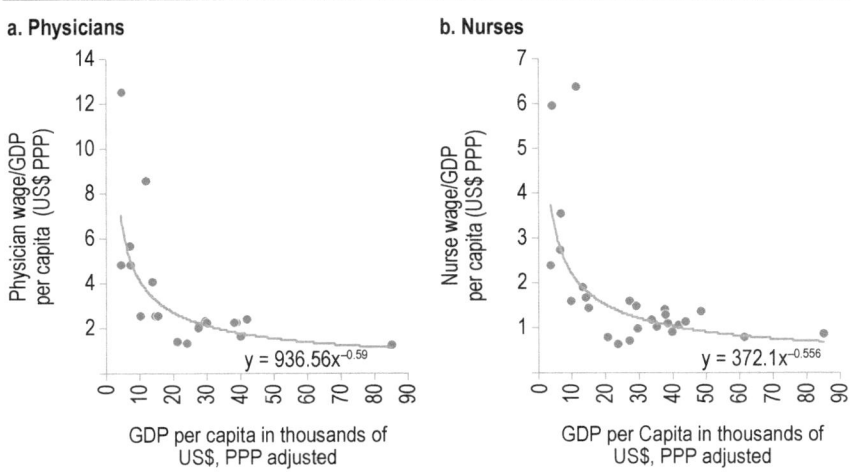

a. Physicians

b. Nurses

Source: OECD (2011) for OECD countries and IDB for Latin American countries.

This level is in line with the lowest number of health professionals associated with a life expectancy around 80 years of age shown in the efficiency frontier of Figure 8.9. Thus, the WHO figure was taken as the benchmark for the number of workers.

Regarding salaries, the same approach used in education is followed. Figures 8.10 panels a and b show the relationship between wages relative to GDP per capita in a country against GDP per capita levels for both physicians and nurses. Fitted values are used as a benchmark to contrast existing wages to determine wage savings.

Putting both worker and wage components together helps determine the efficient wage bill proxy, which can be compared against the actual wage bill to determine total potential savings in the health sector for each Latin American country. The same countries were used in this analysis as in the analysis for education, except for Belize, for which no data were available. Potential savings are smaller than in other sectors, averaging 0.2 percent of GDP. In some countries, however, the savings could be as large as 0.9 percent of GDP.

It All Adds Up

The numbers speak for themselves. Smart adjustments can yield big payoffs. In the targeted areas of energy, social programs, and tax expenditures, overall savings could amount to up to 2 percent of GDP

Figure 8.11 Potential Savings in Targeted Expenditure (Social Programs, Energy, and Tax Expenditure)

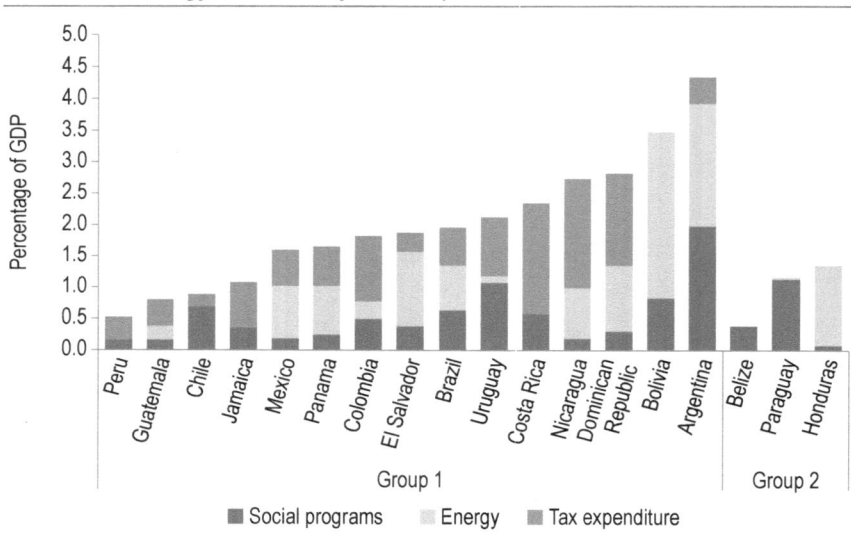

Source: Authors' elaboration based on their own estimates.
Note: For comparability purposes, countries have been split into two groups. Group 1 contains estimates of leakages for countries with data on all three sectors, while Group 2 does not include estimates on tax expenditure leakages.

for the average country—and as high as 4.3 percent of GDP in the most acute cases. Figure 8.11 shows total savings in targeted sectors and their breakdown by sector for the 18 Latin American and Caribbean countries in the sample. Not surprisingly, leakage is somewhat less in social programs than in energy and tax expenditure, since social programs are targeted by design and thus should be less prone to leakage. Thus, savings from leakage in energy and tax expenditures may be larger and easier to fix when choosing among saving opportunities. The challenge for governments is that eliminating leakage will have to be done in ways that do not leave the poor unprotected. This is not an easy task, as governments need to know who the poor are and where they live, and allocate transfers to them directly in order to switch from price subsidies (which are prone to leakage) to income transfers targeted specifically to the poor.

Figure 8.12 presents a breakdown for select countries in the region on potential savings in education and health. Together, these inefficiencies average about 1 percent of GDP—but can be as large as 2.8 percent of GDP for some countries. Estimated inefficiencies average 0.7 percent of

Figure 8.12 **Potential Savings in Education and Health**

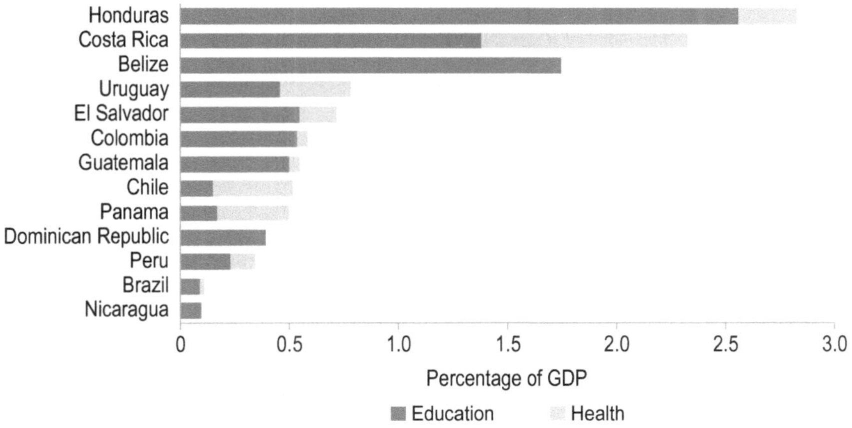

Source: Authors' estimates.
Note: Belize does not include estimates on health leakages.

GDP for education, and about 0.2 percent of GDP for health. Again, there is substantial variation across countries: inefficiencies can be as high as 2.6 percent of GDP in education, and 0.9 percent of GDP in health.

Estimating inefficiencies in spending in sectors with universal coverage is a very difficult task. A complete assessment would ideally control for all the factors that affect outcome variables, such as international assessment scores in education or life expectancy in health. However, given the scope of this study and the restrictions on data availability, only the wage bill was considered in each case, and here too care must be taken to assure efficiency without comprising incentives that attract quality personnel to teaching and health care. The caveats are important but do not make the analysis any less relevant: this is the first comparative analysis of inefficiencies in these sectors for Latin American countries. These estimates are a useful proxy for potential savings in these sectors based on large personnel or wage deviations from selected benchmarks.

The estimates presented in this chapter are a useful starting point for a policy debate on improving the efficiency of both management and public spending in important sectors such as education and health. From here the discussion should be expanded to include additional performance and quality indicators that will allow a more detailed assessment of existing inefficiencies.

Reducing inefficiencies in the five sectors analyzed here could amount, on average, to potential savings in the neighborhood of 3 percent of GDP. Particularly in economies that need to ensure fiscal solvency and make productive investments, these potential savings are significant indeed.

Saving, from the Top Down

Increasing public saving is no easy task, and doing so by raising taxes or slashing expenditures is not only politically unpopular but may be counterproductive as well. For example, increasing taxes may discourage private saving, while across-the-board spending cuts may reduce much-needed public investment and jeopardize the social progress of recent years. But governments do have other options. The first alternative is to correct the entrenched bias in public spending against capital expenditures (which is saving) and in favor of current expenditures (which is consumption). Various political economy and budgeting distortions produce this bias. Acknowledging them and building mechanisms into fiscal rules to overcome the bias can help boost public saving through expenditure switching rather than expenditure reduction.[19]

In addition, the government can save more by spending better. Public saving rates in Latin America and the Caribbean are on average 5 percentage points of GDP lower than in East Asia. The analysis in this chapter suggests that approximately half that gap can be overcome by targeting public expenditures better in areas like energy, social programs, and tax expenditures and by improving efficiency in health and education. Doing so requires analyzing leakages in the budget, dissecting spending by sectors, and searching for potential efficiency gains.

Public saving is not the largest contributor to national saving; however, it is an important one. Governments that want to encourage more saving by the private sector should set the example by using the tools available to them. After two decades of fiscal reforms in Latin America and the Caribbean that have significantly improved fiscal sustainability across the region, it is time to delve into the budgetary reforms that can yield a permanent increase in public saving rates. Saving for development is everyone's responsibility, starting with the government.

Notes

[1]   For a complete assessment of tax policy in Latin America and the Caribbean, see Corbacho, Fretes Cibils, and Lora (2013).

[2]   Roughly half of the increase was allocated to subsidies and transfers, and a quarter to wages and salaries. This points to larger inflexibilities in government expenditure, as salaries, subsidies and transfers are much more difficult to reverse, if needed, relative to public investment.

[3]   The fact that public investment is low and current expenditure is gaining as a share of the budget also has pernicious implications for fiscal sustainability, for at least two reasons. First, any needed adjustment will be increasingly difficult to implement, given the inflexible nature of much of current expenditure. Second, lower public investment may lead to lower growth, thus raising the bar of required primary surpluses in the future.

[4]   As societies age, this effect may become stronger.

[5]   Ardánaz and Izquierdo (2016) follow a framework similar to the one used by Balassone and Kumar (2007) to analyze the cyclicality of total public expenditure. They run separate regressions for changes in real current expenditure and changes in real capital expenditure against a constant and the cyclical component of output performance. A key part of their analysis is that they estimate separate coefficients for the impact of the cyclical component of output, taking into account good times (periods when the cyclical component is positive) compared to bad times (periods when the cyclical component is negative.

[6]   The level of individual income used to define the poor is net of any subsidy they may be receiving from the government. Another popular measure—consistent with several existing studies—is individuals ranked in the lowest 40 percent of the expenditure distribution.

[7]   Such is the case of Data Envelopment Analysis, a concept that will be used in this report.

[8]   For example, idiosyncratic factors may cause a population to assign more importance to education than other countries, as might be the case in some Asian countries.

[9]   The implicit assumption is that expenditure patterns captured in expenditure surveys do not misrepresent or overrepresent the expenditure of the poor relative to that of the nonpoor.

[10] Yet another case is that of subsidies to nonresidential clients in other sectors, which cover a wide range of consumers and firms. For those cases, shares in total consumption of individuals above the poverty line are used to determine leakage. This approach constitutes a lower bound, as only the share of the subsidy to nonresidential sectors that is consumed by the nonpoor is considered leakage. Alternatively, the entire subsidy could be considered a leakage. Even more detailed analysis could use the supply and utilization tables from national accounts data to identify the impact of subsidies on intermediate energy inputs at the sectoral level. However, this approach exceeds the scope of this analysis.

[11] Although some health and education expenditure can be considered social assistance, they are not included in the category of social assistance expenditure.

[12] However, not all of them publish these estimates in a disaggregated form that allows identifying exemptions by type of tax and expenditure; thus, other sources are also used.

[13] These estimates do not consider whether consumers would cut back on these goods and services if they were taxed. Thus they constitute partial equilibrium estimates about additional tax collection that would be obtained once exemptions are eliminated.

[14] DEA analysis was first used by Farrell (1957). For a good introduction to the DEA methodology, see Coelli, Rao, and Battese (1998) and Thanassoulis (2001).

[15] See Joumard, André, and Nic (2010).

[16] This figure updates work by Afonso and Aubyn (2004). Data on the students per teacher ratio are for 2008, four years before students took their exam in 2012, corresponding to the prevailing secondary students per teacher ratio at the time primary students were finishing primary school and before they entered high school.

[17] As such, savings computed here may not be that big because savings in terms of personnel may need to be partly offset by expenditures in training and other activities that could raise teacher productivity to the benchmark level.

[18] Yet another potential source of inefficiency is an excessive number of administrative staff in public education. A similar approach could be used to obtain differences between current expenditure in administrative staff and efficient expenditure in administrative staff.

[19] Peru provides a good example for the region. It established a simple fiscal rule that combines deficit and current expenditure ceilings that created fiscal space to boost public investment. See Carranza, Daude, and Melguizo (2014).

9 Saving Begins at Home

Ultimately, Latin America's low saving rate can be traced back to individual households throughout the region. Why do they—or do they not—save and how? Answering this question is not an easy task. Understanding how people make their saving decisions demands more than an analysis of how the financial system interacts with its individual savers. It requires a closer look into their communities, their homes—and even their minds.

Saving rates in Latin America and the Caribbean are low compared to other regions (Chapter 2). This chapter zooms in on households to find out why people in the region save so little. It evaluates some of the difficulties that households in the region encounter when they try to save, analyzes the effects of these constraints on their financial portfolios, and identifies strategies that may boost household saving rates.

Constraints to Saving

Several factors can limit households' saving choices. These constraints can affect either the choice to save formally or more generally, saving behavior.[1]

Too Hard to Save Formally?

Nothing in life is free, and saving is no exception. When saving is done through a formal financial institution, the monetary costs of managing a saving account make households think twice about opening or using the account, especially when yields do not compensate for these costs.[2] Given high transaction costs—ranging from opening fees and minimum balance requirements to transaction and withdrawal fees—many households find that it simply costs too much to use a financial institution.

In other parts of the world, reducing these monetary costs has proven to be effective in encouraging people to open formal saving products. Subsidies that cut the cost of opening and maintaining a bank account yielded take-up rates (i.e., new accounts opened among those that were offered) as high as 82 percent in Nepal (Prina, 2015) and between 47 percent and 62 percent in Kenya (Dupas et al., 2016; Dupas and Robinson, 2013a). In the Philippines, programs that reduce transaction costs also have had positive, albeit more modest, effects in inspiring people to open formal saving accounts (Ashraf, Karlan, and Yin, 2006). However, better financial conditions such as higher interest rates have had only a limited effect on households' usage of formal saving accounts in Chile (Kast, Meier, and Pomeranz, 2012) and the Philippines (Karlan and Zinman, 2014). Even when financial institutions offer large, subsidized marginal yields, people often respond little to these incentives.

In recent years, various Latin American and Caribbean countries have made major regulatory advances to promote basic or simplified saving accounts with low transaction costs. Other interesting cost-cutting innovations include the expansion of agent banking and the use of virtual technologies to extend the reach of formal financial institutions to underserved geographical areas. Despite their tremendous potential and their rapidly growing popularity in several countries, regulatory challenges and other barriers still limit their expansion. On the one hand, regulatory frameworks that authorize the use of agent banking in the region have developed only slowly. On the other hand, several issues arise when trying to regulate mobile wallets, phone banking and other virtual technologies. In several Latin American and Caribbean countries, regulation deters the use of these technologies since only authorized financial institutions are allowed to collect deposits from the public.[3]

Credible and well-designed regulation may also help address another formidable barrier to formal saving: lack of trust. Latin America's long record of financial crises and bank runs is etched in the memories of potential savers. Following "lack of money," "lack of trust in banks" is the number two reason given for not having a formal account, as reported in the Global Financial Inclusion (Global FINDEX) database (Demirgüç-Kunt and Klapper, 2012). Globally, Latin America and the Caribbean ranks highest among regions in terms of this barrier, well above East Asia and the Pacific (see Figure 9.1). Unfortunately, there is no causal evidence linking the lack of trust in banks with the level of formal savings in an economy. Since trust takes years to build and draws on personal and

Figure 9.1 **Lack of Trust as a Barrier to Open a Formal Bank Account**

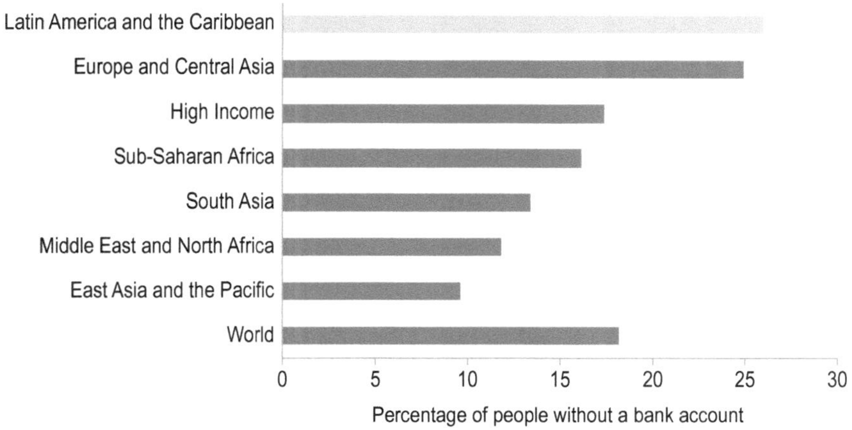

Percentage of people without a bank account

Source: Authors' elaboration based on Global FINDEX dataset (Demirgüç-Kunt and Klapper, 2012).

social history as well as other contextual factors, it is hard to isolate its effect on formal saving rates.

The region's tortuous history of financial crises may not be the only reason behind people's distrust of banks. Information or knowledge gaps may also be to blame. After all, it is hard to ask someone to trust something they do not know or barely understand.

The current state of financial literacy in the region is disappointing. According to a survey by García et al., (2013), the majority of the population in Chile, Colombia, Guatemala, Mexico, and Peru does not understand the term "interest rate." Inflation is another highly misunderstood concept, and thus very few people understand how to factor it into their calculations of the purchasing power of money.

Theoretically, reducing informational gaps should boost the use of formal saving products. However, the actual effect may be disappointing. Survey experiments conducted in Peru, Mexico, and Brazil evaluated the impact of providing poor and middle-income households with information on bank products and yields on the hypothetical choice of opening a formal savings account (Frisancho and Karver, 2016). In all cases, the effect was modest at best.

In general, the effectiveness of interventions to improve financial literacy is discouraging, beyond a few notable exceptions (see Fernandes, Lynch, and Netemeyer, 2014). Traditional financial literacy interventions may be failing not because of the content but because of the delivery strategies used. Standard classroom-like delivery methods have not worked well, but simpler and more agile financial literacy interventions seem promising. Drexler, Fischer, and Schoar (2014) compare two distinct financial literacy programs aimed at microentrepreneurs in the Dominican Republic. The first followed traditional financial education modules in a classroom-like environment. The second was a simplified "rule-of-thumb" program. While the standard accounting program had almost no effect on business financial and profit outcomes, the simplified training resulted in better accounting practices and higher profits.

All in all, the most effective policy by far to increase access to formal saving instruments is removing initial transactional barriers. However, while policy interventions that help reduce transaction costs are effective in persuading people to open accounts, they are far less so in convincing people to use them (see Frisancho, 2016). Most likely, other factors affect household saving decisions more generally. To understand this side of the problem requires nothing less than looking into the minds of Latin American savers and analyzing their cultural and personal biases— a formidable task indeed.

In the Hearts and Minds of Savers

Family and Friends First

It's hard to say no to a family member in need, especially in a culture like that of Latin America that places a high value on the extended family. Despite the insurance benefits that extended networks of family and friends may offer, they can also represent a drain on a household's time and resources and ultimately impose demands on their accumulated stock of savings. These demands are particularly high in Latin America, where private transfers among households represent, on average, 36 percent of per capita labor income (Lee and Mason, 2011a).[4] The high rate of private transfers may also explain the small balances but large cash flows that the relatively poor manage (see Chapter 2). Moreover, the poor spend considerable sums on weddings, festivities, and funerals— celebrations that often include their extended family and/or their social network of friends and neighbors (Collins et al., 2010 and Banerjee and Duflo, 2007). Social pressure to share income and assets may discourage asset accumulation, encourage a fast turnover of resources, or even induce costly behavior such as strategic borrowing to hide resources and preempt requests for transfers (Baland, Guirkinger, and Mali, 2011).

Latin America is not the only place where social pressure affects portfolio allocation (Jakiela and Ozier, 2016). In Kenya, villagers were randomly assigned an initial sum of money and asked to put that money in either a savings account with private balances or an investment account. In the case of the investment accounts, information about their returns could be either public or private, or they could pay a fee to keep the information private. Women, but not men, were willing to forego expected income in order to keep their returns a secret from others in their village. Women with large sums of money and public returns invested 6.5 percent less in a business opportunity than women with less money who could keep the returns private. Essentially, the study finds that women face an average "kinship" tax of about 4 percent of income.[5]

The burden that a social network imposes can be hard to escape. Fear of social shame and ostracism, as well as reciprocity, can be great, especially in close-knit communities. In India, the extent to which households help each other financially, and thus provide interpersonal insurance, varies with social proximity (Chandrasekhar, Kinnan, and Larreguy, 2012). Among very connected households, the level of transfers does not change when a savings instrument is provided. Essentially, family and friends trump personal savings and investment. Thus, the demands of social networks limit the stock of savings the poor can accumulate and divert resources away from productive uses.

In addition to pressure across households, tension between members of the same household also constrains saving. More than one marriage has been strained when one partner makes monetary choices for the household. The reasons for this tension stem from differences between spouses in terms of their bargaining power, intertemporal preferences (Schaner, 2015; Browning, 2000), risk tolerance, or even tastes in consumer goods (Anderson and Baland, 2002). Strategic behavior by both partners can lead to inefficient saving choices.

Differences in saving goals within a household may be explained by differences in the rate at which husbands and wives discount the future. Since women live longer than men and tend to be younger than their husbands, they may well have lower discount rates (Browning, 2000). The prospect of a longer retirement period without their husbands drives women to save more for old age.

In Latin America and the Caribbean, women live an average of 73 years, while men live only 68.9 years. This gap is even wider among developing countries within the region, with females living 77.7 years and males 71.[6] Moreover, women in Latin America tend to marry older men. Among couples with husbands aged between 30 and 50, irrespective of the number of children, about half the households in Brazil consist of husbands who are four or more years older than their wives—almost double the share of households with wives who are the same age or older than their husbands (see Table 9.1). The age gap is similar in Mexico and somewhat less skewed in Peru, but still relatively high.

Viewing households as groups of individuals helps explain the risk sharing arrangements that take place within the unit. By definition, two-person households face less income risk than single-person households dependent on a single source of income. If someone at home loses his or her job, two-person households have to adjust their consumption less than single-person households. In the same vein, two-person households are less affected by the removal of public insurance, such as unemployment insurance, both in terms of savings and the accumulation of assets. Multiple-person households can indeed insure their members by strategizing over labor supply (who in the household will work, at what kinds of work, and when) depending on the generosity of the public insurance available.[7]

In sum, decision-making both within and across households and intra-household insurance mechanisms may lead to suboptimal saving choices. Although it is hard to tackle these issues directly when they constrain saving, they need to be considered in the design of financial services and public insurance programs. For example, in settings where pressure to share with other family members or friends is high, hard

Table 9.1 **Age Differences between Wives and Husbands (percent of households)**

Age difference	Peru		Mexico		Brazil	
	No children	Children	No children	Children	No children	Children
Wife older	24.1	16.4	16.2	17.9	17.9	16.5
Same age	12.9	12.9	10.5	10.4	6.8	8.4
Husband 1–3 years older	26.3	26.8	33.1	31.3	26.5	26.3
Husband 4–5 years older	12.1	13.9	12.7	13.5	15.5	13.5
Husband more than 5 years older	24.5	30.0	27.5	26.9	33.3	35.2

Source: Authors' calculations based on the Base of Pyramid (BoP) Survey.

commitment saving accounts can be useful instruments for households trying to accumulate a stock of savings (Brune et al., 2015).

A Behavioral Economics Tale

Even if there were no constraints to saving formally, saving levels could still suffer if individual biases influenced saving choices. Ultimately, saving is a personal decision subject to an individual's needs, wants, and even personality.

The Penchant for Instant Gratification

The economics and psychology literature have both documented the importance of time preferences in saving decisions (Frederick, Loewenstein, and O'Donoghue, 2002; DellaVigna, 2009). Individuals with present-biased preferences find it extremely hard to postpone consumption, even if it comes at the expense of their future welfare. Thus, they consume today, instead of saving for tomorrow. The more immediate the reward, the harder it is for them to postpone consumption: that is, their preferences may be time-inconsistent. Preferences of this sort lead people to procrastinate in various aspects of their lives: starting a diet, writing a boring report, or renewing a driver's license. They find it particularly hard to save whenever self-control mechanisms are not incorporated into their choices.

Several recent studies have tried to measure the correlation of present-biased preferences with under-saving. These efforts have typically involved small sample sizes in randomized controlled trials or case studies. A noteworthy exception is Wang, Rieger, and Hens (2011), who measure impatience and time discounting in 45 countries, though still relying on small samples of university students (see Box 9.1).

Time preferences may vary by nation or region. Using nationally representative data at the urban level for Peru, Mexico, and Brazil, Frisancho and Karver (2016) measure time preferences by asking individuals to *hypothetically* choose between a small reward today and a larger one in a month. They then compare their answers for the same question but set in a more distant time frame, six to seven months from now. Individuals who choose the smaller reward now rather than waiting for a larger reward in a month, but claim that they would be willing to wait for the larger reward six months from now, are considered time-inconsistent.[8] About 40 percent of the urban population in Mexico, Peru, and Brazil has time-inconsistent preferences. More importantly, about one-third of the urban population in these countries can be considered hyperbolic discounters: they penalize the passage of time more strongly today than they do in the future (see Frisancho and Karver [2016] for more details).

Hyperbolic discounters have a harder time saving because of their present-biased preferences. They also may be more likely to borrow whenever they need cash. In Peru, hyperbolic discounters are 14 percentage points less likely to save than people who are always patient. In Mexico, hyperbolic discounters are 10 percentage points more likely to be indebted than those who are consistently patient. In Brazil, the probability of saving is 8 percentage points lower for hyperbolic discounters relative to people who are always patient (Frisancho and Karver, 2016).

Overall, an important share of the population in Latin America and the Caribbean may benefit from commitment devices that help them save. Those who are conscious of their present-biased preferences will actively demand financial products that help them exercise self-control—like individuals who find a "gym buddy" to motivate them to exercise. People who are not fully aware of these biases could also benefit by being presented with default or opt-out schemes since procrastination itself and/ or inertia will deter or at least delay an active choice to opt out (DellaVigna and Malmendier, 2006). Mandatory pension plans are in essence a way to deal with the tendency to postpone saving for retirement.

Helping people deal with their self-control problems is effective at increasing saving.[9] Since time-inconsistent individuals face a disconnect between their present self and their future self, they need a commitment device to keep up with their initial savings plan. The commitment device can include penalties, such as interest rate reductions or fees. A seminal study by Thaler and Benartzi (2004) shows that behavioral economics can be effectively used to design prescriptive policies: by offering people the option to commit in advance to allocating a portion of their future salary increases toward retirement savings, the program "Save More Tomorrow™" increased saving rates from 3.5 percent to 13.6 percent in a span of 40 months.

A commitment product provided by a bank in the Philippines allowed savers to choose between time-based and amount-based maturities. Among those who opened the account, saving balances increased by over 300 percent relative to the control group. Not surprisingly, savings increased the most among those initially identified as time-inconsistent. These people are precisely the ones whose time preferences are more likely to limit their saving choices in the absence of a commitment device (Ashraf, Karlan, and Yin, 2006).

In settings where the supply of formal products is limited, commitment devices may take the form of informal arrangements, such as saving groups or rotating saving and credit associations (ROSCAs).[10] Members meet to make regular lump-sum contributions that they pool and give to one member of the group in each meeting. These groups are usually formed within an existing social network, which guarantees that the imposed commitment is binding. In Chile, such self-help peer groups were implemented among microentrepreneurs as a commitment device to encourage precautionary savings (Kast, Meier, and Pomeranz, 2012). The number of deposits grew by about 350 percent and savings balances almost doubled among clients in the treatment group.

How strong should the commitments be? Imposing liquidity restrictions that are too strict runs the risk of scaring participants away (Ashraf, Karlan, and Yin, 2006). The trade-off between commitment and flexibility is a recurring issue in the design of financial products and services. Although there is a demand for products that tie one's hands in the future so he can reach his current saving goals, unexpected shocks may force households to break their commitment. In such cases, strong commitment devices may even reduce welfare. The right balance between commitment and flexibility is hard to strike and depends on the setting as well as the specific saving motives of the targeted population and their exposure to uninsured risks. For instance, strong commitment accounts may be more suitable for saving for a specific goal or a planned expenditure/investment, rather than simply for a rainy day (Dupas and Robinson, 2013b).

Commercial commitment products being developed in the region contain a contract specifying a savings plan with a goal to be achieved in a fixed number of installments. Additional incentives are usually offered for those who keep up with their plan, such as preferential interest rates or participation in raffles. Although penalties can also be used to deter individuals from missing an installment, these are rarely implemented, especially when the product is first launched. While some products involve a social commitment, many others rely on individual commitments and/or labelling to help users follow their saving plan.[11]

The Multilateral Investment Fund (MIF) has been promoting individual scheduled saving accounts in the region with varying degrees of commitments and rewards.[12] Preliminary results suggest that take-up rates for commitment devices are high, but usage tends to decline over time. Procrastination or lack of attention reduces the incentives to make deposits over time. Thus, to ensure that people continue to make deposits, they may need additional features built into the product. Using reminders or capitalizing on some of the problem-solving biases discussed in the next section, such as inertia, may be effective tools to increase saving balances among households in the region.[13]

Inertia and Limited Attention: Not All Bad

Most economic models assume that people process all available information in a rational and optimal way. But in real life, people make bad (and conscious) choices. Does this mean they are not rational optimizing agents?

Not necessarily. Psychological or cognitive biases also affect decisions. Sometimes people use less information than is available because it is hard to process—especially when a choice is urgent. Other times, people may act on hunches just because they are overconfident about their own opinion on a given matter. In other words, individuals tend to make decisions based on mental "rules of thumb," or heuristics (Kahneman, Slovic, and Tversky, 1982).[14]

Two such psychological biases are important determinants of saving behavior: inertia and limited attention. The first emerges from a preference for the status quo: the current state is perceived as a reference point and any deviation from it is perceived as a loss. Whenever taking an action imposes some sort of transaction cost, people who prefer the status quo (a tendency toward cognitive inertia) will have a harder time incurring that cost.

Preferences characterized by inertia lead to habits. Some people tend to go to the same places and order the same dishes when they go out for lunch or dinner, for example. These are safe choices; they repeat them because they represent the status quo and they are satisfied with the outcome. Finding a new place to eat or trying a new dish incurs a search cost and poses the risk of not liking the new choice, so there is a tendency not to change. This is why automatic enrollment plans have been successful in many settings, especially in consumer markets. Many promotional campaigns provide a given good or service at a reduced rate for a short period of time, after which automatic enrollment kicks in at the regular rate. Surprisingly, many individuals find it easier to keep paying the higher price than to cancel the service.

Limited attention can also lead to poor choices if information is neglected. In many countries, for example, retail stores must list the final price of their products, including taxes. This is a common practice because consumers tend to forget to factor in the additional cost of taxes when buying goods.

When individuals succumb to limited or selective attention, they are more prone to make mistakes or distort their choices. People can have trouble forecasting their future expenditures, for example, which can affect their saving behavior. Planning tools that force people to list all the elements of their household consumption basket, for instance, can help them pay attention to frequently overlooked details when forecasting their consumption. Evidence from Frisancho and Karver (2016) provides an example along these lines. Households were asked two different questions: "Do you or anyone in the household save regularly?" and "In the last 12 months, have you or anyone in the household saved using […*formal/informal saving instruments…*]." Notably, households respond very differently to these two questions. When asked about whether they save in general, households misreport their actual saving behavior. Among those who claim not to save in general, 39 percent, 23 percent, and 15 percent of the households in Peru, Mexico, and Brazil, respectively, report saving when asked whether they use each possible financial instrument, one at a time.

Inertia and limited attention need not work against saving activity. On the contrary, they can be tapped to actually boost saving levels. First, capitalizing on inertia, the optimal saving level can be made the default. Individuals who tend to prefer the status quo find it harder to opt out of saving. In this way, inertia serves as a constraint for the person to stop saving. Automatic discounts or direct deposits may help mobilize savings in settings where income flows, such as wages, are intermediated by some individual or institution other than the saver. Contributions to pension plans intermediated through the employer seize this opportunity to help people save for retirement. Banks in more financially developed settings have incorporated this feature into several commercial products: an example is automatic deductions for savings for individuals who receive their wages through a bank transfer.

The scant use of electronic transactions as a means of payment in developing countries limits the possibility of using default mechanisms to encourage savings. Nevertheless, recent efforts in the region have targeted cash transfer beneficiaries who receive their grants via direct deposit to a bank account. Default devices linked to remittance receipts is another effective way to capitalize on inertia, since remittance recipients tend to receive an international wire transfer on a regular basis. Whenever income flows through a bank account, additional illiquid accounts can be linked to it to allow the recipient to choose automatic discounts to be saved.

The saving potential of such mechanisms is highlighted by a recent study on the effects of offering direct deposits of the proceeds from cash crop harvests in bank accounts in rural Malawi (Brune et al., 2015). Almost 300 farmers' clubs, each with 10 to 20 members, were randomly assigned to a control group or one of two treatment arms: a direct deposit account and a commitment saving account. The second arm offered the direct deposit account but added an additional illiquid account that allowed farmers to specify an amount to be transferred into it, as well as date-based maturity. Both treatment arms helped increase total savings balances, since all cash crop earnings were automatically saved. However, the commitment account had a much larger effect: while the direct deposit account increased total balances by 280 percent, savings increased 620 percent with the commitment account.

Inertia can also be capitalized on by promoting saving habits among children and youth. Instilling saving habits at a young age can generate new reference points or a status quo that incorporates saving in consumption decisions. Showing young people the value of delaying gratification could be a promising strategy to promote higher savings in Latin America and the Caribbean, where time preferences are biased more toward the present than in other regions.

Financial education for youth can yield important indirect effects beyond financial knowledge, attitudes, and outcomes. First, good financial habits are also linked to better outcomes in schooling, employment, and standards of living. Second, young people can be agents of change in their households, sharing knowledge they acquire with their parents and other siblings (Bruhn et al., 2013).

In Brazil, a financial education program in public high schools improved financial literacy. More importantly, the program seems to have benefited all students, irrespective of their initial level of performance in a financial knowledge exam. Students in the treatment group were on average 12.5 percent more likely to save than the control group. The intervention also improved spending behavior: students in the treatment group were more likely to compare prices, or negotiate prices or payment methods while shopping, and prepare monthly budgets.

Finally, the program also seems to have "trickle up" effects: parents in the treatment group scored higher in a financial literacy exam and were more likely to save (Bruhn et al., 2013).

A recent experiment with young account holders in Colombia explores the roles of limited information, limited self-control, and limited attention on saving behavior with a financial information campaign delivered through short message service (SMS) (Rodríguez and Saavedra, 2015). A large-scale field experiment included three treatment arms in addition to a control group: a financial education campaign with monthly messages; and two treatments with monthly and bimonthly reminders to save. The better targeted reminders to save, regardless of their frequency, had important effects on account balances, mainly by reducing withdrawals. The financial knowledge campaign had no significant effect on account balances, which suggests that informational and knowledge constraints were not binding in this sample.[15]

Lack of attention can also be tackled with appropriate reminders and nudges that help people achieve their saving goals. In daily life, people who know they have a bad memory or lack attention resort to simple tricks to remind themselves of certain events or tasks: wearing a rubber band around their wrists, writing reminders on their hands or arms, placing Post-It notes on the bathroom mirror, or writing to-do lists. Similar strategies may work when it comes to savings. In Bolivia, Peru, and the Philippines, reminders with varying content helped achieve a 6 percent increase in saving balances and a 3 percentage point increase in the probability of reaching a given saving goal (Karlan et al., forthcoming).[16]

The timing and frequency of nudges or reminders may also be important. Certain times of the month or day may be better than others for reminding people to save. If, for instance, the household receives the reminder when cash is scarce, the impact of the nudge could be weak. There may be better times of the day to remind people about their excessive expenditures and their saving goals, such as lunch or dinner time. In some cases, a one-time reminder may not be enough; if so, how many are effective? Finding the right balance between too few reminders and potential "harassment" is another important avenue for future research.

Policy Recommendations: What Really Counts

This chapter suggests three main strategies to promote household saving. First, there is a clear need for financial product innovation in the region to encourage more saving, particularly via formal channels. For example, social constraints to save need to be considered in the design of financial services. Behavioral biases, which also constrain saving for a large share of the population, should also be incorporated in the design of financial products and services.

Second, formal institutions can and should learn from informal mechanisms currently serving the financial needs of poor households. These informal arrangements have emerged to cover the unmet needs of those excluded (and those who exclude themselves) from formal financial services. Formalizing informal mechanisms whenever possible or through potential partnerships with formal institutions can help attract savings into the formal financial system.

Third, focusing on children and youth can foster positive saving habits and potentially affect preferences that could increase saving rates in the future. Since some of the traits that limit saving choices are malleable at younger ages but hard to modify in adults, early interventions may be able to impact time preferences and saving behavior. Given limited empirical evidence, more research is needed, and the research agenda needs to incorporate input from other fields such as neuroscience and psychology.

Product Innovation

Keep It Simple

"The simpler a task, the more likely it is to be done," conclude Karlan, Ratan, and Zinman (2014). Complicated paperwork, hidden fees, long lines to make a deposit, and burdensome trips to the bank all discourage clients from opening an account and/or continuing to use it. In a region where financial literacy is particularly low, financial institutions need to simplify processes to close information gaps that can limit the demand for saving services.

Tackle Behavioral Biases

About one-third of the population in urban Peru, Brazil, and Mexico exhibits hyperbolic time preferences. Moreover, according to the experimental evidence of Wang, Rieger, and Hens (2011) (see Box 9.1), the prevalence of present-biased preferences is higher in Latin America and the Caribbean than in other regions. People with behavioral biases would benefit from commitment devices that would help them save. Consumers who are aware of these behavioral biases have tried to find informal or idiosyncratic ways to deal with them via informal saving mechanisms such as ROSCAs. Formal suppliers of financial services could cater to time-inconsistent consumers with products that help them keep up with their saving goals. Scheduled saving plans and commitment accounts that correctly balance incentives and penalties could be effective instruments to bank the unbanked and help them increase their saving balances.

Among consumers who are not aware of their behavioral biases, introducing default mechanisms in developing financial markets could help them reach their goals. However, the advantages of these mechanisms can be better exploited in settings where income flows are intermediated through formal financial systems. Policymakers and financial institutions that join forces to bank the unbanked are thus a crucial foundation for providing saving products that respond to the needs of the households in the region.

Incorporate Technology

Technology can be helpful not only to simplify processes and transactions but also to help individuals deal with their behavioral biases. Opening accounts and being able to manage them online, for example, may lead to higher take-up and usage rates. Cellphones and the internet facilitate transactions that could otherwise be postponed indefinitely by time-inconsistent individuals. Transferring money from a simplified account to a more illiquid one with a couple of clicks minimizes the role that behavioral biases may play.

Technology can also aid with reminders. The ubiquity of cellphones in the region makes text messages and mobile application software the ideal cost-effective channel to help people save.

Nevertheless, regulation must catch up with innovation. The onus is on financial regulators to ensure that local regulations do not deter the development of new saving products that rely on technology.

Keep Testing

High-income households in Latin America and the Caribbean save a relatively higher fraction of their incomes than poorer households

BOX 9.1. DO GENES AND CULTURE MATTER FOR SAVING?

Several studies have probed differences in saving behaviors across countries and agents to understand if there is a natural propensity to save. A series of studies in the 1970s used factor models to decompose the variance in IQ tests into its genetic and environmental components. However, estimates of the contribution of genetic components from this literature range widely and depend mainly on strong and restrictive assumptions about the factor loadings or about the distribution of the genetic and environmental components.[a]

A noteworthy study on the role of genetics in saving decisions was recently conducted by Cronqvist and Siegel (2015) in Sweden. By exploiting the differences in genes shared among fraternal and identical twins, the study finds that genetic differences explain about one-third of the variation in individual savings rates. Moreover, the study finds that saving rates are negatively correlated with smoking and obesity—behaviors that may also reflect lack of self-control and present-biased preferences—and that this correlation is largely explained by genetic factors.

Another innovative strand of the literature has focused on testing what is referred to as "linguistic relativity," or the Sapir–Whorf hypothesis: Does the structure of a language affect the ways in which its speakers view the world? Can language influence the way speakers think and/or engage in nonlinguistic behaviors such as saving? A recent study by Chen (2013) evaluates whether speakers of languages that disassociate the present from the future have a harder time saving. He first classifies languages into strong and weak future-time reference (FTR) languages, and finds that Spanish and English have strong future time-references, while Chinese has a weak one.[b] In other words, Chinese distinguish the differences between current and future events less strongly than Colombians, who tend to make a very clear distinction between the two.

With this language coding in hand, Chen (2013) finds that the degree of future-time references intrinsic in each language correlates highly with the way in which speakers deal with household and individual intertemporal decisions such as health and saving choices. Furthermore, he shows that linguistic relativity may play an important role in national saving rates: countries with a strong FTR language save about 5 percentage points less per year than comparable countries with weak FTR languages.

Wang, Rieger, and Hens (2011) measure long-term discount rates (δ) and present-bias discount factors (β) in 45 countries around the world. Whenever $\delta=1$, individuals give the same weight to gains/losses today and tomorrow; i.e., they do not penalize future events. Thus, low values of δ signify that they discount the future more heavily relative to the present. Individuals may also discount the future against the present differently depending on when the choice is made. Someone may care about an intertemporal trade-off between today and a week from now, but not so much between four and five weeks from now. Individuals with $\beta=1$, will not exhibit any present bias in their choices

(continued on next page)

BOX 9.1. *(continued)*

Table B.9.1 **Median Long-Term and Present-Bias Discount Factors**

	Long-term discount factor (δ)	Present-bias discount factor (β)
Anglo	0.84	0.76
Middle East	0.80	0.62
East Asia	0.84	0.65
Latin Europe	0.82	0.60
Latin America	**0.82**	**0.59**
Germanic-Nordic	0.84	0.60
Africa	0.77	0.43
East Europe	0.79	0.38

Source: Authors' calculations based on Wang, Rieger, and Hens (2011).
Note: The Anglo region includes Australia, United Kingdom, Ireland, New Zealand, Canada, and the United States. Latin Europe includes France, Portugal, Italy, and Spain.

and will evaluate intertemporal trade-offs in the same light, irrespective of the time for receiving the reward/punishment.

Table B9.1 summarizes the study's results. When grouped by cultural clusters, the median values of the long-term discount rate (δ) remain quite stable across regions, mostly around 0.8. The only exception is Africa, which has a slightly smaller discount factor of 0.77, signaling a less patient attitude in the long term, which is consistent with very low levels of development in the continent. By contrast, there is a great deal of variation in the present-bias discount rate (β) across different cultural clusters. While Latin America and the Caribbean and East Asia have similar long-term discount rates, their present-bias discount rates differ. Latin Americans have a higher prevalence of present-biased preferences. The difference in median β between Latin America and the Caribbean and Anglo cultures is even greater: present-bias discount factors among the latter are almost 30 percent higher than in Latin America and the Caribbean.

[a] For a thorough survey and critique of these studies, see Goldberger (1979).

[b] By contrast, in other Asian countries where multiple languages are spoken, such as Singapore and Malaysia, the main language spoken has a strong future-time reference.

(Chapter 2). This is particularly worrisome because lower income households face greater exclusion from credit and insurance markets, higher income volatility, and greater vulnerability to unexpected income shocks. The poor are also relatively more constrained than the rich in their access to formal saving products due to the higher burden imposed on them by monetary costs or by lower levels of financial literacy.

However, developing and testing prototypes of formal saving products to reach and be used by the poor may not be an appealing enterprise for traditional financial institutions, and it may be extremely costly for nonprofit microfinance institutions that are struggling to survive. After all, the savings that the poor can mobilize amount to modest aggregate sums. This knowledge gap has been more or less covered by the academic community, whose interest in prototypes is increasing, and extensive randomized control trials all over the developing world. Nevertheless, academics' incentives to publish and practitioners' urge to find timely solutions that can be cheaply and quickly tested can limit the extent of experimenting that takes place.

Some efforts to coordinate these two sets of actors have emerged in the past few years. Innovation for Poverty Actions (IPA) has been active in promoting financial inclusion. It has launched several initiatives to connect policymakers and practitioners (matchmaking gatherings) and promote timely research to inform financial inclusion efforts in the developing world. The Multilateral Investment Fund has also served as a laboratory to test financial products and services in the region, with a stronger emphasis on saving products in recent years. As the region and the world as a whole keep changing, these initiatives will be crucial for informing policymakers, practitioners, and financial institutions.

Bridging the Gap between Informal and Formal Mechanisms

Households excluded from formal financial markets meet their demand for financial services by relying on informal mechanisms that are frequently linked to social networks. Although these informal services often charge very high fees and, in some cases, are insecure and unreliable, they remain popular. Some households may even prefer informal services over formal ones for a variety of reasons, such as their convenience, ease of use, and trustworthiness (Lee, Ainslie, and Fathallah, 2012). Providers of informal saving or credit instruments are usually already present in the clients' social network, so access to them is extremely convenient. Moreover, transactions tend to occur without the hassle of paperwork or complicated contracts and are usually enforced by social norms. Despite the risk involved in these unregulated transactions, households seem to perceive them as safer than those in the formal financial systems. These preferences may reflect their distrust of banks and/or confusion and disinformation about regulations and fee structures.

In reality, informal instruments can be very costly or unsafe due to the demands of family and friends and the high probability of loss or theft. Moreover, informal mechanisms tend to be very illiquid as in the case of saving groups or ROSCAS, where the saver must wait until luck or a predetermined schedule of payouts determine if it is his or her turn to receive the pot.

Beyond their proximity to unbanked clients, informal services have several other advantages when reaching the unbanked. They tend to be very flexible and innovative, as they emerge and adapt to the specific needs of the population they serve (Pagura, 2008). *Susu* collectors in Africa, for example, charge a fee to collect very small deposits over the course of a month (sometimes daily) and keep them safe. Households demand these services—which are prohibitively costly for a formal institution to supply—as a way to self-impose a commitment device to save or to keep savings out of the hands of family or friends.

Although financial inclusion efforts tend to focus on providing *formal* financial services, formal financial institutions are starting to link up with informal providers so they can reach clients they would otherwise find extremely hard to serve due to lack of infrastructure and local knowledge.

The "informalization" of formal financial services is happening around the world. In Ghana, two private banks are using *susu* collectors to mobilize savings, while in Jamaica, the Workers Bank created a product that mimics ROSCAs. In the Philippines, formal sector banks extend loans to informal lenders, creating a system of credit-layering that allows them to increase their outreach in rural settings by reducing problems of information, monitoring, and enforcement (Floro and Ray, 1997). In Bolivia, a nonregulated microfinance institution providing nonfinancial services to its clients created over 20 linkages with a variety of actors, including private sector firms such as Western Union and utilities companies. The microfinance institution was then an effective means for formal institutions to reach rural populations (González-Vega and Quirós, 2008).

Even though banking low-income populations may not be profitable per se, banks are realizing that supplying additional financial instruments such as credit and insurance is a very attractive business opportunity. Their ability to serve the poor on a large scale can thus become profitable. After all, the poor are an important share of the population in Latin America and the Caribbean: between 60 percent and 70 percent of the population lives on less than US$10 a day (in purchasing power parity terms).

Formal providers willing to go the extra mile may learn from the successful experiences of informal providers of financial services. First, banks can build on the existing supply of informal financial services. This strategy may help generate trust among unbanked clients, which is an important access barrier in the region.

Second, formal financial institutions can find ways to extend their outreach by merging with or sponsoring other informal providers that have comparative advantages in the market. The formalization of these providers can help reduce the risks and insecurities associated with informal mechanisms. These alliances can also help formal institutions reduce the upfront information and search costs that bancarizing entails.[17] Partnerships with informal institutions that have already assumed the sunk costs of banking someone (including educating the client and building a credit history) may reduce the costs of formal providers trying to reach the unbanked.

Finally, the design of formal products should be inspired by informal products currently being offered, which have been directly shaped by people's demands over time.

Getting an Early Start

Given the importance of behavioral biases to saving, directing interventions at children makes sense. Influencing the behavior of children is certainly easier than changing the bad habits of adults. Evidence from developmental psychology and neuroscience (Henrichs and Van den Bergh, 2015) indicates that self-regulation or self-control is governed by the prefrontal cortex, which can start to develop as early as in utero and continues into early adulthood. Environmental factors can influence both gene expression and neural specialization (Meaney and Szyf, 2005; Henrichs and Van den Bergh, 2015); this opens up the possibility of conducting early interventions among children and youth, while the prefrontal cortex is still developing. Self-control is an important trait for humans in many dimensions of their lives well beyond saving choices; it is thus urgent to learn about interventions that are successful in mediating the perverse effects of genetic predispositions.

However, empirical evidence on interventions that can either generate supportive environments for young people with a higher propensity to save or minimize the effects of genetic predispositions to save little is still scarce. Some exceptions are found in Jamison, Karlan, and Zinman

(2014), Karlan and Linden (2014), and Berry, Karlan, and Pradhan (2012), but their results are far from promising.

Brazil is including financial education in the curriculum of public high schools in the context of a National Strategy for Financial Education (ENEF). Initial results are promising (Bruhn et al., 2013). Several governments in Latin America and the Caribbean are following suit. Education ministers have yet to explore the best way to develop the specific financial literacy component to be included in the public high school curriculum, as well as adequate teaching materials.

Modifying time-preferences or saving attitudes to increase the propensity to save is not an easy task. Little is known about the best time to get started (whether with younger children in primary school and/or older children in secondary school); the length of exposure to environments that are conducive to improving self-control; or the experiences that moderate propensities to save, among others.

Pioneering work along these lines is being undertaken by some nonprofit microfinance institutions in the region, including FINCA Peru and ADRA Peru (see Box 9.2). Monitoring, evaluating, and experimenting along the lines of these efforts is crucial to better understand the impact that early interventions may have on saving choices. More research on the intersection of economics, neuroscience, and psychology is also needed to better understand the effects of environmental factors on genetic traits.

Redefining Financial Inclusion

Financial inclusion has often been viewed narrowly as households' ability to obtain access to credit. For decades, MFIs focused their efforts on easing the credit constraints of poorer households that lacked access to formal financial systems (Angelucci, Karlan, and Zinman, 2015; Banerjee et al., 2015; Banerjee, Karlan, and Zinman, 2015). In recent years, however, the concept of financial inclusion has expanded. Financial inclusion efforts now recognize the role of savings as a development tool and understand that households face strong constraints to save.

The initial focus of financial inclusion was on lifting supply-side constraints by trying to expand the use of formal financial services among the unbanked. Around the developing world, governments energetically promoted simplified saving accounts.[18] These efforts have helped bank the unbanked. However, demand-side constraints also restrict

BOX 9.2. IN PERU, NEVER TOO YOUNG TO SAVE

Microfinance institutions in Latin America and the Caribbean have usually promoted the development of saving habits among their clients, who are primarily
female microentrepreneurs. In recent years, some institutions have extended
their focus to the children and grandchildren of these women by providing
programs and products designed to help children save. In Peru, for example,
FINCA Peru has implemented a program developed by the nongovernmental
organization Aflatoun in rural areas for primary and secondary students and is
providing saving instruments to their clients' children.

Another example in Peru's peri-urban and rural areas is the village banking program of the Adventist Development and Relief Agency (ADRA).
After a few years as a pilot, the institution launched a product designed to
teach children saving habits by directly helping them save. The product is
offered to their clients' children and grandchildren aged 0 to 18. Children
who participate choose a specific saving goal, label a moneybox provided
by ADRA with their goal, and start a cycle of monthly deposits during the
village bank meetings. The children cannot withdraw their funds until they
have reached their goal. In the meantime, they earn interest, as the funds can
be used to extend loans to bank members. The moneyboxes help the children achieve their goals and avoid temptations to withdraw funds between
deposits. ADRA also offers a training component for the children's mothers
and grandmothers that emphasizes the crucial role they play in promoting
their children's saving habits.

Although the effect of the program has not been evaluated, the rapid expansion of the portfolio of young clients is encouraging. Between December
2012 and June 2015, the number of children in the program grew from 882
to 3,831, and total savings accumulated by these young clients increased
sixfold. As of June 2015, the average stock of savings per child was about
US$28.

households' ability to save—particularly through formal instruments.
Even when households have a bank account, they may be unable to
reach their saving goals because of demand-side constraints, such as
social pressure to lend to friends and family, lack of knowledge and/or
information, and behavioral biases.

Any national financial inclusion strategy that seeks to go beyond
counting the number of accounts opened must consider the factors that
limit household savings. On the one hand, formal financial institutions
should continue to design simple, easy-to-use saving products that meet
the demands of households. On the other hand, financial services must
take into account the interaction between saving and credit constraints
in a given market, and the effects on households' financial portfolios

and their demand for financial services. Although credit and saving are often viewed as opposites, they are really two sides of the same coin: households choose to save and borrow simultaneously. When households need money, both instruments provide a tool to finance lump-sum expenditures, since they both require a regular schedule of deposits and facilitate a single withdrawal at a given point in time (Afzal et al., 2015).

Dealing with saving barriers is harder than expanding the presence of banks through agent banking services. Demand-side constraints require well-crafted policy interventions capable of altering behavior. Affecting people's beliefs and preferences is not an easy task, but the potential returns of such interventions may be large—for individuals, households, and the development of their countries.

Notes

[1] Frisancho (2016) summarizes recent experimental evidence on interventions that tackle a variety of saving constraints discussed in this subsection, including transaction costs, lack of trust and regulation, information and knowledge gaps, social pressure and behavioral biases.

[2] See Chapters 3 and 11 for an overview of the main factors that drive up bank costs in Latin America and the Caribbean.

[3] See Chapter 11 for other issues related to regulation barriers.

[4] Nearly two-thirds (65 percent) of the annual consumption of people under 24 in Latin America and the Caribbean is financed by other members of the household, according to National Transfer Account (NTA)'s data. The elderly, on the other hand, give up 12% of their annual consumption in the form of private transfers (see http://www.ntaccounts.org/doc/repository/NTA%20Data%20Sheet.pdf).

[5] These conclusions are drawn from an experiment in Kenya by Jakiela and Ozier (2016). Preliminary results from a similar experiment in Senegal confirm these patterns (Boltz, Marazyan, and Villar, 2015).

[6] Data from the World Bank's World Development Indicators.

[7] See Ortigueira and Siassi (2013) for more details on an intra-household insurance model.

[8] A word of caution is in order. Janssens, Kramer, and Swart (2015) discuss in detail the problems that arise when measuring hyperbolic discounting through hypothetical choices in a one-time cross section. They argue that agents' level of patience may change because their preferences are unstable over time rather than because of present-bias. To measure time inconsistency accurately, the authors recommend relying on a longitudinal design that allows stationarity, time consistency, and time invariance to be disentangled. To the extent that agents incorporate the probability of changing environments in their answers to one-time experiments, future efforts to measure time inconsistency should rely on longitudinal data when possible.

[9] For a model that shows why hyperbolic discounters cannot reach their predetermined choice of savings and how (costly) commitment devices are useful for them, see John (2014).

[10] Versions of this model exist throughout Latin America and the Caribbean. They have a variety of names: *pandero* or *pandeiro* in Peru and

Brazil, *juntas* in the Dominican Republic, *tandas* in Mexico, and *quiniela* in several other countries.

[11] For a review of the available commitment saving products in the region and their current challenges, see Martin (2014).

[12] Multilateral Investment Fund's ProSavings program has financed the development of saving groups as well as individual scheduled savings accounts in the region, with a particular focus on beneficiaries of cash transfer programs and recipients of remittances from abroad.

[13] Thaler and Benartzi's (2004) Save More Tomorrow™ does exactly this: not only are employees given the chance to commit themselves to save in advance, but permanence in the program is made the default option. The design takes into account the role of status quo bias. By doing so, the program has achieved high survival rates: 8 out of 10 participants are still saving even after four pay raises.

[14] Mullainathan and Shafir (2014) highlight that poverty can also impact individuals' ability to process information, manage their time efficiently, or resist temptation, thus limiting their ability to make sound financial choices, forecast, or plan ahead.

[15] This is not surprising, given that this is a selected sample of people who had already opted into the formal financial system.

[16] The Innovation for Poverty Action (IPA) Messaging Project rigorously tests varying contents and methods of delivery of reminders that promote financial inclusion efforts.

[17] The externalities that deter financial institutions from providing the first loan to a poor individual or group with no previous credit history are described in Lanuza (2004). Once the investment to extend a loan to a client is made, other providers in the market have incentives to poach the client and thus avoid the upfront costs paid by the first lender.

[18] An example in India is the Prime Minister's People's Wealth Program, (Pradhan Mantri's Jan-Dhan Yojana), which planned to open 75 million accounts in a first phase that ended August 2015. In Chile, Cuenta RUT, a simplified saving account offered by Banco Estado-Chile's National Bank, has positioned itself as the main means of payment and deposit accounts in the country. Many governments in Latin America and the Caribbean are also paying out conditional cash transfers through basic bank accounts, promoting the bancarization of the poorest segments of the population. Nevertheless,

an ongoing debate rages over the unintended effects of social assistance programs on formal saving choices and trust in the formal financial system. In Argentina and Brazil, for example, the funds deposited into the formal account of beneficiary households are withdrawn whenever the household does not consume the total amount of the transfer during a given time frame. For a discussion on this topic, see Chapter 11.

10 Firm Productivity as an Engine of Saving

Saving rates are relatively low in Latin America and the Caribbean, as is productivity growth. Are these two facts related? Much of this book has argued that indeed, a relationship exists and that the direction of causality runs from savings to productivity, via investment. Low saving rates constrain investment in vital infrastructure such as roads, ports, and telecommunications, which in turn takes its toll on the growth of aggregate total factor productivity (TFP). Without the necessary infrastructure, firms cannot be fully efficient in the production process. Thus, low saving rates impede productivity growth and result in poor economic performance.

However, a second channel relates saving decisions to productivity growth and runs in the opposite direction. This chapter advances—and, more importantly, quantitatively assesses—the idea that productivity growth is not only a fundamental driver of long-run economic growth but, crucially, that it also constitutes an important determinant of saving decisions.

How does this connection from productivity to savings work? Essentially, it's through incentives. Individuals respond to incentives that convince them to postpone consumption today in order to save more and increase their well-being tomorrow. Economies with low TFP growth tend to be economies in which returns to investments are low. Faced with this prospect, firms have little incentive to invest—and households to save. Thus, saving rates will be low, too. In this way, low TFP growth, by providing weaker incentives to save, could be another determinant of the low saving rates observed in the region. The first half of this chapter explores the underlying mechanisms behind this idea, provides empirical evidence in favor of it, and quantifies the mechanism in some Latin American countries.

This causal link from TFP growth to savings is mediated by the financial system. Aggregate TFP is a weighted average of the productivity of individual firms. An economy in which productive firms can increase investment and hire more labor is an economy with high aggregate TFP growth. In order to invest, however, firms need access to financial markets. If instead, financial frictions constrain firms, some productive entrepreneurs may have to stay small until they can save enough to expand. Building up savings takes time; therefore, this process slows down aggregate productivity growth. The second part of the chapter looks at the distribution of private savings in the economy and at the behavior of firm saving in search of evidence that financial frictions distort the incentives to save in the region.

From Japan to the World: The Empirical Link between TFP and Savings

The role of productivity growth as an engine for saving has been well documented in the case of Japan in the 20th century. Chen, İmrohoroğlu, and İmrohoroğlu (2006) showed that the aggregate productivity growth between 1956 and 2000 in Japan explained most of the changes that took place in the country's saving rate during this period.

While the Japanese story is compelling, the real question is whether this pattern is apparent elsewhere around the world and at other points in time. An examination of the data contained in the Penn World Tables, an annual panel of 167 countries spanning the 1950 to 2011 period, provides further evidence of the relationship between saving and TFP growth. Focusing on separate episodes of surges in the saving rate strengthens the case even more.[1]

Episodes of high TFP growth have gone hand in hand with increases in saving rates. Considering 15 episodes of significant, sustained TFP growth; 11 of the 15 were accompanied by an increase in the saving rate as well. Panel a of Figure 10.1 illustrates this phenomenon by plotting TFP, real output per capita, and the saving rate during these episodes. Fifteen years later, on average, TFP had nearly doubled, output per capita had multiplied by a factor of 2.6, and the saving rate had nearly doubled from around 12 percent to 22 percent. Importantly, the increase in the saving rate does not share the same timing as the other two variables, nor does it follow the same smooth path. Instead, the upturn in the saving rate occurs five years after the episode of TFP growth began.

While panel a supports the hypothesis that productivity can be an important determinant of savings, it does not imply that it is the only one. Panel b confirms a positive relationship between the two variables:

on average, episodes in which TFP increased the most also enjoyed the greatest increases in the saving rate. Importantly, though, panel b also reveals that increases in TFP are not the only determinant of savings, nor are they a sufficient condition for boosting the saving rate. In four of the 15 episodes of significant TFP growth identified, the saving rate decreased.

Figure 10.1 Episodes of Surges in TFP

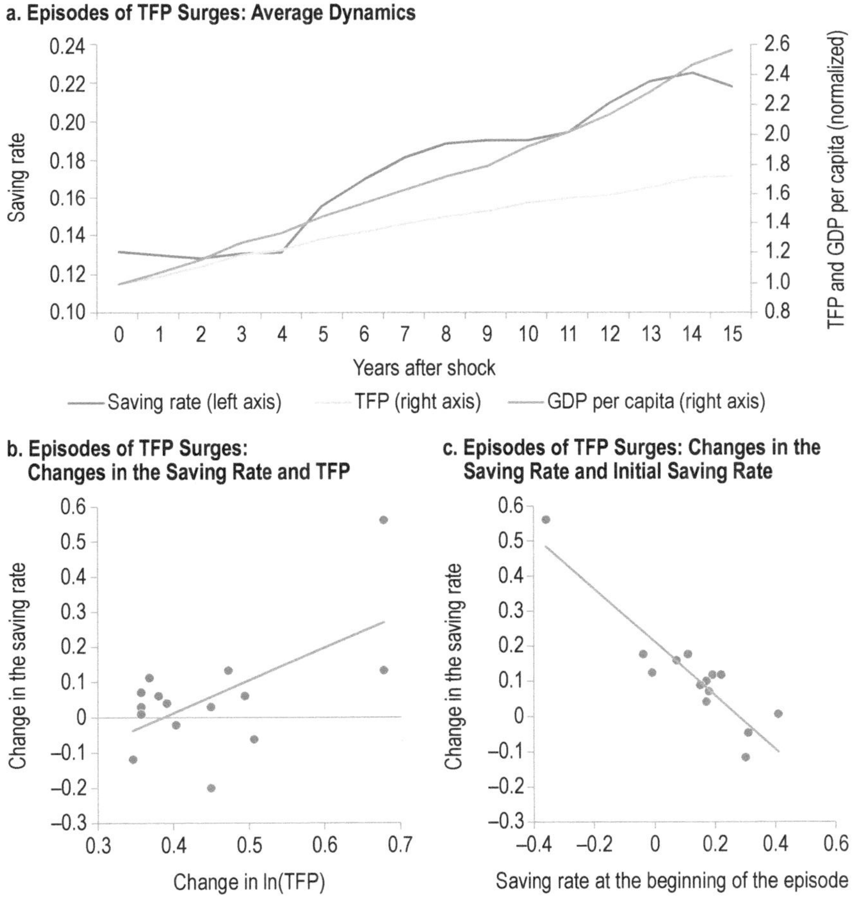

a. Episodes of TFP Surges: Average Dynamics

Saving rate (left axis) ——   TFP (right axis) ——   GDP per capita (right axis)

b. Episodes of TFP Surges: Changes in the Saving Rate and TFP

Change in the saving rate / Change in ln(TFP)

c. Episodes of TFP Surges: Changes in the Saving Rate and Initial Saving Rate

Change in the saving rate / Saving rate at the beginning of the episode

Source: Authors' calculations and Penn World Tables.
Note: In panel a, numbers reported are averages across episodes. TFP and real GDP per capita are normalized to be 1 in the first year of the episode. The horizontal axis represents the years since each episode started. For a list of individual episodes and for methodological details for defining them, see Busso, Fernández, and Tamayo (2016). Panels b and c plot the change in the saving rate during the TFP episode against the change in (log) TFP and the initial rate at the beginning of each of the 15 episodes identified, respectively. The adjusted R-squared of the simple linear regression in panel b is 0.31 and the positive slope has a coefficient of 1.05 with a p-value of 0.018. The adjusted R-squared of the simple linear regression in panel c is 0.82 and the negative slope has a coefficient of –0.84 with a p-value of 0.001. TFP = total factor productivity.

Lastly, panel c presents the change in the saving rate in each episode against the level of the saving rate observed at the beginning of each episode. It reveals a strong negative relationship between the two variables: TFP episodes in which the change in the saving rate increased the most also had a lower saving rate at the beginning of the episode. The four episodes where the saving rate decreased when TFP surged were those with a relatively high saving rate to begin with—above 20 percent.

Another finding is that not all surges in saving rates end up boosting output per capita. Whether a saving rate surge is accompanied by increases in output per capita appears to be related to whether or not TFP increases. This relationship is illustrated in panels a and b of Figure 10.2, in which 22 episodes of large and sustained increases in the saving rate are analyzed. The episodes are divided into those in which TFP increased by less than 10 percent within a decade (panel a), and those in which it increased by at least that (panel b). In the episodes of saving surges characterized by high TFP growth, the saving rate tripled from 10 percent to almost 30 percent within 15 years, while TFP and income per capita increased by a factor of 1.4 and 1.2, respectively. By contrast, in episodes of saving surges characterized by low TFP growth, this variable essentially stagnated alongside income per capita.

This analysis teaches an important lesson: if saving and productivity can foster investment and growth, they should not be studied in isolation. The facts indicate that productivity growth is another important variable when trying to understand the behavior of saving and its contribution to economic growth and well-being. This conclusion is consistent with two empirically documented findings about Latin America: its low saving rates (see Chapter 2) and its persistently low productivity growth (Pagés, 2010).

Incentives to Save

Why do saving decisions depend on investment returns? The mechanism can be understood within the framework of the neoclassical growth model. It has two key building blocks. First, households decide how much to consume and how many hours to work in order to maximize their lifetime well-being. Second, firms combine capital and labor with varying degrees of technical efficiency (productivity). When capital is relatively scarce, firms will want to invest more, driving up the return to investment. Higher investment returns are then passed on to households, inducing them to postpone consumption and increase saving. Thus, saving

Figure 10.2 Episodes of Surges in Saving Rates

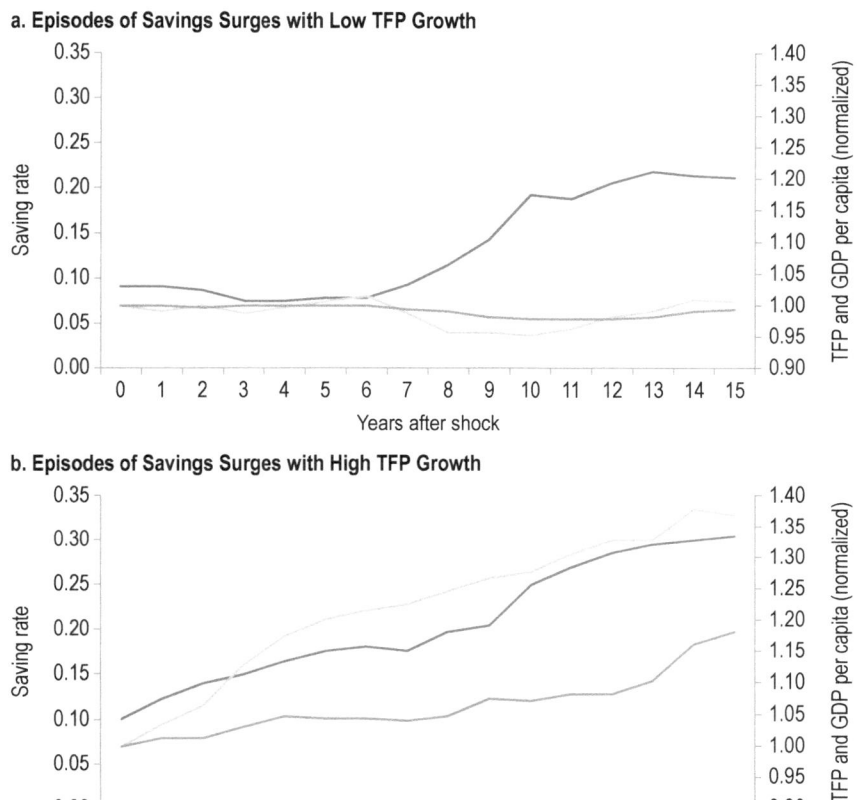

a. Episodes of Savings Surges with Low TFP Growth

b. Episodes of Savings Surges with High TFP Growth

—— Saving rate (left axis)   ——— TFP (right axis)   —— GDP per capita (right axis)

Source: Penn World Tables and authors' calculations.
Note: Numbers reported are averages across 22 episodes of saving rate surges. TFP and real GDP per capita are normalized to be 1 in the first year of the episode. The horizontal axis represents the years since each episode started. Panel a plots averages across 10 episodes in which TFP increased less than 10 percent within a decade. Panel b plots the remaining 12 episodes in which TFP increased by more than that. TFP = total factor productivity.

decisions are determined largely by the returns to investment, which in turn depend on several factors. One of these factors is TFP growth.

Consider the case in which individuals in an economy expect higher productivity growth. This implies that they will be able to extract increasingly larger amounts of output from each unit of capital, effectively increasing investment returns. In this case, individuals will postpone consumption today in order to save, invest, and reap the benefits of the increase in productivity when it comes. The economy's saving rate would increase above the level where it would otherwise have been.[2] In addition to productivity, other factors may also affect returns to investment and saving behavior. First, higher depreciation of capital can reduce the net return of investing because a larger fraction of the capital invested is lost. Second, government taxation of capital income may reduce incentives to save as it reduces after-tax returns. Third, higher government consumption can also be an important drag on the resources available for saving. Lastly, higher population growth requires larger saving efforts in the long run. The relative importance of TFP growth as an engine for saving vis-à-vis these other factors is an open question. The next section quantifies how much each of these forces contributes to explaining the saving rate in three case studies, two of them from Latin America.

Quantifying the Link from Productivity to Saving

To quantify the impact of productivity growth on saving, Chen, İmrohoroğlu, and İmrohoroğlu (2006) use a version of the model described above, fitted to Japanese data. Saving rates are simulated feeding the model with the observed dynamics of TFP growth, as well as the other driving forces that can affect investment returns, namely, population growth, effective rates of capital taxation, and government consumption. The results from this exercise are presented in Figure 10.3 under the label "model with four driving forces." In addition, the figure presents two other simulated saving rates. One of these uses only the series of TFP growth and capital tax rates, leaving government spending and population growth constant ("model with TFP and taxes"). Finally, under the label "model with TFP," only the TFP growth series is used to simulate the saving rate, while keeping the remaining three forces constant. The main conclusion is that the simulated saving rate, using only the observed growth in productivity, properly tracks the evolution of Japan's observed saving rate.

Does this result hold in Latin America too? To answer this question, the model is fitted to Mexico and Chile, much as it was to Japan. These countries provide examples in the region of two contrasting experiences of productivity growth and saving rate dynamics. In Chile and Mexico, productivity suddenly rose and fell around the early-1980s "debt crisis."[3] From the mid-1980s on, both productivity growth and the saving rate recovered in Chile but failed to do so in Mexico.

In addition to actual TFP growth, the model is fed with tax rates, government consumption, and population growth, first jointly and then sequentially. The simulated saving rates for three different scenarios (i.e., the same as in the case of Japan) are reported in panels b and c of Figure 10.3, along with the actual saving rates. A few important observations emerge from the exercise.

Figure 10.3 **Neoclassical Model Predictions of Saving Rates**

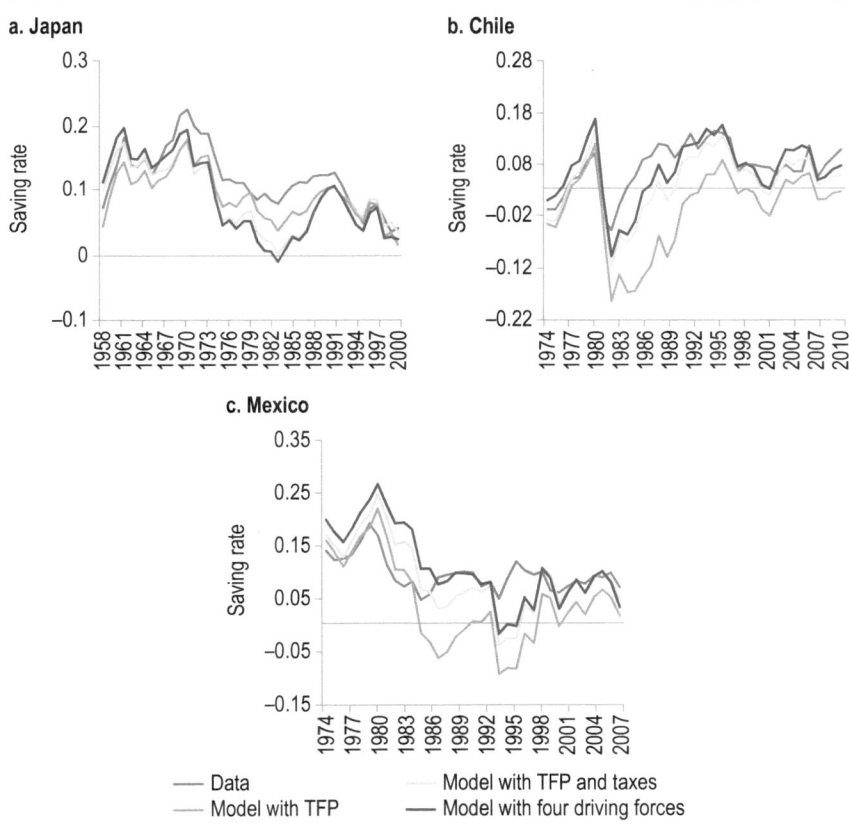

Source: Authors' calculations and Chen, İmrohoroğlu, and İmrohoroğlu (2006).
Note: For Mexico, the parameterization of the model closely follows Kehoe and Meza (2011), who studied Mexico's growth experience during the post-war era. "model with four driving forces" = TFP growth, population growth, government consumption and a tax rate of 53 percent for 1970–88 and 22 percent thereafter. "model with TFP and tax reform" = government consumption and population growth at their sample averages but includes the 1987 "tax reform". "model with TFP" uses the pre-reform tax rate (of 55 percent) for the entire period. The rationale for including a significant drop in the tax rate comes from Mexico's major corporate tax reform in 1987 (Urzúa, 1993). In the case of Chile, the parameterization of the model closely follows Bergoeing et al. (2002). Given the lack of reliable data, capital tax rates were set at 55 percent between 1960 and 1987 and 12 percent thereafter (Bergoeing et al., 2002). Hsieh and Parker (2007) presented compelling evidence that corporate tax rates were lowered by these approximate magnitudes around 1986–87.

First, in the case of Mexico, TFP growth and capital tax rates are able to track the actual saving rate fairly well. In particular, the model with only these two driving forces ("model with TFP and tax reform") is able to account for the rise and fall in the saving rate around the time of the debt crisis and for its subsequent stagnation.[4] Second, while productivity growth helps account for the *dynamics* of the saving rates throughout this period, capital tax rates played an important role in explaining the saving rates *level* in the aftermath of the debt crisis. In the model, capital tax rates serve as a proxy for the investment distortions in the economy. The results show that both TFP growth and these other investment distortions are required to track the evolution of the saving rate in Mexico.

In the case of Chile, the model predicts an increase and then a dramatic drop in the saving rate around the time of the debt crisis in the early 1980s. The series labeled "model with four driving forces" shows that the simulated saving rate can reproduce the major trends in the Chilean saving rate, perhaps even better than for Mexico. In sharp contrast to the Mexican case, in Chile, the saving rate climbed steadily in the years after the crisis and throughout the 1980s and early 1990s. To determine the main driver of this increase, Figure 10.3 compares three saving rates produced by the model. The results are that the strong TFP growth following the crisis of the early 1980s was the main driving force behind the observed saving behavior.[5] Again, capital taxes (i.e., a proxy for broader investment distortions) are important in determining the *level* of the saving rate, perhaps to a larger extent than for Mexico.

To sum up, this analysis uncovers three main lessons. First, as in Japan, the dynamics of productivity help to explain the broad trends in the saving rates of Mexico and Chile. Second, the simulations for both Chile and Mexico support the hypothesis that saving incentives (i.e., investment returns) matter for saving decisions. Finally, and perhaps most importantly, other factors (i.e., investment distortions) play a more central role in explaining the level of saving rates in Chile and Mexico than in Japan. In the real world, these distortions go beyond capital taxes; they also include, for example, distortions in financial markets that raise the cost of credit for firms. There is plenty of evidence that investment distortions are pervasive in the region and should therefore command the attention of policymakers interested in boosting saving.

The Fine Print

Even though the mechanism described above can help rationalize a causal link from productivity growth to saving, it has two potential limitations.[6] First, the model assumes a closed economy setting. Productivity growth would matter less for national saving if countries could perfectly substitute national saving for foreign saving. In a small open economy, foreign capital should flow in with higher productivity growth in search of the higher returns to investment. Hence, investment would be decoupled from national saving. However, evidence of this decoupling has been elusive (see Feldstein and Horioka [1980], and Chapters 4 and 5).[7]

Second, a recent analysis finds that capital flows from rich to poor countries are not only low (as argued by Lucas, 1990), but their allocation across developing countries is at odds with the one predicted by the open economy version of the model described above (Gourinchas and Jeanne, 2013). Not only is the strong positive correlation between productivity growth and foreign capital inflows not observed in the data, in fact there is a negative correlation between the two—a phenomenon known as the "allocation puzzle."

Why doesn't capital flow to countries with higher productivity growth to take advantage of the higher returns to investment? Gourinchas and Jeanne (2013) argue that since individuals can save not only through physical capital but also through financial assets abroad, taxation of returns to physical capital offers an incomplete explanation to the pattern of national saving and capital flows. Instead, large distortions to the accumulation of wealth—saving—rather than to its allocation (between domestic physical capital and foreign financial assets) are responsible for the particular pattern of net capital flows in Latin America (as opposed to, say, countries in Asia that actually subsidize saving). This result validates the idea that in a closed economy a tax on capital income acts also as a tax on saving. It also reaffirms the importance of examining the investment distortions faced by firms in Latin America, an exercise undertaken in the second half of this chapter.

In addition, the model assumes that all firms are homogeneous. This entails studying consumption, labor, and saving decisions from the standpoint of a representative agent (i.e., without distinguishing between firms or households). In particular, who carries out saving decisions is immaterial in the sense that the same results are achieved regardless of whether firms or households save. Acknowledging that agents vary along several dimensions—for instance in terms of wealth and productivity—has two important implications. First, aggregate productivity growth now results from combining the levels and growth rates of individual productivities of all operating firms at a given point in time (see Busso, Fernández, and Tamayo, 2016). Second, the efficient allocation of capital requires institutional arrangements, such as financial markets, for savings to flow across firms and sectors toward their most productive use. That is, with heterogeneous agents, who saves and how much matters.[8] For this reason, the rest of this chapter focuses on heterogeneity and distortions in saving–investment decisions.

Zooming in on Firms' Saving Decisions

Since entrepreneurs, by nature, vary in terms of their ideas and abilities to organize production, firms in the economy have different levels of productivity. Who gets to produce, and how much, matters for aggregate productivity. If a highly productive entrepreneur faces numerous obstacles in financial markets (also known as financial frictions) and thus cannot obtain the credit necessary to fund projects, the firm's growth will be constrained dramatically, as it will need time to accumulate internal funds. This results in lower long-run aggregate productivity growth.

As discussed earlier, low productivity growth provides few incentives for the economy to save. However, while financial frictions hinder productivity growth and thus result in lower aggregate saving, they nonetheless induce productive firms to save (i.e., accumulate internal funds) in order to overcome the lack of access to credit markets; therefore, paradoxically, financial frictions result in a higher share of saving in the economy done by firms (rather than by households). Analyzing the distribution of private saving in the economy, as well as patterns of firm saving, provides evidence that financial frictions distort price signals and incentives to save.

Why do firms save?[9] To begin with, firms must regularly meet cash needs for the ordinary course of business. Since it is costly to convert noncash financial assets regularly into cash for payments, firms need to hold cash to make those payments. Besides this transaction motive, there is a precautionary motive: businesses save so they can react more rapidly to adverse shocks or investment opportunities when access to capital markets is costly or takes time. Finally, and perhaps more importantly, firms save to finance current and future investment.

In contrast to households, which decide to save to increase future consumption, firms decide how much to save and invest to maximize their profits based on the relative costs of internal versus external funding sources.

In an economy without any transaction, bankruptcy, or agency costs, without any distortionary taxes, with symmetric information, and with efficient markets, the capital structure of the firm would be irrelevant for the firm value (Modigliani and Miller, 1958). In such an ideal economy, firms would have no reason to save. If they needed funds to build new plants, buy new machinery, or weather unexpected drops in sales or surges in expenses, they could borrow money from lenders and repay debts in the future. In such an economy, the cost of borrowing (the interest rate) would be the same as the cost of internal funds. In a world with symmetric information, banks, knowing everything that the firm does, would provide those resources if the firm were to find it profitable in the long run; otherwise, the firm would not be willing to borrow money in the first place.

The real world, however, is littered with transaction, bankruptcy, and agency costs; there are distortionary taxes and information frictions; and markets can be inefficient. For the sake of simplicity, these impediments are referred to as "financial frictions." These frictions make external financing relatively more costly than internal financing, thereby increasing incentives for firms to save rather than borrow money from lenders. Information frictions can prevent firms that want to borrow money from finding willing lenders, for whom it is costly to determine the viability of investment projects. This raises the cost of external finance and encourages firms to save. The so-called pecking order theory of finance (Myers and Majluf, 1984) predicts that based on firms' relative cost, it is best for them to use their own savings first, then to use debt, and finally, as a last resort, to issue equity.

Thus, the share of private saving done by firms can be rather large in most economies. Figure 10.4 shows the share of business saving to total private saving computed using national account data (Bebczuk and Cavallo, 2016). It plots information for a subset of countries in Latin America for which data are available, and for three comparison regions/countries: core Europe, the United States, and Germany. Businesses in all regions/countries under consideration are responsible for more than 50 percent of private saving, including Latin America, where the share of private saving by firms is 68 percent.

Figure 10.4 **Share of Corporate Saving in Private Saving**

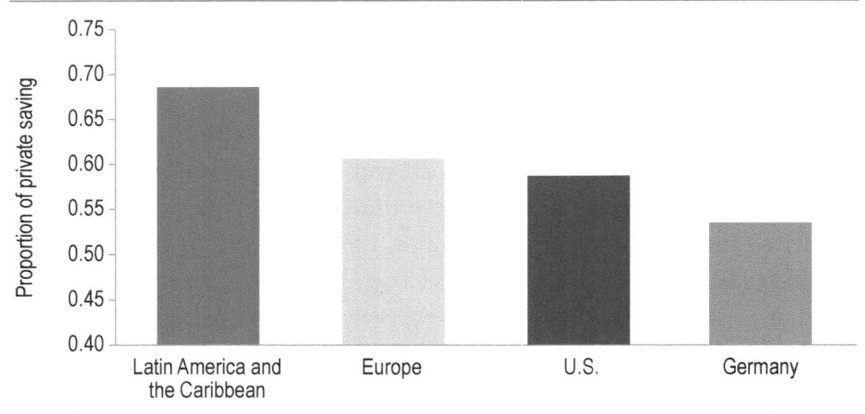

Source: Authors' calculations based on Bebczuk and Cavallo (2016).
Note: Latin America and the Caribbean refer to Brazil, Chile, Colombia, Ecuador, Guatemala, Honduras, and Mexico. Europe refers to Austria, Belgium, France, Italy, the Netherlands, Portugal, Spain, Switzerland, and the United Kingdom. Data are for 2008–12. Private saving is the sum of household and corporate saving.

In most economies, the average firm funds a large proportion of its investment projects using its own saving. Firms in Latin America follow this norm, funding between 45 and 75 percent of their capital with their own savings (see Figure 10.5). Even in Germany, a country with a more developed financial system, the average firm finances 44 percent of its fixed assets with its own savings.[10]

Why do firms in certain economies seem to rely more heavily on their own savings to fund their capital stock? One likely explanation is that their financial systems are underdeveloped. Firms that face fewer binding financial constraints rely less on internal funds to finance their capital investment. They usually face less stringent collateral requirements (Beck, Demirgüç-Kunt, and Maksimovic, 2005, 2008) and, given their size, are typically subject to less severe information asymmetries, resulting in multiple sources of funding (Diamond and Verrecchia, 1991). Figure 10.6 shows that the share of internal funds to finance capital declines with size; it is smaller for larger, less financially constrained firms.

Figure 10.7 utilizes a more direct measure by analyzing actual access to credit. In the scatter plot, each dot represents a country and size category combination. This figure confirms that the greater the access to credit, the smaller the share of investment financed with saving.

Financial frictions seem to be a particularly acute problem in Latin American economies, where financial development is low. Fernández and

Figure 10.5 Firms' Financing with Their Own Savings, Germany and Select Latin American and Caribbean Countries

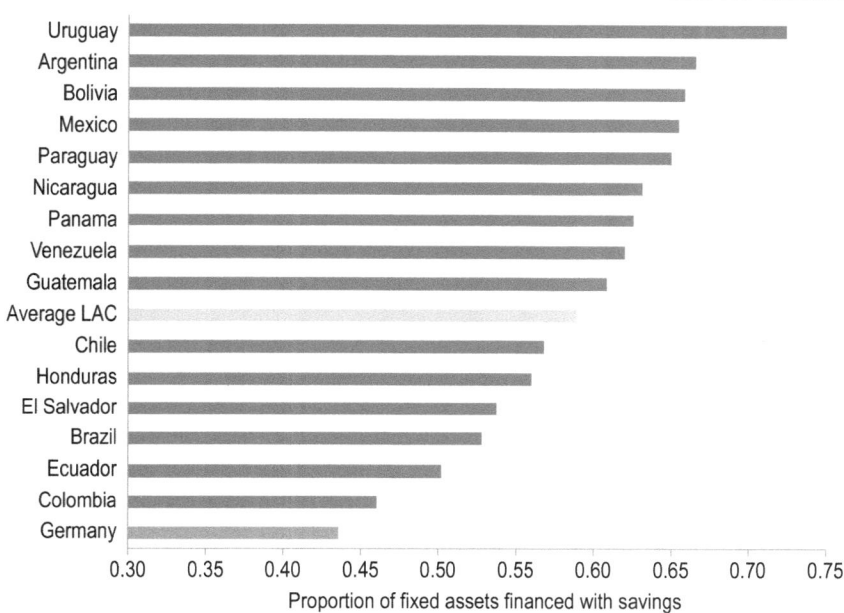

Proportion of fixed assets financed with savings

Source: Authors' calculations based on World Bank Enterprise Survey (WBES). See Busso, Fernández, and Tamayo (2016) for details.
Note: Firm savings are defined as internal funds or retained earnings. LAC refers to Latin America and the Caribbean.

Figure 10.6 Share of Fixed Assets Financed with Savings, by Firm Size

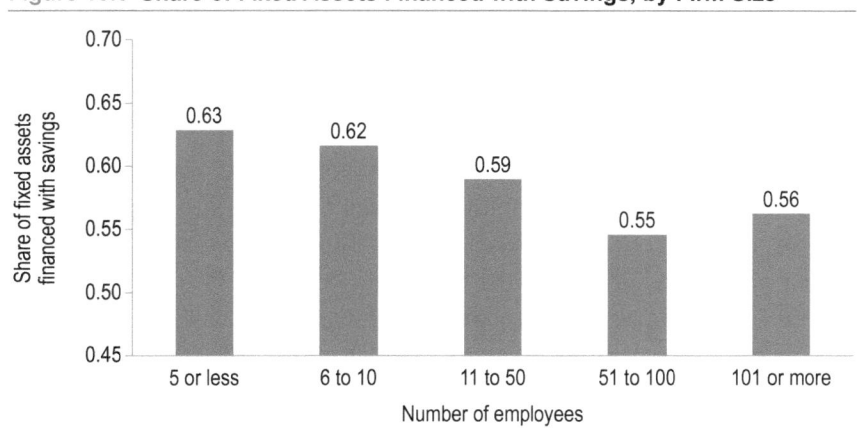

Source: Authors' calculations based on World Bank Enterprise Survey (WBES). See Busso, Fernández, and Tamayo (2016) for details.
Note: Firm savings are defined as internal funds or retained earnings.

Figure 10.7 **Fixed Assets Financed with Savings and Access to Credit**

Source: Authors' elaboration based on World Bank Enterprise Survey (WBES). For a list of countries and other details, see Busso, Fernández, and Tamayo (2016).
Note: Each dot represents a country-bin size combination.

Tamayo (forthcoming) survey the institutional causes of financial underdevelopment and their effect on growth. They pay particular attention to the weak institutions in Latin America which result, for example, in poor creditor protection. Importantly, low financial development could have been a bottleneck in the process of resource reallocation following the large-scale reforms implemented by many countries in the region in previous decades.

Firm Saving: A Way Out for Productive Firms

Firm saving is an imperfect remedy for financial underdevelopment. Saving can help firms overcome financial frictions so they can grow. In this way, saving is related to firm-level productivity and aggregate TFP growth. Firms usually start on a small scale with ideas, low levels of capital, and only a few employees. Small firms learn to organize their business and practices, and with time, realize whether they are productive or not. Not all firms, however, are born equal.

Small, unproductive firms have low marginal products of capital and labor. They have no reason, need, or ability to expand. Depending on how much competition and price distortion they face in their sector, they can survive with low levels of capital. Consequently, they find no need to save much. Their probability of exiting the market in which they operate in any given year is high (Davis, Haltiwanger, and Schuh, 1996). In Latin

America, these firms are usually small, informal, family-owned enterprises that survive mainly because distortions allow them to pay lower input costs or to charge higher prices.

For small, productive firms, however, it is optimal to grow by hiring more labor and acquiring more physical capital. This process of firm growth usually requires long-term investments in the form of new and larger plants that imply substantial resources, and which pay off only gradually over time. Even if the sunk cost of investment is tiny relative to the potential stream of future profits, the firm could expect costs to be very high compared to the meager profits from a small plant. Saving for future investments could be the only way to grow—and this process could take a long time.

Therefore, financial frictions have implications both for aggregate TFP growth and for the level and type of saving done in the economy. To understand why, firms can be classified into three types: small, unproductive firms that remain small or eventually exit the market; small, productive firms that would like to grow but cannot because of financial constraints; and firms that have already jumped to a larger scale.

In an economy with few financial frictions, small, productive firms can borrow substantially to upgrade their plants. Large firms invest to maintain their physical capital. Small, productive firms grow fast, increasing demand for capital and labor, which translates into higher wages and returns to capital accumulation. These price changes have many implications. First, higher wages eventually convince some small, unproductive entrepreneurs to close their plants and become wage employees. Therefore, such an economy has a significant share of large firms. Because productive firms grow fast, the share of small, productive firms is minimal, and there are almost no small, unproductive firms. Since the total factor productivity of the economy is a weighted sum of the productivity of individual firms, this economy enjoys higher aggregate productivity growth. Moreover, higher (equilibrium) investment returns translate into higher incentives for individuals to save. Aggregate savings are higher too.

Now consider an economy with high financial frictions, assuming the same distribution of firm productivities as before. Small, productive firms cannot borrow to upgrade plants and must save a larger portion of the required resources; therefore, they remain small longer. They do not increase labor demand, and wages remain low. They also do not increase demand for capital, and returns to capital accumulation remain low, as well. In such an economy, the mix of firms is very different. There is a smaller share of large firms, a larger share of small, productive firms that want to grow but cannot, and a larger share of small, unproductive firms. Aggregate productivity growth and aggregate savings are lower. The ratio of firm-to-household savings is higher because saving is the only way for firms to upgrade their plants. In that sense, excessive firm saving signals an underdeveloped financial system.

On average, more productive firms tend to save more. More importantly, productive firms without access to credit tend to save more than unproductive firms (see Busso, Fernández, and Tamayo, 2016). This correlation is even stronger among firms that applied for credit but did not secure it yet. In other words, holding the size distribution constant, more productive firms tend to save more. They require capital to grow but cannot access credit.

There is a relatively large, recent literature that formally models the relationships between financial frictions, firm productivity, saving, and aggregate TFP growth along the lines outlined above. For example, Midrigan and Xu (2014) use firm-level data to calibrate a model to South Korea (an economy with low financial frictions), China, and Colombia (two economies with high financial frictions). They show that without firm saving, the costs of financial underdevelopment would be much greater. Financial imperfections have a negative effect on the number and scale of producers that operate in the economy. The ability of firm saving to allow small firms to grow is more limited, precisely because their saving capacity is low.[11]

A Productive Approach to Policy

Two general policy implications are clear. First, when considering policies to promote savings, policymakers should not overlook economic reforms that foster productivity growth. It is no coincidence that episodes of fast TFP growth have been accompanied by increases in the aggregate saving rate and GDP growth, while episodes of savings growth without TFP growth did not lead to GDP growth. There is a reinforcing link whereby more saving can increase growth only if the additional savings is invested in projects that generate high returns and thus enhance productivity growth. Unfortunately, productivity growth has been elusive in Latin America. Policies to promote productivity growth in the region, including those aimed at improving the allocation of resources, promoting competition, and fostering firm innovation, are discussed in Pagés (2010).

Second, since aggregate productivity is a weighted average of the productivity of individual firms, which firms get to produce and how much affects the resulting aggregate productivity growth, and is therefore crucial for generating saving incentives. In particular, severe financial market frictions slow down the dynamics of productive firms significantly, as these firms need to save before they can grow. While this allows productive firms to save more, it also results in losses due to resource misallocation, lower TFP growth, and lower aggregate saving rates. Moreover, labor market and product market distortions might interact with the distortions generated by financial frictions and exacerbate the productivity cost of financial underdevelopment (these interactions are explored in Box 10.1).

Thus, policies to address the underlying causes of financial frictions (which is the focus of the next chapter) can help improve capital allocation, thereby increasing investment returns and saving incentives. In the search for more and, particularly, better saving in Latin America and the Caribbean, alleviating financial frictions can have a quantitatively significant impact.

BOX 10.1. FIRM SAVING, INFORMALITY, DISTORTIONS, AND MISALLOCATION

Latin America has a large number of small, informal, and unproductive firms that face lower costs of inputs or higher product prices because taxes and regulations are not properly enforced (Busso, Fazio, and Levy, 2012). By distorting prices, informality can provide incentives for unproductive firms to grow, even when they would not do so otherwise. The economic inefficiencies generated by these labor and tax distortions can be amplified by the ability of firms to save.

Consider a household that owns a small and relatively unproductive firm, and thus extracts little output from labor and capital. Suppose only labor market distortions exist. This informal firm is less productive than a formal firm in the same sector; it does not pay labor taxes, and therefore it has lower labor costs. For simplicity, assume capital is a complement to labor. Both firms hire labor and capital until the marginal products of these inputs equal their cost. The informal firm, facing lower labor costs, would hire more labor and capital than if resources were efficiently allocated. In an economy with financial frictions, the informal firm is likely to face higher external funding costs than the formal firm. These financial market distortions lessen the misallocation caused by labor market distortions.

This argument ignores the fact that entrepreneurs can overcome financial constraints through saving. If there were financial frictions and no labor mar-

(continued on next page)

BOX 10.1. *(continued)*

ket distortions, then small, informal, unproductive firms would have no reason to save because it would not be optimal for them to grow. However, with labor market distortions, their labor costs would decline, and it could potentially be in the interest of these firms to save in order to acquire capital (which complements labor).

Thus, in a context of preexisting distortions, firm saving can create an additional inefficiency by allowing small, informal firms to work around financial restrictions, and therefore capture more resources (labor and capital) than they would otherwise. Without those preexisting labor distortions, this inefficient cost of savings would not be a factor. Increasing aggregate productivity by reducing misallocation requires reducing preexisting distortions rather than preventing firms from saving, which is probably not feasible.

The additional misallocation cost of firm saving depends critically on the actual amount of capital allocated to small, informal, and unproductive firms and on the shape of these firms' demand for capital. The evidence suggests that this is not a first-order problem, however. In order to estimate the size distribution of capital in the economy, an economic census that covers all firms in that economy is needed. The only country in the region that has such data is Mexico. Busso, Fazio, and Levy (2012) use Mexico's 2008 economic census and find that 90 percent of establishments have fewer than five employees and employ 38 percent of the economy's labor, but only 13 percent of the capital. On the other hand, larger firms with 50 or more employees employ more than 70 percent of the economy's available capital. Data from the National Survey of Microenterprises for Mexico confirm that small firms do not use much capital: the median small firm has a stock value of capital of less than US$1,000. This is consistent with experimental evidence that finds that small, informal firms have a marginal product of capital that is very high for very low levels of capital (de Mel, McKenzie, and Woodruff, 2008) and decreases sharply as firms accumulate small amounts of capital (McKenzie and Woodruff, 2006).

Thus, even though labor and tax distortions are large and can misallocate resources—thereby exacting a high toll on productivity in developing countries (Hsieh and Klenow, 2009; Restuccia and Rogerson, 2008)—they do not seem to increase because of firm saving.

Notes

1. See Busso, Fernández, and Tamayo (2016) for further details about the data and methodology used in this section, the specific criteria used when identifying these episodes, as well as a complete list of them.

2. Busso, Fernández, and Tamayo (2016), which serves as an online appendix to this chapter, presents a full mathematical description of how the neoclassical model works, as well as a simulation following an expected future increase in productivity.

3. Both Mexico and Chile suffered severe debt and financial crises during this time that manifested in collapses of productivity, which the exercise is going to take as given. The main goal is to assess how these events determined the saving decisions during this period.

4. However, when compared to model performance in Chen, İmrohoroğlu, and İmrohoroğlu (2006), the model appears to miss some short-run dynamics. This is expected, given the superior data with which Chen, İmrohoroğlu, and İmrohoroğlu (2006) were able to work. These authors had complete times series of capital tax rates and carefully constructed depreciation series from Hayashi (1989).

5. Cerda et al. (2015) show that a precipitous decline in tax rates on retained earnings (from close to 50 percent in 1985 to 10 percent in 1988) provided plenty of saving incentives in those years.

6. There are also alternative explanations for the link between productivity growth and savings. In fact, Aghion et al. (2009) postulate that low productivity itself may be reinforced by low national saving rates. According to their model, growth in poor countries results from innovations that allow local sectors to catch up with the technology frontier. However, doing so requires the cooperation of a foreign investor who is familiar with the frontier and a domestic entrepreneur who is familiar with the local conditions. National savings allow the local entrepreneur to take an equity stake in this cooperative venture, thus mitigating potential agency problems.

7. Chapter 5 provides evidence about the imperfect substitutability between national and foreign saving. In addition, de la Torre and Ize (2015), who argued for the presence of transaction costs that would make foreign and domestic savings imperfect substitutes, have recently confirmed this for Latin America.

[8] Notice that, with perfect financial markets, heterogeneity has no real effect since all firms could freely borrow to quickly attain their optimal size. Likewise, imperfect financial markets without heterogeneity revert back to the neoclassical world (see Busso, Fernández, and Tamayo, 2016).

[9] See Bebczuk and Cavallo (2016) for a complete treatment of this issue.

[10] This result is similar to the one presented in Kawamura and Ronconi (2015). The main difference is that in this chapter, data from the WBES is reweighted in order to keep constant the size distribution of firms across countries. This is done to prevent differences in the sampling frame of each country from affecting the results. See Busso, Fernández, and Tamayo (2016) for more details.

[11] Buera, Kaboski, and Shin (2011) use a similar model to explain the relationship between aggregate total factor productivity and financial development across countries. They assume that after production, entrepreneurs could renege on borrowing contracts. This imperfect enforceability of contracts introduces a financial friction that distorts the allocation of capital across firms and their entry/exit decisions, reducing aggregate productivity growth. In their model, forward-looking self-financing (i.e., saving) can alleviate the resulting misallocation. However, it is more difficult to self-finance on a larger scale with larger financing needs. Thus, large-scale sectors (such as manufacturing) are affected more by financial frictions than smaller-scale sectors (such as services). The variation in financial development explains 80 percent of the difference in output per worker between Mexico and the United States.

11 Breaking the Vicious Circle: Financial Policies for High-Quality Saving

This book argues that Latin America and the Caribbean suffers from two interrelated problems: saving is low, and those meager savings are used inefficiently. The two problems are connected and reinforced by the financial system—the set of institutions through which resources are channeled from savers to investors in the economy.

Figure 11.1 traces these connections. To start with, low saving in Latin America means that only a small flow of funds becomes available to firms and individuals that need to invest. This limited supply of loanable funds, in turn, limits the growth of the financial industry, resulting in high unit costs to channel funds between lenders and borrowers (the process of financial intermediation). High costs compound other distortions in financial markets, such as the poor quality of credit information and weak protection of property rights. As a result, the available savings in the economy are misallocated: for example, the firms that receive credit from banks are not necessarily the most productive ones, or the ones with the greatest productive potential, but rather those that can pledge collateral. The inefficient use of resources in the economy, in turn, is a main determinant of the region's low productivity (Pagés, 2010). Finally, low productivity is the other side of the coin of low returns to investment and saving (See Chapter 10). Not surprisingly, given the low returns to saving that prevail in the region, savings—and the financial intermediation of available savings—are also low.

The circle ends where it began: Latin America and the Caribbean is a region of low saving with undeveloped financial systems. Breaking this vicious circle requires concerted policy actions to improve

Figure 11.1 The Vicious Circle of Low Saving and Inefficient Financial Intermediation

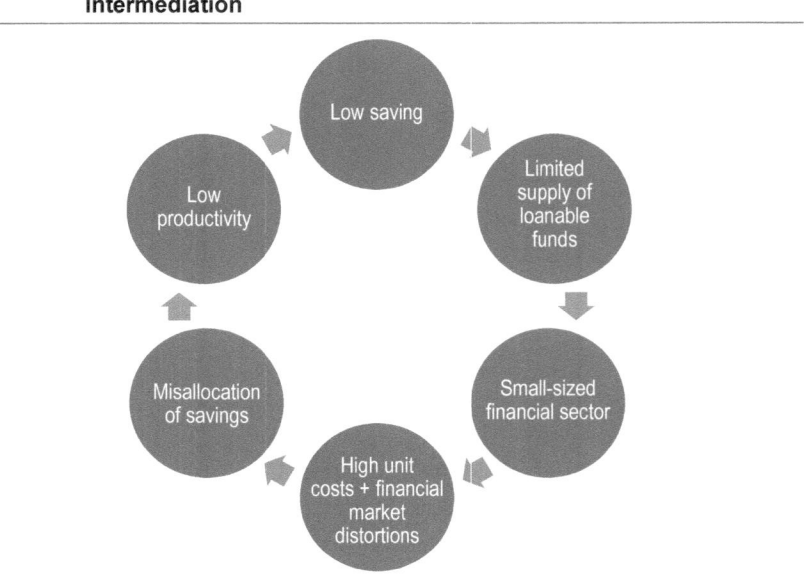

Source: Authors' elaboration.

financial intermediation. This chapter discusses two policy avenues that can help break the circle: (1) reducing financial market frictions to improve the efficiency of intermediation; and (2) encouraging more extensive use of formal financial saving instruments to reduce unit costs of operation.

Toward a Well-Oiled Financial Machine

In an ideal world with frictionless, competitive financial markets, resources flow toward the most productive investment projects, and the returns of these projects are reflected in the interest rate paid to savers. That is, ideally, developed and competitive financial markets lead to high returns to capital and low interest rate spreads, which translate into high returns for savers. Instead, the low productivity of capital[1] and the very high interest rate margins between what is charged to lenders and what depositors receive illustrate how far the region is from such an ideal world (see Figure 11.2).[2] Financial systems across the region do not intermediate savings efficiently; on the contrary, these financial systems are small and fragmented between formal and informal institutions (see Chapter 3).

Figure 11.2 **The Spread between Lending and Deposits by Region, 2006–13 Average**

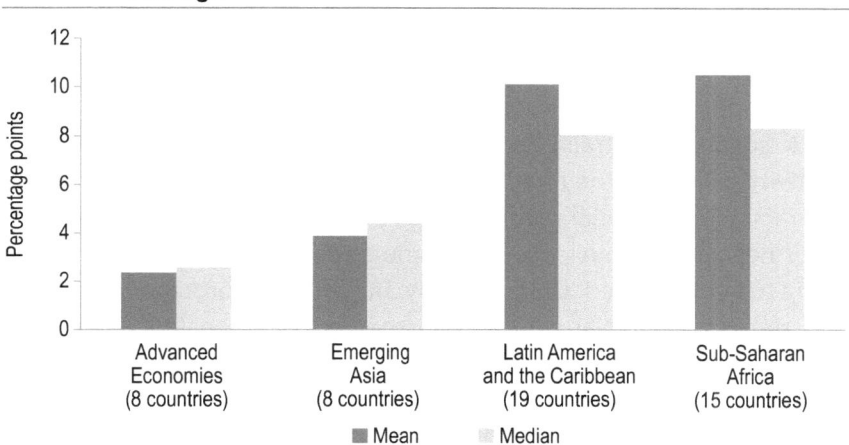

Source: Authors' calculations based on World Bank Global Financial Development Database.
Note: Interest rate spread is the interest rate charged by banks on loans to private sector customers minus the interest rate paid by commercial or similar banks for demand, time, or savings deposits. The terms and conditions attached to these rates differ by country, however, limiting their comparability. See endnote 3 of chapter 2 for the list of countries in each country group.

Financial market distortions and low productivity are intertwined because financial frictions typically undermine the efficient allocation of savings. Misallocation of resources suppresses productivity in the region to about half its potential (Pagés, 2010). If productivity were higher, not only would accumulated savings be used more efficiently, but savings would accumulate more quickly in response to the higher returns prompted by the productivity boost.

At least two types of financial frictions are common in the region and reduce productivity growth. First, financial intermediaries lack good quality information about potential borrowers. With little information upon which to base their decisions, lenders are essentially flying blind; thus, they charge more to cover their risks and raise the margins of financial intermediation. As problems of asymmetric information can divert savings from their most productive uses, reforms that improve information sharing should enhance resource allocation and efficiency. While the region has made good progress in this respect—especially in extending the coverage of credit bureaus—the quality and timeliness of the information available through such bureaus is relatively low in some countries.[3] While credit information is abundant in some countries, it is scarce in others because the legal environment does not favor the storage and exchange of this valuable resource (see Frisancho, 2012). On average the regulatory framework (i.e., rules affecting the scope, accessibility, and quality of credit information available through public or private credit registries) is less conducive to information sharing in Latin America and the Caribbean than in other regions of the world (see Table 11.1).

A second constraint to financial market development and productivity growth in the region relates to the cost of enforcing financial contracts. For financial relationships to thrive, the obligations of each party need to be explicit, and an impartial enforcing agent must be ready to act if needed. Unfortunately, the effective protection of property rights in financial contracts in the region is weak. Column 2 in Table 11.1 illustrates how Latin America and the Caribbean lags behind Advanced Economies and other emerging market countries in the enforcement of legal rights. This raises the cost of financial intermediation in the region. It also feeds mistrust in the financial system because the weak protection of property rights affects both creditors and debtors.[4] If assets must be pledged as collateral to signal creditworthiness to deal with enforcement problems or information gaps, wealthy but unproductive entrepreneurs may gain access to finance, while poor but productive ones may remain excluded from or underserved by credit markets (see Buera, Kaboski, and Shin, 2011).

To address the underlying distortions, regulatory and institutional reforms are necessary. Several successful reforms have been launched in the region. Bankruptcy reforms in Brazil (2004–05), Colombia (2011), and more recently Chile (2014) appear to be reducing the costs of

Table 11.1 Institutional Credit Market Indicators, Average 2014–2016

Region	Depth of credit information index[a] (0–8)	Strength of legal rights index[b] (0–12)
Latin America and the Caribbean	5.8	4.4
Advanced economies	6.7	6.1
Other emerging countries	6.4	5.0

Source: Authors' calculations based on World Bank (2016).
[a] Depth of credit information index measures rules affecting the scope, accessibility, and quality of credit information available through public or private credit registries. The index ranges from 0 to 8, with higher values indicating the availability of more credit information, from either a public registry or a private bureau, to facilitate lending decisions.
[b] Strength of legal rights index measures the degree to which collateral and bankruptcy laws protect the rights of borrowers and lenders and thus facilitate lending. The index ranges from 0 to 12, with higher scores indicating that these laws are better designed to expand access to credit.
See endnote 3 of chapter 2 for the list of countries in advanced economies and Latin America and the Caribbean. Other emerging economies includes countries from emerging Asia and Sub-Saharan Africa.

enforcing financial contracts. At least in the case of Brazil, reforms have increased access to credit, especially for smaller firms (Araujo, Ferreira, and Funchal, 2012). Likewise, the recent introduction of collateral registries for movable assets in some countries aims to break the link between wealth and access to finance because they enable working capital and some forms of firm income to be pledged as collateral. In 2006, Peru introduced a law governing guarantees for moveable collateral, and Colombia introduced a similar law in 2013–14. Such policies have helped firms—especially smaller and younger ones—access bank financing under better terms (Love, Martínez Pería and Singh, 2013).

The high fixed costs that characterize financial markets create additional barriers to efficient financial intermediation. High fixed costs create natural incentives for industry concentration, which may lead to uncompetitive practices. While there is plenty of evidence of consolidation in the financial industry in Latin America over the past few decades, there is no compelling evidence that such consolidation or the subsequent increase in concentration has reduced competition (Gelos and Roldós 2004; IDB, 2004; Levy Yeyati and Micco, 2007). If anything, standard measures of market power show that, at least in some countries, market power in loan and deposit markets has fallen over time (Williams, 2012). On the other hand, concentration in the banking industry does appear to impair cost-efficiency (Tabak, Fazio, and Cajueiro, 2011). Such inefficiencies can persist only if various factors prevent additional suppliers from entering the market. Chapter 3 discussed how the combination of high fixed costs and income inequality may limit the size of the financial system in Latin America and the Caribbean because banks naturally locate only in areas where enough customers can afford service costs. One way to weaken the link between high fixed costs of operation and industry concentration is to expand the customer base. More customers would help reduce the unit costs of operations, making it more profitable for other financial institutions to enter the industry.

Broadening the Base

Savings in the region are channeled through a variety of formal and informal saving vehicles (see Chapter 3). Given this variety, traditional financial inclusion efforts have focused on access: opening bank accounts for the unbanked. This is a necessary first step, but is not enough to encourage formal (financial) saving.

About 55 percent of the adult population still do not own accounts in formal financial institutions. Why not? According to the 2014 Global Findex Database (World Bank, 2014b), many people say such accounts are too expensive, require too much documentation to open, or are in a financial system they do not trust (see Figure 11.3).

Among people who already own an account, only 31 percent use it to deposit some of their savings, and only 26 percent use it to deposit all of their savings. Why don't people save more through the financial system? Limited physical coverage of banking networks, lack of trust in banks, and high service fees are important constraints to save formally (see Chapter 9). These factors act as pecuniary and nonpecuniary costs that reduce the effective returns to formal saving. With limited returns, no wonder savers shy away from the formal financial system as a saving vehicle. How can these problems be resolved?

Reducing Service Costs

Financial institutions pass the high average (unit) costs of operating on to their customers, and thus reduce the effective returns that savers receive. In the financial services industry, the scale of operation matters:

Figure 11.3 Reasons Why People Do Not Have a Formal Bank Account, by Region, 2014

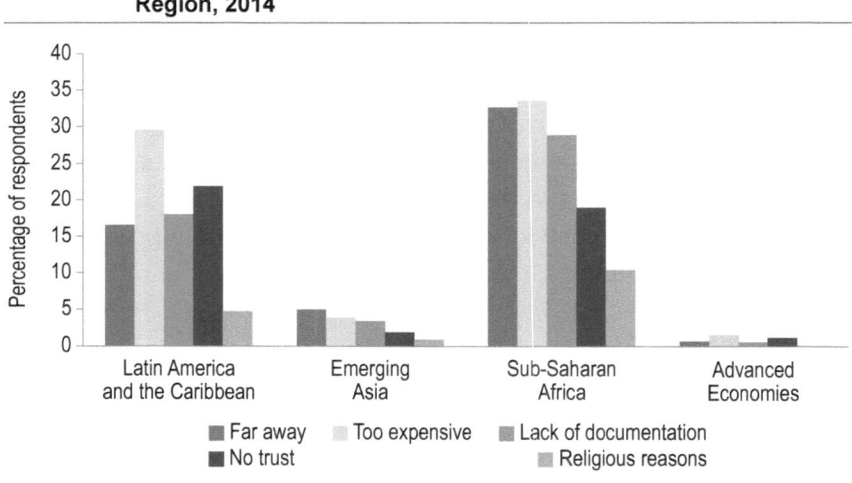

Source: Authors' calculations based on World Bank (2014b).
Note: Bars show percentage of respondents who do not have an account at a financial institution and why. Percentages add up to more than 100 percent in some regions because some respondents gave more than one reason. See endnote 3 of chapter 2 for the list of countries in each country group.

if suppliers of financial services can spread fixed costs (for physical branches, reserves needed to meet regulatory capital requirements, and so on) over a greater volume of users, unit costs fall.[5]

Currently, only high-income households can afford the high unit service costs of financial services in the region. Excluding a large bloc of potential customers reinforces the "smallness" problem, creating a vicious circle of small customer base, high unit costs, and financial exclusion.

Traditionally, governments around the world have sought to expand the user base of financial services by simply letting demand drive the growth of the financial system. More recently, however, governments—particularly those in the developing world—have tried to incorporate potential users of financial services, by channeling large transactional markets, such as government transfers, through the formal financial system.

These strategies may have been successful at increasing ownership of formal saving instruments. Ownership of a formal saving account increased to 45 percent of the region's adult population in 2014 from 34 percent in 2011—a 33 percent increase (World Bank's Global Findex Database). Account ownership increased more in Latin America and the Caribbean than in any other region in the world (see Figure 11.4).

Figure 11.4 Penetration of Formal Savings Accounts, 2011 vs. 2014

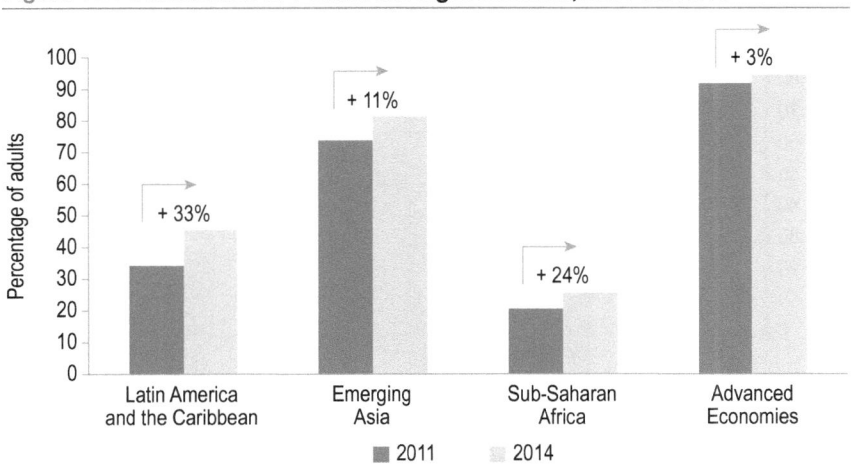

Source: Authors' calculations based on World Bank Findex Database.
Note: Account penetration is the percentage of respondents older than 15 years of age who had an account at a financial institution. See endnote 3 of chapter 2 for the list of countries in each country group. Data available only for 2011 for Paraguay, Trinidad and Tobago, Central African Republic, Comoros, Gabon, Lesotho, Liberia and Swaziland and only for 2014 for Belize, Norway, Switzerland, Ethiopia and Namibia.

Efforts to expand the customer base can help reduce unit costs, which in turn may encourage more saving. Quasi-experimental evidence demonstrates a causal effect of financial access on saving behavior. For example, people who received their conditional cash transfers (CCTs) in Mexico as a deposit to their bank account increased their total savings by 60 percent, on average, compared to those who received transfers in cash (Ubfal, 2013). This increase in total savings—which included formal and informal instruments—was driven mainly by higher formal savings.

Despite considerable effort to increase financial inclusion, there is still room for improvement on several fronts. On the one hand, Latin America and the Caribbean still has the world's lowest fraction of government transfers paid through formal financial instruments (Figure 11.5). Countries like Bolivia, El Salvador, and Jamaica still have a long way to go to meet even the regional average.

On the other hand, most beneficiaries of social programs in the region who are paid through bank accounts withdraw the money all at once, whether they need the money then or not. This percentage is higher than in other regions. To some extent, this practice may be due to design problems and misinformation. For example, in 2009, Colombia's CCT program, Familias en Acción, began paying beneficiaries

Figure 11.5 Government Transfers Paid through the Financial System

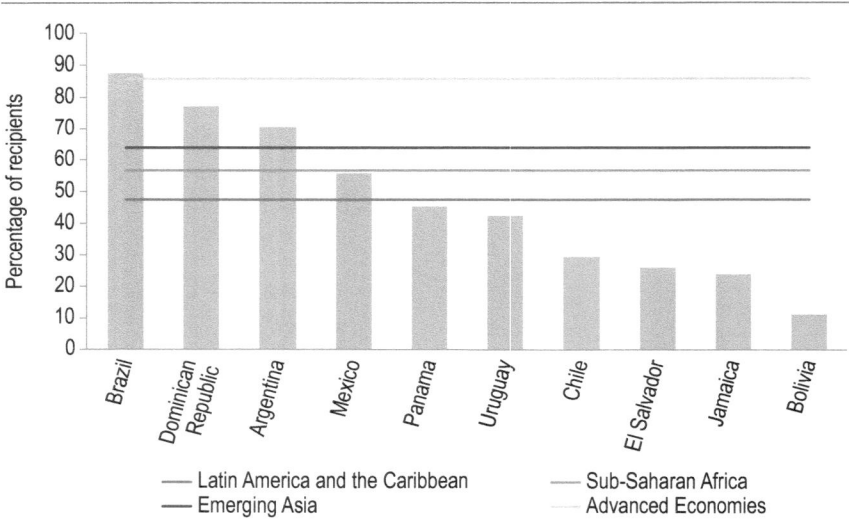

Source: Authors' calculations based on World Bank (2014b).
Note: Variable denotes the percentage of transfer recipients older than 15 years who received government transfers into an account at a financial institution or card in the past 12 months. See endnote 3 of chapter 2 for the list of countries in each country group.

through basic saving accounts at a state-owned bank. According to data from the government agency in charge of promoting financial access, Banca de Oportunidades, over 90 percent of beneficiaries were receiving the transfers through an account at the state-owned bank by 2012. Yet, over 40 percent of beneficiaries in Bogotá, the main urban center, thought their subsidy money was at risk if left in the bank account (when it really was not). Similarly, many beneficiaries did not know that the bank account used to deposit the CCT did not have a maintenance fee, and most of the recipients did not know that the accounts paid them interest (Maldonado and Tejerina, 2010). In Brazil, most beneficiaries of social programs receive transfers through a limited purpose instrument (electronic card), which as of 2012 required them to withdraw the funds within 60 days of receiving them.

These examples suggest that providing more information to recipients about how bank accounts work and paying attention to program design can help overcome the tendency to withdraw all the funds at once. This would help beneficiaries move a step closer to using the bank accounts for saving rather than for purely transactional purposes.

Keeping it Simple

Governments across the region have encouraged the financial industry to design and offer saving instruments with a varying mix of functions, costs, and requirements to make them more attractive. Simplified versions of the traditional saving account (sometimes called simplified accounts or basic accounts) are becoming increasingly popular. While the specific characteristics vary from one country to another, three features distinguish these instruments: they provide limited services, including ceilings on balances and transactions; financial institutions charge low (or no) fees and require low (or no) minimum balances; and they require less documentation than traditional accounts.

Many regulators in Latin America have embraced the effort to popularize saving products along these lines. Before implementing further policies to directly influence the features and price of saving products, policymakers should have a clear diagnosis of why innovation and cost reduction have not already taken place. If the problem is that these simplified products are not profitable to banks, for example, then mandating commercial banks to supply them would require public subsidies. Without the subsidies, commercial banks could try to compensate for the losses by either making other financial products more expensive or by making it more difficult for potential clients to open the simplified accounts. Alternatively, if the problem is bad regulation or red tape, regulatory reforms would be needed.

The specific case in each country depends on country-specific circumstances. All in all, Latin America and the Caribbean still lags behind other regions in terms of the ease with which financial institutions can offer saving products, and potential customers face more requirements to open bank accounts. According to the Economist Intelligence Unit's Global Microscope, Latin America and the Caribbean as a region on average fares worse than East Asia and Sub-Saharan Africa in these two areas, although a great deal of variation exists across countries.[6]

Mexico is at the forefront of efforts in the region to introduce simplified accounts. In 2011, Mexico introduced a tiered system for the requirements and costs of opening and using bank accounts. Customers with relatively limited saving and transaction needs (in volume) need not go to the branch or provide any form of identification to open an account. Importantly, the system complies with anti-money laundering principles. Within two years, the number of simplified accounts in commercial banks reached 12 million (Faz, 2013). Other countries in the region are following suit; for instance, in 2015 Costa Rica introduced a three-tiered system of accounts whose costs and requirements are proportional to the balances and transactions permitted.

Despite their potential, simpler accounts per se may not be enough to encourage more financial saving. The obstacles that impede ownership of formal saving instruments may be quite different from those that constrain their use as saving vehicles. Furthermore, in some cases, simplified saving products may not be profitable; financial institutions will find it worthwhile to promote them only if they foresee users "graduating" to more complex financial products.

Fostering a Culture of Saving

Despite the increase in the number of bank accounts across the region in the past decade, the increase in the percentage of people who claim to save through formal financial institutions has been more modest. Saving through formal accounts rose to 16.4 percent of adults in 2014 from 13.9 percent in 2011 (Figure 11.6), an 18 percent increase, according to the World Bank's FINDEX Database. Still, despite the increase, the

Figure 11.6 **Saving through Formal Accounts, 2011 vs. 2014**

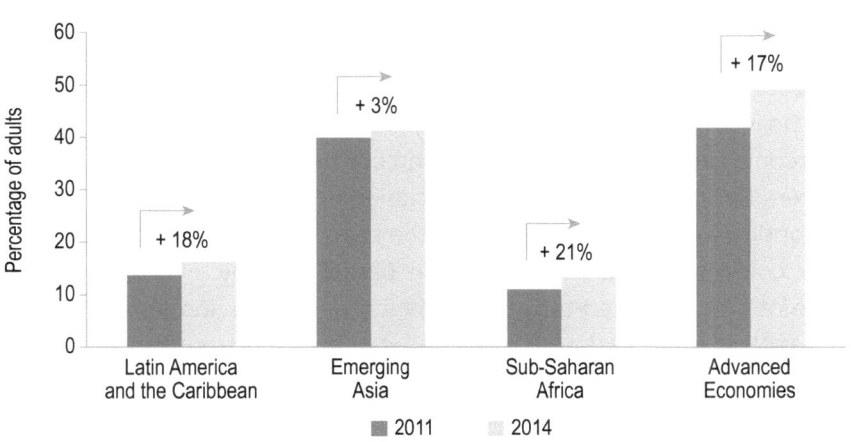

Source: Authors' calculations based on World Bank (2014b).
Note: Measured as the percentage of respondents older than 15 years who saved at a financial institution in the past 12 months.
See endnote 3 of chapter 2 for the list of countries in each country group, restricted here depending on data availability. Data available only for 2011 for Paraguay, Trinidad and Tobago, Central African Republic, Comoros, Gabon, Lesotho, Liberia and Swaziland and only for 2014 for Belize, Norway, Switzerland, Ethiopia and Namibia.

region lags behind Emerging Asia and Advanced Economies, and is only slightly better-off than Sub-Saharan Africa.

More can be done to encourage financial saving by leveraging the government's efforts to expand financial inclusion. Given that lack of trust in banks is a problem in the region, the accounts used to deliver government transfers can be complemented with tools to build people's confidence in the system. As discussed in Chapter 9, lack of trust is sometimes linked to misinformation. For example, to the extent that mistrust reflects potential customers' belief that balances can disappear if the money is not withdrawn, then tools that allow customers to consult balances frequently and free of charge, such as debit cards or other electronic means, can help build user confidence over time.

Experimental evidence shows that people save more after they gain confidence in the system. Bachas, Gertler, Higgins and Seira (2015) study a sample of Oportunidades-Progresa beneficiaries who received a debit card along with their bank account in 2009–11. Beneficiaries could check their account balances as frequently as they wanted, free of charge. Over time, beneficiaries consulted their balances less and made fewer withdrawals. One year after receiving the "treatment" debit card, beneficiaries had reduced consumption and increased formal saving by similar amounts (meaning that they channeled all the new saving to formal saving). With less cash in hand, the beneficiaries consumed fewer temptation goods (such as alcohol and tobacco), further reinforcing the increase in saving.

Delivering social transfers through term-saving instruments can help overcome behavioral and social saving constraints. For instance, policymakers in Colombia offered beneficiaries of conditional cash transfers the option to set aside a fraction of the transfer in a term deposit, which they could withdraw after a certain period of time. Households that were offered the fixed-term instrument saved more and invested more in health and education than those who received transfers through a standard deposit account (Barrera-Osorio et al., 2011).

Financial education is also important. Thanks to financial education, combined with delivery of government transfers through bank accounts, beneficiaries of Familias en Accion in Colombia saved more (Núñez Méndez et al., 2012). Similarly, in 2009, Peru started paying government transfers through formal accounts at the state-owned Banco de la Nación. From the beginning, the strategy included a financial education module that assured savers that balances left in the bank account were not at risk. The fraction of beneficiaries with low balances fell from close to 80 percent to less than 10 percent after one year (Trivelli, Montenegro, and Gutiérrez, 2011). A recent impact evaluation of the program (Boyd and Aldana, 2015) finds that financial education has a positive and sizable impact on the probability of saving, and on the probability of saving formally in a nearby bank. The program also helped to formalize saving as beneficiaries gradually transferred their informal savings to the bank account provided by the conditional cash transfer program (Rosen, 2010).

International remittances channeled by migrant workers to their home countries represent another sizable transactional market that remains largely outside the formal financial system. Although every dollar of remittances must, at some point, go through the financial system of the home country, this connection may be limited to the money transfer operator and the bank that carries out the currency conversion. Intermediating remittances through the formal financial system can bolster economic efficiency and individual welfare through various channels. To begin with, the sheer size of remittance flows presents an opportunity to increase the volume of resources and transactions administered by local financial systems, thereby helping to lower unit service costs.[7]

Another important feature of remittances is that they are spaced out in intervals, and arrive in sizable sums (they are "lumpy"). This pattern creates an inherent demand for savings. Researchers estimate that about 20 percent of remittances in developing countries are used for saving or investment. Furthermore, remittances are the point of entry for many remitters and their families to the formal financial system. Financial intermediaries can use remittances as a stepping stone to identify other sources of income for their new customers, which in turn can induce them to increase their lending to customers.

Innovative products and channels have considerable potential to turn remittances into financial saving. Commercial banks in El Salvador have been particularly keen on reducing transaction costs and offering flexible ways to send and collect remittances. Experimental evidence from El Salvador shows that giving remitters greater control over the accounts has the potential to increase savings by over 50 percent (Ashraf et al., 2015).

Greater control by migrants over savings accounts in their home countries can increase both the take-up rates and balances in savings accounts. In a randomized field experiment conducted by Ashraf et al., (2015), Salvadoran migrants in the Washington, DC area were assigned to different savings account options in El Salvador, or received no offer of any new financial product in the comparison group. Each option varied the degree of control participants could exert on the new accounts that were offered at Salvadorian Banks.

The results provide evidence that migrants value and take advantage of opportunities to exert control over savings in their home country. Migrants were much more likely to open savings accounts in El Salvador, and accumulate more savings at the new accounts, if they were assigned to the option offering the greatest degree of monitoring and control. The average savings in a 12-month period increased from US$186 in the comparison group to US$282 in accounts opened in the migrant's own name. The evidence suggests that these numbers represented increases in total savings rather than shifts in saving mechanisms.

Banks in El Salvador have also devised various ways to extend mortgage loans to migrants in their home country. Some banks are even offering microcredit lines at preferential rates with no further requirement than the proof of remittances received.

Clearly, making more progress in terms of encouraging financial saving may require more than just opening bank accounts. It will require complementary interventions focusing on financial education, building trust in financial institutions, and innovation in product design. The success of these policies in terms of creating and sustaining a culture of formal savings will also depend on the functioning of the entire financial ecosystem.

Banking—The Old Fashioned Way

Technological and financial innovations like simplified accounts can make it easier to open bank accounts, but the availability of a bank branch, where potential customers can make regular deposits and withdrawals, can also encourage saving. Bruhn and Love (2014) show that the almost overnight expansion of Banco Azteca to become the second largest network of branches in Mexico inspired a sudden boom in saving accounts in the municipalities in which Banco Azteca began operations. Similarly, expansion of the state-owned financial institution, Patronato del Ahorro Nacional, in 1993 increased households' saving rate by over 3 percentage points (from around 14 percent to 17 percent), with bigger surges among poorer households (Aportela, 1999).

The problem is that opening up physical branches, particularly in remote locations, can be very costly for financial institutions. Remote locations are by definition likely to bring in relatively few customers.

Over the years, policymakers have tried to create incentives for financial institutions to reach relatively small and distant communities. In Latin America, the deployment of physical infrastructure has relied heavily on the expansion of public banks. In Mexico, for instance, BANSEFI started a US$150 million program in 2002 to strengthen the efficiency and outreach capacity of 19 small savings and credit institutions. A core aspect of the program was the development of an information technology system linking 180 offices of these institutions and BANSEFI´s own 551 branches (Taber, 2004). This allowed BANSEFI to increase its coverage from 28 percent of municipalities in 2006 to 98 percent in 2013. In Chile, approximately 21 percent of the branches of Banco Estado are in regions with fewer than 1 million inhabitants. In Colombia, over 24 percent of the branches of Banco Agrario are located in cities with less than 1 million inhabitants.

India undertook one of the largest branch expansion programs in the world in the 1980s. To obtain a license to open a branch in a location that already had one or more branches (a "banked location"), a bank had to open branches in four eligible "unbanked locations." This process had a sizable positive impact on mobilizing saving and accumulating capital (Burgess and Pande, 2005), although it is unclear whether these benefits outweighed the very significant costs of the decade-long strategy.

Creating incentives for private institutions to open more branches can be even more challenging, and potentially expensive. High income inequality (as discussed in Chapter 3) and limited competition in the financial industry can reinforce this lack of incentives. Therefore, governments should have a clear diagnosis of the reasons for the low physical penetration and weigh all the policy options, including direct subsidies and changes to competition policy, where necessary.

More than Brick-and-Mortar Banking

A complementary approach to opening brick-and-mortar branches is promoting the use of alternative banking channels, such as agent networks. This form of branchless banking has the potential to promote financial saving by providing services at a lower cost, and with greater flexibility, than traditional banking to a broader customer base.

Bank agents are nonfinancial retailers that offer basic financial services under the name of a financial services provider. They are access points to the formal financial system. Policymakers around the world are searching for new ways to offer saving instruments through branchless channels. In Kenya, for example, the Retirement Benefits Authority (RBA) introduced a retirement saving plan in 2009 for informal workers, who could contribute through mobile money providers. The plan succeeded in promoting formal saving (McKay and Pickens, 2010).

In Latin America, the popularity of bank agents has increased as regulatory frameworks have adapted, and as information technologies have allowed the massive use of portable devices (mobile phones, portable terminals) to carry out financial transactions. The region has the highest number of "pure" bank agents per 100,000 inhabitants (bank agents that directly link the customer with the financial institution without an e-money issuer or a telecom company mediating this relationship). Brazil leads the expansion of agent networks, with 208 agents per 100,000 inhabitants (see Table 11.2). The path for Brazil to become the regional leader was cleared in 1999 with a central bank resolution that instituted *correspondente* (correspondent) relationships, which allow banks to establish agreements with nonbanking firms to provide financial and payment services. With the proliferation of agents in Brazil, the financial industry has been able to enter into increasingly more remote and less densely populated areas (Assunção, 2013).

In Chile, bank agents became popular even before appropriate regulation was put in place in 2010. A pilot program launched in 2005 by the state-owned Banco Estado was the precursor of the current Chilean model, which now has 118 agents per 100,000 inhabitants. Colombia introduced regulation for bank agents in 2006 and launched an ambitious government subsidy program in 2007, under which banks would bid to place their agents in certain municipalities previously chosen by a government agency (Banca de Oportunidades). Households and small businesses were 13 percent and 8 percent more likely, respectively, to use formal savings products in municipalities covered by the program

Table 11.2 **Coverage of Bank Agents, Select Latin American Countries and Various Regions**

	Agents per 100,000 inhabitants	Agents per 1000 sq km
Brazil	208.2	44.1
Colombia	115.3	43.1
Chile	118.0	23.9
Peru	69.2	14.8
Ecuador	49.2	27.3
Guatemala	43.7	54.7
Mexico	22.7	12.9
Venezuela	10.3	3.1
Paraguay	5.7	0.9
El Salvador	1.0	2.7
Bolivia	0.8	0.1
East Asia and Pacific	32.3	36.3
Eastern Europe and Central Asia	25.0	2.7
Latin America and the Caribbean	100.7	26.8
Middle East and North Africa	50.2	32.8
South Asia	57.6	221.9
Sub-Saharan Africa	5.2	3.0
Developed countries	18.8	3.7

Source: Authors' calculations based on Cámara, Tuesta and Urbiola (2015) and the World Development Indicators.
Note: Developed countries include Australia, Canada, New Zealand, United States and Western Europe. Data for regions correspond to 2014; data for individual countries are for 2013.

compared to peer individuals in a control group of municipalities (Econometría and SEI, 2011).

Despite progress, important gaps remain and there is ample room for improvement. First, Latin America is very large, and while the region ranks first in terms of agents per 100,000 habitants, it has relatively few bank agents per 1,000 square kilometers compared to other developing regions. Thus, many geographical areas remain without coverage. Second, the pervasive use of cash in the region makes transactions through bank agents expensive. Given the risks and costs of carrying cash over long distances, banks that operate networks need physical branches near the agent's area of influence. This in turn suggests that most agent networks must be operated by banks with an already existing, large brick-and-mortar branch network.

To solve these problems, policymakers should encourage the entry of independent agent networks. They can reach more customers, particularly in remote areas, and also promote competition among financial institutions (de Olloqui, Andrade, and Herrera, 2015). Furthermore, expanding the range of services that agents can provide to include retail payments and remittances can also help financial institutions achieve a sustainable scale of operation.

Dialing up Technology

The widespread adoption of mobile technologies can also promote branchless banking.[8] Financial accounts associated with a mobile phone number, or operated exclusively through mobile phones, are usually simpler to set up and cheaper to use than standard bank accounts. Depending on the country's specific regulations, mobile accounts typically do not require a minimum deposit or a minimum balance. They do not charge an administrative fee, and they do not charge users for a certain number of transactions per month (cash withdrawals, balance inquiries).

Mobile technology helps overcome one of the main obstacles currently facing bank agent networks in Latin America: the need to operate groups of agents through nearby branches. However, a parallel platform for financial services does have transaction costs associated with the high use of cash in the region. Potential customers that use cash for their everyday transactions have to convert that cash into electronic deposits and vice-versa (i.e., a process known as "cash-in-cash-out", or CICO). Thus, for mobile technologies to effectively complement bank agents, the costs of CICO have to decline. Doing so requires a combination of specialization in the provision of CICO services (for example, through specialized providers that can connect final users with multiple financial institutions) and encouraging less use of cash for daily transactions (so that CICO is less frequent).

The good news is that mobile phone penetration in Latin America and the Caribbean is high by international standards: unique subscriber penetration in the region was 52 percent in 2014—the highest among developing regions (Almazán and Frydrych, 2015). However, Latin America still lags behind other developing regions in terms of using mobile technologies for financial services. With a few exceptions, such as Mexico, in most countries in the region, the ownership of mobile accounts is less than what would be expected given the penetration of mobile phone subscriptions, the physical coverage of the financial system, and the fraction of people residing in remote areas. More importantly, in most countries, the use of such accounts to receive money (the most prevalent use of mobile accounts everywhere) is less than what would be expected given the penetration of mobile accounts (see Figure 11.7).

As shown in Figure 11.7, more people in Mexico have a mobile account and use it than would be expected given the penetration of mobile telephony and the current physical coverage of the banking system. An important contributing factor is that in 2012 Mexico became the first country in the world to ease the anti-money laundering regulations for bank accounts linked to mobile phones, while still complying with the new recommendations of GAFI (Money Laundering Financial Action Group) on low-risk products (Alonso et al., 2013).

Colombia is a noteworthy case because it still has low penetration of mobile accounts, but it ranks among the highest in the region in terms of regulation of digital financial services according to the 2015 Global Microscope.

In Peru, the regulator introduced a simplified process for opening financial products in 2011. In 2012, an electronic money law was passed that creates a new license for specialized operators, allowing nonfinancial service providers to enter, and thus increasing competition. As a result, in a rather unprecedented coordination effort, the Peruvian bankers' association, ASBANC, is building a single platform that can be used by all parties involved in providing these services, including telecommunication companies.

Figure 11.7 **Penetration and Use of Mobile Accounts**

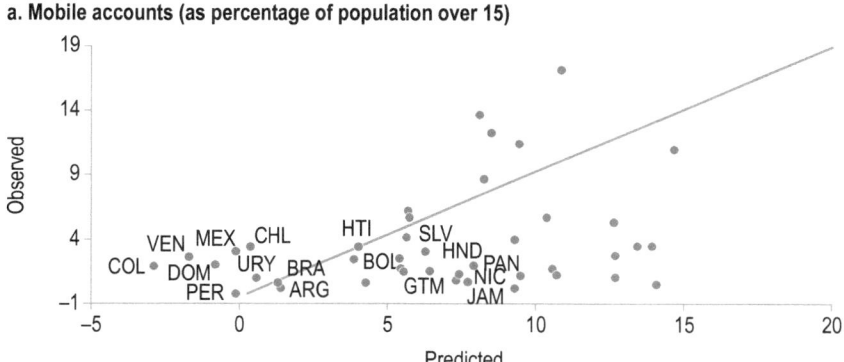

a. Mobile accounts (as percentage of population over 15)

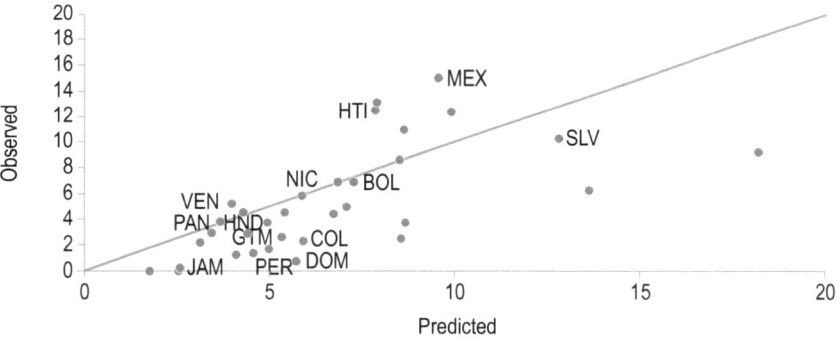

b. Received domestic remittances through a mobile phone
(as percentage of recipients of remittances over 15)

Source: Authors' calculations based on World Bank (2014b) and World Develompent Indicators database (World Bank).
Note: The left panel plots the observed values for the fraction of adults with a mobile account (penetration) against those predicted by a linear regression using mobile phone penetration, bank branch and ATM per km2 and urbanization rate. The predictions in the right panel are for the use of mobile accounts (receiving domestic transfers) with mobile account penetration as sole regressor. Countries in sample: Argentina, Benin, Bolivia, Botswana[a], Brazil, Burkina Faso, Burundi, Cameroon, Chad, Chile, Colombia, Democratic Republic of the Congo, Dominican Republic, El Salvador, Gabon, Ghana, Guatemala, Guinea, Haiti, Honduras, Indonesia, Jamaica, Kenya[a], Madagascar, Malawi, Malaysia, Mali, Mauritius, Mexico, Namibia, Nicaragua, Niger, Nigeria, Panama, Peru, Republic of the Congo, Rwanda, Senegal, South Africa, Tanzania[a], Thailand, Togo, Uganda[a], Uruguay, Venezuela, Zambia and Zimbabwe.[a]
[a] These countries are in the sample but are not shown; their predicted or observed values are greater than 20 percent.

In Paraguay, a novel feature of the regulation is that balances on mobile accounts that have been inactive for 90 days or more must be automatically transferred to a savings account at a formal financial institution.

Further policy interventions should support the development of the market for mobile banking specifically and the digital finance environment more generally. Such policies should build upon past achievements and current market conditions. Thus, they may differ from one country to another. Andrade and Mas (2015) describe at least five different scenarios under which the market for digital finance should flourish. The different policy avenues should be contingent on issues such as whether a big player is already taking most of the market and asymmetric regulation is required (as in Kenya) or whether a public agency is already working on reducing the use of cash among savers.

Specific policies can add dynamism to the digital finance market in the short term. For instance, they can address the need for specialized providers to enter the market (de Olloqui, Andrade, and Herrera, 2015). This, in turn, requires developing appropriate regulation for the use of existing mobile infrastructure by entrants. Likewise, promoting interoperability among platforms (so that users can make transfers to and from accounts at different mobile finance providers and between platforms and traditional bank providers) is a key element in the effort to increase the scale of operations and lower service costs. More flexible and complex financial services through mobile phones will also require enhancing mobile network capabilities.

Financial Saving beyond Banking

Latin America has a bank-centered financial system and banks and capital markets are complements rather than substitutes in financial markets (see Chapter 3). Therefore, policies that encourage the growth of bank-centered financial systems may also support the development of capital markets in the region, even though the exact way and pace at which each grows will vary according to the idiosyncrasies of each country.

However, specific aspects related to capital markets can help break the vicious circle of low saving and inefficient use of existing savings (shown in Figure 11.1).

One of these is pension funds, which are becoming increasingly important asset managers in many countries across the region (Bebczuk, 2015b). Assets managed by private pension systems exceed 50 percent of GDP in Chile (an early reformer). They are also already high in Colombia, Mexico, and Peru, and are projected to continue growing. While these sums are still low compared to Advanced Economies, they are nonetheless sizable. This pool of capital is potentially important for funding productive investments like infrastructure because pension funds accumulate long-term savings in domestic currency. However, the funds accumulated in pension funds are not always invested efficiently. For example, the risk profile of infrastructure investment projects is attractive for investors with long-term horizons, such as pension funds (see Chapter 4). However, on average, only about 2 percent of the total portfolio of pension funds in Latin America and the Caribbean is invested directly in infrastructure projects. This compares to between 5 and 7 percent of such investment portfolios in Australia and Canada. Conversely, a relatively high share of pension fund portfolios is invested in government bonds in Latin America and the Caribbean. In some countries, the problem is compounded by the fact that the lack of alternative financing options increases governments' temptation to capture the resources of institutional investors in order to cover their own current financing needs.[9] To reverse this pattern, two changes are needed. First, the supply of "investible assets" must expand through regulatory and institutional reforms that turn infrastructure into an asset class (see Chapter 4). Second, countries in the region should review pension fund investment allocation rules and regulations to enable and promote more investment diversification (see Chapter 7).

In addition, underdeveloped insurance markets in the region limit the opportunities for portfolio managers of pension funds and other asset managers to improve the risk-return profile of investment projects. A case in point is the collapse of Monoline insurance, which provided insurance to infrastructure bonds. This has severely limited the opportunities for prospective investors to mitigate risk. Deepening and strengthening insurance markets through regulatory and institutional reforms is yet another way to promote the development of capital markets in the region.

Creating a Virtuous Circle

Saving is low in Latin America and the Caribbean, and only a small fraction of the savings generated is channeled to the rest of the economy via an efficient financial system. Financial systems across the region are small and inefficient. Encouraging efficient financial saving requires concerted efforts on the demand and supply sides of financial services.

To expand the customer base of financial services, financial inclusion policies should be upgraded from the traditional focus on opening bank accounts toward an approach that encourages the use of the formal financial system as the main saving vehicle. Encouraging more formal financial saving, however, does not guarantee the efficient use of those savings. The resources must be channeled to enterprises with higher productive potential. Financial inclusion policies must be coupled with reforms that reduce distortions in financial markets to ensure that resources flow to the most productive—or potentially productive—uses.

Latin America and the Caribbean is caught in a vicious circle—but there is an alternative. The option is a virtuous circle (Figure 11.2) that begins with a culture of saving that generates higher savings for both firms and individuals to invest. The larger supply of loanable funds feeds the growth of the financial system, which can then lower its costs for lenders and borrowers alike. Lower costs are accompanied by regulatory reforms that strengthen property rights and expand credit information. Capital is allocated more efficiently to productive firms that grow, employ more workers in the formal economy, and feed overall economic growth. Gainfully employed people in formal jobs earn enough to invest in their own and their children's health and education and prepare for their retirement. A healthier, more educated workforce and a financial

Figure 11.8 The Virtuous Circle of High Saving and Efficient Financial Intermediation

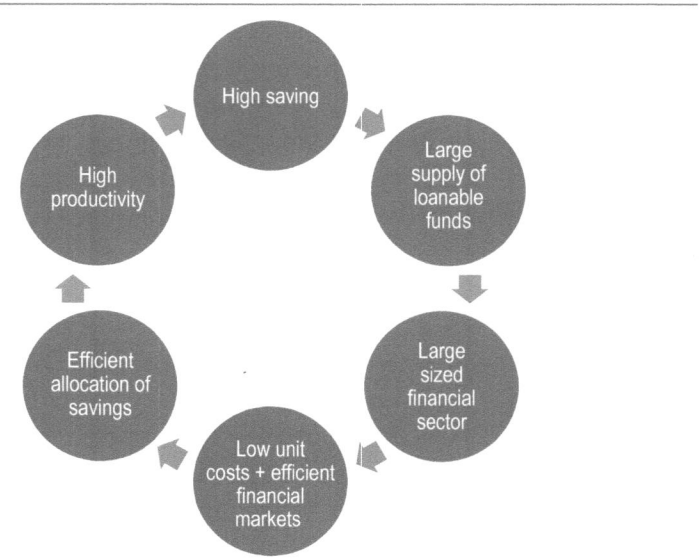

Source: Authors' elaboration.

system capable of supporting the investment needs of an expanding productive base fuel productivity. Higher productivity provides greater returns to investment and saving and, thus, encourages even more and better saving.

Despite the financial deregulation and reforms of recent decades, financial systems in Latin America and the Caribbean remain very shallow by international standards. Undeniably, the region has made notable progress in recent years. However, the region is still far from breaking into the virtuous circle. Fixing the system is not an easy task, but it is an important one. If Latin America and the Caribbean hopes to grow and prosper in a sustainable and equitable manner, its governments and citizens must learn how to generate and use saving for development.

Notes

[1] The aggregate marginal product of capital in the region is below that of Advanced Economies and Emerging Asia, according to calculations using a methodology that corrects marginal products for the effect of the relative price of capital (Caselli and Feyrer, 2007). For the median country in Latin America, the estimated marginal product of capital is 8.4 percent, while it is 11.1 percent in Advanced Economies and 9.3 percent in Emerging Asia.

[2] In addition to having to deal with financial market frictions and competition issues, firms in the region may be inherently more volatile and risky, which could justify the persistence of high interest rate spreads. While this issue has not been properly researched, the relatively high profitability of the financial industry in Latin America and the Caribbean does not appear consistent with this hypothesis.

[3] Coverage is measured as the percent of adults covered by the credit bureau. Research by Martínez Pería and Singh (2014) suggests that after the introduction of a credit bureau—but not a credit registry—firms can access loans from banks more easily, at lower cost, and at longer maturities. As predicted by theory, the effects are more pronounced for smaller firms, which tend to be less transparent and less experienced.

[4] A comprehensive review of the consequences of weak property rights in financial intermediation can be found in Fernández and Tamayo (forthcoming).

[5] Economies of scale can also be achieved by coordinating suppliers. A clear example of the cost structure under which financial institutions operate is their use of network-specific technologies. Physical branches, automated teller machines (ATMs), and mobile phone applications are often developed to function for a single institution or a small set of providers. Expanding the network to other suppliers (to increase the volume of users) would reduce unit costs; however, that would require coordination so that all providers/users would contribute their fair share to setting up and maintaining the system. The lack of coordination is a market failure that may warrant policy intervention.

[6] Among many other things, the Global Microscope asks local experts to grade the ease with which saving products may be offered based on existing practices and regulations such as interest rate restrictions and account opening requirements. See : www.eiu.com/microscope2015

[7] In Latin America and the Caribbean, personal remittances received amount to about 6 percent of GDP, on average. For some countries, remittances (as a percent of GDP) are significantly higher (World Development Indicators Database)

[8] A comprehensive review of some of the issues covered in this section can be found in Chong (2011).

[9] Becerra, Cavallo, and Scartascini (2012) show that, in countries where governments have lower state capabilities, governments are more likely to direct credit to finance their own operations, thereby curtailing credit to the private sector.

References

Aaron, H. 1966. "The Social Insurance Paradox." *Canadian Journal of Economics and Political Science* 32(03) August: 371–74.

Acemoglu, D., and F. Zilibotti. 1997. "Was Prometheus Unbound by Chance? Risk, Diversification, and Growth." *Journal of Political Economy* 105(4) August: 709–51.

Afonso, A., and M. St. Aubyn. 2005. "Non-Parametric Approaches to Education and Health Efficiency in OECD Countries." *Journal of Applied Economics* 8(2) November: 227–46.

Afzal, U., G. d'Adda, M. Fafchamps, S. Quinn, and F. Said. 2015. "Two Sides of the Same Rupee? Comparing Demand for Microcredit and Microsaving in a Framed Field Experiment in Rural Pakistan." September. Available at http://web.stanford.edu/~fafchamp/sargodha.pdf. Accessed November 2015.

Aghion, P., D. Comin, and P. Howitt. 2006. "When Does Domestic Saving Matter for Economic Growth?" NBER Working Paper no. 12275. National Bureau of Economic Research, Cambridge, MA.

Aghion, P., D. Comin, P. Howitt, and I. Tecu. 2009. "When Does Domestic Saving Matter for Economic Growth?" Working Paper no. 09–080. Harvard Business School, Boston, MA.

Aguila, E. 2011. "Personal Retirement Accounts and Saving." *American Economic Journal: Economic Policy* 3(4) November: 1–24.

Aizenman, J., E. Cavallo, and I. Noy. 2015. "Precautionary Strategies and Household Saving." *Open Economies Review* 26(5) November: 911–39.

Aizenman, J., B. Pinto, and A. Radziwill. 2007. "Sources for Financing Domestic Capital: Is Foreign Saving a Viable Option for Developing Countries?" *Journal of International Money and Finance* 26(5) September: 682–702.

Alaimo, V., M. Bosch, D. Kaplan, C. Pagés, and L. Ripani. 2015. *Empleos para crecer*. Washington, DC: Inter-American Development Bank.

Allen, F., and D. Gale. 2000. *Comparing Financial Systems*. Cambridge, MA: MIT Press.

Almazán, M., and J. Frydrych. 2015. "Mobile Financial Services in Latin America and the Caribbean: State of Play, Commercial Models, and Regulatory Approaches." Report. GSMA, London.

Alonso, J., C. Amuedo-Dorante, and L. Juárez. 2015. "The Effect of Non-Contributory Pensions on Saving in Mexico." Inter-American Development Bank, Washington, DC. Unpublished.

Alonso, J., A. Arellano, and D. Tuesta. 2015. "Factors that Impact on Pension Fund Investments in Infrastructure under the Current Global Financial Regulation." Paper presented at the Wharton School conference, 2015 Symposium: Implications of the New Regulatory Order for Retirement System Risk Management, April 30–May 1, Philadelphia, PA.

Alonso, J., S. Fernández de Lis, C. Hoyo, C. López-Moctezuma, and D. Tuesta. 2013. "Mobile Banking in Mexico as a Mechanism for Financial Inclusion: Recent Developments and a Closer Look into the Potential Market." BBVA Research Working Paper no. 13/20. Banco Bilbao Vizcaya Argentaria, Madrid.

Anderson, R. W., and K. Jõeveer. 2012. "Bankers and Bank Investors: Reconsidering the Economies of Scale in Banking." Financial Markets Group Discussion Paper no. 712. Department of Finance, London School of Economics and Political Science, London.

Anderson, S., and J.-M. Baland. 2002. "The Economics of ROSCAS and Intrahousehold Resource Allocation." *Quarterly Journal of Economics* 117(3) August: 963–95.

Andrade, S. G., and I. Mas. 2015. "A Digital Money Grid for Modern Citizenship: Latin American Scenarios, 2015–25." Inter-American Development Bank, Washington, DC; and Tufts University, Medford, MA. Available at http://papers.ssrn.com/sol3/papers.cfm?abstract_id=1725103&download=yes. Accessed February 2016.

Angelucci, M., D. Karlan, and J. Zinman. 2015. "Microcredit Impacts: Evidence from a Randomized Microcredit Program Placement Experiment by Compartamos Banco." *American Economic Journal: Applied Economics* 7(1) January: 151–82.

Aportela, F. 1999. "Effects of Financial Access on Savings by Low-Income People." Paper. Research Department, Banco de México, Mexico City. Available at http://citeseerx.ist.psu.edu/viewdoc/download?doi=10.1.1.194.5270&rep=rep1&type=pdf. Accessed February 2016.

Araujo, A. P., R. V. X. Ferreira, and B. Funchal. 2012. "The Brazilian Bankruptcy Law Experience." *Journal of Corporate Finance* 18(4) September: 994–1004.

Ardánaz, M., and A. Izquierdo. 2016. "Cycles and Public Expenditure in Latin America: Current Expenditure Increases for the Good Times but Capital Expenditure Cuts for the Bad Times?" Inter-American Development Bank, Washington, DC. Unpublished.

Arrow, K. J., and M. Kurz. 1970. *Public Investment, the Rate of Return, and Optimal Fiscal Policy.* Baltimore, MD and London: Johns Hopkins University Press.

Aschauer, D. A. 1989. "Is Public Expenditure Productive?" *Journal of Monetary Economics* 23(2) March: 177–200.

Ashraf, N., D. Aycinena, C. Martínez A., and D. Yang. 2015. "Savings in Transnational Households: A Field Experiment among Migrants from El Salvador." *Review of Economics and Statistics* 97(2) May: 332–51.

Ashraf, N., D. Karlan, and W. Yin. 2006. "Tying Odysseus to the Mast: Evidence from a Commitment Savings Product in the Philippines." *Quarterly Journal of Economics* 121(2) May: 635–72.

Assunção, J. 2013. "Eliminating Entry Barriers for the Provision of Banking Services: Evidence from 'Banking Correspondents' in Brazil." *Journal of Banking and Finance* 37(8) August: 2806–11.

Attanasio, O. P., A. Bonfatti, S. Kitao, and G. Weber. 2015. "Global Demographic Trends, Capital Mobility, Saving and Consumption in Latin America and the Caribbean (LAC)". IDB Working Paper no. 586. Department of Research and Chief Economist, Inter-American Development Bank, Washington, DC.

Attanasio, O. P., and A. Brugiavini. 2003. "Social Security and Households' Saving." *Quarterly Journal of Economics* 118(3) August: 1075–1119.

Attanasio, O. P., L. Picci, and A. E. Scorcu. 2000. "Saving, Growth, and Investment: A Macroeconomic Analysis Using a Panel of Countries." *Review of Economics and Statistics* 82(2) May: 182–211.

Attanasio, O. P., and S. Rohwedder. 2003. "Pension Wealth and Household Saving: Evidence from Pension Reforms in the United Kingdom." *American Economic Review* 93(5) December: 1499–1521.

Bachas, P., P. Gertler, S. Higgins, and E. Seira. 2015. "Banking on Trust: Debit Cards, Cash Transfers, and Savings in Mexico." Paper presented at the University of San Francisco's Economics Guest Speaker Seminar, November 5, San Francisco, CA.

Bagehot, W. 1873. *Lombard Street: A Description of the Money Market.* London: Henry S. King and Co. Available at http://oll.libertyfund. org/titles/128. Accessed March 2016.

Bailliu, J. N., and H. Reisen. 1998. "Do Funded Pensions Contribute to Higher Aggregate Savings? A Cross-Country Analysis." *Review of World Economics (Weltwirtschaftliches Archiv)* 134(4) December: 692–711.

Baland, J.-M., C. Guirkinger, and C. Mali. 2011. "Pretending to Be Poor: Borrowing to Escape Forced Solidarity in Cameroon." *Economic Development and Cultural Change* 60(1) October: 1–16.

Balassone, F., and M. S. Kumar. 2007. "Cyclicality of Fiscal Policy." In M. S. Kumar and T. Ter-Minassian, eds., *Promoting Fiscal Discipline.* Washington, DC: International Monetary Fund.

Banerjee, A. V., and E. Duflo. 2007. "The Economic Lives of the Poor." *Journal of Economic Perspectives* 21(1) Winter: 141–68.

Banerjee, A. V., E. Duflo, R. Glennerster, and C. Kinnan. 2015. "The Miracle of Microfinance? Evidence from a Randomized Evaluation." *American Economic Journal: Applied Economics* 7(1) January: 22–53.

Banerjee, A., D. Karlan, and J. Zinman. 2015. "Six Randomized Evaluations of Microcredit: Introduction and Further Steps." *American Economic Journal: Applied Economics* 7(1) January: 1–21.

Banks, J., R. Blundell, and S. Tanner. 1998. "Is There a Retirement-Savings Puzzle?" *American Economic Review* 88(4) September: 769–88.

Barr, N. 2002. "Reforming Pensions: Myths, Truths, and Policy Choices." *International Social Security Review* 55(2) April–June: 3–36.

Barr, N., and P. Diamond. 2006. "The Economics of Pensions." *Oxford Review of Economic Policy* 22(1) Spring: 15–39.

———. 2009. "Reforming Pensions: Principles, Analytical Errors and Policy Directions." *International Social Security Review* 62(2) April–June: 5–29.

Barrera-Osorio, F., M. Bertrand, L. L. Linden, and F. Pérez-Calle. 2011. "Improving the Design of Conditional Transfer Programs: Evidence from a Randomized Education Experiment in Colombia." *American Economic Journal: Applied Economics* 3(2) April: 167–95.

Barro, R. J. 1974. "Are Government Bonds Net Wealth?" *Journal of Political Economy* 82(6) November–December: 1095–1117.

Baxter, M., and M. J. Crucini. 1993. "Explaining Saving–Investment Correlations." *American Economic Review* 83(3) June: 416–36.

Bebczuk, R. 2015a. "Pension Reform and Saving in Latin America and the Caribbean (LAC)." Inter-American Development Bank, Washington, DC. Unpublished.

———. 2015b. "Wealth, Financial Intermediation, and Saving in Latin America and the Caribbean." IDB Discussion Paper no. 406. Capital Markets and Financial Institutions Division, Inter-American Development Bank, Washington, DC.

Bebczuk, R., and E. Cavallo. 2016. "Is Business Saving Really None of Our Business?" *Applied Economics* 48(24): 2266–84.

Bebczuk, R., L. Gasparini, J. Amendolaggine, and N. Garbero. 2015. "Understanding the Determinants of Household Saving: Micro Evidence for Latin America." IDB Technical Note no. 843. Department of Research and Chief Economist, Inter-American Development Bank, Washington, DC.

Bebczuk, R., and A. R. Musalem. 2006. "Pensions and Saving: New International Panel Data Evidence." Working Paper no. 61. Departamento de Economía, Facultad de Ciencias Económicas, Universidad Nacional de La Plata, La Plata, Argentina.

Becerra, Ó., E. Cavallo, and I. Noy. 2015. "The Mystery of Saving in Latin America." IDB Working Paper no. 615. Department of Research and Chief Economist, Inter-American Development Bank, Washington, DC.

Becerra, Ó., E. Cavallo, and C. Scartascini. 2012. "The Politics of Financial Development: The Role of Interest Groups and Government Capabilities." *Journal of Banking and Finance* 36(3) March: 626–43.

Beck, T., A. Demirgüç-Kunt, and V. Maksimovic. 2005. "Financial and Legal Constraints to Growth: Does Firm Size Matter?" *Journal of Finance* 60(1) February: 137–77.

———. 2008. "Financing Patterns around the World: Are Small Firms Different?" *Journal of Financial Economics* 89(3) September: 467–87.

Beneke, M., N. Lustig, and J. A. Oliva. 2015. "El impacto de los impuestos y el gasto social en la desigualdad y la pobreza en El Salvador." IDB Technical Note no. 775. Fiscal and Municipal Management Division, Inter-American Development Bank, Washington, DC.

Berger, A. N., and L. J. Mester. 1997. "Inside the Black Box: What Explains Differences in the Efficiencies of Financial Institutions?" *Journal of Banking and Finance* 21(7) July: 895–947.

Bergoeing, R., P. J. Kehoe, T. J. Kehoe, and R. Soto. 2002. "A Decade Lost and Found: Mexico and Chile in the 1980s." *Review of Economic Dynamics* 5(1) January: 166–205.

Berry, J., D. Karlan, and M. Pradhan. 2012. "Evaluating the Efficacy of School-Based Financial Education Programs in Ghana." Presentation delivered at the Impact and Policy Conference: Evidence in Governance Financial Inclusion and Entrepreneurship, September 1, Bangkok.

Berstein, S., M. Bosch, and M. L. Oliveri. 2016. "Promised and Affordable Replacement Rates in LAC Pension Systems in 2015 and 2100: Methodology and Determinants." IDB Technical Note no. 964. Department of Research and Chief Economist, Inter-American Development Bank, Washington, DC.

Berstein, S., and C. Cabrita. 2007. "Los determinantes de la elección de AFP en Chile: nueva evidencia a partir de datos individuales." *Estudios de Economía* 34(1) June: 53–72.

Berstein, S., and R. A. Chumacero. 2006. "Quantifying the Costs of Investment Limits for Chilean Pension Funds." *Fiscal Studies* 27(1) March: 99–123.

Berstein, S., O. Fuentes, and F. Villatoro. 2013. "Default Investment Strategies in a Defined Contribution Pension System: A Pension Risk Model Application for the Chilean Case." *Journal of Pension Economics and Finance* 12(04) October: 379–414.

Berstein, S., G. Larraín, F. Pino, and E. Morón. 2006. "Chilean Pension Reform: Coverage Facts and Policy Alternatives [with Comments]." *Economía* 6(2) Spring: 227–79.

Berstein, S., M. Morales, and A. Puente. 2015. "Rol de un seguro de longevidad en América Latina: casos de Chile, Colombia, México y Perú." Paper presented at the Thirteenth International FIAP Seminar, Los sistemas de pensiones multipilares: invirtiendo en el futuro, September 24–25, Montevideo.

Berstein, S., and A. Puente. 2015. "Sistemas de pensiones: diseños alternativos en América Latina." In Asociación de Aseguradores de Chile, ed., *Nueve miradas expertas: escáner a las rentas vitalicias. Los éxitos, los riesgos y las grandes oportunidades del futuro.* Santiago: Asociación de Aseguradores de Chile, A.G.

BlackRock. 2015. "Infrastructure Rising: An Asset Class Takes Shape." New York, NY. Available at https://www.blackrock.com/investing/literature/whitepaper/infrastructure-rising-an-asset-class-takes-shape.pdf. Accessed December 2015.

Bloom, D. E., D. Canning, and J. Sevilla. 2001. "Economic Growth and the Demographic Transition." NBER Working Paper no. 8685. National Bureau of Economic Research, Cambridge, MA.

Blyde, J. S., C. Daude, and E. Fernández-Arias. 2010. "Output Collapses and Productivity Destruction." *Review of World Economics (Weltwirtschaftliches Archiv)* 146(2) June: 359–87.

Boadway, R. 2015. "Tax Policy for a Rent-Rich Economy." *Canadian Public Policy* 41(4) December: 253–64.

Bodie, Z. 1990. "Pensions as Retirement Income Insurance." *Journal of Economic Literature* 28(1) March: 28–49.

Boltz, M., K. Marazyan, and P. Villar. 2015. "Preference for Hidden Income and Redistribution to Kin and Neighbors: A Lab-in-the-Field Experiment in Senegal." PSE Working Paper no. 2015-15. Paris-Jourdan Sciences Économiques (Paris School of Economics), Paris. Available at https://halshs.archives-ouvertes.fr/halshs-01157710/document. Accessed December 2015.

Borio, C., and P. Disyatat. 2011. "Global Imbalances and the Financial Crisis: Link or No Link?" BIS Working Paper no. 346. Monetary and Economic Department, Bank for International Settlements, Basel, Switzerland.

Bosch, M., S. Berstein, F. Castellani, M. L. Oliveri, and J. M. Villa. 2015. "Diagnóstico del sistema previsional colombiano y opciones de reforma." IDB Technical Note no. 825. Labor Markets and Social Security Unit, Inter-American Development Bank, Washington, DC.

Bosch, M., Á. Melguizo, and C. Pagés. 2013. *Better Pensions, Better Jobs: Towards Universal Coverage in Latin America and the Caribbean*. Washington, DC: Inter-American Development Bank.

Bosch, M., and M. L. Oliveri. 2015. "Labor Market and Poverty Impacts of Non-Contributory Pensions: The Case of Argentina's Moratorium." Inter-American Development Bank, Washington, DC. Unpublished.

Boyd, C., and Ú. Aldana. 2015. "Evaluación del Programa 'Promoción del ahorro en familias JUNTOS'." Paper. Instituto de Estudios Peruanos, Lima. Unpublished.

Browning, M. 2000. "The Saving Behaviour of a Two-Person Household." *Scandinavian Journal of Economics* 102(2) June: 235–51.

Bruhn, M., L. de Souza Leão, A. Legovini, R. Marchetti, and B. Zia. 2013. "The Impact of High School Financial Education: Experimental Evidence from Brazil." Policy Research Working Paper no. 6723. World Bank, Washington, DC.

Bruhn, M., and I. Love. 2014. "The Real Impact of Improved Access to Finance: Evidence from Mexico." *Journal of Finance* 69(3) June: 1347–76.

Brune, L., X. Giné, J. Goldberg, and D. Yang. 2015. "Facilitating Savings for Agriculture: Field Experimental Evidence from Malawi." NBER

Working Paper no. 20946. National Bureau of Economic Research, Cambridge, MA.

Bucheli, M., N. Lustig, M. Rossi, and F. Amábile. 2014. "Social Spending, Taxes, and Income Redistribution in Uruguay." *Public Finance Review* 42(3) May: 413–33.

Buera, F. J., J. P. Kaboski, and Y. Shin. 2011. "Finance and Development: A Tale of Two Sectors." *American Economic Review* 101(5) August: 1964–2002.

Buera, F. J., and Y. Shin. 2013. "Financial Frictions and the Persistence of History: A Quantitative Exploration." *Journal of Political Economy* 121(2) April: 221–72.

Burgess, R., and R. Pande. 2005. "Do Rural Banks Matter? Evidence from the Indian Social Banking Experiment." *American Economic Review* 95(3) June: 780–95.

Busso, M., M. V. Fazio, and S. Levy. 2012. "(In)Formal and (Un)Productive: The Productivity Costs of Excessive Informality in Mexico." IDB Working Paper no. 341. Department of Research and Chief Economist, Inter-American Development Bank, Washington, DC.

Busso, M., A. Fernández, and C. Tamayo. 2016. "Firm Productivity as an Engine of Saving." IDB Technical Note no. 963. Department of Research and Chief Economist, Inter-American Development Bank, Washington, DC.

Butelmann, A., and F. Gallego. 2000. "Ahorro de los hogares en Chile: evidencia microeconómica." *Economía Chilena* [Central Bank of Chile] 3(1) April: 5–24.

Cabrera, M., N. Lustig, and H. E. Morán. 2015. "Fiscal Policy, Inequality, and the Ethnic Divide in Guatemala." *World Development* 76(December): 263–79.

CAF (Development Bank of Latin America). 2009. *Caminos para el futuro: gestión de la infraestructura en América Latina*. Economic and Development Report Series. Caracas: CAF.

———. 2013. *La infraestructura en el desarrollo integral de América Latina: IDeAL 2013*. October. Bogotá: CAF.

Calderón, C., and L. Servén. 2003. "The Output Cost of Latin America's Infrastructure Gap." In W. Easterly and L. Servén, eds., *The Limits of Stabilization: Infrastructure, Public Deficits, and Growth in Latin America*. Palo Alto, CA: Stanford University Press and Washington, DC: World Bank.

———. 2004. "Trends in Infrastructure in Latin America, 1980–2001." Policy Research Working Paper no. 3401. World Bank, Washington, DC.

———. 2010. "Infrastructure in Latin America." Policy Research Working Paper no. 5317. World Bank, Washington, DC.

Calderón-Madrid, Á. 1998. "Explicaciones de la caída del ahorro privado en México desde tres perspectivas." IDB Working Paper no. R-346. Inter-American Development Bank, Washington, DC.

Callen, T., and C. Thimann. 1997. "Empirical Determinants of Household Saving: Evidence from OECD Countries." IMF Working Paper no. 97/181. Asia and Pacific Department, International Monetary Fund, Washington, DC.

Calvo, G. A., A. Izquierdo, and R. Loo-Kung. 2006. "Relative Price Volatility under Sudden Stops: The Relevance of Balance Sheet Effects." *Journal of International Economics* 69(1) June: 231–54.

Calvo, G. A., A. Izquierdo, and L.-F. Mejía. 2004. "On the Empirics of Sudden Stops: The Relevance of Balance-Sheet Effects." *Proceedings* [Federal Reserve Bank of San Francisco] 2004(June).

Calvo, G. A., L. Leiderman, and C. M. Reinhart. 1996. "Inflows of Capital to Developing Countries in the 1990s." *Journal of Economic Perspectives* 10(2) Spring: 123–39.

Cámara, N., D. Tuesta, and P. Urbiola. 2015. "Extending Access to the Formal Financial System: The Banking Correspondent Business Model." BBVA Research Working Paper no. 15/10. Banco Bilbao Vizcaya Argentaria, Madrid.

Campos, J., T. Serebrisky, and A. Suárez-Alemán. 2015. "Time Goes By: Recent Developments on the Theory and Practice of the Discount Rate." IDB Technical Note no. 861. Infrastructure and Environment Sector, Inter-American Development Bank, Washington, DC.

Canuto, O. 2014. "Liquidity Glut, Infrastructure Finance Drought and Development Banks." *Capital Finance International* (Autumn): 14–18.

Carpena, F., S. Cole, J. Shapiro, and B. Zia. 2015. "The ABCs of Financial Education: Experimental Evidence on Attitudes, Behavior, and Cognitive Biases." Policy Research Working Paper no. 7413. World Bank, Washington, DC.

Carranza, L., C. Daude, and Á. Melguizo. 2014. "Public Infrastructure Investment and Fiscal Sustainability in Latin America: Incompatible Goals?" *Journal of Economic Studies* 41(1): 29–50.

Caselli, F., and J. Feyrer. 2007. "The Marginal Product of Capital." *Quarterly Journal of Economics* 122(2) May: 535–68.

Catão, L. A. V., and G. M. Milesi-Ferretti. 2014. "External Liabilities and Crises." *Journal of International Economics* 94(1) September: 18–32.

Cavallo, E., E. Fernández-Arias, and M. Marzani. 2016. "Varieties of Saving and Crises." IDB Technical Note no. 1047. Department of Research and Chief Economist, Inter-American Development Bank, Washington, DC.

Cavallo, E., E. Fernández-Arias, and A. Powell. 2014. "Is the Euro-Zone on the Mend? Latin American Examples to Analyze the Euro Question." *Journal of Banking and Finance* 47(C) October: 243–57.

Cavallo, E., and M. Pedemonte. Forthcoming. "What Is the Relationship between National Saving and Investment in Latin America and the Caribbean?" *Economía* [LACEA].

Cavallo, E., A. Powell, M. Pedemonte, and P. Tavella. 2015. "A New Taxonomy of Sudden Stops: Which Sudden Stops Should Countries Be Most Concerned About?" *Journal of International Money and Finance* 51(C) March: 47–70.

Cavallo, E., G. Sánchez, and P. Valenzuela. 2016. "Gone with the Wind: Demographic Transitions and Domestic Saving." IDB Working Paper no. 688. Department of Research and Chief Economist, Inter-American Development Bank, Washington, DC.

CDE (Center for Demography and Ecology), PAHO (Pan American Health Organization), NIA (National Institute on Aging), and CDHA (Center for Demography of Health and Aging). 2002. "Encuesta salud, bienestar y envejecimiento (SABE)." Survey. CDE and CDHA, University of Wisconsin-Madison, Madison, WI; PAHO, Washington, DC; and NIA, National Institutes of Health, Bethesda, MD. Available at http://www.ssc.wisc.edu/sabe/data.html. Accessed February 2016.

CELADE (Latin American and Caribbean Demographic Center). 2015. "Estimaciones y proyecciones de población a largo plazo 1950–2100. Revisión 2015." CELADE, Economic Commission for Latin America and the Caribbean (ECLAC), Santiago. Available at http://www.cepal.org/es/estimaciones-proyecciones-poblacion-largo-plazo-1950–2100. Accessed February 2016.

Cerda, R., R. Fuentes, G. García, and J. I. Llodrá. 2015. "Understanding Domestic Savings in Chile." IDB Working Paper no. 626. Department of Research and Chief Economist, Inter-American Development Bank, Washington, DC.

Cerra, V., and S. C. Saxena. 2008. "Growth Dynamics: The Myth of Economic Recovery." *American Economic Review* 98(1) March: 439–57.

Chandrasekhar, A. G., C. Kinnan, and H. Larreguy. 2012. "Informal Insurance, Social Networks, and Savings Access: Evidence from a Lab Experiment in the Field." Consortium on Financial Systems and Poverty, Chicago, IL. Available at http://www.cfsp.org/publications/working-papers/informal-insurance-social-networks-and-savings-access-evidence-lab-exper#.Vm3fpoRq7Og. Accessed December 2015.

Chen, K., A. İmrohoroğlu, and S. İmrohoroğlu. 2006. "The Japanese Saving Rate." *American Economic Review* 96(5) December: 1850–58.

Chen, M. K. 2013. "The Effect of Language on Economic Behavior: Evidence from Savings Rates, Health Behaviors, and Retirement Assets." *American Economic Review* 103(2) April: 690–731.

Chong, A., ed. 2011. *Development Connections: Unveiling the Impact of New Information Technologies*. Development in the Americas series. New York, NY: Palgrave Macmillan and Washington, DC: Inter-American Development Bank.

Chong, A., and C. Pagés. 2010. "Taxes and Productivity: A Game of Hide and Seek." In C. Pagés, ed., *The Age of Productivity: Transforming Economies from the Bottom Up*. Development in the Americas series. New York, NY: Palgrave Macmillan and Washington, DC: Inter-American Development Bank.

Clements, B., D. Coady, M. Soto, F. Eich, A. Kangur, J. Kapsoli, K. Kashiwase, M. Nozaki, B. Shang, and V. Thakoor. 2011. "The Challenge of Public Pension Reform in Advanced and Emerging Economies." Paper. Fiscal Affairs Department, International Monetary Fund, Washington, DC.

Coelli, T., D. S. P. Rao, and G. E. Battese. 1998. *An Introduction to Efficiency and Productivity Analysis*. New York: Springer.

Coeurdacier, N., S. Guibaud, and K. Jin. 2015. "Credit Constraints and Growth in a Global Economy." *American Economic Review* 105(9) September: 2838–81.

Coeurdacier, N., and H. Rey. 2013. "Home Bias in Open Economy Financial Macroeconomics." *Journal of Economic Literature* 51(1) March: 63–115.

Collins, D., J. Morduch, S. Rutherford, and O. Ruthven. 2010. *Portfolios of the Poor: How the World's Poor Live on $2 a Day*. Princeton, NJ: Princeton University Press.

Commission on Growth and Development. 2008. "The Growth Report: Strategies for Sustained Growth and Inclusive Development." Report. World Bank, Washington, DC.

Committee on International Economic Policy and Reform. 2012. "Banks and Cross-Border Capital Flows: Policy Challenges and Regulatory Responses." Report. Brookings Institution, Washington, DC.

Corbacho, A., V. Fretes Cibils, and E. Lora, eds. 2013. *More than Revenue: Taxation as a Development Tool*. Development in the Americas series. Washington, DC: Inter-American Development Bank and New York, NY: Palgrave Macmillan.

Corbo, V. 1998. "Government Policy, Saving and Growth in Latin America." In S. Borner and M. Paldam, eds., *The Political Dimension of Economic Growth: Proceedings of the IEA Conference Held in San José, Costa Rica*. Volume 119. London: Palgrave Macmillan.

Coronado, J. L. 1998. "The Effects of Social Security Privatization on Household Saving: Evidence from the Chilean Experience." Finance and Economics Discussion Series Paper no. 1998–12. Board of Governors of the Federal Reserve System, Washington, DC.

Cronqvist, H., and S. Siegel. 2015. "The Origins of Savings Behavior." *Journal of Political Economy* 123(1) February: 123–69.

Cruces, J. J. 2016. "Argentina's Residential Real Estate Sector: A Magnet for Savings amidst Mistrust in Traditional Investment Vehicles." IDB Technical Note no. 911. Department of Research and Chief Economist, Inter-American Development Bank, Washington, DC.

Davis, E. P. 2002. "Prudent Person Rules or Quantitative Restrictions? The Regulation of Long-Term Institutional Investors' Portfolios." *Journal of Pension Economics and Finance* 1(02) July: 157–91.

Davis, S. J., J. C. Haltiwanger, and S. Schuh. 1996. *Job Creation and Destruction*. Cambridge, MA: MIT Press.

de la Torre, A., and A. Ize. 2015. "Should Latin America Save More to Grow Faster?" Policy Research Working Paper no. 7386. World Bank, Washington, DC.

de Mel, S., D. McKenzie, and C. Woodruff. 2008. "Returns to Capital in Microenterprises: Evidence from a Field Experiment." *Quarterly Journal of Economics* 123(4) November: 1329–72.

de Mello, L., and N. Mulder. 2006. "Fiscal Adjustment in Latin America: Trends and Stylised Facts." In L. de Mello, ed., *Challenges to Fiscal Adjustment in Latin America: The Cases of Argentina, Brazil, Chile and Mexico*. Paris: OECD Publishing.

de Olloqui, F., G. Andrade, and D. Herrera. 2015. "Inclusión financiera en América Latina y el Caribe: coyuntura actual y desafíos para los próximos años." IDB Discussion Paper no. 385. Capital Markets and Financial Institutions Division, Inter-American Development Bank, Washington, DC.

Della Croce, R., and S. Gatti. 2014. "Financing Infrastructure—International Trends." *OECD Journal: Financial Market Trends* 2014(1): 123–38.

Della Croce, R., and J. Yermo. 2013. "Institutional Investors and Infrastructure Financing." OECD Working Paper on Finance, Insurance and Private Pensions no. 36. OECD Publishing, Paris.

DellaVigna, S. 2009. "Psychology and Economics: Evidence from the Field." *Journal of Economic Literature* 47(2) June: 315–72.

DellaVigna, S., and U. Malmendier. 2006. "Paying Not to Go to the Gym." *American Economic Review* 96(3) June: 694–719.

Demirgüç-Kunt, A., and L. Klapper. 2012. "Measuring Financial Inclusion: The Global Findex Database." Policy Research Working Paper no. 6025. World Bank, Washington, DC.

Dewatripont, M., and J. Tirole. 1994. *The Prudential Regulation of Banks*. Cambridge, MA: MIT Press.

DeYoung, R. 2010. "Scale Economies Are a Distraction." *The Region* [Federal Reserve Bank of Minneapolis] 24(3) September: 14–16.

Diamond, D. W., and R. E. Verrecchia. 1991. "Disclosure, Liquidity, and the Cost of Capital." *Journal of Finance* 46(4) September: 1325–59.

Diamond, P. A. 1965. "National Debt in a Neoclassical Growth Model." *American Economic Review* 55(5, Part 1) December: 1126–50.

Didier, T., and S. L. Schmukler, eds. 2014. *Emerging Issues in Financial Development: Lessons from Latin America*. Washington, DC: World Bank.

Djankov, S., T. Ganser, C. McLiesh, R. Ramalho, and A. Shleifer. 2010. "The Effect of Corporate Taxes on Investment and Entrepreneurship." *American Economic Journal: Macroeconomics* 2(3) July: 31–64.

Drexler, A., G. Fischer, and A. Schoar. 2014. "Keeping It Simple: Financial Literacy and Rules of Thumb." *American Economic Journal: Applied Economics* 6(2) April: 1–31.

Dupas, P., S. Green, A. Keats, and J. Robinson. 2016. "Challenges in Banking the Rural Poor: Evidence from Kenya's Western Province." In S. Edwards, S. Johnson, and D. N. Weil, eds., *African Successes: Modernization and Development*. Volume 3. Chicago, IL: University of Chicago Press.

Dupas, P., and J. Robinson. 2013a. "Savings Constraints and Microenterprise Development: Evidence from a Field Experiment in Kenya." *American Economic Journal: Applied Economics* 5(1) January: 163–92.

———. 2013b. "Why Don't the Poor Save More? Evidence from Health Savings Experiments." *American Economic Review* 103(4) June: 1138–71.

Eckler. 2014. "Review of Cost of Government Pensions in Barbados." Eckler Consultants and Actuaries, Christ Church.

ECLAC (United Nations Economic Commission for Latin America and the Caribbean). 2014a. "Base de datos de inversiones en infraestructura económica en América Latina y el Caribe, 1980–2012." Santiago. October. Available at http://www.cepal.org/es/notas-informativas/base-de-datos-de-inversiones-en-infraestructura-economica-en-america-latina-y-el. Accessed December 2015.

———. 2014b. "La nueva era demográfica en América Latina y el Caribe: la hora de la igualdad según el reloj poblacional." Document presented at the First Meeting of the Presiding Officers of the Regional Conference on Population and Development in Latin America and the Caribbean, November 12–14, Santiago.

———. 2015a. "CEPALSTAT." Databases and Statistical Publications. ECLAC, Santiago. Available at http://estadisticas.cepal.org/cepalstat/WEB_CEPALSTAT/Portada.asp. Accessed February 2016.

———. 2015b. "Inversión/Gasto social en América Latina y el Caribe." Database. Social Development Division, ECLAC, Santiago. Available at http://dds.cepal.org/gasto/indicadores/. Accessed February 2016.

Econometría and SEI (Sistemas Especializados de Información). 2011. "Evaluación de impacto: acceso a servicios financieros en los municipios intervenidos por el Programa de Inversión Banca de las Oportunidades (2007–2010)." Report. Government of Colombia, Bogotá.

Ehlers, T. 2014. "Understanding the Challenges for Infrastructure Finance." BIS Working Paper no. 454. Monetary and Economic Department, Bank for International Settlements, Basel, Switzerland.

EIU (Economist Intelligence Unit). 2014. "Evaluating the Environment for Public-Private Partnerships in Latin America and the Caribbean: The 2014 Infrascope." Index and study. EIU, New York, NY.

El Mekkaoui de Freitas, N., and J. Oliveira Martins. 2014. "Health, Pension Benefits and Longevity: How They Affect Household Savings?" *Journal of the Economics of Ageing* 3(April): 21–28.

Estache, A., T. Serebrisky, and L. Wren-Lewis. 2015. "Financing Infrastructure in Developing Countries." *Oxford Review of Economic Policy* 31(3–4) Autumn–Winter: 279–304.

Fajnzylber, E., G. Plaza, and G. Reyes. 2009. "Better-Informed Workers and Retirement Savings Decisions: Impact Evaluation of a Personalized Pension Projection in Chile." Working Paper no. 31. Superintendencia de Pensiones, Santiago.

Farrell, M. J. 1957. "The Measurement of Productive Efficiency." *Journal of the Royal Statistical Society: Series A (General)* 120(3): 253–90.

Fay, M., and M. Morrison. 2007. *Infrastructure in Latin America and the Caribbean: Recent Developments and Key Challenges*. Washington, DC: World Bank.

Faz, X. 2013. "Mexico's Tiered KYC: An Update on Market Response." Blog post. Consultative Group to Assist the Poor (CGAP), Washington, DC. June 25. Available at http://www.cgap.org/blog/mexicos-tiered-kyc-update-market-response. Accessed February 2016.

Feldman, R. J. 2010. "Size and Regulatory Reform in Finance: Important but Difficult Questions." *The Region* [Federal Reserve Bank of Minneapolis] 24(3) September: 8–9.

Feldstein, M., and P. Bacchetta. 1991. "National Saving and International Investment." In B. D. Bernheim and J. B. Shoven, eds., *National Saving and Economic Performance*. Chicago, IL: University of Chicago Press.

Feldstein, M., and C. Horioka. 1980. "Domestic Saving and International Capital Flows." *Economic Journal* 90(358) June: 314–29.

Fernandes, D., J. G. Lynch, Jr., and R. G. Netemeyer. 2014. "Financial Literacy, Financial Education, and Downstream Financial Behaviors." *Management Science* 60(8) August: 1861–83.

Fernández, A., and C. E. Tamayo. Forthcoming. "From Institutions to Financial Development and Growth: What Are the Links?" *Journal of Economic Surveys*.

Fernández-Arias, E., and R. Hausmann. 2001. "Is Foreign Direct Investment a Safer Form of Financing?" *Emerging Markets Review* 2(1) March: 34–49.

Fernández-Arias, E., and D. Lombardo. 1998. "Private External Overborrowing in Undistorted Economies: Market Failure and Optimal Policy." IDB Working Paper no. 369. Inter-American Development Bank, Washington, DC.

Ferreira, F. H. G., J. Messina, J. Rigolini, L.-F. López-Calva, M. A. Lugo, and R. Vakis. 2013. *Economic Mobility and the Rise of the Latin American Middle Class*. Washington, DC: World Bank.

FIAP (Federación Internacional de Administradoras de Fondos de Pensiones). 2015. "Estadísticas históricas." Database. FIAP, Santiago. Available at http://www.fiap.cl/prontus_fiap/site/edic/base/port/series.html. Accessed February 2016.

Finkelstein, A., and J. Poterba. 2004. "Adverse Selection in Insurance Markets: Policyholder Evidence from the U.K. Annuity Market." *Journal of Political Economy* 112(1) February: 183–208.

Floro, M. S., and D. Ray. 1997. "Vertical Links between Formal and Informal Financial Institutions." *Review of Development Economics* 1(1) February: 34–56.

Franks, J., C. Mayer, and L. Renneboog. 2001. "Who Disciplines Management in Poorly Performing Companies?" *Journal of Financial Intermediation* 10(3–4) July: 209–48.

Frederick, S., G. Loewenstein, and T. O'Donoghue. 2002. "Time Discounting and Time Preference: A Critical Review." *Journal of Economic Literature* 40(2) June: 351–401.

Frisancho, V. 2012. "Signaling Creditworthiness in Peruvian Microfinance Markets: The Role of Information Sharing." *B.E. Journal of Economic Analysis and Policy* 12(1) October: 1–43.

———. 2016. "How to Raise Household Savings in LAC: Constraints and Best Practices." IDB Technical Note no. 962. Department of Research and Chief Economist, Inter-American Development Bank, Washington, DC.

Frisancho, V., and J. Karver. 2016. "Financial Inclusion in Latin America and the Caribbean." Inter-American Development Bank, Washington, DC. Unpublished.

Galiani, S., P. Gertler, and R. Bando. 2014. "Non-Contributory Pensions." NBER Working Paper no. 19775. National Bureau of Economic Research, Cambridge, MA.

Gandelman, N. 2015a. "A Comparison of Saving Rates: Micro Evidence from Seventeen Latin American and Caribbean Countries." IDB Working Paper no. 602. Department of Research and Chief Economist, Inter-American Development Bank, Washington, DC.

———. 2015b. "Do the Rich Save More in Latin America?" IDB Working Paper no. 588. Department of Research and Chief Economist, Inter-American Development Bank, Washington, DC.

García, N., A. Grifoni, J. C. López, and D. Mejía. 2013. "Financial Education in Latin America and the Caribbean: Rationale, Overview and Way Forward." OECD Working Paper on Finance, Insurance and Private Pensions no. 33. OECD Publishing, Paris.

Gelos, R. G., and J. Roldós. 2004. "Consolidation and Market Structure in Emerging Market Banking Systems." *Emerging Markets Review* 5(1) March: 39–59.

Gill, I. S., T. Packard, and J. Yermo. 2005. *Keeping the Promise of Social Security in Latin America*. Palo Alto, CA: Stanford University Press; and Washington, DC: World Bank.

Goldberger, A. S. 1979. "Heritability." *Economica* 46(184) November: 327–47.

González-Rozada, M., and H. Ruffo. 2015. "Non-Contributory Pensions and Savings: Evidence from Argentina." Inter-American Development Bank, Washington, DC. Unpublished.

González-Vega, C., and R. Quirós. 2008. "Strategic Alliances for Scale and Scope Economies: Lessons from FADES in Bolivia." In M. E. Pagura, ed., *Expanding the Frontier in Rural Finance: Financial Linkages and Strategic Alliances*. Rugby, Warwickshire, UK: Practical Action Publishing.

Gourinchas, P.-O., and O. Jeanne. 2013. "Capital Flows to Developing Countries: The Allocation Puzzle." *Review of Economic Studies* 80(4) October: 1484–1515.

Granda, C., and F. Hamann. 2015. "Informality, Saving and Wealth Inequality in Colombia." IDB Working Paper no. 575. Department of Research and Chief Economist, Inter-American Development Bank, Washington, DC.

Grigoli, F., A. Herman, and K. Schmidt-Hebbel. 2014. "World Saving." IMF Working Paper no. 14/204. Western Hemisphere Department, International Monetary Fund, Washington, DC.

———. 2015. "Saving in Latin America and the Caribbean: Performance and Policies." IMF Working Paper no. 15/108. Western Hemisphere Department, International Monetary Fund, Washington, DC.

Grout, P. A., W. L. Megginson, and A. Zalewska. 2009. "One Half-Billion Shareholders and Counting: Determinants of Individual Share Ownership around the World." Paper. Available at http://ssrn.com/abstract=1364765. Accessed January 2016.

Hall, C. D. 2014. "Actuarial Analysis of the Sustainability of the National Insurance Scheme (NIS) in Jamaica." Eckler Consultants and Actuaries, Kingston.

Hansen, E., and R. Wagner. 2015. "Multinationals Stockpiling Cash: Exploring a Commodity Boom." IDB Working Paper no. 580. Department of Research and Chief Economist, Inter-American Development Bank, Washington, DC.

Hayashi, F. 1989. "Is Japan's Saving Rate High?" *Quarterly Review* [Federal Reserve Bank of Minneapolis] 13(2) Spring: 3–9.

Heller, P. S. 1989. "Aging, Savings, and Pensions in the Group of Seven Countries: 1980–2025." *Journal of Public Policy* 9(02) April: 127–55.

HelpAge International. 2015. "Global AgeWatch Index 2015." Database. HelpAge International, London. Available at www.helpage.org/global-agewatch/. Accessed February 2016.

Henrichs, J., and B. R. H. Van den Bergh. 2015. "Perinatal Developmental Origins of Self-Regulation." In G. H. E. Gendolla, M. Tops, and S. L. Koole, eds., *Handbook of Biobehavioral Approaches to Self-Regulation*. New York, NY: Springer-Verlag.

Hernani-Limarino, W., W. Jiménez, and G. Mena. 2015. "Evolution, Importance and Correlates of Household Savings in Bolivia." Working Paper no. 10/2015. Fundación ARU, La Paz, Bolivia.

Hernani-Limarino, W., and G. Mena. 2015. "Intended and Unintended Effects of Unconditional Cash Transfers: The Case of Bolivia's *Renta Dignidad*." IDB Working Paper no. 631. Department of Research and Chief Economist, Inter-American Development Bank, Washington, DC.

Hess, D. 2005. "Protecting and Politicizing Public Pension Fund Assets: Empirical Evidence on the Effects of Governance Structures and Practices." *UC Davis Law Review* 39(1) November: 187– 227.

Higgins, S., and C. Pereira. 2014. "The Effects of Brazil's Taxation and Social Spending on the Distribution of Household Income." *Public Finance Review* 42(3) May: 346–67.

Holzmann, R. 2013. "Global Pension Systems and Their Reform: Worldwide Drivers, Trends and Challenges." *International Social Security Review* 66(2) April–June: 1–29.

Holzmann, R., and R. Hinz (with H. von Gersdorff, I. Gill, G. Impavido, A. R. Musalem, R. Palacios, D. Robolino, M. Rutkowski, A. Schwarz, Y. Sin, and K. Subbarao). 2005. *Old-Age Income Support in the 21st Century: An International Perspective on Pension Systems and Reform*. Washington, DC: World Bank.

Hopt, K. J. 2011. "Comparative Corporate Governance: The State of the Art and International Regulation." *American Journal of Comparative Law* 59(1) Winter: 1–73.

Hsieh, C.-T., and P. J. Klenow. 2009. "Misallocation and Manufacturing TFP in China and India." *Quarterly Journal of Economics* 124(4) November: 1403–48.

———. 2014. "The Life Cycle of Plants in India and Mexico." *Quarterly Journal of Economics* 129(3) August: 1035–84.

Hsieh, C.-T., and J. A. Parker. 2007. "Taxes and Growth in a Financially Underdeveloped Country: Evidence from the Chilean Investment Boom." *Economía* [LACEA] 8(1) Fall: 1– 53.

Hurst, E., G. Li, and B. Pugsley. 2014. "Are Household Surveys Like Tax Forms? Evidence from Income Underreporting of the Self-Employed." *Review of Economics and Statistics* 96(1) March: 19–33.

IDB (Inter-American Development Bank). 2004. *Unlocking Credit: The Quest for Deep and Stable Bank Lending.* Economic and Social Progress in Latin America: 2005 Report. Washington, DC: IDB.

———. 2008. "Social Protection Surveys in Mexico and Peru." IDB, Washington, DC.

IMF (International Monetary Fund). 2009. "Debt Bias and Other Distortions: Crisis-Related Issues in Tax Policy." Paper. Fiscal Affairs Department, IMF, Washington, DC. Available at https://www.imf.org/external/np/pp/eng/2009/061209.pdf. Accessed February 2016.

———. 2015. "World Economic Outlook." Database. IMF, Washington, DC. October. Available at https://www.imf.org/external/pubs/ft/weo/2015/02/weodata/download.aspx. Accessed February 2016.

Inderst, G. 2013. "Private Infrastructure Finance and Investment in Europe." EIB Working Paper no. 2013/02. European Investment Bank, Luxembourg.

Inderst, G., and F. Stewart. 2014. "Institutional Investment in Infrastructure in Developing Countries: Introduction to Potential Models." Policy Research Working Paper no. 6780. World Bank, Washington, DC.

Infrastructure Canada. 2007. "Infrastructure and Productivity: A Literature Review." Report. Research and Analysis Division, Infrastructure Canada, Ottawa, ON, Canada.

Ionescu, L., and E. A. Robles. 2014. "Update of IOPS Work on Fees and Charges." IOPS Working Paper on Effective Pensions Supervision no. 20. International Organisation of Pension Supervisors (IOPS), Paris.

IOPS (International Organisation of Pension Supervisors). 2010. "IOPS Principles of Private Pension Supervision." IOPS, Paris. Available at http://www.iopsweb.org/principlesandguidelines/IOPS-principles-private-pension-supervision.pdf. Accessed February 2016.

———. 2011. "Pension Supervisory Authorities and Financial Education: Lessons Learnt." IOPS Information Paper no. 1. IOPS, Paris.

———. 2012. "Toolkit for Risk-Based Pensions Supervision: Case Study: Netherlands." IOPS, Paris.

Izquierdo, A., and E. Kawamura. 2015. "Public Expenditure: Is There a Bias against Public Investment? A Political Economy Explanation." Paper presented at the 2015 LACEA Annual Meeting, October 15–17, Santa Cruz, Bolivia.

Izquierdo, A., R. Loo-Kung, and F. Navajas, coords. 2013. *Resistiendo el canto de las sirenas financieras en Centroamérica: una ruta hacia un gasto eficiente con más crecimiento*. Washington, DC: Inter-American Development Bank.

Jakiela, P., and O. Ozier. 2016. "Does Africa Need a Rotten Kin Theorem? Experimental Evidence from Village Economies." *Review of Economic Studies* 83(1) January: 231–68.

Jamison, J. C., D. Karlan, and J. Zinman. 2014. "Financial Education and Access to Savings Accounts: Complements or Substitutes? Evidence from Ugandan Youth Clubs." NBER Working Paper no. 20135. National Bureau of Economic Research, Cambridge, MA.

Janssens, W., B. Kramer, and L. Swart. 2015. "Be Patient When Measuring Hyperbolic Discounting: Stationarity, Time Consistency and Time Invariance in a Field Experiment." Discussion Paper no. 2015–097/V. Tinbergen Institute, Amsterdam.

Jaramillo, M. 2014. "The Incidence of Social Spending and Taxes in Peru." *Public Finance Review* 42(3) May: 391–412.

Jeanne, O., and A. Korinek. 2010. "Excessive Volatility in Capital Flows: A Pigouvian Taxation Approach." *American Economic Review* 100(2) May: 403–07.

Jemio, L. C., and O. Nina. 2016. "Saving and Investment Behavior in Bolivia: Evidence from a Flow-of-Funds Analysis." IDB Technical Note no. 895. Department of Research and Chief Economist, Inter-American Development Bank, Washington, DC.

Jiménez, L. F., and S. Manuelito. 2013. "Rasgos estilizados de la relación entre inversión y crecimiento en América Latina y el Caribe, 1980–2012." Macroeconomics of Development Series no. 136. United Nations Economic Commission for Latin America and the Caribbean (ECLAC), Santiago.

Jiménez-Martín, S. 2014. "The Incentive Effects of Minimum Pensions." *IZA World of Labor* 2014(August) 1–10.

John, A. 2014. "Just a Few Cents Each Day: Can Fixed Regular Deposits Overcome Savings Constraints? Evidence from a Commitment Savings Product in Bangladesh." Economic Organisation and Public Policy Discussion Paper no. 51. London: London School of Economics and Political Science.

Joumard, I., C. André, and C. Nicq. 2010. "Health Care Systems: Efficiency and Institutions." OECD Economics Department Working Paper no. 769. OECD Publishing, Paris.

J.P. Morgan Asset Management and Af2i (Association Française des Investisseurs Institutionnels). 2014. "Guide to Infrastructure Investing." Available at http://www.jpmorganassetmanagement.ch/DE/dms/Guide_to_infrastructure_investing_[MKR]_[CH_EN].pdf. Accessed December 2015.

Juárez, L. 2009. "Crowding out of Private Support to the Elderly: Evidence from a Demogrant in Mexico." *Journal of Public Economics* 93(3–4) April: 454–63.

Kahneman, D., P. Slovic, and A. Tversky, eds. 1982. *Judgment under Uncertainty: Heuristics and Biases*. Cambridge, UK: Cambridge University Press.

Karlan, D., and L. L. Linden. 2014. "Loose Knots: Strong versus Weak Commitments to Save for Education in Uganda." July. Available at http://www.povertyactionlab.org/publication/loose-knots-strong-versus-weak-commitments-save-education-uganda. Accessed January 2016.

Karlan, D., M. McConnell, S. Mullainathan, and J. Zinman. Forthcoming. "Getting to the Top of Mind: How Reminders Increase Saving." *Management Science*.

Karlan, D., A. L. Ratan, and J. Zinman. 2014. "Savings by and for the Poor: A Research Review and Agenda." *Review of Income and Wealth* 60(1) March: 36–78.

Karlan, D., and J. Zinman. 2014. "Price and Control Elasticities of Demand for Savings." January. Available at http://karlan.yale.edu/sites/default/files/savingselasticities_2014_01_v9.pdf. Accessed January 2016.

Kast, F., S. Meier, and D. Pomeranz. 2012. "Under-Savers Anonymous: Evidence on Self-Help Groups and Peer Pressure as a Savings Commitment Device." NBER Working Paper no. 18417. National Bureau of Economic Research, Cambridge, MA.

Kawamura, E., and L. Ronconi. 2015. "Firms' Investment and Savings in Latin America: Stylized Facts from the Enterprise Survey." IDB Working Paper no. 638. Department of Research and Chief Economist, Inter-American Development Bank, Washington, DC.

Ke, D., L. Ng, and Q. Wang. 2010. "Home Bias in Foreign Investment Decisions." *Journal of International Business Studies* 41(6) August: 960–79.

Kehoe, T. J., and F. Meza. 2011. "Catch-up Growth Followed by Stagnation: Mexico, 1950–2010." *Latin American Journal of Economics* 48(2) November: 227–68.

Kohli, H. A., and P. Basil. 2011. "Requirements for Infrastructure Investment in Latin America under Alternate Growth Scenarios: 2011–2040." *Global Journal of Emerging Market Economies* 3(1) January: 59–110.

Kotlikoff, L. J. 1988. "Intergenerational Transfers and Savings." *Journal of Economic Perspectives* 2(2) Spring: 41–58.

Kotlikoff, L. J., and A. Spivak. 1981. "The Family as an Incomplete Annuities Market." *Journal of Political Economy* 89(2) April: 372–91.

Lane, P. R., and G. M. Milesi-Ferretti. 2007. "The External Wealth of Nations Mark II: Revised and Extended Estimates of Foreign Assets and Liabilities, 1970–2004." *Journal of International Economics* 73(2) November: 223–50.

Lanuza, P. 2004. "Making Sense of the Commercialization of Microfinance in Latin America: Lessons for Nicaragua." Paper. St. Antony's College, Oxford, UK. Available at http://www.microfinancegateway. org/sites/default/files/mfg-en-case-study-making-sense-of-the-commercialization-of-microfinance-in-latin-america-lessons-for-nicaragua-2004.pdf. Accessed January 2016.

Lasso, F. 2006. "Incidencia del gasto público social sobre la distribución del ingreso y la reducción de la pobreza." Paper presented at the Central Bank of Colombia's Weekly Economics Seminar, November 17–18, Medellín, Colombia.

Lee, P., P. Ainslie, and S. Fathallah. 2012. "Embracing Informality: Designing Financial Services for China's Marginalized." Report. Reboot, New York, NY.

Lee, R. D., and A. Mason. 2011a. "Generational Economics in a Changing World." *Population and Development Review* 37(s1) January: 115–42.

———, eds. 2011b. *Population Aging and the Generational Economy: A Global Perspective*. Cheltenham, GL, UK and Northampton, MA,

USA: Edward Elgar Publishing; and Ottawa, ON, Canada: International Development Research Centre.

Levine, R. 2005. "Finance and Growth: Theory and Evidence." In P. Aghion and S. N. Durlauf, eds., *Handbook of Economic Growth*. Volume 1A. Amsterdam: North-Holland.

Levy, S. 2008. *Good Intentions, Bad Outcomes: Social Policy, Informality, and Economic Growth in Mexico*. Washington, DC: Brookings Institution.

Levy Yeyati, E., and A. Micco. 2007. "Concentration and Foreign Penetration in Latin American Banking Sectors: Impact on Competition and Risk." *Journal of Banking and Finance* 31(6) June: 1633–47.

Levy Yeyati, E., and J. Zúñiga. 2015. "Varieties of Capital Flows: What Do We Know?" Faculty Research Working Paper no. 15–025. John F. Kennedy School of Government, Harvard University, Cambridge, MA.

Llerena Pinto, F. P., M. C. Llerena Pinto, M. A. Llerena Pinto, and R. Saá. 2015. "Social Spending, Taxes and Income Redistribution in Ecuador." CEQ Working Paper no. 28. Center for Inter-American Policy and Research (CIPR) and Department of Economics, Tulane University, New Orleans, LA; and Inter-American Dialogue, Washington, DC.

Loayza, N., A. M. Oviedo, and L. Servén. 2005. "The Impact of Regulation on Growth and Informality: Cross-Country Evidence." Policy Research Working Paper no. 3623. World Bank, Washington, DC.

Loayza, N., K. Schmidt-Hebbel, and L. Servén. 1999. "What Drives Private Saving across the World?" Working Paper no. 47. Central Bank of Chile, Santiago.

López-Murphy, P., and A. R. Musalem. 2004. "Pension Funds and National Saving." Policy Research Working Paper no. 3410. World Bank, Washington, DC.

Lora, E. 2007. "Public Investment in Infrastructure in Latin America: Is Debt the Culprit?" Working Paper no. 595. Inter-American Development Bank, Washington, DC.

Love, I., M. S. Martínez Pería, and S. Singh. 2016. "Collateral Registries for Movable Assets: Does Their Introduction Spur Firms' Access to Bank Financing?" *Journal of Financial Services Research* 49(1) February: 1–37.

Lucas, Jr., R. E. 1990. "Why Doesn't Capital Flow from Rich to Poor Countries?" *American Economic Review* 80(2) May: 92–96.

Lustig, N., and C. Pessino. 2013. "Social Spending and Income Redistribution in Argentina during the 2000s: The Rising Role of Noncontributory Pensions." CEQ Working Paper no. 5. Center for Inter-American Policy and Research (CIPR) and Department of Economics, Tulane University, New Orleans, LA; and Inter-American Dialogue, Washington, DC.

Lustig, N., C. Pessino, and J. Scott. 2014. "The Impact of Taxes and Social Spending on Inequality and Poverty in Argentina, Bolivia, Brazil, Mexico, Peru, and Uruguay: Introduction to the Special Issue." *Public Finance Review* 42(3) May: 287–303.

Maldonado, J. H., and L. Tejerina. 2010. "Investing in Large Scale Financial Inclusion: The Case of Colombia." IDB Technical Note no. 197. Social Protection and Health Division, Inter-American Development Bank, Washington, DC.

Marín, A. G., and R. Schwabe. 2013. "Bank Competition and Account Penetration: Evidence from Mexico." Working Paper no. 2013-14. Banco de México, Mexico City.

Martin, X. 2014. "Inclusive Commitment Savings in Latin America and the Caribbean." Study. Multilateral Investment Fund, Inter-American Development Bank, Washington, DC. Available at http://www.pro-savings.org/sites/default/files/CONSOLIDADO%20ingles.pdf. Accessed January 2016.

Martínez Pería, M. S., and S. Singh. 2014. "The Impact of Credit Information Sharing Reforms on Firm Financing." Policy Research Working Paper no. 7013. World Bank, Washington, DC.

Mayer, C. 1996. "Corporate Governance, Competition and Performance." OECD Economics Department Working Paper no. 164. OECD Publishing, Paris.

———. 1998. "Financial Systems and Corporate Governance: A Review of the International Evidence." *Journal of Institutional and Theoretical Economics* 154(1) March: 144–76.

McDonald, K., C. Ansley, A. Coleman, M. Holm, J. McDermott, P. Mersi, and S. Toplis. 2011. "Saving New Zealand: Reducing Vulnerabilities and Barriers to Growth and Prosperity." Report. The Treasury, Government of New Zealand, Wellington.

McKay, C., and M. Pickens. 2010. "Branchless Banking 2010: Who's Served? At What Price? What's Next?" Focus Note no. 66. Consultative Group to Assist the Poor (CGAP), Washington, DC.

McKenzie, D. J., and C. Woodruff. 2006. "Do Entry Costs Provide an Empirical Basis for Poverty Traps? Evidence from Mexican Micro-enterprises." *Economic Development and Cultural Change* 55(1) October: 3–42.

McKinsey Global Institute. 2013. "Infrastructure Productivity: How to Save $1 Trillion a Year." Report. McKinsey and Company, New York, NY.

Meaney, M. J., and M. Szyf. 2005. "Environmental Programming of Stress Responses through DNA Methylation: Life at the Interface between a Dynamic Environment and a Fixed Genome." *Dialogues in Clinical Neuroscience* 7(2) June: 103–23.

Meléndez, M. 2014. "CEQ Master Workbook: Colombia." November 21. Tulane University, New Orleans, LA.

Mester, L. J. 2010. "Scale Economies in Banking and Financial Regulatory Reform." *The Region* [Federal Reserve Bank of Minneapolis] 24(3) September: 10–13.

Midrigan, V., and D. Y. Xu. 2014. "Finance and Misallocation: Evidence from Plant-Level Data." *American Economic Review* 104(2) February: 422–58.

Milevsky, M. A. 2013. *Life Annuities: An Optimal Product for Retirement Income*. Charlottesville, VA: Research Foundation of CFA Institute.

———. 2015. *King William's Tontine: Why the Retirement Annuity of the Future Should Resemble Its Past*. New York, NY: Cambridge University Press.

Miranda Pinto, J. 2013. "Proyección de pensión personalizada en Chile: evaluación de su impacto en la decisión de jubilación." *Estudios de Economía* 40(2) December: 211–45.

Modigliani, F., and M. H. Miller. 1958. "The Cost of Capital, Corporation Finance and the Theory of Investment." *American Economic Review* 48(3) June: 261–97.

Morton, M., J. Klugman, L. Hanmer, and D. Singer. 2014. "Gender at Work: A Companion to the *World Development Report on Jobs*." Report. Gender and Development Unit, World Bank, Washington, DC.

Mullainathan, S., and E. Shafir. 2014. *Scarcity: The New Science of Having Less and How It Defines Our Lives*. New York, NY: Picador.

Musalem, A. R., and P. Souto. 2009. "Unveiling the Governance of National Public Pension Funds." Working Paper no. 34. Center for Financial Stability, New York, NY.

Myers, S. C., and N. S. Majluf. 1984. "Corporate Financing and Investment Decisions When Firms Have Information that Investors Do Not Have." *Journal of Financial Economics* 13(2) June: 187–221.

National Academies of Sciences, Engineering, and Medicine. 2015. *The Growing Gap in Life Expectancy by Income: Implications for Federal Programs and Policy Responses*. Washington, DC: National Academies Press.

Núñez Méndez, J., N. Salazar, L. Cuesta, C. Castañeda, G. Rivas, and J. Castillo. 2012. "Primer seguimiento de la evaluación de impacto del piloto del Programa de Promoción de la Cultura del Ahorro." Report. FEDESARROLLO, Bogotá.

OECD (Organisation for Economic Co-operation and Development). 2007. "Encouraging Savings through Tax-Preferred Accounts." OECD Tax Policy Study no. 15. OECD Publishing, Paris.

———. 2009. "OECD Guidelines for Pension Fund Governance." OECD, Paris. Available at http://www.oecd.org/pensions/private-pensions/34799965.pdf. Accessed January 2016.

———. 2011. *Government at a Glance 2011*. Paris: OECD Publishing.

———. 2012. "A Policy Roadmap for Defined Contribution Pensions." In *OECD Pensions Outlook 2012*. Paris: OECD Publishing.

———. 2014a. "Pension Markets in Focus: 2014 Edition." Annual report. OECD, Paris. Available at http://www.oecd.org/daf/fin/private-pensions/Pension-Markets-in-Focus-2014.pdf. Accessed February 2016.

———. 2014b. "Social Expenditure Database (SOCX)." Database. OECD, Paris. Available at http://www.oecd.org/social/expenditure.htm. Accessed February 2016.

———. 2015a. "Can Pension Funds and Life Insurance Companies Keep Their Promises?" In *OECD Business and Finance Outlook 2015*. Paris: OECD Publishing.

———. 2015b. *G20/OECD Principles of Corporate Governance*. Paris: OECD Publishing.

———. 2015c. "Pension Markets in Focus: 2015 Edition." Annual report. OECD, Paris. Available at http://www.oecd.org/daf/fin/private-pensions/Pension-Markets-in-Focus-2015.pdf. Accessed February 2016.

Ortigueira, S., and N. Siassi. 2013. "How Important Is Intra-Household Risk Sharing for Savings and Labor Supply?" *Journal of Monetary Economics* 60(6) September: 650–66.

Pagés, C., ed. 2010. *The Age of Productivity: Transforming Economies from the Bottom Up*. Development in the Americas series. New York,

NY: Palgrave Macmillan and Washington, DC: Inter-American Development Bank.

Pagura, M. E., ed. 2008. *Expanding the Frontier in Rural Finance: Financial Linkages and Strategic Alliances.* Rugby, Warwickshire, UK: Practical Action Publishing.

Paz Arauco, V., G. Gray Molina, E. Yáñez Aguilar, and W. Jiménez Pozo. 2014. "Explaining Low Redistributive Impact in Bolivia." *Public Finance Review* 42(3) May: 326–45.

Perrotti, D. E., and R. J. Sánchez. 2011. "La brecha de infraestructura en América Latina y el Caribe." Natural Resources and Infrastructure Series no. 153. United Nations Economic Commission for Latin America and the Caribbean (ECLAC), Santiago.

Piazzesi, M., and M. Schneider. 2012. "Inflation and the Price of Real Assets." Paper. Stanford University, Stanford, CA; and National Bureau of Economic Research (NBER), Cambridge, MA. Available at http://web.stanford.edu/~piazzesi/inflationAP.pdf. Accessed February 2016.

Poterba, J. M. 1987. "Tax Policy and Corporate Saving." *Brookings Papers on Economic Activity* 18(2): 455–503.

Powell, A., coord. 2013. *Rethinking Reforms: How Latin America and the Caribbean Can Escape Suppressed World Growth.* 2013 Latin American and Caribbean Macroeconomic Report. Washington, DC: Inter-American Development Bank.

———. 2015. "Boring Banks, Safe Economies?" *Ideas Matter* (blog), Inter-American Development Bank, Washington, DC. June 25. Available at http://blogs.iadb.org/ideasmatter/2015/06/25/boring-banks-safe-economies/. Accessed January 2016.

———. 2016. "Banks, Financial Markets and Financial Inclusion in Latin America." IDB technical note. Inter-American Development Bank, Washington, DC. Unpublished.

Powell, A., and M. Székely. 2015. "Financial Access and Household Behavior: Evidence from Mexico." Inter-American Development Bank, Washington, DC. Unpublished.

Prina, S. 2015. "Banking the Poor via Savings Accounts: Evidence from a Field Experiment." *Journal of Development Economics* 115(C) July: 16–31.

Rajan, R. G., and L. Zingales. 2003. "Banks and Markets: The Changing Character of European Finance." NBER Working Paper no. 9595. National Bureau of Economic Research, Cambridge, MA.

Ramey, G., and V. A. Ramey. 1995. "Cross-Country Evidence on the Link between Volatility and Growth." *American Economic Review* 85(5) December: 1138–51.

Rancière, R., A. Tornell, and F. Westermann. 2006. "Decomposing the Effects of Financial Liberalization: Crises vs. Growth." *Journal of Banking and Finance* 30(12) December: 3331–48.

Ravallion, M. 2003. "Measuring Aggregate Welfare in Developing Countries: How Well Do National Accounts and Surveys Agree?" *Review of Economics and Statistics* 85(3) August: 645–52.

Restuccia, D., and R. Rogerson. 2008. "Policy Distortions and Aggregate Productivity with Heterogeneous Establishments." *Review of Economic Dynamics* 11(4) October: 707–20.

Rodríguez, C., and J. E. Saavedra. 2015. "Nudging Youth to Develop Savings Habits: Experimental Evidence Using SMS Messages." CESR-Schaeffer Working Paper no. 2015–018. University of Southern California, Los Angeles, CA.

Rofman, R., and M. L. Oliveri. 2012. "Pension Coverage in Latin America: Trends and Determinants." Social Protection and Labor Discussion Paper no. 1217. World Bank, Washington, DC.

Röhn, O. 2010. "New Evidence on the Private Saving Offset and Ricardian Equivalence." OECD Economics Department Working Paper no. 762. OECD Publishing, Paris.

Rojas-Suárez, L., and M. A. Amado. 2014. "Understanding Latin America's Financial Inclusion Gap." Working Paper no. 367. Center for Global Development, Washington, DC.

Rosen, B. 2010. "The Experience of Participants in Both an Incentivized Savings and CCT Program in Rural Peru." Study. Proyecto Capital, Instituto de Estudios Peruanos, Lima.

Ruiz, C. 2013. "From Pawn Shops to Banks: The Impact of Formal Credit on Informal Households." Policy Research Working Paper no. 6634. World Bank, Washington, DC.

Ruiz-Tagle, J., and D. Contreras. 2014. "CEQ Master Workbook: Chile." August. Tulane University, New Orleans, LA.

Saad, P. M. 2011. "Demographic Trends in Latin America and the Caribbean." In D. Cotlear, ed., *Population Aging: Is Latin America Ready?* Washington, DC: World Bank.

Samuelson, P. A. 1958. "An Exact Consumption-Loan Model of Interest with or without the Social Contrivance of Money." *Journal of Political Economy* 66(6) December: 467–82.

Sandoval-Hernández, J. 2012. "The Impact of Pension Reforms on Mexican Household Saving." Paper. College of Charleston, Charleston, SC. Unpublished.

Sauma, P., and J. D. Trejos. 2014. "Gasto público social, impuestos, redistribución del ingreso y pobreza en Costa Rica." CEQ Working Paper no. 18. Center for Inter-American Policy and Research (CIPR) and Department of Economics, Tulane University, New Orleans, LA; and Inter-American Dialogue, Washington, DC.

Schaner, S. 2015. "Do Opposites Detract? Intrahousehold Preference Heterogeneity and Inefficient Strategic Savings." *American Economic Journal: Applied Economics* 7(2) April: 135–74.

Scott, J. 2014. "Redistributive Impact and Efficiency of Mexico's Fiscal System." *Public Finance Review* 42(3) May: 368–90.

SENAMA (Servicio Nacional del Adulto Mayor). 2009. "Estudio nacional de la dependencia en las personas mayores." Report. SENAMA, Ministry of Social Development, Government of Chile, Santiago.

Serebrisky, T. 2014. "Sustainable Infrastructure for Competitiveness and Inclusive Growth: IDB Infrastructure Strategy." Report. Inter-American Development Bank, Washington, DC.

Serebrisky, T., D. Margot, A. Suárez-Alemán, and M. C. Ramírez. 2015. "What Do We Know about Investment and Saving in Latin America and the Caribbean?" Paper. Inter-American Development Bank, Washington, DC.

Serebrisky, T., A. Suárez-Alemán, D. Margot, and M. C. Ramírez. 2015. "Financing Infrastructure in Latin America and the Caribbean: How, How Much and by Whom?" Report. Inter-American Development Bank, Washington, DC.

Sirri, E. R., and P. Tufano. 1995. "The Economics of Pooling." In D. B. Crane, K. A. Froot, S. P. Mason, A. F. Perold, R. C. Merton, Z. Bodie, E. R. Sirri, and P. Tufano, eds., *The Global Financial System: A Functional Perspective*. Boston, MA: Harvard Business School Press.

Souto, P., and A. R. Musalem. 2012. "Assessing the Governance and Transparency of National Public Pension Funds." *Review of European Studies* 4(2) June: 148–67.

Standard & Poor's. 2015. "Global Infrastructure Investment: Timing Is Everything (And Now Is the Time)." Standard & Poor's Ratings Direct (January 13). Available at http://www.tfreview.com/sites/default/files/SP_Economic%20Research_Global%20Infrastructure%20Investment%20(2).pdf. Accessed January 2016.

Subsecretaría de Previsión Social [Undersecretariat of Social Security]. 2002. "Bases de datos EPS." Social Protection Survey database. Subsecretaría de Previsión Social, Government of Chile, Santiago. Available at http://www.previsionsocial.gob.cl/subprev/?page_id=7518. Accessed February 2016.

Székely, M., P. Mendoza, and J. Karver. 2015. "Understanding Domestic Saving in Latin America and the Caribbean: The Case of Mexico." IDB Working Paper no. 606. Department of Research and Chief Economist, Inter-American Development Bank, Washington, DC.

Tabak, B. M., D. M. Fazio, and D. O. Cajueiro. 2011. "Profit, Cost and Scale Efficiency for Latin American Banks: Concentration-Performance Relationship." Working Paper no. 244. Research Department, Central Bank of Brazil, Brasília.

Taber, L. (with C. Cuevas). 2004. "Integrating the Poor into the Mainstream Financial System: The BANSEFI and SAGARPA Programs in Mexico." In Consultative Group to Assist the Poor (CGAP) and World Bank, eds., *Scaling up Poverty Reduction: Case Studies in Microfinance*. Washington, DC: CGAP and World Bank.

Terry, D. F., and S. R. Wilson, eds. 2005. *Beyond Small Change: Making Migrant Remittances Count*. Washington, DC: Inter-American Development Bank.

Thaler, R. H., and S. Benartzi. 2004. "Save More Tomorrow™: Using Behavioral Economics to Increase Employee Saving." *Journal of Political Economy* 112(S1) February: S164–S187.

Thanassoulis, E. 2001. *Introduction to the Theory and Application of Data Envelopment Analysis: A Foundation Text with Integrated Software*. New York: Springer.

Tovar, J., and M. Urrutia. 2014. "Household Savings in Colombia 1997–2011." Inter-American Development Bank, Washington, DC. Unpublished.

Trivelli, C., J. Montenegro, and M. C. Gutiérrez. 2011. "Un año ahorrando: primeros resultados del programa piloto 'Promoción del Ahorro en Familias JUNTOS'." Working Paper no. 159. Instituto de Estudios Peruanos, Lima.

Trujillo, V., and S. Navajas. 2014. "Financial Inclusion in Latin America and the Caribbean: Data and Trends." Paper. Multilateral Investment Fund, Inter-American Development Bank, Washington, DC.

Ubfal, D. 2013. "The Impact of Financial Access for Beneficiaries of Social Programs in Mexico." Paper presented at the 2013 LACEA-LAMES Annual Meetings, October 31, Mexico City.

United Nations. 2013. "World Population Prospects: The 2012 Revision." DVD-ROM. Population Division, Department of Economic and Social Affairs, United Nations, New York.

———. 2015. "World Population Prospects: The 2015 Revision." Database. Population Division, Department of Economic and Social Affairs, United Nations, New York. Available at http://esa.un.org/unpd/wpp/. Accessed February 2016.

Urzúa, C. M. 1993. "Tax Reform and Macroeconomic Policy in Mexico." Working Paper no. X–1993. Centro de Estudios Económicos, El Colegio de México, Mexico City.

Wang, M., M. O. Rieger, and T. Hens. 2011. "How Time Preferences Differ: Evidence from 45 Countries." Discussion Paper no. 2011/18. Department of Business and Management Science, Norwegian School of Economics, Bergen, Norway.

WHO (World Health Organization). 2006. *The World Health Report 2006: Working Together for Health*. Geneva, Switzerland: WHO.

———. 2015. *World Report on Ageing and Health*. Geneva, Switzerland: WHO.

Williams, J. 2012. "Efficiency and Market Power in Latin American Banking." *Journal of Financial Stability* 8(4) December: 263–76.

World Bank. 1994. *Averting the Old Age Crisis: Policies to Protect the Old and Promote Growth*. New York, NY: Oxford University Press.

———. 2011. "Supporting Infrastructure in Developing Countries." Report. MDB Working Group on Infrastructure, World Bank, Washington, DC.

———. 2014a. *Global Financial Development Report 2014: Financial Inclusion*. Washington, DC: World Bank.

———. 2014b. "Global Findex Database." Database. Available at http://datatopics.worldbank.org/financialinclusion/. World Bank, Washington, DC. Accessed February 2016.

———. 2015a. *Global Financial Development Report 2015–2016: Long-Term Finance*. Washington, DC: World Bank.

———. 2015b. "World Development Indicators." Database. World Bank, Washington, DC. Available at http://data.worldbank.org/indicator/NE.GDI.FTOT.CD. Accessed February 2016.

———. 2016. *Doing Business 2016: Measuring Regulatory Quality and Efficiency*. Thirteenth edition. Washington, DC: World Bank.

World Bank and PwC (PricewaterhouseCoopers). 2015. "Paying Taxes 2016." Report. Available at https://www.pwc.com/gx/en/paying-taxes-2016/paying-taxes-2016.pdf. Accessed February 2016.

World Economic Forum. 2006. *The Global Competitiveness Report 2006–2007*. Geneva, Switzerland: World Economic Forum.

———. 2010. *The Global Competitiveness Report 2010–2011*. Geneva, Switzerland: World Economic Forum.

———. 2014. *The Global Competitiveness Report 2014–2015*. Geneva, Switzerland: World Economic Forum.

Yang, T., and O. S. Mitchell. 2008. "Public Sector Pension Governance, Funding and Performance: A Longitudinal Appraisal." In J. Evans, M. Orszag, and J. Piggott, eds., *Pension Fund Governance: A Global Perspective on Financial Regulation*. Cheltenham, GL, UK and Northampton, MA, USA: Edward Elgar Publishing.

Index